THE SALVATION OF ISRAEL

A volume in the series

Medieval Societies, Religions, and Cultures
Edited by M. Cecilia Gaposchkin and Anne E. Lester

A list of titles in this series is available at cornellpress.cornell.edu.

THE SALVATION
OF ISRAEL

JEWS IN CHRISTIAN ESCHATOLOGY
FROM PAUL TO THE PURITANS

JEREMY COHEN

CORNELL UNIVERSITY PRESS
Ithaca and London

First published 2022 by Cornell University Press

Printed in the United States of America

Library of Congress Cataloging-in-Publication Data

Names: Cohen, Jeremy, 1953– author.
Title: The salvation of Israel : Jews in Christian eschatology from Paul to the Puritans / Jeremy Cohen.
Description: Ithaca [New York] : Cornell University Press, 2022. | Series: Medieval societies, religions, and cultures | Includes bibliographical references and index.
Identifiers: LCCN 2021054779 (print) | LCCN 2021054780 (ebook) | ISBN 9781501764721 (hardcover) | ISBN 9781501764769 (pdf) | ISBN 9781501764752 (epub)
Subjects: LCSH: Judaism (Christian theology)—History of doctrines. | Christianity and other religions—Judaism. | Judaism—Relations—Christianity. | End of the world—History of doctrines. | Antichrist—History of doctrines.
Classification: LCC BT93 .C645 2022 (print) | LCC BT93 (ebook) | DDC 261.2/6—dc23/eng/ 20220128
LC record available at https://lccn.loc.gov/2021054779
LC ebook record available at https://lccn.loc. gov/2021054780

Contents

Acknowledgments

My work on this project commenced some three decades ago, before the end of the last millennium, and it has developed over time, benefiting from the assistance, advice, and feedback of many. At the Israel Institute of Advanced Studies in Jerusalem in 2000–2001, Ora Limor and I organized a research group on the subject "Millennial Pursuits: Apocalyptic Traditions and Expectations of the End among Medieval Jews and Their Neighbors." Among the numerous colleagues who participated in our seminars and reacted helpfully to my ideas, Ora Limor, Israel Yuval, Alexander Patschovsky, Bianca Kühnel, Ram Ben-Shalom, Bernard McGinn, and Felicitas Schmieder generously afforded me their time and assistance, allowing me to profit from their expertise and insight, both then and during the years that have ensued. Alexander Patschovsky graciously expended much energy in sending me source materials unavailable in Israel. And, owing to the efforts of Ram Ben-Shalom and others, our text-reading workshops evolved into the Israel Open University's still vibrant "Text and Context" seminars, where I continue to benefit from the suggestions and reactions of fellow medievalists and early modernists at various Israeli universities.

This book touches an array of subjects, time periods, and genres of sources, and I offer heartfelt thanks to the anonymous readers of the manuscript for Cornell University Press and to dozens of colleagues to whom I turned for help and who responded willingly and patiently with invaluable guidance. Among many, many others, these include Renana Bartal, Benjamin Braude, Haim Hames, Martha Himmelfarb, Alexandra Johnston, David Katz, Beatrice Kitzinger, Deeana Klepper, Katrin Kogman-Appel, Sara Lipton, David Nirenberg, Sarit Shalev-Eyni, Alison Stones, Debra Higgs Strickland, Carol Symes, Kyle Thomas, and Tuly Weisz. Among my doctoral students and research assistants over the past decades, I thank Yosi Yisraeli, Avital Davidovich-Eshed, Roni Cohen, Tali Berner, Dorit Reiner, Marianne Naegli, Montse Leira, and Pablo Bornstein, most of them now established, credentialed historians in their own right, for their dedicated support. Yosi Yisraeli gave generously of his time to read and react to a nearly final draft of the entire book.

Since that millennial year in Jerusalem, I pursued my research at numerous libraries and institutions on several continents. I extend special thanks to my hosts at the Institute for Advanced Study in Princeton, Johns Hopkins University, the Katz Center for Advanced Judaic Studies at the University of Pennsylvania, and the Oxford Centre for Hebrew and Jewish Studies, for their fellowships, hospitality, and assistance during sabbatical and other leaves. Most recently, the book took shape during a sabbatical at Dartmouth College and the Harvard Center for Jewish Studies, where my hosts Susannah Heschel, David Stern, and their staffs contributed roundly to an inordinately productive semester in their midst.

I acknowledge the generous funding of the Israel Science Foundation (grants 722/99 and 683/13). At Tel Aviv University, the financial support of the Abraham and Edita Spiegel Family Foundation Chair for European Jewish History and the Chaim Rosenberg School of Jewish Studies and Archaeology facilitated the pursuit of my research and its publication. And, over the course of many years, the staff of the Goldstein-Goren Diaspora Research Center has given me invaluable logistical support and advice. Cecilia Gaposchkin and Anne Lester, editors of the new Medieval Societies, Religions, and Cultures series at Cornell University Press, have contributed to this book with their enthusiastic interest and encouragement, as have Mahinder Kingra, Bethany Wasik, Susan Specter, Marian Rogers, and their colleagues at the Press, with their consistently congenial assistance and their editorial expertise.

Finally, my thanks to my wife, my children, their spouses, and my grandchildren for their love, unfailing support, and their patience throughout the many years of the life of this project.

Part 1 draws extensively from and expands my earlier study "The Mystery of Israel's Salvation: Romans 11:25–26 in Patristic and Medieval Exegesis," *Harvard Theological Review* (December 20, 2005), reused here with the permission of the Harvard Divinity School and Cambridge University Press. In chapter 3, in the subsection "Thomas Aquinas," I have drawn extensively from my earlier study "Supersessionism, the Epistle to the Romans, Thomas Aquinas, and the Jews of the Eschaton," reused here with permission: Copyright 2017, *Journal of Ecumenical Studies*, vol. 52.4. All rights reserved. An earlier version of chapter 7 appeared as Cohen, "Synagoga Conversa: Honorius Augustodunensis, The Song of Songs, and Christianity's 'Eschatological Jew,'" *Speculum* 79 (2004): 309–340, and I thank the Medieval Academy of America for permission to reuse this material here.

THE SALVATION OF ISRAEL

Introduction

This book studies Christianity's "eschatological Jews"—the Jews of the end of days as imagined by Christian writers and artists—in ancient, medieval, and early modern times. Despite the centuries that distance us from these sources, the questions and issues that they raise have not gone away. They persist in drawing attention, and even in leaving their mark on contemporary American politics and foreign policy, as they did when the United States moved its embassy in Israel from Tel Aviv to Jerusalem in 2018. To offer the opening prayer at the ceremony inaugurating the new embassy, the State Department invited an evangelical pastor known for his earlier declarations that "you can't be saved being a Jew," and that Judaism numbers among those non-Christian religions that "lead people to an eternity of separation from God in hell." The same pastor, however, now understood the significance of the Jerusalem embassy in unabashedly apocalyptic terms. He addressed God in saying that "Israel has blessed this world by pointing us to you," and that President Trump, who implemented the plan for moving the embassy, "stands on the right side of you, O God, when it comes to Israel."[1]

Christians believe that Jesus is the Christ, the messiah promised by God to his people Israel, and, when Jews refuse to acknowledge Jesus as their savior, their denial raises challenging questions. If not Jesus, then whom *do* the Jews expect to redeem them? What lies in store for Jews who at present fail to acknowledge the truth of Christianity? Many Christians over the course of history have reasoned that, if the Jews do not await the coming of the true messiah, then they must be awaiting a false one: not Christ, but Antichrist. Pinning their hopes on this demonic imposter, they should arguably suffer the same eternal punishment that awaits him. And yet, how would this bear on the promise of redemption and national restoration that the Jews' ancestors received from God long ago? Will God ultimately return the Jews to their homeland and admit them into the kingdom of heaven? Does God renege on his commitments? The apostle Paul, perhaps the founder of Christianity as we know it, answered forthrightly: their present disbelief notwithstanding, eventually all of the people of Israel will be saved.

Christian responses to these questions have evolved over time, though they began to take shape at the earliest moments of the Christian experience, when the end of days appeared to loom ominously on the horizon. The original followers of Jesus, themselves observant Jews who clung to their beliefs in him despite the setback of his death, evidently expected a swift resolution to their crisis. The book of the Acts of the Apostles in the New Testament records in its opening verses that after the crucifixion, Jesus commanded his disciples to remain in Jerusalem. One day, when he appeared among them within days or weeks thereafter, they pressed him: "Lord, is *this* the time when you will restore the kingdom to Israel?" (Acts 1:6). Yet Jesus's return—or, as Christians have termed it, the second coming of Christ—did not materialize, either on that day or even during the lifetimes of these disciples as they assumed it would, and the new community's anticipations for the eschaton underwent dramatic change during the ensuing generations. Among the many factors that shaped the history of these ideas, I single out several.

First, postponing the fulfillment of apocalyptic expectations required doctrinal justification and other creative measures for sustaining the commitment and solidarity of the community. Believers needed to appreciate their present situation not as a crippling setback or defeat, but as a necessary stage in the divine plan. Second, Jesus's Jewish disciples needed to explain to themselves and to others why most Jews did not share their conviction that Jesus was their savior. How is it that the majority of God's chosen people had deserted him? Whom would the future prove right, and how? Third, within two decades after the crucifixion, the apostle Paul appeared on the scene and quickly assumed a leading role in defining and disseminating the new faith. He offered Gentiles full membership alongside Jews in the newly founded messianic kingdom, and, as the first Christian century wore on, non-Jews constituted an increasingly significant element in Jesus-believing communities. Paul had never met the living Jesus, and he beckoned pro-spective believers to undergo a conversion much like his own. His call for each individual to experience a spiritual rebirth in the crucified Christ miti-gated, at least somewhat, the urgency of the earthly reappearance of a liv-ing human Christ, and it may well have allowed the faithful to cope better with delays in Christ's second coming. Fourth, the destruction of Jerusalem and the Jewish temple by the Romans in the year 70 proved traumatic for all Jews, including the persistently Torah-observant Jews in the Jesus-believing communities, who continued to yearn for the restoration of Jerusalem to a sovereign, Jewish, Davidic kingdom. How should these Jews who accepted Jesus as their savior confront their new circumstances, especially as other voices among the believers discerned in the destruction of Jerusalem a divinely wrought punishment of the Jews for rejecting Jesus, the teachings of Paul, and the new covenant of grace that they had inaugurated? And fifth, these and other developments contributed to the gradual, but seemingly irre-versible, separation—the parting, or partings, of the ways as scholars have termed it—between Jews and Christians, a process that spanned the first sev-eral centuries. As this process continued, not only did Christians view them-selves and their communities as the fulfillment of Israel's messianic hopes, but they defined their own religious identity and beliefs in contrast to those of Jews and Judaism. The Jew became for Christians the quintessential other.

From the earliest stages in their history, Christian messianic longings man-ifested deeply ingrained ambivalence concerning the Jews and their eschato-logical destiny. Would the Jews ultimately find salvation in Christ come the end of time and the culmination of God's plan for human history? Or, in the cosmic struggles between the forces of evil and good leading up to the final redemption, would the Jews continue to reject the true savior and ally them-selves with his Satanic nemesis, their own messianic pretender, none other than Antichrist? Either one of these outcomes—the ultimate conversion of the Jews or their ultimate alliance with Antichrist, who would lead them to damnation—could confirm the claims of Christians in their polemical encounter with Judaism. They were not mutually exclusive, and both made their way into the traditions of Christian eschatology that the church fathers bequeathed to posterity. Particular theologians could lean in one direction or the other, but, most commonly, they integrated both into their doctrine concerning the end of days. As the learned scholar Bede, writing in England around 700, observed, "We have two very certain indicators of the approach of the Day of Judgement, namely the conversion of the Jewish people, and the reign and persecution of Antichrist," whose rise to power the Jews will support.[2]

In the pages that follow I propose to explore the history of Christian ambivalence concerning the Jews of the end of days, or, as I have labeled them here, Christianity's "eschatological Jews." In an earlier book published over two decades ago, I investigated the complex character of medieval Christianity's "hermeneutical Jew," a virtual Jew constructed to play a role in a properly ordered Christian view of the world. Hermeneutical Jews, as depicted most importantly in the "Jewish witness" doctrine of Augustine of Hippo, contribute to Christendom during the present stage in salvation history, between the first and second comings of Christ. These Jews, their observance of the Mosaic law, their Old Testament Scriptures, and their dispersion and subjugation in Christendom validated the church's claims to have legitimately fulfilled, rather than abandoned, God's covenant with biblical Israel. A construction spawned by the dictates of an ambivalent Christian theology, the hermeneutical Jews embody much of the imperfection of the present age, similarly serving as the "other" in opposition to which Christians identified themselves and elaborated their reading of the Bible. As I endeavored to show, Augustine's hermeneutical Jews eventually proved incompatible with the "real" Jews of the European Middle Ages and the Talmudic literature underlying their postbiblical Judaism; yet their impact and their legacy endured.[3]

This new book, then, serves as sequel to its predecessor, focusing on Christian ambivalence toward Jews and Judaism in expectations of the end time, beyond their place in the *saeculum* or the imperfect world of the present. Our topic is a vast one, virtually limitless. I have confined the investigation to several key trajectories, and I make no claim to have included all churchmen who contributed to this story or all noteworthy instances of any given phenomenon. Yet I have selected lines of inquiry both for their importance and for their interest, inasmuch as they draw selectively on a range of sources: exegetical and topical, theological and literary, academic and popular, textual and visual. I have aimed throughout to illuminate the complexity of the issues by way of example and thus to trigger further conversation, rather than to bring discussion to any definitive conclusion.

Beginning with Paul himself and extending just beyond the Middle Ages, part 1 of this book considers milestones in the interpretation history of the Pauline prediction that, ultimately, all Israel will find salvation. Paul's prophecy in his Epistle to the Romans anticipates an eschatological fusion of Gentiles and Jews grounded in salvation in Christ. Dating from two to three decades after the crucifixion, this conviction also reflects how the rift between Jews who rejected Jesus and those (Jews and non-Jews) who believed in him played a formative role in the development of Christian theology: this rift underscored the unredeemed nature of the world at present; the final redemption depended on its resolution. The approach of these first three chapters will be an exegetical one, as they move from the meaning of Paul's prophecy in Romans to its interpretation among select medieval and early modern readers. Though the review dwells primarily on biblical commentaries, which at times make for difficult reading, it should also exemplify how Christian eschatology emerged directly from, and depended overwhelmingly on, a careful reading of biblical prophecy, from both Old Testament and New. This, too, warrants appreciation.

In the three chapters that follow, part 2 will investigate the linkage between the Jews and the primary agents of cosmic evil, Satan and Antichrist, that figures in Christian expectations of the end time. While Scripture certainly nourished ideas concerning Antichrist, discussion will break loose from the confines of biblical commentary, in order to follow Antichrist and his Jewish connections in a wider variety of sources. We shall touch first on scattered references to Antichrist in the New Testament and then on the Antichristology of the church fathers. Next we shall examine the writings of medieval churchmen and their apocalyptic visions, the Tiburtine Sibyl and Pseudo-Methodius among them, from Augustine to Joachim of Fiore and the bearers of Joachim's legacy. We shall then turn to portrayals of Antichrist in more popular literature of the later Middle Ages, along with his appearances on the medieval stage and in illustrations of manuscripts and incunabula.

Finally, part 3 considers medieval and early modern writers who do not fit neatly into either part 1 or part 2. In biblical commentaries, sermons, and even in pastoral and missionary treatises, their exceptional voices broke with existing precedent in developing the role of the eschatological Jew, at times extending it into new, uncharted territory. They demonstrate hitherto unappreciated possibilities in Christian eschatology, especially in its yearning for a happy end that would reinstate the Jews within the community of God's elect.

Few aspects of religions shed light on the character and the self-understanding of their adherents as much as their expectations for the end of time. Bridging the present with idealized portraits of the past and utopian visions of the future, eschatology derives from the vital core of a religion's theology, sociology, and culture, and it has consistently served as one of the most potent agents of social change in Jewish, Christian, and Muslim civilization. No less important, messianic beliefs give expression to social criticism in a broad range of contexts. They evince dissent on the one hand and mold attitudes toward nonconformists and dissenters on the other hand. In the case of nonbelievers, eschatology fixes their significance in an overall scheme of human history and conditions interaction with them as that history unfolds. Although most of the sources studied in this book have figured, often repeatedly, in earlier scholarly research, the systematic investigation of the eschatological Jew as such has not. My notes and bibliography attest to far-reaching indebtedness to previous studies. Still, as this book wrestles with the dual role of the Jews in Christian expectations for the end of days, and, above all, with the complexities of such Christian ambivalence regarding the Jews from the church fathers until the Puritans, I hope to illuminate a dimension of the Jewish-Christian encounter that has not received the attention it deserves. The book hopes to foster awareness and discussion, and, even beyond its selectivity in focusing on particular sources as opposed to others, it knowingly leaves important issues for future consideration, from the role of eschatology in the literary corpora of particular authors to the reception and influence of their ideas considered here. I plan to return to such questions in more delimited studies over the years to come, and I hope that others will see fit to do the same.

PART I

All Israel Will Be Saved

> So that you may not claim to be wiser than you are, brothers, I want you to understand this mystery: a hardening has come upon part of Israel, until the full number of the Gentiles has come in. And so all Israel will be saved; as it is written [Isaiah 59:20–21, 27:9], "Out of Zion will come the Deliverer; he will banish ungodliness from Jacob." "And this is my covenant with them, when I take away their sins." (Romans 11:25–27)

Our story begins with these words of the apostle Paul, which, probably more than any other verses from Scripture, fashioned Christian expectations for the Jews of the end time. Few words of Paul have failed to evoke extensive scholarly debate, especially as conflicts over the meaning of Paul's teaching—not the sayings of Jesus—account for most of the important differences between various Christian sects, traditions, and churches. These words in Romans prove no exception. To the contrary, their importance and continued contemporary relevance for Christian theologians only intensifies debate over Paul's original intentions.

Without aiming to resolve any of the long-standing disputes in the vast scholarly literature on Paul, chapter 1 situates these verses in the larger context of the Epistle to the Romans, the scheme of salvation history proposed in Romans 9–11 in particular, and the range of appreciations of that scheme in modern studies of Paul. The messages Paul transmitted to future generations were fraught with ambiguity, and even as subsequent Christian readers of Romans have grappled with its problems and inconsistencies, they interpreted Paul through the lenses of their own theologies and worldviews. Their readings do not necessarily reveal Paul's original purpose, but they do illustrate the meaning found in Paul by his successors and the significance of the Pauline legacy they helped to mold. Chapter 2 carries this story through to the beginning of the fifth century, highlighting some of the most significant Romans commentaries authored by Greek and Latin church fathers: those of Origen, John Chrysostom, Ambrosiaster, and Pelagius above all. Chapter 3 surveys the interpretation history of Romans in the Latin West, from Augustine, Gregory the Great, and others in the early medieval period, to Peter Abelard and Thomas Aquinas during the High Middle Ages, to select Catholic and Protestant exegetes of the later Middle Ages and the early modern period. Most options for understanding Paul had found expression by then, and investigators in our own age must invariably seek to unravel the riddles of Pauline doctrine by engaging the exegesis of his late ancient and medieval heirs.

CHAPTER 1

Paul and the Mystery of Israel's Salvation

Paul's letters in the New Testament number among the oldest Christian writings to have survived, and, although he himself probably had no such intention, his legacy laid the groundwork for the emergence of Christianity as a distinct religion and for the partings of the ways between Jewish and Jesus-believing religious communities. Nevertheless, most of the details of his life remain shrouded in obscurity. While the book of the Acts of the Apostles devotes much attention to Paul's career, experts have wisely questioned the reliability of the account that it relates. The seven New Testament epistles that most regard as genuinely Pauline offer the only reliable basis for insight into this elusive, enigmatic, inordinately creative, and charismatic Hellenistic Jewish thinker; yet these letters regularly attest to a brilliant, impassioned preacher much more than to a consistent systematic theologian. One finds it difficult to define the conclusive Pauline view on many centrally important theological issues—with the Jews and their destiny figuring prominently among them.[1] The scholarly literature investigating Paul and his theological concerns knows no limits. Without presuming to offer solutions to the manifold problems arising in any attempt to "make sense" out of Paul, I have focused this consideration of Paul's predictions for the Jews of the eschaton on some of the many interdependent questions that converge in such a discussion.

Our analysis of Paul here will treat chapters 9–11 of Romans, where he addresses the role of Israel in the divine plan for the world's salvation most directly; these chapters bristle with ambiguity that itself reflects the grounding of Paul's own enterprise in his reading of the Bible. Paul neither initiated nor ended this exegetical discourse, and we shall return to several of its subsequent phases as this book progresses, but he himself encountered biblical texts and traditions much older than he, traditions with which he struggled continuously in mapping his scheme of salvation history. As various experts have underscored, Romans 9–11 resembles "a complex choral symphony . . . of potentially discordant scriptural voices,"[2] and "the theology of Romans is the result of the encounter with the Old Testament."[3] Over half of the citations from the Hebrew Bible in Paul's letters appear in Romans;[4] and indeed, as Richard Hays proposed, the epistle "is most fruitfully understood as an intertextual conversation between Paul and the voice of Scripture, that powerful ancestral presence with which Paul grapples."[5] As a result, beginning our story with Paul admittedly obscures the prior stages of a conversation in which Paul participated no less than he innovated. Yet the ensuing history of Christian ideas that concerns us commences with him.

Textual Ambiguities

Several overlapping uncertainties prove particularly significant in that conversation, and I quote Romans 9–11 at length in view of its importance for all that will follow in this book.

Ethnic and Spiritual Israel, the Remnant, and the Rest

Among the questions raised by Paul's prediction in Romans that "all Israel will be saved" (11:26), the most immediate is, Who qualifies as Israel? In the second verse of Romans 9, Paul expresses "great sorrow and unceasing anguish" for his fellow Jews who, presumably, have rejected salvation in Christ, and he explains:

> For I could wish that I myself were accursed and cut off from Christ for the sake of my own people, my kindred according to the flesh. They are Israelites, and to them belong the adoption, the glory, the covenants, the giving of the law, the worship, and the promises; to them belong the patriarchs, and from them, according to the flesh, comes the Messiah. (9:3–5)

These words seem to leave no doubt that even Jews outside Paul's Jesus-believing community retain their special status as God's chosen people, Israel. But the verses that follow immediately restrict inclusion in Israel to those who had inherited God's promises of salvation to the ancient Hebrew patriarchs.

> For not all Israelites truly belong to Israel, and not all of Abraham's children are his true descendants; but "it is through Isaac that descendants shall be named for you." This means that it is not the children of the flesh who are the children of God, but the children of the promise are counted as descendants. (9:6–8)

Paul thus appears to disavow God's election of Abraham's physical descendants *qua Israel*, but not without some hedging. Further on, in Romans 9:27–28, he notes: "Isaiah [10:22–23] cries out concerning Israel, 'Though the number of the children of Israel were like the sand of the sea, only a remnant of them will be saved; for the Lord will execute his sentence on the earth quickly and decisively.'" Then, concluding this chapter in his epistle, Paul recapitulates (9:30–31): Gentiles who did not seek salvation through observance of the law of Moses have attained it through faith in Christ. Yet Israel, the Jews who sought salvation through the law and not through faith, has fallen.

Although the prophecy of Isaiah suggests that most of the Jews, labeled the children of Israel, would forfeit their elect status, some, a remnant, would in fact be saved. Who constitutes this remnant? Have these Jews already been saved, or did their salvation pertain to future, perhaps eschatological events? Moreover, how does the "remnant" (*to kataleimma* in Greek, *reliquiae* in the Latin Vulgate) of Romans 9:27 relate to Paul's subsequent uses of similar terms? Reaffirming in Romans 11 that God has not rejected his people, Paul invokes the divine assurance to the ancient Israelite prophet Elijah on Mt. Tabor that he, in fact, did not stand alone in his refusal to worship the pagan god Baal, but that others remained with him.

> I ask, then, has God rejected his people? By no means! I myself am an Israelite, a descendant of Abraham, a member of the tribe of Benjamin. God has not rejected his people whom he foreknew. Do you not know what the scripture says of Elijah [1 Kings 19:14–18], how he pleads with God against Israel? "Lord, they have killed your prophets, they have demolished your altars; I alone am left, and they are seeking my life." But what is the divine reply to him? "I have kept for myself seven thousand who have not bowed the knee to Baal." So too at the present time there is a remnant, chosen by grace. (Romans 11:1–5)

What, then, happened to the others, who did not remain among God's elect? "Israel failed to obtain what it was seeking. The elect obtained it, but the rest (*hoi loipoi, caeteri*) were hardened" (11:7). Finally, in the passage cited at the very beginning of our discussion, Paul declares that "a hardening has come upon part (*apo merous, ex parte*) of Israel" (11:25). The language of Romans might suggest a qualitative difference between the "remnant" of the elect destined for salvation and the "rest" of Israel that were "hardened" temporarily,[6] but additional reflection can quickly befog it. For if the whole of Israel to be saved includes the part that was hardened or blinded, what does Paul intend when, earlier in this chapter (11:10), he invokes the exhortation of Psalm 69:24, "Let their eyes be darkened so that they cannot see, and keep their backs forever bent." If God punished this remaining and disbelieving part of Israel *forever*, how can the apostle include it within the whole of Israel to be saved? Additionally, Paul does not specify if Isaiah's prophecy of the salvation of Israel's remnant pertains to past or to future eschatological events, that is, to the first or second coming of Christ. If to the future, what, if anything, distinguishes the salvation of this remnant from all Israel's salvation predicted in Romans 11:25–26?

Mystery: Reversal, Jealousy, Restoration

Paul declares that the hardening and ultimate salvation of Israel pertain to a mystery (*mysterion, mysterium*), some of which he elaborates to the Jesus-believing recipients of his letter, lest they "be wise in their own conceits" (Romans 11:25), but which he never explains in full. Apparently, the mystery comprises God's plan for the redemption of humankind, a blueprint for salvation history replete with irony, paradox, and reversal, that Paul addresses in Romans 9–11.

In Romans 9, Paul's new criteria for inclusion in a reconstituted, spiritual Israel and his remarks on the inscrutability of divine justice underlie his declaration that faithful Gentiles have largely replaced the Jews as God's chosen people, at least for the time being.

> What if God, desiring to show his wrath and to make known his power, has endured with much patience the objects of wrath that are made for destruction? And what if he has done so in order to make known the riches of his glory for the objects of mercy, which he has prepared beforehand for glory—including us whom he has called, not from the Jews only but also from the Gentiles? As indeed he says in Hosea [2:23, 1:10[7]]: "Those who were not my people I will call 'my people,' and

her who was not beloved I will call 'beloved.'" "And in the very place where it was said to them, 'You are not my people,' there they shall be called children of the living God." (Romans 9:22–26; there follows immediately Paul's citation of Isaiah to the effect that only a remnant of Israel will be saved)

So far, the rationale for the reversal in the destinies of Jews and Gentiles appears coherent, if not fully understandable in all of its depth. Chapter 9 thus concludes, as we have seen, that Gentiles have attained righteousness in their faith, while Israel has lost it in its observance of the law.[8] Romans 10 eventually returns to these themes, reaffirming that "there is no distinction between Jew and Greek. . . . 'Everyone who calls on the name of the Lord will be saved'" (10:12–13); additional references to the Hebrew Bible (Deuteronomy 32:21 and Isaiah 65:1–2) then reinforce the reversal in the relationship between Israel and the nations.

Romans 11, however, complicates matters. Here, as noted, Paul appears to retreat from his statements on the displacement of Jews by Gentiles, declaring emphatically that God has not rejected his people, that the whole lump of dough and the branches stemming from the roots of Israel retain their sanctity and that all Israel will be saved. More interesting still, the apostle highlights God's use of the Gentiles to arouse jealousy among the Jews, disclosing another dimension to the mystery of salvation history.

So I ask, have they stumbled so as to fall? By no means! But through their stumbling salvation has come to the Gentiles, so as to make Israel jealous. Now if their stumbling means riches for the world, and if their defeat means riches for Gentiles, how much more will their full inclusion mean! Now I am speaking to you Gentiles. Inasmuch then as I am an apostle to the Gentiles, I glorify my ministry in order to make my own people jealous, and thus save some of them. For if their rejection is the reconciliation of the world, what will their acceptance be but life from the dead! (Romans 11:11–15)

Evidently, the Jews needed to fall in order to allow for the salvation of the Gentiles, "the reconciliation of the world," and jealousy then needs to prod the Jews to return to God, which will signify the consummation of the divine master plan, leading to nothing less than "life from the dead." As Paul emphasized to his Roman correspondents in his famous parable of the olive tree (11:17–24), if its natural branches (the Jews) could be broken off to make room for the grafting of wild branches (Gentiles), so too could they be restored. Does this mysterious plan suggest that the Jews simply functioned as pawns in the divine blueprint for human history, alternatively allowing for the salvation of the nations in their fall and for the final redemption in their conversion? Could God not have realized the redemption of the world in any other way? What constitutes the intrinsic significance of Israel's salvation? Paul leaves these questions largely unanswered.

Divine and Human Responsibility

The relationship between grace, predestination, and free will in determining the fate of a human being weighs heavily on Paul throughout much of the epistle; in and of itself, this vast, intricate, perplexing, and foundationally important issue lies outside the bounds of the present inquiry. Nonetheless, one can readily understand how the question of the Jews' moral responsibility for the divinely wrought punishment of their "hardening"—or, the extent to which God punished them for transgressions that were intentional—does bear upon interpretations of Romans 11:25–26 and the ultimate salvation of Israel. Here, again, one has trouble finding consistency in Paul's teaching. Romans 9:18 propounds the inscrutability of divine justice: "So then he has mercy on whomever he chooses, and he hardens the heart of whomever he chooses." The concluding verses of Romans 10, however, suggest that the basis for the Jews' rejection lay in their own intention.

> So faith comes from what is heard, and what is heard comes through the word of Christ. But I ask, have they not heard? Indeed they have. . . . Again I ask, did Israel not understand . . .? Then Isaiah [65:1–2] is so bold as to say, "I have been found by those who did not seek me; I have shown myself to those who did not ask for me." But of Israel he says, "All day long I have held out my hands to a disobedient and contrary people." (Romans 10:17–21)

Adding still further to the confusion, Paul proceeds in Romans 11:8–10 to invoke Isaiah 29:10 ("The Lord has poured out upon you a spirit of deep sleep, he has closed your eyes"), Deuteronomy 29:4 ("To this day the Lord has not given you a mind to understand, or eyes to see"), and, as we have noted, Psalm 69:23 ("Let their eyes be darkened so that they cannot see"). Should one conclude that the blindness and obstinacy of the Jews derive from God's decree, so that the Jews might not bear complete responsibility for their continuing error? Or, perhaps, if the Jews' error and punishment preceded their blindness, and not vice versa, they must unquestionably assume such responsibility. Presumably, the extent to which the Jews bear direct moral responsibility for their punishment will contribute to the extent that they must willfully mend their ways before the removal of their "hardening" and before the salvation of all Israel.[9]

Alongside these several questions and ambiguities, one must recognize the high stakes involved in the interpretation of our passage, beyond the exegesis of Romans per se. "The final destiny of ethnic Israel," one investigator has written, "is both a sensitive and important topic. It is sensitive, because it involves real people and real outcomes. It is important, because it involves God's promises and God's integrity."[10] Paul's instruction concerning the place—and identity—of Israel in the divine economy of salvation bears directly not only on the status of the Jews, who in the past were readily identifiable as Israel, but also on that of Christians, who claim to have replaced them as the true Israel of the present. To what extent and in whom have God's ancient promises to the Hebrew patriarchs of Israel withstood the trauma of the Jews' refusal to accept the truth of Christianity? How, in their dealings with Jews living in their midst and under their dominion, must Christians acknowledge Israel's former election? Looking forward to the future, must Christians preserve the Jewish people precisely so that they can convert at the end time, thereby fulfilling Paul's prophecy in its ostensibly literal meaning?

The Epistle to the Romans and Its Present-Day Interpreters

Unanswered questions like these abound, questions that intersect with ongoing, often heated debates among New Testament scholars concerning Paul and his letter to Rome. Their various viewpoints defy any effort at formulating a consensus or manageable summary, and we can only touch briefly on some of them.[11]

The Epistle and Its Author

Scholars agree overwhelmingly that Paul himself wrote the Epistle to the Romans, that he wrote it as he prepared for a journey to the western Mediterranean that would likely include a stop in Rome, and that it dates from the later years of Paul's active career, perhaps from the very late 50s. Though it appears first (owing to its length) among the Pauline epistles in the New Testament canon, Paul evidently wrote Romans last.

Disagreement still ensues, however, concerning the Roman believers in Jesus addressed in the letter—whether or not they included Jews—although progressively more recent studies have tended to discern a Gentile profile of Paul's audience. As opposed to earlier generations of Pauline scholarship that viewed Romans 9–11 as distinct, perhaps even detachable, from the bulk of the letter, many—though not all—investigations of the last decades have "reinstated" these chapters, not only as an authentic part of the original composition, but even, perhaps, as expressing the central part of its message.[12] The logic of the progression from one section of the epistle to the next may still be grounds for dispute, but inasmuch as many more exegetes now tend to affirm the integrity of the letter as a whole, a thorough analysis of any passage or section must naturally consider its place within the entirety of the book.[13] Recent research has also explored the complexity and sophistication of the rhetoric of Romans: multiple voices, including those of Paul's putative interlocutors; veiled but deliberate allusion to key biblical intertexts; and the conscious use of rhetorical devices and ploys typical of literary genres in the Hellenistic world. How ought such sensitivity to Pauline rhetoric to inform the interpretation of his teaching on the Jews of the end time?

By way of example, let us look quickly at a very small handful of scholarly positions. One refreshingly novel, pioneering trajectory in recent research literature, an approach espoused in works by John Gager, Stanley Stowers, Paula Fredriksen, and others, depicts Paul as firmly anchored in his Judaism, on the one hand, and his Epistle to the Romans as addressed directly to formerly pagan, that is non-Jewish, believers in Jesus, on the other hand. These Gentile believers in Jesus have the upper hand in the Roman community, and Paul strives to prevent them from ostracizing the Jews. A quarter century ago in his *Rereading Romans*, Stowers offered a probing rhetorical analysis of Romans to argue that the epistle and its ostensibly polemical portrayal of Jews and Judaism addressed a deliberately constructed Gentile reader, not a Jewish readership at all.[14] Gager applauded Stowers's reading,[15] and just several years ago Fredriksen concurred emphatically.

> The reading of Romans that I offer here, in short, assumes that Paul's letter speaks to the gentiles; that he addresses gentile issues and problems; that he mobilizes a rhetorical gentile to make his points; and that he authorizes his case to these Christ-following Roman gentiles (whom he has never met, 15.22–23) by invoking his divine appointment as apostle to gentiles. Romans speaks most directly not to the justification of sinners in general, but to the justification specifically of gentiles-in-Christ.

In Romans Paul declares in a resounding fashion that God has graciously included all nations in his imminent redemption of the Jews, Paul's "kinsmen according to the flesh" (9.4, 11.26). As Fredriksen sees it, Paul's salvation of all Israel, expected along with the impending second coming of Christ, would invariably include "Christ-following Jews no less than Christ-following Gentiles," and he sought to convey precisely this message to his non-Jewish correspondents.[16]

As we shall soon see, these scholars part company on other issues, but they share the voiced conviction that the traditional Christian, markedly anti-Jewish reading of Paul from Augustine to Luther and beyond—as one who condemned the Jews and their law—has distorted our understanding of Romans. A fair, balanced assessment of Romans, they maintain, requires our disentanglement from nearly two millennia of interpretation history, an exegetical tradition that transformed Paul into the Christian that he was not, and that bore on the relations between Jews and Christians in ways that Paul neither imagined nor desired, often with tragic historical consequences.[17]

One need not incline outspokenly toward the Stowers-Gager-Fredriksen direction in order to commend disentanglement from distortions of Paul in the history of biblical interpretation. Nor does disentanglement, in and of itself, invalidate those traditional interpretations as distortion, and traditional interpretations still flourish. Some leading Pauline scholars insist that Paul directed his letter to Jews and Gentiles alike among the Roman Christians, seeking to illustrate the polar opposition between observance of the law and faith in Christ and to distance these Jews from their ancestral practices. One distinguished reviewer of *Rereading Romans* actually accused Stowers of transmuting Paul into a present-day religious pluralist that he certainly was not, advancing a theological agenda attuned to the sensitivities of our own day, not Paul's.

> His presuppositions rise to the surface in sentences like the following. . . : "The idea of Paul saying that the law, with its divinely ordained institutions, cannot make Jews acceptable to God becomes absurd" (p. 190). One can only reply that some of us have thought for many thousands of minutes about how these writings functioned among Jews in Paul's time and have spent equal time contemplating Paul's letters, which drive us to conclude that he does indeed question the adequacy of the law, however theologically "absurd" that may seem to some.[18]

In a similar vein, two recent magisterial commentaries on Romans by prominent New Testament scholars insist that the issues, problems, and tensions of Jewish-Christian interaction lie at the heart of the epistle, which

Paul addressed to Jewish believers in Christ as much as he did to Gentiles. In their respective ways, Douglas Moo and Richard Longenecker contend that Jewish homiletic overshadows Greco-Roman rhetoric in Romans 9–11, chapters in which Paul wrestles with apparent contradictions between God's earlier election of a Jewish Israel and his adoption of the Gentiles among those chosen for salvation. For Longenecker, the rhetoric of a "Jewish remnant theology" propels the presentation of Paul's ideas in Romans 9–11.[19] For Moo, "Israel's unbelief of the gospel" constitutes the core issue of Romans 9–11,

> for it raises the question of the continuity of salvation history: Does the gospel presented in the NT genuinely "fulfill" the OT and stand, thus, as its natural completion? Or is the gospel a betrayal of the OT . . .? We need to hear Paul's careful and balanced answer to these questions. He teaches that the gospel is the natural continuation of OT salvation history. . . . But at the same time, he teaches that the gospel is also the fulfillment of salvation history—against the Judaizing tendency to view the gospel in terms of the torah.[20]

Such a reading might well situate Romans at the foundation of the Jewish-Christian debate as it developed throughout late antiquity and the Middle Ages.

The New Perspective on Paul: First-Century Judaism, *Sonderweg*, and Supersession

This difference of scholarly opinion offers a small taste of a foundationally important concern in the study of Paul over the last half century. Though our interest lies not with the research literature on Paul per se, we must consider the approach that has come to occupy center stage in many academic discussions since the publication of E. P. Sanders's groundbreaking *Paul and Palestinian Judaism: A Comparison of Patterns of Religion* in 1977, an approach that James Dunn dubbed "The New Perspective on Paul" in 1983. Subsequent studies of Paul's epistles could rarely avoid taking sides concerning the New Perspective, which, owing to its popularity and plentiful variations, has proven difficult to encapsulate in simple terms and has itself become the subject of numerous investigations.[21]

Proponents of the New Perspective have argued that we can no longer appreciate the first-century Judaism that figures so significantly in Paul's letters in the terms that later Christian theologians depicted it, from the church fathers through the Middle Ages and Reformation and even beyond. How did these theologians portray it? To paraphrase one writer's succinct summary of this age-old consensus,

> Paul's letters and his biography in Acts demonstrate that his own conversion led him to his doctrine of justification by faith;
> this doctrine constitutes the most essential tenet of Christianity; it portrays Christianity and Judaism as contradictory and mutually exclusive;
> and, while Christianity affirms that humans require divine grace to achieve righteousness, Judaism teaches that humans must merit salvation through their observance of God's law.

At the bottom line: Jewish "theology that endorses 'salvation by works' reflects a bad religion because it denies the grace of God."[22]

The wisdom of appreciating the Judaism of the late Second Temple period on its own terms might appear compelling to twenty-first-century readers, but old myths certainly do die hard, and a community of readers can rarely extricate itself from a long-standing, predominant mentality that underlies its religious convictions without considerable difficulty. One impetus for struggling with this difficulty has derived from collective pangs of guilt among Christians from a wide spectrum of churches in the wake of the Holocaust, guilt that has prodded New Testament scholars to wonder: Must not prevalent, sanctioned interpretations of the New Testament, perhaps even Scripture itself, share in the responsibility for antisemitism and its genocidal consequences during World War II? A leading advocate of the New Perspective, Terence Donaldson acknowledged the sobering impact of the Holocaust and its aftermath on Christian scholarship: "As they came to realize the extent of Christian complicity in the 'final solution . . .,' Christian scholars were driven to undertake a new and chastened examination of New Testament statements concerning Jews and Judaism, those of Paul included." In this reappraisal, Donaldson concluded, Romans 11 figures prominently but ambiguously, at once facilitating a Christian revaluation of ethnic Israel, and yet suggesting that "the (Gentile) church owes its existence to the rejection of Israel, God having rejected the one and put the other in its place." These last ideas indeed nourished the *adversus Judaeos* tradition of ancient and medieval Christianity and "thus contributed in no small measure to the legacy of Christian anti-Semitism."[23]

The New Perspective has recast first-century Judaism as offering salvation through faith and the election of divine grace, and not, at least not in the first instance, solely through the meritorious observance of God's law.

Second Temple Judaism embodied considerably more than the spiritless, archaic, and arcane legalism that classical Christian tradition perceived in it. It surely required Jews to observe the precepts of the Torah meticulously, but perhaps, as some have argued, as a means of retaining one's elect status, perhaps as a means for marking boundaries between Jews and others, but not as the exclusive path to salvation.[24] Beyond this reappraisal of first-century Judaism, investigators have also reconsidered how Paul perceived his own Judaism. Here one finds disagreement in the New Perspective camp. Some contend that Paul himself appreciated Judaism for what it was, and not for what his successors made it. Others, however, acknowledge that Paul condemned the legalism, the merit-based view of justification through works that he vehemently denounced in offering the Gentiles redemption through the saving power of the cross.[25]

The New Perspective has aroused extensive, serious opposition, not at all limited to fundamentalist voices of the Christian Right. Some resist lowering the profile of legalism and merit-based salvation in first-century Judaism, and still more believe that Paul definitely broke with his Jewish past precisely on those grounds. Again by way of example, even as he concurred with Sanders that Paul offered salvation *in Christ* to Jews no less than to Gentiles, Stephen Westerholm summarized his opposition to the New Perspective—especially its reassessment of Paul's view of Judaism—in an essay published twenty-five years after Sanders's book.

> Paul finds the basic [Jewish] principle of the "righteousness of the law" in Scripture itself, so that what he rejects can scarcely be confined to perceived misunderstandings . . . among his contemporaries. The law, *as* law, is meant to be observed: only so can the life and blessings that it promises be enjoyed. But (the post-Damascus) Paul [that is, Paul after his conversion] believes that human beings, at enmity with God and in slavery to sin, have neither the ability nor the inclination to submit to God's law.

As a consequence, "a new divine act of creation is needed before people can be 'put right' with God." At the bedrock of Paul's belief in Christ and his "doctrine of justification" lie his unshaking convictions that no human works do help in meriting salvation. Justification can and must "be received (by faith) as a gift of God's grace."[26] The classic anti-Jewish reading of Paul, Westerholm has continued to argue in his "The New Perspective at Twenty-Five" and in subsequent publications as well, remains largely, though not entirely, correct.[27]

At the end of the day, many New Testament scholars find themselves and their own theological perspectives in Paul and his doctrine. As some have observed, the "Old Perspective" academic establishment "for many years had read Paul as if he were a sixteenth-century Christian trying to assuage his conscience rather than a first-century Jewish-Christian apostle who was trying to incorporate Gentiles into the kingdom of God as full citizens along with Jews."[28] On the other hand, proponents of the New Perspective might fashion Second Temple Judaism in the image of their own liberal Protestantism, constructing it in a manner congenial both to Paul and to themselves. "Paul, and indeed the rabbis and teachers of Second Temple Judaism who preceded him," one writer notes astutely, "turn out to have been 'anonymous Protestants'" of a contemporary vintage.[29]

One particularly controversial outgrowth of the New Perspective that many of its leading proponents, including Sanders himself, have not espoused has direct impact on our concerns: the notion that, as self-proclaimed apostle to the Gentiles, Paul's condemnation of the observance of Mosaic law applied solely to non-Jews, who could find salvation only through their faith and the gift of God's grace. In this line of reasoning, the covenant that God had struck with the Jews at Sinai remains intact. Jews have their own special route, a *Sonderweg* in the terminology of New Testament studies, for achieving righteousness. As a result, two parallel roads lead to redemption: the covenant of Sinai struck with and for the Jews alone, and faith in the saving power of Jesus's crucifixion for the Gentiles. One cannot overemphasize the ramifications of this reading of Paul: Gentiles, to be sure, need not convert to Judaism and observe the law in order to find salvation in Christ. Jews, however, *need not convert to Christianity*. They may find redemption in their Jewish observance, outside of faith in Christ![30]

The meaning of Romans 11, and verses 25–27 above all, lies at the heart of the *Sonderweg* argument: God's ultimate salvation of his *Jewish* people of Israel will occur—imminently!—in tandem with that of the Gentiles, in accordance with his respective plans and covenants for the two distinct communities. Given modern liberal, pluralistic sensitivities, the notion that Paul did not condition the redemption of the Jews on their confession of Christian faith has evoked considerable sympathy. Yet it has unquestionably elicited more opposition than support and may even have induced scholars to explain their resistance to the New Perspective more clearly.

Simply put, *Sonderweg* reads supersessionism or replacement theology— that Christ's new covenant of grace supplants and invalidates the old covenant of the Torah—out of Paul's message. But is this defensible? We mention three problems by way of example.

- In view of Paul's critique of Torah-observance as a viable route to salvation in the preceding chapters of Romans, how can one explain the following statement by Paul in Romans 9:30–31?

  > Gentiles, who did not strive for righteousness, have attained it, that is, righteousness through faith; but Israel, who did strive for the righteousness that is based on the law, did not succeed in fulfilling that law? Why not? Because they did not strive for it on the basis of faith, but as if it were based on works. They have stumbled over the stumbling stone. . . .

What is this stumbling stone that stands in the way of the Jews' salvation, if not the misguided Jewish conviction, one that nourishes their lack of faith, that one merits salvation through observance of the Torah's commandments?

- How can one otherwise explain the failure, the stumbling, and the rejection of Israel in Romans 11:7–15 that we already encountered?
- Read straightforwardly, Romans 11 appears to glorify the fusion of Jewish identity and heritage with faith in the new covenant of grace. The *Sonderweg*'s two-covenant theory that limits salvation in Christ to non-Jews leaves little room for Jewish Christianity.

Though ecumenically minded souls might applaud the tolerant pluralism that the *Sonderweg* school attributes to Paul, can one maintain such an understanding of Paul without reading present-day sensitivities into the text of Romans (and the other Pauline epistles) written nearly two thousand years ago?[31]

Alternatively, does Romans render Paul a supersessionist? Diametrically opposed to the *Sonderweg* reading of Paul stands the replacement theology typically attributed to him by the church fathers, medieval theologians, and leading Reformers like Luther and Calvin. Numerous contemporary scholars continue to understand Paul and his letter to the Romans as supersessionist.[32] Here again we encounter challenging and perilous language, given the hazards of delineating the relationship between New and Old Testaments in our post-Holocaust age. As one Catholic scholar has acknowledged, "It is now widely agreed among Christian theologians that being a supersessionist is a bad thing."[33] Another Pauline scholar and retired Anglican bishop has observed that supersessionism "is now waved around as a magic wand to cast a spell of guilty silence over any suggestion that Paul might have meant what he said . . ., namely that the answer to Jewish salvation is the new covenant established through Jesus Christ."[34] But what does the term really mean? A recent book posits the following:

> Supersessionism rests on two core beliefs: (1) national Israel has some-how completed or forfeited its status as the people of God and will never again possess a unique role or function apart from the church; and (2) the church is now the true Israel that has permanently replaced or superseded national Israel as the people of God.

Put simply and powerfully with regard to Jewish-Christian relations, super-sessionism teaches that *"the New Testament church is the new Israel that has forever superseded national Israel as the people of God."*[35] Many later readers of Paul understood him to teach precisely this, and not a few respected scholars still hold that he did. But did he himself intend to do so? What does Romans impart concerning the ultimate destiny of Israel—national Israel, a spiritu-ally reconstituted Israel, or both—at the end of time?

"All Israel": Interpretive Possibilities and Pitfalls

Closing the circle, we return to Paul's prophecy of Romans 11:26 with which we began: When "the full number of the Gentiles has come in . . ., all Israel will be saved." Advances in Pauline scholarship over the last decade or two have only broadened and intensified difference of opinion on the meaning and ramifications of these words. A recent survey of scholarly opinion distin-guishes between three prominent exegetical trajectories: (1) the *Jewish escha-tological* view "that 'all Israel' comprises some totality of the Jewish people and involves a mass-conversion of Jews"; (2) the *ecclesiastical* view, in which "'all Israel' refers to the multiethnic church"; (3) the *Jewish-remnant* view, in which "'all Israel' refers to all ethnic Jews who are saved by faith in the Mes-siah throughout the church age."[36]

Yet not even this list finds room for every significant pattern of inter-pretation. How, for example, should one categorize the *Sonderweg* line of interpretation, which maintains that the Jews can find salvation through their observance of the Torah? Or the view that "all Israel" means the pre-viously hardened part of ethnic Israel that will ultimately see the light?[37] In all three of the options listed just above, a redeemed Israelite is a Jesus-believing Israelite. Additionally, where should one place the view that Jews will surely find salvation through belief in Jesus Christ, but that such belief will develop within the framework of their Judaism, requiring no conversion from one religion (or faith system) to another?[38] Especially in the second and third options on our list, when will Paul's prediction of the salvation of Israel materialize—or has it materialized already, or perhaps at least begun to materialize? And, if all this will occur approaching the end of days, exactly when in Paul's eschatological timetable—only upon the second coming of Christ, or perhaps earlier—will it happen? For "Paul speaks of a *parousia*, inaugurated by the removal of the restrainer, a rebellion and the revelation of the man of lawlessness, terminating with the resurrection of believers and the destruction of the man of lawlessness followed by the establishment of a kingdom."[39] Moreover, each of the three options itself allows for considerable variation. In the *Jewish eschatological* view, for instance, exactly what "totality" of ethnic Israel will find salvation: a totality (or majority or even just a large number) of individuals, or a newly reunited fellowship of the twelve Israelite tribes? Will the multiethnic church of the *ecclesiastical* view include Jews and Gentiles on an equal footing, or will Jews take priority over Gentiles, or vice versa?[40] What will become of all the remaining Jews in the *"Jewish-remnant"* view, those who have not, or not yet, confessed their faith in Jesus and the new covenant of grace?

The virtually limitless range of possibilities testifies to the numerous difficulties—exegetical, theological, and historical—entailed in ascribing a particular position to Paul himself. In the final analysis, Paul remains elusive. He defies an easy, straightforward reading. Nonetheless, one can highlight a prominent—one writer has termed it "epochal"—development in Pauline studies of the last generations: the reinstatement of ethnic Israel (namely, the Jews) in interpretations of Romans. If most earlier authorities chose "to emphasize how God had rejected Israel or made Israel's plight a negative example from which the church should learn," the last half century has witnessed a dramatic shift in underscoring the enduring value Paul attributed to the Jews and their role in the drama of the end time.[41] Though they represent an array of denominations and theological temperaments, the great majority of experts cited here would probably, each in their own particular fashion, subscribe to this consensus.

Debate over the correct understanding of Romans 9–11 shows no sign of abating. The stakes remain as high as ever, and, though daunting, the mass of studies on Paul cannot fail to impress on a reader how the reading of an enigmatic ancient Jewish preacher weighs heavily on religious ideas and sensitivities throughout the Christian world, today just as in the past.[42] As a historian and a Jew, I find this phenomenon fascinating, highly informative, and even moving.

In many ways, our foray into Pauline scholarship blurs the difference between primary and secondary sources in a book such as this. Historians once enshrined that presumably fundamental difference among the most basic working assumptions of their craft. Many now have difficulty maintaining the distinction. In the ensuing chapters of this book, we shall see that the modern scholars discussed and cited here followed directly in the footsteps of their patristic, medieval, and early modern predecessors.[43] Their conclusions concerning Paul may differ considerably. Yet, like their predecessors in earlier historical periods, they continue to wrestle with the problems of understanding Paul in light of their own theological convictions and denominational affiliations. They remain deeply invested—personally, religiously, and ideologically—in the process and results of their research. They must surely accommodate the doctrine of Paul as they best understand it. Somehow, Paul and his doctrine must also accommodate them. Paul's meaning derives from his interpreters no less than from Paul himself.

CHAPTER 2

The Pauline Legacy

From Origen to Pelagius

> This text is the basis of the common opinion that, at
> the end of the world, the Jews will return to the faith.
> However, it is so obscure that, unless one is willing
> to accept the judgment of the fathers who expound
> the apostle in this way, no one can, so it would seem,
> obtain a clear conviction from this text.
>
> —Martin Luther, *Lectures on Romans*[1]

As Martin Luther noted in his own comments
on Romans, the obscurities of Paul's prophecy of the salvation of Israel well
overshadow the clarity of its meaning. Varied understandings of virtually
every significant term in Romans 11:25–26—the mystery, the hardening of
Israel, the full number of the Gentiles, and the salvation of all Israel—as
well as the place of these verses in the broader context of Romans 9–11 have
yielded divergent implications for the construction of the Jews in Christian
theology. Owing to the suggestion that the Jews must endure in order to
convert at the end of days, interpretations of these passages could also bear
on regulation of the status of the Jews in Christendom. At any point in the
annals of Christianity, such disparity has characterized perceptions of Jews
of the past, present, and future, and the Christian sense of continuity and
discontinuity in the history of Israel. In this chapter and the next, we shall
visit select interpretations of Romans, chosen from among scores of extant
patristic and medieval commentaries for their diversity, interest, and influence, seeking to understand how Christian theologians wrestled with the
predictions and puzzles that Paul had bequeathed to them.[2] Our list may
prove surprising for those commentaries it includes and those it excludes.
Yet it will allow us to see that Paul's interpreters pursued the import of his
epistle in different directions, and, in their efforts to clarify his intentions as

they understood them, they frequently compounded the ambiguities of the biblical text at least as much as they resolved them.

Origen

"Origen of Alexandria is, depending on whom you ask, either one of the Church's greatest Fathers, or one of its greatest heretics."[3] In view of his frequently controversial doctrine and his monumental works of biblical exegesis, he was a pivotal figure in the early development of Christian theology. Almost as much as Paul himself, Origen (ca. 184–ca. 253) occupies center stage in this phase of our story. The first truly scientific exegete among the church fathers, he established biblical commentary as a lasting, major genre of Christian ecclesiastical literature. His encounter with Judaism and the rabbinic texts of his day, in Alexandria and even more so in Caesarea, was arguably more serious and extensive than that of any other patristic scholar. Origen undoubtedly sought to unravel ambiguity in Paul's eschatological prognosis, but the depth and complexity of his analysis of Romans 9–11, at least in the extant Latin translation of his commentary by Rufinus of Aquileia (340–410), had the opposite effect, leaving uncertainties that he perceived in the text a permanent fixture in Christian tradition.[4]

Opening his comments on Romans 9–11, Origen places Paul's prophecy that all Israel will be saved in the limelight of his exposition. He affirms confidence in the ultimate salvation of the Jews, even as the apostle redefines the identity of Israel. Paul's efforts to save the Jews, in fact, outstripped those of Moses himself, who had implored God to forgive his sinful people and, if not, to expunge Moses's name from his book. While the descendants of the Israelites whom Moses took out of Egypt "who had received the promised land still wander away from it as exiles banished from their home, hear what Paul says about Israel: 'Brothers,' he says, 'I do not want you to be ignorant of this mystery, whereby blindness has come upon part of Israel until the full number of the Gentiles has come in. And so all Israel will be saved.'"[5] Origen quotes this prophecy again and yet again,[6] and on its basis he seeks to integrate the substance of these three chapters in Romans. He suggests that Paul's exposition of God's intricate plan for salvation history in general, and of the relationship between Israel and the nations of the world in particular, will culminate in this glorious forecast, which serves to direct the flow of Paul's argument in this part of the epistle. As we ourselves have seen, however, the road from the opening of Romans 9 to the end of Romans 11 hardly lacks its confusing twists and turns. How did Origen address the obscurities in these chapters of the epistle that we discussed in the previous chapter?

Ethnic and Spiritual Israel, the Remnant, and the Rest

Strikingly confident in God's enduring commitment to the Jews, Origen must clarify Paul's distinction between the "sons of the flesh" and "the sons of the promise" among Abraham's descendants on the one hand, and his adamant insistence that God has not abandoned ethnic Israel ("Has God rejected his people? By no means!") on the other hand. God's ancient promises to Israel of the flesh, Origen maintains, now find fulfillment in the newly constituted Israel of the spirit, even as the Jews somehow retain their status as Israelites. Origen explains that Paul cries out

> on behalf of his brothers related to him according to the flesh, who are Israelites inasmuch as theirs were the adoption as sons, the law, and the promises—wishing that he be cursed in their place. Of them he says that the divine word has not been voided, namely, that the promise made them has not been annulled. For he who was the true Israelite not only descended from Abraham according to the flesh (for it is not the children of the flesh who are the children of God) but also descended from Abraham according to the promise of faith—he has received God's promises. For many are of Israel's stock, but not all of them are called Israel.[7]

More simply put, there are Israelites and there are Israelites. Not all those from Abraham's progeny are *named* or *called* Israel (*Israhel appellantur*). Though ethnically Israelite, not everyone *can properly be referred to as an Israelite* (*Israhel non potest dici*). One must differentiate between the Jew who has not seen the light and the Jew who has; only the latter qualifies a *true* Israelite (*verus fuerit Israhel*). Origen subsequently returns to this distinction between Israelites in general and the true Israelite: "Everyone who descends from the stock of Israel is called Israel, though one who sees God[8] with a pure spirit and a sincere heart is a true Israelite." And he proceeds to point out inconsistencies in the formulations of Paul himself, "in one instance referring to Israel according to the flesh, in another referring not at all to Israel in the flesh—as here, where, stating that God did not reject his people and wishing to explain the nobility of the Israelite soul, he said: 'I myself am an Israelite.'"[9]

Nobility of faith, purity of heart, and sincerity—not nobility of lineage—distinguish the spiritual Israel destined for salvation. As Origen concludes succinctly, "Such then is the remnant deriving from the election of grace" (*reliquiae quae secundum electionem gratiae factae sunt*).[10] At the same time, however, Origen holds that Paul differentiated between *two categories of Israelites* among the single, presumably Jewish people of Israel itself.

> The Apostle thus divides Israel into two parts, one of which, that which has found what it sought, he calls "the election," while the other, that which not only did not find what they sought but have been blinded by a sluggish spirit, he calls "the rest." Indeed, he says that God gave them "eyes that they would not see and ears that they would not hear, down to this very day," that is, until the end of the present age.[11]

Where lies the difficulty? On the basis of these overlapping but different distinctions, Origen does not clarify who constitutes the *reliquiae*, the remnant that Isaiah prophesied would be saved and that Paul suggested already were saved.[12] Was it the *largely non-Jewish Israel of the spirit*—God's people now from among the Gentiles[13]—or those *few believing Jewish Israelites*? Very many from among the people of Israel would be "objects of wrath, made for destruction."[14] One can identify the rest of Israel that God has blinded (*reliquus Israhel*),[15] closing off their hearts to the truth until "the end of the present age," either with the *Jewish nation of carnal Israel* or with the *remainder of the Jews* who have no faith in Christ.

Mystery: Reversal, Jealousy, Restoration

Complicating matters further, Origen takes pains to delimit the extent of *carnal* Israel's rejection, making guardedly positive mention of the salutary nature of the Jews and their role in God's historical plan, error and guilt notwithstanding. Origen understands Paul to mean that Jewish Israel stumbled temporarily but did not fall permanently. Its temporary lapse facilitated the salvation of the Gentiles. The Gentiles' conversion, in turn, will instill jealousy in Israel and ultimately rouse the Jews to believe in Christ. Albeit counterproductively, inasmuch as they neither believe nor understand the truth of Christianity, the Jews retain their religious fervor, zealously cherishing and pondering the law that God gave them.[16] Their alienation from God accordingly serves his purposes; it has not deprived them of their inheritance forever. Despite the Jews' rejection of Jesus and his apostles, the potential for restoration and renewal remains inherent within them.

Even more important, for all his denigration of the Jews and their observance—and historians have debated the extent to which he was benign or hostile toward Jews and Judaism[17]—Origen insists that their reintegration into the people of God remains a vital, indispensable component of the final redemption.

> For now, while all the Gentiles are making their way toward salvation, the treasures of God are being collected from the multitude of the faithful. But as long as Israel remains in its unbelief, the fullness of the Lord's portion will still not be considered complete; for the people Israel are missing from the whole. Yet when the plenitude of the Gentiles shall enter and Israel shall come to salvation through faith in the new age, that very people which had been first will, in coming very last, somehow complete that fullness of God's inheritance and portion. Thus, it is called "the fullness," because, in the very last days, it will supply what had been missing in God's portion.[18]

Completion—achievement of the "fullness" (*plenitudo*)—of the divine portion depends on the entry of both the full number of the Gentiles and the people of Israel into the community of the faithful.[19]

This interdependence of the fate of the Gentiles and that of the Jews, Origen elaborates, embodies the "mystery" that Paul wished to unravel to his readers. The initial election, the subsequent rejection, and the final reconciliation of Israel comprise vital elements of the divine economy of salvation; without them, God's plans for the redemption of humankind would remain unfulfilled. As long as Israel remained the sole bearers of God's covenant, "we Gentiles," Origen explained, had no access to God's inheritance or share in the rights to his scepter. Therefore God allowed blindness to come upon "not all but some" of the people of Israel, diverting them with the enticements of sin, and thereby making room for the Gentiles to share in the divine inheritance. Nonetheless, "when the plenitude of the Gentiles shall be achieved and Israel, envying their salvation, shall begin to dispel blindness of heart from herself and to perceive Christ, the true light, with her own elevated eyes, and so in keeping with earlier prophecies Israel, now roused, shall seek the salvation she had lost when blinded," the divine plan will be fulfilled.[20] At the core of the mystery, God uses the stumbling and disenfranchisement of the Jews to facilitate the salvation of the Gentiles, even as he anticipates the more wondrous salvation that the Jews' reinstatement will entail at the end of days. "It would appear absurd if, when their offense gave reconciliation to the world, their recovery would not confer something greater and far superior to the world."[21]

Yet, even here, despite Origen's intent to elaborate and to clarify, doubt and ambiguity remain. What, or who, is the part of Israel overcome by blindness? Origen gives the impression of a lesser part—"a part, that is, not all, but some" (*ex parte, id est non omnibus sed aliquibus*)—rather than a majority. If so, must one conclude that the (presumably greater) part of Israel *not overcome by blindness* represented a majority of the Jewish people? This would not comport with Origen's previous intimations that the saved remnant (*reliquiae*) of the Jews not blinded by God were relatively few in number, far fewer than the relative portion of the Gentiles that had come to have faith.[22] Alluding to the scriptural adage (Tobit 12:7) that "it is good to conceal the mystery of the king," Origen suggested that Paul had, perhaps, deliberately left his prophecy opaque and perplexing, just as a mystery should be: "The Apostle wanted this passage to be considered like mystery such that the faithful and the perfect might secretly hide its meaning among themselves as the mystery of God and not revealing it to the imperfect and less worthy."[23]

Divine and Human Responsibility

In Origen's commentary on Romans 9–11, although issues of human will and predestination in and of themselves do not bear heavily on the more central question of Israel's redemption, Israel's blindness and ignorance of the truth do figure significantly in the mystery of God's plan for human salvation. Surely, Origen maintains, people do sinful things of their own free will. He therefore deems Israel "inexcusable" for its rejection of God's truth and God's son.[24] Addressing the Jews, he declares: "If you do not wish to listen to us preaching, you now are to blame if, when you listen, you do not believe, and when you do not believe, you do not call out, and when you do not call out, you cannot be saved."[25] Still, the Jews do not sin deliberately. They remain ignorant of the truth that they have rejected; as we have noted, they maintain their zeal for God, misguided though that zeal might be. "However much they may have entangled themselves in so many evils of their own sins, nevertheless, a zeal and jealousy for God is in them," and this, Origen maintains, has led Paul in his epistle to pray for their ultimate salvation.

> They have a zeal for God that is not based on knowledge. . . . "Being ignorant of the righteousness that comes from God," they have submitted to their own sense of righteousness. It is of little benefit to have zeal for God and not to have understanding of zeal. After all, the Jews thought that they were acting with zeal for God when they sacrilegiously trespassed against the Son of God because they were zealots without knowledge.[26]

Ignorant of divine righteousness, they zealously sought righteousness as they, mere mortals, wrongfully perceived it.

Given their error, one might even reason that the Jews' present blindness constitutes not only a divinely wrought punishment but also a means for reducing the sinfulness in their rejection of Jesus. Origen explains that people use their bodily eyes to gaze upon good things or evil things—to lift them up toward God in heaven or to gaze upon worthless earthly pursuits (like the amusements of the circus and the theater). So too one can fix one's spiritual eyes either on the truth of God's word or on ways of fighting against the truth and against faith in Christ. Thus did Paul invoke Deuteronomy 29:4, imploring God to give the Jews "eyes so that they might not see the points of [their] perverted interpretation and ears so that they might not hear, that is the teachers of deception," in order to make them less guilty! Origen challenges his readers: Shouldn't one construe Paul as "one who wishes them things by which their sins might be reduced? For it is far better not to comprehend than to comprehend incorrectly."[27] Such an appreciation of God's blinding of "the rest of Israel" (reliquus Israhel—namely, those who have rejected Jesus) comports with Paul's insight into the divine mystery, that the Jews have merely stumbled temporarily in their sin, rather than fallen forever as the devil Lucifer had fallen. Accordingly, "their conversion will occur at the end of the present age, when the fullness of the Gentiles shall enter, and all Israel will be saved; but for that one [Lucifer] who is said to have fallen from the heaven, there will be no conversion at the end of the present age."[28] Until that end time, Origen bids us:

> Consider the wisdom of God in these matters, how for him not even misdeeds and setbacks occur pointlessly. Rather, although an individual offends by the free will of his own disposition, the supervision of divine wisdom makes it happen that the very thing by which some are impoverished through the harm of their own negligence makes others rich.[29]

"All Israel": The Fullness of the Gentiles and the Salvation of the Jews

If Origen, as we have noted, fails to explain precisely what part of Israel will succumb to blindness, he has similar difficulty deciphering Paul's prediction that "all Israel will be saved."

> What is this "all Israel" that will be saved, and what will this plenitude of the Gentiles will, God alone knows. . . . But this can also comport with our understanding: Just as Israel cannot achieve salvation so long

as it remains Israel according to the flesh and does not become a true Israelite fashioned according to the Spirit, apprehending God with the soul, neither can all of the Gentiles be saved unless they be found within the fullness, whatever is designated as the "plenitude" by the Apostle.[30]

Origen proposes a measure of parity between the conversion of "the full number of the Gentiles" and the salvation of "all Israel." Both will signify the culmination of human history, bringing God's plan for human salvation to its final fulfillment. Both represent qualitative as well as quantitative designations, defying any immediate, simplistic definition, although the progression of Origen's commentary up until this point in Romans 11 bespeaks the conviction that the "rest of Israel" (*reliquus Israhel*), blinded upon their initial rejection of Jesus, will ultimately be restored.

In the sentences that follow, however, Origen appears to reverse himself, thereby adding to our uncertainty: "He [Paul] does not say that such blindness had befallen all Israel, but only part. . . . For 'there is a remnant, chosen by grace. . . .' So, then, that remnant in its blessedness is comparable to the plenitude of the Gentiles; but the rest of Israel who have been blinded are comparable to the Gentiles who could not become part of the plenitude." Origen then offers the exegete seemingly clear-cut advice for sorting matters out.

> Therefore, what is found in the discourses of the prophets concerning the promises, texts of blessing, if these things concern Israel, they pertain to that remnant which was chosen; if about the Gentiles, they refer to the plenitude. Yet whatever disagreeable things are said about Israel, they certainly apply to the rest who have been blinded; yet if about the Gentiles, they surely concern those who are outside the plenitude.[31]

Origen thus draws a parallel between the full number of Gentiles and the *remnant of Israel*—not to *"all Israel"*—to be saved at the end time. This, in turn, might imply that just as there will, evidently, remain some unconverted, and therefore unsaved, Gentiles not part of this fullness, so will those many blinded Jews (*reliquus* or *residuum Israhel*)[32] belonging not to the presumably small "remnant" (*reliquiae*) of Israel remain unsaved at the end! Along with unbelieving Gentiles, they will suffer "torments and purifying punishments," no less than the fire of hell.[33]

At the end, will all Israel be saved, or only the remnant? Origen only begins to hint at a possible solution to this puzzle, although this, too, puzzles no less than it clarifies. He proceeds to suggest that the infernal punishments intended for those not included in "the full number of the Gentiles" or in "all Israel" will not last forever. How long will this "purging" endure? Again, only Christ knows.[34] Yet the fires of hell do purge and purify, suggesting that they will rehabilitate their victims. Does Origen mean, somehow, to add an additional, posteschatological stage to his expectations for the end time? Will the entry of "the full number of the Gentiles" at the end of days lead to the salvation of "all Israel," such that those errant Gentiles and Jews not included in these categories and yet suffering the torments of hell and themselves, at last, might be saved?[35] It may well. In any event, Origen does appear to maintain that the Jewish people as a whole will regain their status as a community of God's faithful, that all Jews will ultimately be saved.[36]

From the days of the church fathers until our own, Origen and the constellation of ideas that we label Origenism have consistently provoked controversy and division—with the doctrine of universalism, belief in the ultimate salvation of all rational souls (apokatastasis), among the most hotly debated of all.[37] If Origen taught that God would ultimately save everyone, what significance should we assign his efforts to demonstrate that he would eventually save the Jews? Why, one scholar has asked, belabor the issue, as we have done in the preceding pages?[38]

Here I would answer directly: above all, because Origen himself saw fit to do so. He himself deemed his painstaking interpretation of Romans 9–11 necessary, and he thereby intensified the spotlight on the ultimate—and essential—conversion of the Jews in Christian eschatology. Though often suspect in Western Christianity from the time that his works circulated in their Latin translation, Origen and his ideas had a pervasive and enduring influence.[39] In this book, Origen assumes importance not only for the distinctive interpretations of his monumental commentary on Romans, but also for his contribution to the interpretive enterprise that followed him. Subsequent Christian exegesis of Romans resounds with quotations, paraphrases, and echoes of his comments. Wrestling with Paul's prophecy of the salvation of Israel, Origen demarcated the hazardous exegetical playing field, as it were, for subsequent commentators who elaborated their understanding of Romans and its teaching concerning the "eschatological Jew."

Fathers of the Antiochene School

Most other surviving patristic commentaries on Romans pale in comparison with Origen's—in the depth of their exposition of chapters 9–11, in the level of their commitment to grapple with the exegetical problems inherent in the text, and in the extent of their concern with the issue of Israel's salvation.

Some addressed the matter of Israel's free will and resulting responsibility for their crimes against God, while others considered the logic underlying God's plan for salvation history, but few grappled in earnest with the difficulties implicit in Paul's prophecy that "all Israel will be saved." In his penchant for a systematic comprehensiveness and the ambiguity that often resulted therefrom, Origen, as we have suggested, appears to have delineated the range of problems and interpretive strategies available to his successors, Eastern and Western alike. These later commentators, in turn, selected and highlighted particular issues that engaged them the most.

John Chrysostom

We turn here to the works of two more Greek patristic authors. Though their commentaries on Romans 9–11 might lack the fascinating—if at times confounding—exegetical thoroughness of Origen's, they do illustrate the degree to which Christian exegesis of the New Testament and anti-Jewish polemic may or may not have proven interdependent. To one side of Origen, as it were, one can adduce the Romans commentary of John Chrysostom (347–407), well known for his avid campaign against Christian Judaizers in his city of Antioch and for the series of eight acrimonious sermons "Against the Jews" that he delivered in 386 and 387. If Origen had sought somehow to retain the duality of Israel and the nations throughout his scheme of salvation history, Chrysostom endeavored to erect an insurmountable barrier between communities of Jews and Christians. While we remember Origen for his interest in Jewish exegetical traditions and his interaction with rabbinic scholars of his day, Chrysostom hardly leaves us the impression that Jews and Judaism could enrich his Christianity. Thus did he preach against the Jews to his flock in Antioch: "Where Christ-killers gather, the cross is ridiculed, God blasphemed, the father unacknowledged, the son insulted, the grace of the spirit rejected."[40] No doubt that times had changed since Origen, that Christianity's victory in the Roman world fueled the aggressiveness of a churchman with pastoral responsibilities like Chrysostom, and that the metropolitan context of Antioch itself (still home to a dynamic Jewish community) contributed to the passion of Chrysostom's rhetoric. Yet personality, temperament, and theology influenced exegesis no less than these contextual factors, and Paul's predictions for "all Israel" afford an instructive case in point.

Alongside Origen's commentary, Chrysostom's homilies on Romans number among the acclaimed works of Christian biblical interpretation. For Johannes Quasten, renowned patristics scholar of the twentieth century, they were "by far the most outstanding patristic commentary on this Epistle and the finest of all Chrysostom's works."[41] Margaret Mitchell considered Chrysostom "Paul's most prolific commentator and avid admirer from the patristic period."[42] Several other scholars have actually praised Chrysostom for a balanced, restrained approach toward the Jews in his commentary on Romans. One investigator writes that in contrast to the anti-Jewish sermons, the Romans commentary establishes Chrysostom as "a man of his time," manifesting "an approach which is truly theological and much more worthy [than those polemical sermons] of the great Antiochean's name."[43] Another writer notes that while Augustine and others read ethnic Israel out of God's plan for the final redemption, Chrysostom retained a place for them and is, therefore, "a refreshing exception to this line of interpretation."[44] Nonetheless, one can very reasonably defend a diametrically opposed assessment of Chrysostom's Romans commentary, arguing that here John "engages in a consistent denunciation of Judaism," leveling unsparing criticism of the Jews' observance of the law and their unforgivable sin of rejecting Jesus, thus stripping them of any preferred status in the eyes of God. While the hope for Israel's salvation afforded Romans 9–11 cohesiveness as the thematic climax of Paul's epistle, Chrysostom "found it possible to support his understanding of the epistle as a whole only by means of a systematic disparagement of Judaism."[45]

Chrysostom could not but uphold Paul's teaching regarding the Jews, that "many have already believed, and more are likely to believe," thus attaining forgiveness from sin. And although "this has been promised, but has never yet happened in their case, nor have they ever enjoyed the remission of sins by baptism, certainly it will come to pass."[46] Nevertheless, as much as Origen's commentary strikes an ambivalent note concerning the Jews, Chrysostom's strikes a consistently strident one, especially in its review of those chapters that concern us.[47] Without mention of Origen, Chrysostom evidently strove to neutralize the dimension of his interpretation that one might label positive or supportive in its attitude toward the Jews, as one sees in the following.

- Chrysostom minimizes, discounts, or overlooks Paul's own Jewishness.[48] As opposed to Origen, who learned from the beginning of Romans 9 that because the apostle, in all earnest, offered himself to be cursed, "he gained salvation for his [Jewish] brothers,"[49] Chrysostom leaves his readers with a different message. Notwithstanding Paul's expressions of affinity to Judaism, "surely we do not therefore assert him to be a Jew, but upon this very score to be perfectly free from Judaizing, and clear of it, and a genuine worshipper of Christ. As then when you see him circumcising and sacrificing, you do not therefore condemn him as Judaizing, but upon this very score have the best reason for crowning him as quite an alien to Judaism."[50]

- Here one finds none of the salutary, redeeming qualities that Origen highlighted in the Jewish character. If Paul seems to allude to such positive attributes of the Jews or their enviable status in the eyes of God, Chrysostom explains this as a rhetorical ploy: "He does not take his aim at them, without first divesting them of a suspicion they had, lest, then, he should seem to be addressing them as enemies."[51] For example, where Paul acknowledges that the Jews retain a genuine zeal for God, Chrysostom alerts his reader that in fact the apostle "is now going again to rebuke them more vehemently than before," and he alludes, as he does throughout his comments on Romans 9–11, to the subterfuge in the epistle's rhetoric: "Observe how adroitly he favors them in the word, and yet shows their inopportune obstinacy."[52]

- Both Origen and John Chrysostom affirmed that the Jews acted of their own free will. Yet while Origen held that the Jews sinned out of ignorance, even if such ignorance did not render them inexcusable, Chrysostom displayed no such sympathetic understanding.

> But of Israel he [God] says, "All day long I have held out my hands to a disobedient and contrary people" (Romans 10:21), here meaning by "day" the whole period of the former dispensation. But the stretching out of the hands means calling and drawing them to him, and inviting them. Then to show that the fault was entirely their own, he says "to a disobedient and contrary people." You see what a great charge this is against them! For they did not obey him even when he invited them, but they disaffirmed him, and that when they saw him doing such, not once or twice or thrice, but constantly. . . . It was from their own temper that ruin had befallen them, and . . . they are wholly undeserving of pardon. For though they had both heard and understood what was said, still not even then were they minded to come to him.[53]

Likewise, while Origen understood God's blinding and deafening of the Jews—with "eyes that they would not see and ears that they would not hear"—as a means of containing the Jews' guilt for rejecting Jesus, Chrysostom writes that Paul "is but finding fault with their contentious spirit. For when they had eyes to see the miracles, and were possessed of ears to hear that marvelous teaching, they never used these as were fitting."[54]

- When Paul appears to emphasize the continuing sanctity and worth of the people of Israel in the divine economy of salvation, Chrysostom understood Paul as ostensibly preaching kindly to them[55] while in fact intensifying their condemnation. Unlike Origen's, in Chrysostom's reading neither the fall nor stumbling of ethnic Israel facilitated the redemption of the Gentiles—only their own genuine faith did. For Chrysostom, Paul's parable of the olive tree and the breaking off of its cultivated (Jewish) branches to accommodate the grafting of wild (Gentile) branches in Romans 11:17–24 underscores the rejection of Israel and the adoption of the Gentiles much more than it seeks to maintain a place for the Jews in God's plan.

- When he arrived at Romans 11:26 in his commentary, how, then, did Chrysostom treat Paul's prophecy that "all Israel will be saved"? By ignoring it almost completely! This second half of the verse warrants no comment whatsoever on the future salvation of all Israel; Chrysostom's commentary does not even cite it here. Earlier in his comments on Romans 11:11—"Have they stumbled so as to fall? By no means!"—Chrysostom explains:

> You see how he is attacking them again, and under the expectation of some moderation he proves them guilty of confessed sins. But let us see what even by way of allayment he does devise for them. Now what is the allayment? "When the fullness of the Gentiles," he says, "shall have come in, then shall all Israel be saved," at the time of his second coming and the end of the world. Yet this he does not say at once. But since he had made a hard onset upon them, and linked accusations to accusations, bringing prophets in after prophets crying aloud against them . . . ,

Paul again took a step back and, for the sake of correct appearances, reached out a seemingly appeasing hand toward the Jews.[56]

- Moreover, in reviewing the rhythm of the mysterious path that God had ordained for human history, Chrysostom emphatically ascribed primacy to the Gentiles, not the Jews. The latter were relative latecomers to the community of the elect.

> He shows here that the Gentiles were called first. Then, as they would not come, the Jews were elected, and the same result

occurred again. For when the Jews would not believe, again the Gentiles were brought over. And he does not stop here, nor does he draw the whole to a conclusion at their rejection, but at their having mercy shown them again. See how much he gives to those of the Gentiles, as much as he did to the Jews before. For when you, he said, disobeyed as Gentiles, then the Jews came in. Again, now that they have disobeyed, you have come in.[57]

In a word, the Gentiles have always taken precedence in God's plan for human redemption, so much so that the Jews were "of the class of parasites (i.e. guests), rather than those [Gentiles] in uncircumcision." For if Abraham "was justified and crowned while in uncircumcision, the Jews came in afterwards; Abraham is then the father first of the uncircumcised, who through faith appertain to him, and then of those in the circumcision."[58] In truth, argues Chrysostom, Paul ranks a Gentile believer in Christ even higher than Abraham in his or her election and faith.

So great is the power of spiritual words. For of one of the Gentiles, one who was recently come near, one who had done no works, he not only says that he is in nothing inferior to the Jew who believes (i.e. as a Jew), but not even to the patriarch, but rather, if one must give utterance to the wondrous truth, even much greater. For so noble is our birth, that his faith is but the type of ours.[59]

Granted, hopes Chrysostom, that the Jews will not perish forever, they will eventually be drawn to God out of jealousy for the Gentiles who had replaced them. Still, the Jews' fall appears much more permanent and difficult to reverse than it did in Origen's commentary. Addressing his Gentile audience, John recapitulates: "Now consider: you were disobedient, and they were saved. Again, they were disobedient, and you have been saved. Yet you have not been so saved as to recede again, like the Jews, but so as to draw them over through jealousy while you remain."[60]

Theodore of Mopsuestia

Known for its historical-literal orientation and its departure from the allegorizing tendencies of Origen and the Alexandrian "school" of biblical interpretation, the opposing Antiochene school did not always give expression to the markedly anti-Jewish tones of John Chrysostom in his exposition of Romans. Chrysostom's friend and colleague Theodore of Mopsuestia (ca. 350–428) also numbered among the deans of the Antiochene exegetes; yet he did not use his commentary on Romans as a vehicle for anti-Jewish polemic. To the contrary, he affirmed the centrally important contribution of the people of Israel to the redemption of humankind, both in the past and in the future, in terms at least as emphatic as Origen's, at times perhaps even more so. Jews served as catalysts for the salvation of the Gentiles, not in their falling away from God but in their faith in him, in their establishment of the early church, and in their preaching of the doctrine of Christ. "For what is there of the fine things by which the Gentiles are dignified," Theodore questioned rhetorically, "that is not from the Jews?"[61] And the Jews will continue to occupy center stage and play a leading role in the progression of salvation history. Following Origen but not Chrysostom, for instance, Theodore wrote that Hosea's prophecy of reversal cited by Paul in Romans 9:25–26 refers not to the replacement of the Jews by the Gentiles but to the future restoration of the Jews themselves.

> The Apostle uses the present quote from Hosea not as if the prophecy were about the Gentiles who were to be saved, for it clearly refers to Jews. . . . In this manner he also rejected Jews when they were corrupt in mind and, because of [their] nature, unwilling to be reverent, and he claimed them again when their ways were changed.[62]

Not the Gentiles, as one can easily understand Paul's prophecy (in Romans 11:11)—and so did we and Origen understand him[63]—but those Jews who already have faith in Christ will arouse the envy of their coreligionists and ultimately induce them to return to God.

> It is clear that he will not consider them rejected who desire to believe, for he has not only admitted those who believed, but has also shown them to be teachers of the world. For the statement, "so as to make Israel jealous" is not about the Gentiles, as some think, but about the Jews, in order to show that they also can be admitted if they desire to believe.[64]

In the same vein, Theodore understood Paul to assert that if a few believing Jews have already brought so many Gentiles into the faith, certainly the belief of all of the Jews would expedite the salvation of the entire world. For Theodore, it goes virtually without saying that "all Israel" to be saved in Romans 11:25–26 includes both "those who are naturally related to Israel, that is, the Jews (*Ioudaioi*), and those who are made worthy of the name through faith, that is those of the Gentiles.[65]

Two Latin Fathers

Few Latin fathers before Augustine left us commentaries on Romans, and this chapter closes with a look at the exegesis of two noteworthy church-men in the Latin West. As opposed to their Eastern counterparts already considered here, who probably encountered Jews more regularly, and in significantly greater numbers, these two writers displayed only a secondary interest in the Jews of the end time.

Ambrosiaster

Situated between Origen and his Greek successors discussed above and the Latin exegetes of the late ancient and medieval periods considered in the next chapter stands an anonymous church father whom subsequent writers mistakenly confused with Ambrose of Milan (who himself had rather little to say about the eschatological Jew) and whom scholars have come to remember as "Ambrosiaster." Writing early in the last third of the fourth century, Ambrosiaster composed the first complete Latin commentary on the epistles of Paul, before Rufinus translated the commentaries of Origen. Although one knows virtually nothing concerning the identity or career of this writer, his works manifest considerable erudition, and his thorough, systematic exposition of Romans surpassed that of any other Latin father. Ambrosiaster's commentary added new dimensions to the Western under-standing of Pauline teaching concerning the Jews, perpetuating and com-pounding ambiguities that we have already encountered. It appears to have done so independently, without merely following the example of Origen, and on purely exegetical grounds, unencumbered by pressing considerations of anti-Jewish ideology or polemic.[66]

Ambrosiaster recognized and addressed many of the same issues raised by Romans 9–11 that engaged Origen, but his resolution of those issues, while reminiscent of Origen's, nevertheless differed. Ambrosiaster evidently had difficulty understanding how Paul elicited sympathy and even praise for the Jews if God had rejected them, and, though affirming Paul's expectations for the salvation of Israel, he did not share Origen's resounding confidence, stated and unstated, that God would ultimately redeem the Jews as a people. For his part, Ambrosiaster proposed to distinguish between various catego-ries of Jews within the people of Israel as a means of explaining the osten-sibly inconsistent statements of Paul. Such a pattern of distinction runs like a unifying thread throughout Ambrosiaster's commentary on Romans 9–11, and yet, while it avoids some of the inconsistency of Origen's interpretation, it remains perplexing on other grounds.

Addressing Paul's anguish on behalf of his apostate Jewish kinsmen at the beginning of Romans 9 and then his self-consoling proposal that not all Jews qualify as true Israelites, Ambrosiaster reasons that Paul grieved

> only for these who disbelieved on account of jealousy; they still can believe. . . . For those predicted to be unbelievers, however, one should not grieve very much, because they were not predestined for life. The foreknowledge of God determined [Latin *decrevit*] long ago that they should not be saved. Who laments for someone who is believed to be long dead? When the Gentiles, who were previously without God, slipped in and accepted the salvation which the Jews lost, anguish is aroused. But then in turn it is calmed, because the Jews themselves are the cause of their own ruin.[67]

Ambrosiaster's comment conveys at least three ideas that figure significantly in his explication of the Jews' role in the divine economy of salvation. First, not all Jews of the future were predestined to believe, only some. Second, one must differentiate between the present disbelief of these two categories of Jews: some failed to believe because of their envy (*per invidiam minime crediderunt*), and these retain the potential for belief and salvation; yet for those inherently lacking in faith (*incredulis*), there remains no hope for the future. And third, divine foreknowledge notwithstanding, those doomed to perdition bear the responsibility for their own fate.

These notions reappear as Ambrosiaster's commentary on Romans unfolds. In one particularly important passage, where Paul highlights the blindness imposed upon Israel as punishment for its rejection of Jesus and his gospel, Ambrosiaster thus differentiates between two classes of people.[68] One class deliberately rejects the truth.

> There is one type that because of their own ill will is blinded forever, in order that they may not be saved. They are possessed of such ill will to the point that they say they do not understand what they hear even though they do understand. . . . They were blinded, so that thereafter they would be unable to believe and be saved. They were supported in their wish, so that because they declared what they knew was true to be false, they thereafter did not understand what is true. As a result, the falsehood they desired they held to be true.

The second class rejects the truth in error, owing to a misguided zeal to uphold their ancestral ways.

There is another type of people that, in following the righteousness of the law, do not accept Christ. Because they do so not out of the jealousy of an evil will (*non per invidiam malae voluntatis*), but out of a mistaken zeal for the tradition of their fathers, they are blinded temporarily. . . . For that reason they are blinded, so that once the Gentiles have been admitted to their promise, they may return to the faith of God out of their own zeal, when they become jealous of the Gentiles. Because some of the Jews resisted the savior out of zeal for the law, not out of ill will but rather out of ignorance, they were not blinded forever.

Ambrosiaster repeatedly employs this interpretive strategy of differentiating between Jews blinded temporarily and permanently in his exposition of Romans 9–11: in explaining the distinction between the remnants of Israel destined for salvation and the rest of Israel doomed to damnation (9:27, 11:2–5, 11:8–10); in understanding Paul's limited praise for the Jews (10:1–4); and in elaborating Israel's ultimate salvation (11:25–26). For all that he may have wished to minimize the problems that we may have encountered in a reading such as Origen's, however, these do persist, and on multiple grounds.

The Remnant and the Rest

First, Ambrosiaster's comments raise questions concerning the remnants of Israel that, according to the prophecy of Isaiah adduced by Paul, would be saved, whereas the rest would not. *Who* were these remnants, and *when* would they receive the faith and salvation? Ambrosiaster explains: "So the prophet says that out of a huge multitude only believers, whom God foreknew, are saved."[69] Here, then, Ambrosiaster identifies those Jews predestined by God for salvation with the *reliquiae* of Isaiah's famous prophecy, although, using the present tense, he does not specify whether this prophecy of their salvation referred to past or future events—the first or second coming of Christ. Most Christian exegetes, Origen included, tended to understand the remnant of Israel in Romans 9:27 as those Jews who still number among God's chosen now that the Gentiles have replaced the Jews as the larger community of God's faithful. From Paul's perspective as interpreted by these exegetes, then, Isaiah's prophecy applied to the past, to the first coming of Christ. The prediction had already been fulfilled, perhaps even in the person of Jesus the Jew himself. Yet Ambrosiaster's standing distinction between those Jews blinded temporarily and those blinded permanently—that is, those preordained for salvation and those destined for perdition—suggests that these destinies have yet to materialize, that they will materialize at some time in the presumably eschatological future.[70] Did Ambrosiaster therefore differentiate between three classes of Jews: (1) those predestined for salvation and already saved (Isaiah's *reliquiae*), (2) those predestined for future salvation but at present blinded by their envy, and (3) those predestined for ultimate damnation? Or, contrary to the general consensus of opinion, did Ambrosiaster read Isaiah's prophecy of the remnant as unfulfilled, applying to the future?

Although the latter alternative might prove simpler and more consistent for Ambrosiaster, he appears to have opted for the former, more complicated and confusing interpretation. At the beginning of chapter 11, he portrayed Paul—in reaffirming God's commitment to the children of Abraham—as differentiating between "that part of Israel *[that] has been saved*, the part that God foreknew would be saved," and "the part of Israel that has been assigned to perdition on account of persistent unbelief *[that] could still be saved*."[71] Ambrosiaster had set out, one would think, to distinguish between two categories of Jews; yet the complexities of Paul's epistle seem to yield three: those saved already, those yet to be saved, and those never to be saved.

Blindness, Ignorance, Error, Envy, Malevolence

Second, Ambrosiaster appears to have contradicted himself with regard to the rationale for this distinction between various classes of Jews. As noted above, his comments on Romans 9 assert that some Jews failed to believe because of their envy (*invidia*), while others, owing to their ill will, were inherently incapable of believing (*increduli*). Expounding Romans 10, however, he explains precisely which Jews Paul praised for their devotion to God in spite of their ignorance of Christ: "The apostle says that out of ignorance they did not believe in Christ; for they indeed had a zeal for God. But because they were unaware of God's will and plan, they acted against the one whom they professed to defend. The apostle is speaking about those who out of error rather than the malevolence of envy (*non malivolentia invidiae*) failed to accept Christ."[72] Previously he noted that the Jews overcome by jealousy / *invidia* still retained the ability to believe and would eventually be saved; now, and again while commenting on Romans 11, he writes that the envious Jews in particular qualify as malignant and damned. Furthermore, as we have seen, Ambrosiaster refers to both of these groups as blind,[73] but only to one of them as ignorant.[74] At the same time, in the continuation of the passage from which we just quoted, he finds authoritative support for his distinction in Acts 3:17: "The apostle Peter also speaks of them [namely, Jews who failed to accept Christ because of their error and not out of the malevolence of envy (*non malivolentia invidiae*)]: 'I know, brothers, that you acted in ignorance, as did also your rulers.'"[75]

Ambrosiaster has here adduced a verse that both he and most medieval Christian exegetes after him understood as bearing upon the intentions of those Jews responsible for Jesus's crucifixion: Did the Jews who killed Jesus understand the magnitude of their crime—that is, did they realize that they were taking the life of their messiah and the son of God? Ambrosiaster, Augustine, and others typically used terms like "ignorance" and "blindness" almost interchangeably in explaining the error of the Jews, while those who later came to condemn the Jews for perpetrating their crime intentionally asserted that the Jews *knew*, not that they were blind. Once again, although the possibility remains that Ambrosiaster allowed for a third, intermediate alternative—of Jews blinded, but whose blindness derived from envy,[76] not from ignorance or error—it does not appear to comport well either with his own understanding of the intentions of Jesus's Jewish killers or with that of most subsequent Latin exegetes.[77]

THE MYSTERY AND ITS RATIONALE

Third, as he explains Paul's prophecy concerning "all Israel," Ambrosiaster alludes only briefly to the "mystery" in God's plan for salvation history, which Origen had expounded in depth as a recurring pattern of reversal, replacement, and reinstatement that would culminate in the final redemption of the world at large. Ambrosiaster surely acknowledges, as we have seen, that "for that reason they are blinded, so that once the Gentiles have been admitted to their promise, they may return to the faith of God out of their own zeal, when they become jealous of the Gentiles."[78] Yet he displays relatively little interest in Romans 11:11–15, in which Paul discusses the rationale for God's mysterious plan, allotting it not even two pages in (the printed edition of) his commentary, as opposed to the eleven pages that they receive in Origen's. And addressing Romans 11:25–26, Ambrosiaster merely reiterates how some Jews, blinded by their misguided but well-intentioned zeal for the law, will eventually regain their free will and return to Christ after jealously observing the Gentiles in possession of the promise given to Abraham. "All Israel" and "the full number" or "fullness" of the Gentiles—terms so important, and difficult, for Origen—receive no comment, and readers must simply answer for themselves those questions left unanswered by Paul. One can well infer that those other Jews, blinded by their ill will toward God and predestined never to have faith, will never return and be saved, although on this, too, Ambrosiaster equivocates, suggesting:

> Although the Jews have sinned gravely in rejecting the gift of God and are worthy of death, nevertheless because they are the children of exemplary people, whose privileged position and meritorious conduct garnered many blessings from God, they will be received with joy when they return to the faith, since God's love for them is kindled by the memory of their fathers.[79]

In the following sentences, Ambrosiaster interprets "the gifts and the calling of God are irrevocable" or, as in the Old Latin and Vulgate, "without repentance" in Romans 11:29 to mean "the gift of God forgives sins freely in baptism,"[80] that is, without expressions of penitence. Yet if he thus raised the possibility that the Jews need not repent in order to be saved, the fact remains that they must become Christian and have faith in Christ.[81]

In all, Ambrosiaster's reading of Romans 9–11 hinges much more on matters of heavenly foreknowledge, human will, and divine justice than on the dialectical interaction between Israel and the nations at the heart of God's plan for salvation history.

Pelagius

Though deemed heretical in Catholic tradition for his belief that human nature still (even after the fall) has the power to do good, refrain from evil, and thereby, albeit with the indispensable help of God's grace, merit salvation, Pelagius (ca. 354–ca. 420) and his extensive interpretation of Romans 9–11 rightfully assume a place in our story. A British monk who spent the last decades of the fourth century and the first decade of the fifth in Rome, Pelagius probably encountered the Latin translation of Origen's Romans commentary soon after its publication in 406, and he may well have read Ambrosiaster's as well. Not surprisingly, in view of the central importance of free will, human responsibility, and divine foreknowledge in Romans, his own commentary on the epistle was the longest of his works. It led him to build upon some of the key ideas of his predecessors and yet depart radically from their expectations for the last days. Like Origen, Theodore of Mopsuestia, and Ambrosiaster, Pelagius accorded the Jews a distinctive primacy in God's plans for human redemption. Even more than other fathers who preceded him, he developed the notion that humans have free will and ultimately earn the fate that they deserve, divine foreknowledge of their destiny notwithstanding. With regard to Paul's predictions for the redemption of Israel, however, Pelagius drained it of its eschatological significance.

In addressing Romans 11, Pelagius suggests that the salvation of all the Gentiles did not entail the complete disenfranchisement of the Jews but signaled equivalence in the status of both peoples in the eyes of God. Moreover, Pelagius understands the prophecy of all Israel's salvation in Romans 11:26 (*omnis Israhel salvus fieret*) to have materialized already: "all Israel was saved," not "all Israel will be saved." Otherwise, he elaborated, one would have to understand Paul's citation (in Romans 11:26) from Isaiah (59:20) to refer to the future as well, and this leads to an untenable conclusion.

> Some interpreters regard all these as future events. To these one must reply: Then this prophecy—"the Deliverer" of Israel "will come from Zion"—has yet to take place, and Christ will come again to set them free; and, if they have been blinded temporarily by God, and not by themselves, what will come of those who perish now as unbelievers?[82]

The position of those who postpone the salvation of Israel to the end time, such that in large measure the Jews remain deprived of salvation until then, renders God's blinding of Israel grossly unjust in the eyes of Pelagius. For if God has purposefully distanced the Jews from salvation for the duration of the present era, what will come of those denied the opportunity to have faith of their own accord, as people must in order to save their souls?[83]

Pelagius thus effectively sidesteps the question of how many Jews are included in the Israel *to be saved*, stripping the divine mystery of Romans 11:25 of its commonly presumed eschatological resolution. While Israel's blindness afforded the Gentiles the appropriate occasion for their salvation (*occasionem eis salutis*), neither does Pelagius view this blindness as signifying a wholesale rejection of the Jews and their law, nor does he consider the displacement of the Jews necessary to make room for the Gentiles. On the contrary, God wished to bring the Gentiles into the fold for the express purpose of wooing the Jews. "They were not broken off for your sake," Paul writes the Romans of the Jews, "but you were grafted in because of the fact that they were broken off."[84] In other words, rather than save the Gentiles instead of the Jews, God sought to level the distinction between them, emphasizing that the same essential human condition—the inherent capability of *achieving* justification through faith with the help of God's grace along with a (not insurmountable) propensity for sin—characterized them all.

Indeed, without overlooking the importance of the gift of God's grace, Pelagius's commentary suggests that divine rejection and election correspond directly to the just deserts of those concerned, and that such status can fluctuate in accordance with human merit and demerit. God "has not rejected everyone, he says, and not forever, but only those who do not believe, and as long as they do not believe."[85] And again, specifically of the Jews: "They have not fallen away completely and beyond hope. . . . He loved them so much that the Gentiles were called for their salvation, so that when they saw that the Gentiles were allowed into the kingdom of God, they might perhaps repent more readily."[86] Jews who do not number among the elect thus bear responsibility for their own rejection: "Israel as a whole has not obtained righteousness, because it did not seek it by faith but thought that it was justified solely by works of the law, though it disregarded the greatest commandments of the law." And, when "God gave them a sluggish spirit, eyes that would not see," their blindness did not constitute the punishment that other church fathers had reckoned it, but the essential state that they had brought upon themselves and from which they could extricate themselves.

> The Scripture says: "Before a man are life and death; and whichever pleases him will be given to him" (Ecclesiasticus 15:18)—clearly, so as not to eliminate freedom of choice. It is therefore God's prerogative to allow them the spirit of stupefaction that they desired, for they have always disbelieved the words of God. Indeed, if they had wanted to have a spirit of faith, they would have received it. But even today Christians who doubt the resurrection and reward or Gehenna have sought a similar spirit for themselves, for in this passage the prophet was addressing both unbelievers and sinners.[87]

Placing present-day Israel and the nations of the world on a par, Pelagius thus brings us full circle. Israel sinned, bringing blindness upon itself. God redeemed the Gentiles, essentially for Israel's sake. Now that their redemption has occurred, Jews and Gentiles share the same status. Those who fail to believe share in the same blindness, the same spirit of confusion to which the apostle had alluded. Of these, those who will to repent have the ability to do so, and, with the help of God, they can re/join the community of the elect. The reference of Romans 11:26 to the salvation of "all Israel" refers to developments already transpired, to the very establishment of Christianity. Simply put, it refers to the inauguration of a new basis for achieving salvation, the basis of faith. "Both transgression and faithlessness seized Israel to such an extent that the time came when all the Gentiles were given access to life. All of Israel, thus, was being saved in the same way as the full number of the Gentiles—by faith alone—so that, because they had been equals in transgression, they were equals in Christ."[88] How many Jews will ultimately avail themselves of the new opportunity open to them? For Pelagius, that question appears to have no bearing on the essential meaning of Romans.

CHAPTER 3

The Latin West

From Augustine to Luther and Calvin

Romans 9–11 and the eschatological role of the Jews generally did not receive the same probing consideration in the works of the later Latin fathers and their medieval successors as they did in the commentaries of Origen and Ambrosiaster. Instead, one finds that subsequent Western theologians borrowed extensively from the interpretations of their predecessors, and that inconsistency continues to abound in their commentaries. Although the question of Israel's place in the divine economy of salvation hardly lost its currency during the Middle Ages, other issues—the nature and effects of original sin, and the tension between predestination and divine justice, for example—evidently overshadowed the questions concerning us at present in the eyes of the epistle's commentators. The "Jewish questions," in turn, proceeded to spark discussion within the framework of avowedly anti-Jewish polemical treatises as well as in other exegetical and theological contexts. Against the backdrop of this general assessment, again we proceed to focus selectively on trends, individuals, and exceptions worthy of our attention.

Augustine

Most important and influential of the Latin church fathers, Augustine of Hippo (354–430) did not complete a systematic commentary on Romans. His interests in the epistle focused chiefly on the interplay of divine election and grace and the human will in determining the call to faith, much more than on Paul's prediction of the salvation of Israel. Nonetheless, as with so many other questions of theology and biblical interpretation, Catholic attitudes toward the Jews and Judaism among them, Augustine contributed roundly to prevailing trends in the Christian interpretation of Romans 9–11 during the millennium that followed him.[1]

In contrast to those of Pelagius, Augustine's comments on Romans restore the salvation of "all Israel" to the end time, in a manner that expresses his debt to both Origen and Ambrosiaster. Echoing Origen's rationale for the alternating pattern of rejection and election for Jews and Gentiles outlined by Paul in Romans 9–11, Augustine explains in a letter to Paulinus of Nola that the "mystery" of Romans 11:25 bears upon the reason why it pleases God "to allow those to be born, to increase and multiply, those who he foreknew would be wicked, even if he himself did not make them wicked." Augustine here affirms that while God might work in a way that defies simple explanation on our part, all that transpires in terrestrial history gives expression to the wondrous objectives of his creation: "His design is deeply hidden, whereby even in making a good use of the wicked for the benefit of the good, he exalts the omnipotence of his goodness, since, just as their evil constitutes bad use of his good works, so does his wisdom make good use of their evil works."[2]

How, then, do the fall and final restoration of the Jews serve the interests of the divine master plan? Paul's denial in Romans 11:11 that the Jews have "stumbled so as to fall" intends not to underscore the reversibility of their fall—which for some might in fact prove irreversible—but its ultimately beneficial quality. The Jews have not fallen purposelessly; rather, their fall facilitates the salvation of the Gentiles.[3] Yet here Augustine takes his explanation one step further than Origen's. Referring Paulinus to Romans 11:28, where Paul indicates to the Gentiles that "as regards the gospel they [the Jews] are enemies of God, for your sake," Augustine elaborates: "Now, the price of our redemption is the blood of Christ, who could manifestly not be killed except by his enemies. Here is the use of wicked men for the benefit of the good."[4] Not only did the fall of the Jews make room for the Gentiles in the community of God's faithful, as Origen had explained the mystery, but the Jews' central role in spilling the salvific blood of Christ, specifically, served God's purposes well.

On the question of the eschatological destiny of the Jews, however, Augustine's letter to Paulinus appears to have taken a step away from Origen's position, blending it with ideas of Ambrosiaster. Quoting Romans 11:25–26, Augustine endeavors to understand the partial nature of Israel's blindness.

> He said [that Israel was blinded] "in part," because not all of them were blinded; there were some among them who recognized Christ. But the fullness of the Gentiles comes in among those who have been called according to the plan. And so all Israel shall be saved, inasmuch as from among the Jews and from among the Gentiles who have been called according to the plan, they more truly constitute Israel . . ., while he calls those others "Israel according to the flesh." Then he inserts the testimony of the Prophet: "He who delivers and banishes ungodliness from Jacob will come from Zion, and this will be my covenant with them, when I take away their sins"—not, indeed, those of all the Jews, but of the elect.[5]

We have seen how Origen himself noted that the "true Israelite . . . sees God with a pure mind and a sincere heart,"[6] while many who number among Israel of the flesh do not. Similarly, Origen acknowledged that just as only God knows who and how many will number among the plenitude of the Gentiles, so does the precise numerical extent of "all Israel" remain a riddle. But, while Origen still belabored the need for the people of Israel to return to God in order to bring his plan for human history to its perfect fulfillment, giving the impression that the Jews as a people will be saved, Augustine suggested otherwise, at least in his letter to Paulinus. Augustine's eschatological Israel is here a reconstituted Israel; it is "more truly Israel," including both Jews and Gentiles. Accordingly, one can perceive in this passage a threefold classification of the Jews along lines laid down by Ambrosiaster. Some Jews recognized Christ; blindness struck the rest, and, of these, God will save some, the elect, in the end; the others will remain unsaved. "All Israel," then, should not mean all Jews, but rather a composite entity including Jews and non-Jews. When Paul invokes biblical prophecies like that of Psalm 69:23–4, "Let their eyes be darkened so that they cannot see, and make their loins tremble continually," he referred not to all the Jews: "These indictments do not concern those who believed in Christ at that time . . ., nor those who have believed in Christ up to the present or who, henceforth, up to the end of the world, will believe in Christ, that is, the true Israel who will see the Lord face to face. For they are not all Israelites who are sprung from Israel."[7] Similarly, with regard to Paul's ensuing declaration (Romans 11:28, quoted just above) that "as regards the gospel they [the Jews] are enemies for your sake, but as regards election they are beloved for the sake of their ancestors," Augustine clarified emphatically that these are two distinct groups of Jews.

Are those enemies who died in their enmity, and those from among the Jews who still die as adversaries of Christ, are they elected and beloved? Not at all, and what person, however stupid, would say this? But both of these terms, though contrary to one another, that is, "enemies" and "beloved", apply, not indeed to the same individuals, but nonetheless to the same Jewish people and to the same posterity of Israel according to the flesh.[8]

Thus formulated, the Augustinian position seems fairly clear and comprehensible, but, at the same time, it might well appear counterintuitive. Augustine's acclaimed doctrine of Jewish witness, which defined and highly valued the continuing, *present* role of the Jewish people in the divine economy of salvation, could understandably lead one to expect its eventual salvation.

As for their present dispersion through almost all the lands and peoples, it is by the providence of the true God, to the end that when the images, altars, groves and temples of the false gods are everywhere overthrown, and the sacrifices forbidden, it may be demonstrated by the Jewish scriptures how this was prophesied long ago. Thus the possibility is avoided that, if read only in our books, the prophecy might be taken for our invention.[9]

This Augustinian teaching, which underlay the Catholic Church's policy of toleration for Jews and Judaism in Christendom, nourished—and was nourished by—the notion that blind ignorance prevented the Jews from recognizing Jesus as messiah and God. We recall that when Ambrosiaster divided the Jews blinded for their rejection of Jesus into two sets, those who would be saved and those who would not, he identified these groups with those who sinned out of blind error and those who sinned out of malice, respectively. Augustine, too, may have deliberated as to the degree of guilt incurred by the Jews who rejected their savior,[10] but, when it came to their part in the crucifixion, he generally insisted that the Jews who crucified Jesus did not recognize him as their messiah or as divine.[11] Just as the fall of the Jews, deriving from their role in the crucifixion, once contributed to the salvation of world at large, so too does their survival in the present; therefore, Augustine teaches, God mandated that survival in his express command (Psalm 59:12) "Slay them not, lest my people forget."[12] If the Jewish people of the past and the present have functioned collectively in accordance with the divine interest, couldn't one reasonably think similarly concerning the Jews of the end time, to whom Elijah will come to preach a true, spiritual understanding of the law? Had not Paul himself declared: "If their rejection means the reconciliation of the world, what will their acceptance mean but life from the dead?" Indeed, as Augustine acknowledges, "That in the last days before the judgment the Jews are to believe in the true Christ, that is, in our Christ, is a frequent topic on the lips [lit., in the sermons] and in the thoughts [lit., hearts] of believers."[13] No less a devotee of Augustine than the twelfth-century Joachim of Fiore understood him to have taught precisely that.[14] Augustine himself, however, may not have drawn the conclusions we and others might have anticipated, even if some presume to think that he did.[15]

Patterns of Interpretation in the Middle Ages

Based on the spectrum of diverse, ambivalent, and often inconsistent patristic opinion that we have encountered thus far, we can track several recurring tendencies in the Latin exegesis of the Middle Ages, mindful that any given writer might well find a place on multiple lists. Pelagius's interpretation of Romans enjoyed a measure of popularity among some later writers, whether or not they recognized the dangerously Pelagian nature or heretical source of their arguments and took steps to "correct" their own commentaries accordingly. The sixth-century Cassiodorus (d. ca. 585), for example, positively declares that one cannot merit the gift of divine grace, and to assert otherwise "is Pelagian";[16] and he allows, albeit far less emphatically, for the conversion of Israel at the end of days.[17] He followed Pelagius, however, on a number of counts: the initial advent of Christ resulted in equivalence between the status of Jews and Gentiles.[18] God's wish for such parity (rather than a preference for the Gentiles over the Jews) underlay his rejection of Israel.[19] And the Jews once willed not to have faith in Jesus,[20] just as they must will to regain it, even if the will of penitent sinners alone does not entirely suffice to facilitate their salvation.[21] In a commentary on Romans erroneously attributed to Jerome, Cassiodorus's contemporary John the Deacon reiterates verbatim the Pelagian argument that Paul's prophecy of Israel's salvation had already been realized.[22] A pseudo-Augustinian Romans commentary of the ninth century also borrows extensively from the commentary of Pelagius,[23] whose ideas even find an echo in the writings of Pablo de Santa María at the beginning of the fifteenth century.[24]

Yet the majority of Western medieval theologians wavered between the positions of Origen, Ambrosiaster, and Augustine that we have considered, offering little new insight to the understanding of eschatological expectations for Israel in the Epistle to the Romans.[25] Some surely followed Augustine in understanding "all Israel" in Romans 11:26 as including only those Jews and Gentiles who have faith in Christ come the end time. These converted Jews and non-Jews would be saved, while the others would not. Stating that the end time would bring parity between Jews and Gentiles, the ninth-century Sedulius Scottus hints that, inasmuch as a great many, but not all, Gentiles would be saved in the "fullness" envisioned by Paul in Romans 11:25, the same would hold true for the Jews.[26] Atto of Vercelli (885–961) makes this conclusion explicit, adopting the Augustinian notion of a reconstituted Israel that would embody remnants of carnal Israel alongside many Gentiles.[27]

Others, however, continued in the direction of Origen and identified Israel with the Jewish people, thus persisting in according the Jews primacy in the divine economy of salvation. Such an identification, admittedly, did not require an emphatic, explicit declaration that God would ultimately save each and every Jew. One could speak collectively of the Jewish or Israelite people, of Synagoga, of Judea, or simply of "the Jews" and convey essentially the same impression. Addressing Job 38:41 ("Who provides for the raven its prey, when its young ones cry to God, and wander about for lack of food?") in his *Moralia on Job*, for instance, Gregory the Great (d. 604) identifies the raven with the Jews and its young as the apostles, who originated in their midst.

> Thus is it written: "until the full number of the Gentiles come in, and so all Israel will be saved"—because the holy apostles strove especially hard first to preach to those that heeded them and then to present the example of the converted Gentiles to those that resisted them. . . . When the Jewish people sees the Gentiles converted to God through the efforts of the preachers, it ultimately grows ashamed at the foolishness of its disbelief. Then it understands the teachings of its holy scripture, when it recognizes that they became clear to the Gentiles even before themselves. . . . With the travels of the apostles throughout the world completed, it finally accepts spiritually those things of which it had long deprived itself owing to the constraints of its perfidy.[28]

Several hundred years later, the ninth-century Haymo of Auxerre found additional support for the "mystery" of Romans 11 in 1 Corinthians 15:46: "It is not the spiritual which is first but the physical [*carnale*, although the Vulgate reads *animale*], and then the spiritual"; so, too, will the fullness of the physical Gentile church enter the faith before the more spiritual Synagoga.[29] And early on in the twelfth century, Herveus of Bourg-Dieu explained that the blindness imposed upon part of the Jews induced them to crucify Jesus, in ignorance of his identity. Yet when the fullness of the Gentiles will embrace faith in Christ, such blindness will end, and the remaining Jews will find salvation; empowered by the preaching of Elijah (himself a Jewish prophet!) and Enoch, they will resist the onslaught of Antichrist to which many non-Jews will fall prey. "In the end they will convert, even if now they are our enemies."[30] One finds nearly identical views in the twelfth-century Romans commentaries of William of Saint-Thierry[31] and Peter Lombard,[32] and in the *Glossa ordinaria*.[33]

Yet among those who insisted on the Jewish composition of Paul's Israel, some still imposed limitations and criteria in determining who would eventually be saved. The same Haymo of Auxerre just mentioned notes in a different context that Synagoga would believe only *ex parte*.[34] Haymo's contemporary and fellow Benedictine monk Rabanus Maurus cites Ambrosiaster to the effect that only those Jews blinded by their error, not by malice, would be saved.[35] Late in the eleventh century, Bruno the Carthusian similarly limited the number of Jews within "all Israel,"[36] affirming that one must understand collective terms like "fullness" and "all" not quantitatively but qualitatively. Notable twelfth-century churchmen followed in this direction, including Peter the Venerable of Cluny[37] and Otto of Freising,[38] who afford examples of how the ramifications of interpreting Romans extended far beyond exegetical literature per se. One should note how Ambrosiaster's distinction between those predestined for salvation and those not so predestined among the currently unredeemed people of Israel thus found echoes over the course of the Middle Ages, particularly as issues of human intentionality grew more pressing in their own right. Furthermore, while Ambrosiaster does not appear to have had a well-developed polemical agenda, others did. As I have demonstrated elsewhere, the differentiation between disbelief originating in blindness and unintentional error and that deriving from ill will came to figure significantly in medieval reevaluations of the guilt of the Jews responsible for Jesus's crucifixion.[39]

Within this group of churchmen, Peter Abelard sparks particular interest; many of the ideas we have encountered resonate in his commentary on Romans, along with others that we have not yet seen. Owing to the curiosity evoked by Abelard's explication of Romans 11:26, we quote it at some length. Abelard notes that "the remnant" of the Jews destined for salvation in Romans 9:27 could refer to the Jews who already found salvation in Christ or "the simple and ignorant among the people who were cast away among them" but will eventually see the light.[40] Ultimately, after the entry of the plenitude of the Gentiles prophesied in Romans 11:25, he writes,[41]

> all Israel [will be saved], namely, according to their individual tribes. Therefore, many will be converted in the end, by the preaching of Enoch and Elijah.[42] Nevertheless, not all will be converted, since the truth says to them concerning the Antichrist [John 5:43], "Another will come in his own name, and you will receive him," so that not all the

Jews will be converted at the end of the world, just as they were not at the coming of Christ, but only the Lord's remnant.

Gravitating toward an Augustinian position, Abelard evidently maintains that the all of Israel to be saved includes representatives of all twelve Israelite tribes but not the twelve tribes in their entirety. Otherwise, how could one understand Jesus's own prediction that the Jews will ultimately join the ranks of Antichrist? Abelard then adduces a letter of Jerome to confirm that Isaiah's prophecy of "a remnant will be saved" means "Although the multitude did not believe, nevertheless a few will." He also quotes prophetic forecasts of doom and redemption planned by God for the end of days cited by Isidore of Seville in *De fide catholica contra Iudaeos* and brings Isidore's own conclusion:

> All these passages pertain to the carnal kingdom of that people or to its worship, because they will be beyond repair. For those promises of repair which the word of their [prophets] expresses are promised to that portion of the Jews which will believe on God. For not all the Jews are to be redeemed, and not all will be saved. But all those who are to be chosen by faith will be saved.[43]

Surprisingly, then Abelard hesitates, noting that this might not entail what Paul in fact intended in his epistle.

> The Apostle himself, where he says and so all Israel will be saved, also seems to agree with some of the saints who say that at the end they will be converted through the preaching of Elijah and Enoch, either according to all the tribes (we should not understand it individually, as we said), or perhaps those who at first acknowledged the Antichrist when he restored the Judaic rites, and who were corrected later through the preaching of Enoch and Elijah.

Abelard suggests that, in Paul's view, the Jews might eventually respond to the preaching of Elijah and Enoch and convert—either as representatives of the twelve tribes or perhaps en masse, meaning those who will first succumb to Antichrist and then acknowledge the truth in the message of Elijah and Enoch. Offsetting the weight of the evidence first adduced from Jerome and Isidore, Abelard then cites some of his predecessors, the "saints" mentioned in the preceding paragraph, who envisioned a more collective salvation of the Jews of the eschaton.

- Gregory the Great: "At the end all Israel will run together to faith when the preaching of Elijah is recognized."

- Remigius of Auxerre: the Jewish "captivity will be ended with the preaching of Elijah and Enoch, since all the Jews will believe in Christ at their preaching."
- Haymo of Auxerre: "He will turn ungodliness from Jacob fully, just as it is written, 'And he will redeem Israel from all his sins,' and when the fullness of the Gentiles has gone in, then all Israel will be saved."

His own preferred forecast notwithstanding, does Abelard concede that Paul appeared to predict otherwise? As one approaches the later Middle Ages, Christian expectations for eschatological Israel remain rife with uncertainty and ambiguity.

From Thomas Aquinas to the Early Reformers

Thomas Aquinas

The greatest of medieval European theologians, still revered by Roman Catholics as their leading doctrinal authority, Thomas Aquinas himself contributed to this ambiguity and helped to bequeath it to generations of scholars who followed him. Indeed, Thomas steered a relatively conservative, balanced course with regard to the status of Jews and Judaism in a properly ordered Christian society. Yet some historians, I among them, have recently linked aspects of Thomistic teaching to the growing intolerance toward the Jews that characterized late medieval Europe, while other writers, most prominently present-day Catholic theologians, have sought to cleanse Thomas of all traces of supersessionism, even recommending his teaching as a basis for interfaith dialogue today. Thomas's commentary on Romans, chapters 9–11 in particular, lies at the heart of this discussion, especially with its concern for two issues that engaged the apostle Paul: first, the relation between the Jews and the people of Israel in the divine economy of salvation; and second, expectations for the Jews at the end of days.

How does Thomas's Romans commentary define the role of the Jews in salvation history?[44] While it innovates but little in its substance, the formulation and expression of its ideas bear noteworthy characteristics. Early on in his commentary, Thomas asserts that the term "Jew" is an honorable one (225). The Jews' privileged state in receiving the law encompasses their "being the race to whom the law was given" and the advantages that accrued from instruction in the law and from its observance (224). The exemplary precept of circumcision served to remit original sin, and it benefited the Jew if he observed the law, "just as profession benefits religious clergy, if they observe the rule" (238). No less emphatically, however, Aquinas qualifies that these benefits of circumcision applied "to the time before the passion of Christ," not thereafter (239). Moreover, inasmuch as "he is not a real Jew who is one outwardly, nor is true circumcision something external and physical" (Romans 2:28), the benefits of the law now relate to him who is a Jew "inwardly (*abscondito*), that is, whose *heart* is possessed by the precepts of the law." In all, "inward Judaism and circumcision prevail over the outward" (245).

Nonetheless, though teaching that true Jews and circumcision are inward in the heart and not outward in the flesh—just as Paul had explained the identity of Israel—Aquinas appears to qualify his assertions. He turns to Paul's declaration that they retain value and prerogatives in the eyes of God, and in his plan for salvation: "They have an advantage both in contemplating divine matters . . . and in the provision of temporal things. . . . They have further advantages relating to their ancestors, to the promises, and to their offspring" (249). No matter how egregious the unbelief and ingratitude of the Jews toward God, "if the Jews' prerogative were taken away[45] on account of the unbelief of some, it would follow that man's unbelief would nullify God's faithfulness—which is an unacceptable conclusion" (253). No matter how serious the crime, "God's justice, which entails keeping his promises, is not changed on account of sin" (257). In a word, "man's sin does not exclude God's faithfulness" (259).

When he arrives at Romans 9, Aquinas focuses his concern, like Paul's, on the eschatological. He notes that the apostle seeks to promote the honor of Christ "which would be enhanced by the conversion of the Jews" (740), and his attention then turns again to the special dignity or greatness of the Jews. This derives first from their descent "from the stock of Jacob, who was called Israel" (743). Second, it encompasses an array of blessings and benefits, which we might best enumerate schematically.

1. Spiritual benefits.
   a. In the present—their adoption as sons of God (Romans 9:4): "Hence it says in Exodus: 'Israel my first-born son.' This refers to spiritual men (*spirituales viros*) who arose among that people"; that is, it refers to those Jews who have seen light.
   b. In the future—the glory of the sons of God promised them.
2. Figural benefits, of which three are figures of present spiritual benefit (*tria sunt figura praesentis spiritualis beneficii*). Nothing in Thomas's formulation redirects the focus away from these "spiritual men" just mentioned.
   a. The testament, meaning either the "pact of circumcision" or "the new covenant preached first to the Jews."[46]

b. The law given through Moses

c. Divine worship

3. That blessing that "pertains to future glory": God made them many promises of earthly reward, "but by these temporal goods spiritual goods were prefigured" (744).

4. The dignity of their descent from "those ancestors who were especially acceptable to God" (745).

5. The greatness of their descendant Jesus (746).

Once again, albeit now at greater length, Thomas elaborates how the dignity of the Jews pertains not to Israel of the flesh but to Israel of the spirit.

> After asserting the greatness of the Jews, the Apostle now shows that it did not refer to those who descended according to the flesh from the ancient patriarchs but to the spiritual progeny chosen by God. First, he shows that this greatness arises from God's selection; second, that this selection applies in equal measure to Jews and Gentiles (748).

Thomas expands at length on Paul's comments pertaining to divine election and predestination: of Abraham's children—and Isaac's too—"one was chosen, and the other rejected" (756). In the case of Isaac's twin sons, Esau and Jacob, though born of the same physical union, one was predestined for the eternal love of God, the other to eternal rejection, such that the elder would ultimately serve the younger (Genesis 25:23).

> It can be taken figuratively so that by the elder is understood the Jewish people, who were the first to receive the adoption of sons . . ., and by the younger is understood the Gentiles, who were called to the father later and were signified by the prodigal son. The elder people in this case serve the younger, inasmuch as the Jews are our book-bearing slaves (capsarii), preserving the books from which the truths of our faith are drawn (761).

The rejection of the Jews involves no injustice on God's part; owing to their crimes, they deserve destruction. On the contrary, their continued survival, "the fact that he preserves their life proceeds from his exceeding goodness" (781). For "the sin of the Jews was greater than that of the men of Sodom. . . . Consequently, it was an act of divine mercy that the Jews were not totally exterminated as were the Sodomites" (806). And what of the promises and benefits that once distinguished the Jews: divine adoption, love, deliverance from original sin through circumcision, and more? Emphasizing Paul's citation of Hosea (1:10) in Romans 9:26, Thomas replied concerning the Gentiles now of the true faith. Though once unfit to receive the blessings of divine sonship, divine love, and liberation from the yoke of original sin through circumcision, now, "even among the believing Jews (*etiam apud Iudaeos credentes*)," these Gentiles shall be called the "sons of the living God" (800).

Addressing Romans 10, Thomas affirms that the present fallen state of the Jews is neither universal nor unprofitable nor irreparable (813), and he assesses the ignorance underlying the unbelief of the Jews (815–22, 845–57), a subject falling largely beyond the purview of this book.[47] Turning to Romans 11, however, Thomas veers toward the heart of our present concerns. Though the Jews as a people have fallen from divine election, God has not rejected them "in their entirety" (*totaliter*), since he has not rejected those chosen and predestined (*praedestinatos*) for a better fate (861–63). Paul cited Scripture[48] to the effect that "the remainder of the people," those who "have been blinded because of their malice," bear the lot of God's rejection. And Thomas notes, "To this the Apostle adds on his own, 'until this present day,' because *they will see and hear at the end of the world, when the hearts of the children will be converted to the hearts of the fathers*" (872–75; emphasis mine). Additionally, the fall of the Jews has proven exceedingly valuable.

> This can be understood in three ways. In the first way, that by their offense, which they committed in killing Christ, the salvation of the gentiles was obtained through the redemption of Christ's blood. . . .[49] In the second way, it can be understood of the trespass by which they rejected the teaching of the apostles, with the result that the apostles preached to the gentiles. . . . In a third way it can be understood as meaning that on account of their impenitence they have been scattered among all the nations. Everywhere, as a result, Christ and the church had testimony to the Christian faith from the books of the Jews—testimony for converting the gentiles, who could have suspected that the prophecies concerning Christ, which the preachers of the faith brought forward, were fabricated, if they had not been proven by the testimony of the Jews. Hence it is said in Psalm 58[59]:12, "He shows me concerning my enemies, that is the Jews, 'Slay them not, lest my people forget, scatter them by your might'" (881).

Contrary to scholars who have argued that Aquinas dissociated himself from the Augustinian doctrine of Jewish witness and the construction of the biblical Jew that nourished it,[50] Thomas here reaffirms that doctrine but subsumes Augustine's hermeneutically crafted Jew into his appreciation of Pauline eschatology, upholding, in general terms at least, the optimistic outlook expressed by the apostle in Romans 11:12–16. In Thomas's words, "If for the benefit of the whole world God permitted the Jews to do wrong and be diminished, much more will he repair their destruction for the benefit of the whole world."

What, then, constituted the mystery of the Jews' contribution to the drama of the end time?

> [If] the loss of the Jews occasions the reconciliation of the world, inasmuch as we have been reconciled to God through the death of Christ, what shall the acceptance be if not . . . that it will make the gentiles rise to life? For gentiles are the believers who will grow lukewarm . . . or will fall away entirely, being deceived by the Antichrist. These will be restored to their primitive fervor by the converted Jews (*Iudaeis conversis in pristinum fervorem restituentur*). And just as the gentiles were reconciled owing to their [the Jews'] enmity, so after the conversion of the Jews, the end of the world then imminent, there will be a general resurrection, through which men will return from the dead to immortal life. (890)

With regard to the second coming of Christ, just like the first, the non-Jewish addressees of Romans must recall that "Judea did not receive salvation from the gentiles, but just the reverse: 'salvation is from the Jews' (John 4:22)" (897). Just as God's rejection of the Jews once facilitated the salvation of the Gentiles upon the foundation of the church, so too will they, upon their future conversion, facilitate the Gentiles' prevailing over the deceptions of Antichrist and their return to the faith. Finally, Aquinas explains the promise of Paul that blindness will persist among the Jews "until the fullness of the gentiles will come in, and so all Israel will be saved."

> It should be noted that the word "until" (*donec*) can signify the cause of the blindness of the Jews. For God permitted them to be blinded, in order that the full number of the gentiles come in. It can also designate the termination, namely, that the blindness of the Jews will endure up to the time when the full number of the gentiles will come to the faith. This comports with what follows concerning the future rehabilitation of the Jews, when he says "and then," that is when the fullness of the gentiles shall have entered, "all Israel will be saved," not some as now, but all, universally. (916; and cf. 882)

Contrary to the difficulty previously encountered in converting Jews, Thomas echoes earlier voices[51] in highlighting "the ease with which the Jews will be converted at the end of the world" (919). The fulfillment of God's promises will mark the culmination of his plan for saving the world; nothing can undermine that plan, "because God does not change his mind" (924).

This brief review allows for highlighting several issues as bearing most directly on our subject. First, *who comprises the people of Israel?* On the one hand, Thomas reiterates Paul's affection for his people, as well as the irrevocability of God's promises to the Jews, perhaps suggesting the correspondence, if not absolute identity, of the Jews with Israel. On the other hand, the singular greatness of the Jews (*dignitas Iudaeorum*)—notwithstanding its repeated mention in Romans—"does not refer to those who descended according to the flesh from the ancient patriarchs but to the spiritual progeny chosen by God" (748). Or, expressed otherwise, although Paul bemoans the fall of his Jewish kinsmen and prays for their rehabilitation in Christ, Aquinas shows that he takes pains to assign God's ancient promises to the true Israelites, to "those who are upright and see God by faith" (750). This applies to the status of their privileged origin and descent from both Abraham and Jacob/Israel; to their adoption as sons of God; and to the figural benefits bestowed on Israel that "are *figures* of present spiritual benefit" rather than intrinsically spiritual benefits themselves: the pact of circumcision, the law given to Moses, and the worship of God (744). Inasmuch as some have highlighted this passage as denoting the continued election of the Jews and enduring value of their pact of circumcision in the divine economy of salvation,[52] we should take care in its precise elucidation.[53] For the implication that many ethnic Jews no longer qualify as genuine Jews (beyond their exclusion from the true Israel) exceeds the claims of Paul, at least in its terminology; it may well hint at the increasingly hostile anti-Jewish polemic of twelfth- and thirteenth-century Christendom, which distinguished between true biblical Israelites and inauthentic postbiblical Jews. As for "the blessing which pertains to the future glory" elaborated in the Old Testament, here, too, Thomas makes clear that "by these temporal goods spiritual things were prefigured" (744), in a manner comporting with the tolerant stance of the *Summa theologiae* toward the practice of Judaism in Christendom.

> Although unbelievers may sin in their rites, they may be tolerated, on account of some good that results or some evil that is avoided. Thus from the fact that the Jews keep their ceremonies, which once foreshadowed the truth of the faith we now hold, there follows this good—that our very enemies bear witness to our faith, and that what we believe is set forth as in a figure (*quasi in figura*).[54]

Simply put, Christians may tolerate the practice of Judaism inasmuch as it still directs one toward Christ.[55]

And second, *what constitutes the eschatological role of the Jews?* Beyond the "mystery" of the fall, the alienation, the blindness, and the displacement of carnal Israel that in Paul's eyes facilitated the salvation of a reconstituted, spiritual Israel, Aquinas affirmed the witness doctrine of Augustine concerning the role of the Jews at present. As noted above, God intended the Jews to function in Christendom as enslaved book-bearers, guarding the Scriptures that authenticate the truth of Christianity (761), so that their dispersion in exile, books in hand, would overcome doubts concerning the authenticity of biblical testimony (881). Nonetheless, Thomas's Romans commentary sounds more hopeful than Augustine concerning the future salvation of the Jews. Although Thomas stops short of concluding that each and every Jew will be saved, one can expect the redemption of the full complement of those elected by God in this regard; for "if they are dear to God, it is reasonable that they be saved by God" (923). Thomas's expectation that these converted Jews will restore Gentile victims of Antichrist to their Christian faith (890), even if not grounded in the teachings of Augustine, recalls hopes for the eschatological Jew voiced by more recent, twelfth-century churchmen—like Herveus of Bourg-Dieu and Peter Abelard, both mentioned above—as well as others, like Honorius Augustodunensis, whom we shall meet later in this book.[56]

Mindful of the virtually unchallengeable deference that Catholic theologians accord to Thomistic doctrine, reminiscent of the commitment of Christian scholars in general to the teaching of the apostle Paul, we end this discussion of Thomas with the following conclusions. Thomas's appraisal of the Jews and Judaism in his commentary on Romans, much like that in the *Summa theologiae,* which I have considered elsewhere, and much like that of Paul himself, resounds with ambiguity.[57] Yet the historian reading Paul and Thomas ought well to confront such ambiguity without imposing a present-day theological agenda on either one. Setting out, as some might have done, because "we require additional confirmation . . . that Thomas, at the very least, is not anti-Jewish," and concluding precisely that "Thomas is not anti-Jewish: he remains faithful to the plot line established by Paul,"[58] does not advance the cause of open-minded historical investigation.

In all, though Thomas discusses the Jews, their present state, and the fate that awaits them at the end of time in a tone considerably milder than some of his predecessors, his interpretation of the Pauline epistle breaks little, if any, new ground. Most important, Thomas maintains the ambiguity that resounds throughout Romans. On the one hand, God chose the Jews, the nation of Israel, to play a critically important role in facilitating his salvation of the world and accorded them a singular status in keeping with that role: dignity, prerogatives, and promises for the future that distinguish them from others. On the other hand, these benefits now pertain to genuine Jews of the heart, Israelites of the spirit—whether of Jewish birth or not—who have seen the light and subscribed to the new covenant of grace. Has ethnic Israel fallen from its once elect status? Yes, but hardly incurably or irreparably. Has God forever rejected his once beloved Jewish people? Certainly not in its entirety. He has not rejected those among the Jews specifically chosen and predestined for salvation (861–63, 872), and one can look forward to the collective salvation of "all Israel" at the end time (contrasted with the previous salvation of select, individual Jews—*non particulariter sicut modo, sed universaliter omnes*, 916), even if that collective does not include every single Jew. Unlike the Jews of the present age, these Jews of the eschaton will be converted with ease, and, as noted, they themselves will help secure victory in the final struggle against Antichrist.

Though his commentary on Romans did not address the nature of Jewish guilt in the crucifixion of Jesus in any meaningful way, it did, perhaps ineluctably, touch upon the nature of Jewish guilt in the rejection of Christianity and whether it derived from ignorance or intention. As we saw in the previous chapter, the Romans commentary of Ambrosiaster linked those Jews truly ignorant of the truth of Christianity with those destined for salvation, while those whose malevolence underlay their lack of faith will suffer eternal damnation. Some other commentaries, the *Glossa ordinaria* included (on Romans 11:7), hinted in such a direction but hardly addressed the issues in any systematic fashion.[59] Thomas, I have shown in earlier studies,[60] elsewhere condemned the Jewish leaders of Jesus's day for willfully murdering their savior and God. Here in his Romans commentary as well, he invokes the notion of voluntary ignorance that undergirded this argument. Commenting on Romans 10:18—"Have they not heard?"—Aquinas explained: "After showing [cf. 813] that the fall of the Jews is pitiable, because they sinned from ignorance, here the Apostle shows that their fall is not entirely excusable; because their ignorance was not invincible or rooted in necessity, but somehow voluntary" (845). Yet just as Augustine's doctrine of Jewish witness and the policy of "slay them not" that it entailed did not lead to an inclusive forecast of Jewish salvation at the end time, so too did Thomas's more inclusive expectation not negate the elements of the new, thirteenth-century evaluation of contemporary Judaism as entailing deliberate, mortally sinful rejection of God's word. Just as one cannot read that evaluation directly into his Romans commentary, so should one not read it out of the Thomistic synthesis, despite its inconsistencies and hesitations.[61]

From Late Medieval to Early Modern Exegetes

During the remaining centuries of the Middle Ages and the first generations of the Reformation, Christian commentators on Romans departed minimally from the prevailing patterns of interpretation in all that concerned the eschatological Jew, and this chapter ends with a few select points of interest.[62] The Franciscan Nicholas of Lyra, well known for his valuation of Rashi and Jewish exegetical tradition in his *Postillae* on Hebrew Scripture, followed mainly in the footsteps of Thomas Aquinas, rather than those of Augustine, predicting the collective salvation of the Jewish people at the end of the world—"many more" (*multo magis*) than the small remnant that already converted to Christianity.[63] Echoing the view of Thomas and others who preceded him that the Jews of the end time would participate in the struggle against Antichrist, Nicholas maintained that they would willingly sacrifice their lives (*mortem suscipient*) in combating the eschatological villain.[64]

Exegetes of the Protestant Reformation and Catholic Restoration blazed few new trails in their explication of Romans 9–11. Early in the sixteenth century, the renowned Catholic humanist Erasmus of Rotterdam extended his biblical interpretation to a broader readership in his pioneering paraphrases of Scripture. In the paraphrase on Romans, where he passionately assumes the voice of the apostle, Erasmus commends the zeal, albeit a misguided zeal, that led the Jews to reject Jesus: "I cannot excuse their unbelief, but nevertheless to some extent something can be alleged as a pretext for their sin."[65] Though known for his hostile, intense condemnation of Jews and Judaism in other contexts, he then enthusiastically anticipates the conversion and salvation of the Jews at the end time.

> I shall reveal a certain secret to you, my brothers. . . . This blindness came upon the Jewish people, but not upon all of them and not forever. A good many of them do acknowledge Christ, and others will persist in their own blindness only until the number of Gentiles, for whom the fall of the Jews has now opened an access, has been filled. But when they see that the whole earth abounds in the profession of the Christian faith, that they await that messiah of theirs in vain, that their city, temple, sacred things, and people have been dispersed and scattered, they will finally begin to regain their vision and to acknowledge their own error, and they will understand that Christ is the true messiah. And thus all of the Israelites will be restored to salvation, although now part of them have fallen away from it.[66]

Although "very many" of the Jews "do not accept the gospel of Christ but adhere to the letter of the law and are thus the enemies of God," their holy ancestry and nationality will facilitate their conversion despite their fall—"if they recover their senses."[67]

In the similarities and differences between their interpretations of Romans 9–11, Martin Luther and John Calvin exemplify the ambiguity in the medieval exegetical tradition that they inherited. Both described God's election of the Jews and the benefits accruing from that election at considerable length. Calvin displayed the influence of John Chrysostom in his reading of Pauline rhetoric concerning the Jews,[68] and he followed Augustine in conceiving eschatological Israel (the "all Israel" to be saved) as a blended entity of Jews and non-Jews—even if the Jews would retain a measure of primacy as God's "first-born."[69] Luther, for his part, looked forward to the collective conversion of Jewish Israel. Though he generally preferred Augustine (to the medieval Scholastics) on matters of sin, grace, and justification in Romans, Luther broke with Augustine, continuing to view the Jews as simultaneously elect and rejected. Referring to that "part of the dough offered as first fruits" (Romans 11:16), Luther explained:

> To understand the apostle rightly, we must know that what he says extends over the lump of the Jewish people and has reference to the good ones among them of the past as well as of the present and the future. Even if some among them are rejected, the whole lump must be honored because of the elect, just as any community must be honored because of the good ones among its members, even though the wicked outnumber them.[70]

Luther took further issue with Augustine's contention that no human being, "however stupid," would consider the Jewish enemies of Christ at once both beloved and rejected.[71] Luther adamantly asserted otherwise: the very same Jews are holy lump and cut-off branches.

> [They] are "fullness" and "diminution," and, likewise, they are enemies for the sake of the Gentiles" and "yet greatly beloved for the sake of their fathers." Again and again, the Scripture says diverse things about them on account of the diversity that prevails among them. This sounds as if the apostle wanted to regard them one and all personally as enemies and beloved friends, inasmuch as, though he distinguishes between individual persons, he emphasizes that they belong to the same lump.[72]

Luther thus taught straightforwardly: "The Jews who expelled Christ to the Gentiles, where he now reigns, will come back to him in the end."[73] This objective ranked so high on God's eschatological agenda that he intended the "stumbling" and rejection of the Jews, even more than as a means to draw the Gentiles into the faith, as a means of saving the Jews through the jealousy that would arise among them. Admittedly, "their fall is the salvation of the Gentiles; yet this was not its final purpose, but the fact that they fell was to induce them to emulate the good of those who rose up. . . . They would not let themselves be so stimulated if he said that he had given the Gentiles something worthless or that the Jews had not lost anything."[74] One might consider Luther's stance impressively clear. Yet some three decades after delivering his lectures on Romans, Luther wrote in his scathing anti-Jewish diatribe, *Vom Schem Hamphoras*:

> In sum, they are the devil's children damned to hell. . . . Some, so inclined, may still hope for that whole gang as they wish. I have no hope there anymore and know of no writings concerning such hope. We cannot even convert the majority of Christians and have to be satisfied with a small number; it is therefore even less possible to convert these children of the devil! Although there are many who derive the crazy notion from the 11th chapter of the Epistle to the Romans that all Jews must be converted, this is not so. St. Paul meant something quite different.[75]

Precisely what did Paul mean? Luther does not explain.

Exegesis and the Eschatological Jew

Many great Christian theologians hedged their bets, so to speak, accommodating multiple, even contradictory, viewpoints on the salvation of eschatological Israel. In appropriating teachings of their predecessors, commentators on Romans sought to minimize dissonance in the exegetical traditions of their church, even as their own writings perpetuated the difficulties in deciphering Paul's predictions for the Jews of the end time. Peter Abelard, for one, explained that God would ultimately save only representatives of the twelve Israelite tribes, but he immediately adduced the opinions of other "holy men" who maintained that "all Israel" denoted the Jewish people in its entirety. Thomas Aquinas observed that the Gentiles at the end of time would be saved "entirely or for the most part," and he implied that the Jewish people would be saved in a similar manner, "not some as now, but all, universally." And Martin Luther, in the passage quoted at the opening of the previous chapter, proclaimed the nigh impossibility of a precise, incontrovertible understanding of "all Israel will be saved."

The early seventeenth-century Flemish Jesuit Cornelius à Lapide offers a fitting and helpful distillation of the patristic and medieval Christian interpretation of Scripture with which to conclude this survey.[76] In his commentary on Romans 11:25, Cornelius states that once the Gentiles are called to salvation, "all the Jews are to be enlightened, to believe, and to be saved." Several sentences later, however, he indicates that this plenitude of the Gentiles signifies a specific number—apparently not each and every Gentile individual—and immediately adds: "Thus, in their wake, all Israel will be saved, and from the respective plenitudes of Gentiles and Jews there will rise and stand one complete and perfect church." Although Cornelius unhesitatingly interprets "Israel" as the Jews, the parity between the collectives of Gentiles and Jews destined for salvation and inclusion in the eschatological church might lead one to infer that the plenitude of the Jews to be saved likewise represents a particular number of Jews, and is not necessarily all-inclusive.

Assimilating the indecisiveness of the patristic and medieval exegetical tradition that he inherited, Cornelius thus enumerates three conflicting approaches to the understanding of "all Israel" in his comments on Romans 11:25–26. First, he writes, some of the church fathers understood all Israel "not carnally, but spiritually," referring to all believers destined to be saved from among *both Jews and Gentiles*. Offering a second interpretation that Cornelius found preferable to the first, others asserted that all Israel means all Jews, such that "at the end of the world all Jews without exception shall be converted and saved." Third, Cornelius explains that "all Israel" can mean "almost all, [that] very many from among the individual tribes of Israel, except for the tribe of Dan [of which Antichrist will be born[77]], will be converted and saved." Curiously, although it reminds one of Abelard, Cornelius cites no earlier proponent of this third alternative interpretation, which he avowedly likes the best. Moreover, his stated preference hardly tallies with his unqualified opening comment on Romans 11:25 that "*all the Jews* are to be enlightened, to believe, and to be saved."

Cornelius's summary of the exegetical alternatives for Romans 11:25–26 sheds light on the linkage between Christian eschatology and biblical interpretation. Just as the Augustinian doctrine of toleration for the contemporary Jew as constructed in medieval Christian theology—whom I have elsewhere dubbed Christianity's "hermeneutical Jew"[78]—derived from a particular exegetical outlook and found justification in particular biblical proof texts, so, too, did Christian expectations for the Jew of the end time stem from the interpretation of Scripture. Polyvalence in Scripture comported well with a multiplicity of interests and perspectives among its interpreters, and, much like its hermeneutical Jew, Christianity's "eschatological Jews" evoked inconsistency and ambivalence in the attempts of churchmen to define their character and role. The blend of Paul's prophecy of the salvation of Israel with commonly assumed connections between the Jews and Antichrist understandably generated a wide range of alternative eschatological scenarios, as will become evident in part 2 of this book.

Part II

The Jews and Antichrist

As the world awaited the onset of the third millennium some two decades ago, the Baptist Reverend Jerry Falwell, one of the most prominent leaders of the Christian Right in the United States, shared his thoughts concerning Antichrist and his imminent appearance.

> "Is he alive and here today?" he asked. "Probably. Because when he appears during the Tribulation period he will be a full-grown counterfeit of Christ. Of course he'll be Jewish. Of course he'll pretend to be Christ. And if in fact the Lord is coming soon, and he'll be an adult at the presentation of himself, he must be alive somewhere today. . . ."
>
> Mr. Falwell said . . . that he did not intend his statement to be anti-Jewish. He said he meant only that the Antichrist must be Jewish because Jesus Christ was a Jew. "If he's going to be the counterfeit of Christ, he has to be Jewish," Mr. Falwell said.[1]

In response to the outcry evoked by his words in various quarters, Falwell asserted that his words reaffirmed age-old Christian tradition, and one indeed finds varied expressions of that tradition as one looks progressively farther back in time.

For example, in the twentieth century, the Jewish Antichrist figured prominently in Nazi propaganda.[2] Hundreds of years earlier, in an explicit

FIGURE 1. The conception of Antichrist. *Von dem Endkrist*, fol. 3r. Strasbourg, 1482. Call number *KB+ 1482 (Antichrist. Legend. Von dem Endkrist). Rare Book Collection. The New York Public Library. Astor, Lenox, and Tilden Foundations.

woodblock illustration (fig. 1), a late fifteenth-century German biography of Antichrist depicts his conception as resulting from an incestuous union between a Jewish man and his daughter.[3]

One century earlier, a vernacular German work related the following.

> The Antichrist shall be born in Babylon of the Jewish people, from the lineage of a patriarch, called Dan, and shall be born out of wedlock and circumcised like a Jew. . . . Afterwards, when he is so arrogant that he says he is Christ, God's son, the angel will disown him and the Devil will appropriate him. The Red Jews, who are locked up, come out and follow him. They will rebuild the Temple at Jerusalem and worship him as a god and say, he is Christ, and our Lord Jesus Christ was the Antichrist.[4]

And in the most popular medieval work on Antichrist, the tenth-century French monk Adso of Montier-en-Der had already incorporated elements of this narrative in a brief biography of the eschatological villain.

> As our authors say, the Antichrist will be born from the Jewish people, that is, from the tribe of Dan, as the Prophet says: "Let Dan be a snake in the wayside, an adder on the path." He will sit in the wayside like a

serpent and will be on the path in order to wound those who walk in the paths of justice and kill them with the poison of his wickedness.[5]

Such linkage between Antichrist and the Jews certainly betrays a conception of Judaism as standing in stark contrast to Christianity, much like thesis and antithesis. The two are mutually exclusive. Both cannot be true. Corroboration of one bespeaks the refutation of the other, and vice versa. The Christian image of the Jew as the "other" par excellence nourishes and intensifies in the identification of the Jews with the eschatological enemies of God. Although the Jews were never his sole eschatological foes, the urgencies of Christian apocalypticism, which itself owed much to its Jewish heritage, surely accentuated the stark contrasts between the Jews and the true believers destined for salvation at the end of days.

Yet a word of caution is in order as we set out on our journey. Though rife with antagonism and negative stereotypes, Christianity's portrayal of the Jews and Antichrist is nonetheless far from simple or homogeneous. Rather, these imagined eschatological Jews give expression to a classic Christian ambivalence, in which a desperate longing for the reintegration of Judaism and Christianity often accompanies and tempers deeply rooted antagonism and hatred. As Reverend Falwell himself made clear,

> The Jews are God's chosen people, and we are, as Christians, miraculously connected to them. . . . I sincerely love the Jewish people. I honestly believe that, as a Christian, it is my responsibility to honor and revere the people God chose as His own. However, my love and respect of the Jewish people cannot alter the prophetic truths of the Bible. Keep looking to the skies, my friends. He is returning soon![6]

CHAPTER 4

Antichrist and the Jews in Early Christianity

"The history of the Antichrist follows the history of Christ like a shadow."[1] And yet, while countless people might speak of Antichrist, no one can say for sure who he is or where he comes from. Since Wilhelm Bousset first published his classic study, *The Antichrist Legend*, in 1895, historians of religion have investigated, revisited, and repeatedly debated the history of the Christian idea of Antichrist. What were its roots? When, where, and under what circumstances did it take shape? How should one rank the importance of its various components? Many investigators have advanced opposing, albeit well-formulated and instructive arguments, and we intend here neither to review them systematically nor to resolve definitively the issues over which they disagree. Rather, we shall focus on the Jewish dimensions of the Antichrist myth, from its Jewish sources to the Jewish identity and attributes of Antichrist and his followers.[2]

From Jewish to Christian Scripture

No matter what particular stance one takes concerning Antichrist, one must appreciate that Christian eschatology had roots in the religion of biblical Israel and in Jewish apocalyptic thought and literature of the Second Temple period—in the Judaism that spawned and nurtured Christianity.[3] Messianic prophecies of the Hebrew Bible inculcated belief in God's future salvation of Israel. They highlighted the role of the redeemer-king, the *mashiach*, the messiah or anointed one, a term that translated into Greek as *Christos*. Moreover, in a variety of ways, these prophecies envisioned enemies of God and of the messiah who would attempt to thwart God's salvation of the elect in advance of the end of days. Simply put, whether one does or does not view the idea of Antichrist as grounded *primarily* in the teachings of the Hebrew Bible, that idea should certainly have felt at home in the matrix of those teachings. Several clear-cut examples illustrate how Christianity's eschatological villain unquestionably had forerunners in the legacy of biblical Israel.

In his farewell address prior to their entry into the promised land, Moses warns the children of Israel against false prophets and deceivers from among themselves, villains who will seek to lead the people astray, away from God and the laws of the covenant.

> If prophets or those who divine by dreams appear among you and promise you omens or portents, and the omens or the portents declared by them take place, and they say, "Let us follow other gods," whom you have not known, "and let us serve them," you must not heed the words of those prophets or those who divine by dreams; for the Lord your God is testing you, to know whether you indeed love the Lord your God with all your heart and soul. . . . If anyone secretly entices you— even if it is your brother, your father's son or your mother's son, or your own son or daughter, or the wife you embrace, or your most intimate friend—saying, "Let us go worship other gods . . .," show them no pity or compassion and do not shield them. (Deuteronomy 13:1–8)

As Wayne Meeks pointed out, Moses's admonition presages the "Man of Lies" and evil teacher of the Dead Sea Scrolls, ideas still prevalent among various sectarian Jewish groups of the first Christian century and similar to that of their false prophet and anti-messiah.[4]

The seer Daniel, the Hebrew Bible's own apocalyptic visionary, foresaw the coming of a tyrannical ruler who would follow the heyday of the four great earthly kingdoms of the ancient Near East.

> At the end of their rule, when the transgressions have reached their full measure, a king of bold countenance shall arise, skilled in intrigue. He shall grow strong in power, shall cause fearful destruction, and shall succeed in what he does. He shall destroy the powerful and the people of the holy ones. By his cunning he shall make deceit prosper under his hand, and in his own mind he shall be great. Without warning he shall

destroy many and shall even rise up against the Prince of princes. But he shall be broken, and not by human hands. (Daniel 8:23–25)

While the strength, arrogance, and rebelliousness of this ruler clearly allude to the Seleucid king Antiochus Epiphanes as perceived by the traditional Jews whom he persecuted during the 160s B.C.E., later readers of Daniel eventually understood this passage as a prediction of Antichrist. So too did they read Daniel's elaboration of the tyrant's evil reign several chapters later.

> Forces sent by him shall occupy and profane the temple and fortress. They shall abolish the regular burnt offering and set up the abomination that makes desolate. He shall seduce with intrigue those who violate the covenant. . . . The king shall act as he pleases. He shall exalt himself and consider himself greater than any god, and shall speak horrendous things against the God of gods. He shall prosper until the period of wrath is completed, for what is determined shall be done. He shall pay no respect to the gods of his ancestors . . . ; he shall pay no respect to any other god, for he shall consider himself greater than all. (Daniel 11:31–37)

Finally, among apocryphal texts of the "intertestamental" period that bridge and blur the divide between Judaism and Christianity, the Sibylline Oracles—dating from the centuries preceding and following the Romans' destruction of the temple in Jerusalem—include many of the key features of the Antichrist myth.[5] Books 3–5, evidently among the Jewish components of the collection, appear to forecast an eschatological tyrant, a villain who will wreak havoc throughout the world, upsetting political, social, and natural orders before his defeat and destruction at the hands of God (3:611–15).

> A great king will come from Asia, a blazing eagle,
> who will cover the whole land with infantry and cavalry.
> He will cut up everything and fill everything with evils.
> He will overthrow the kingdom of Egypt. He will take out
> all its possessions and ride on the broad back of the sea.
> Then they will bend a white knee on the fertile ground
> to God the great immortal king
> but all handmade works will fall in a flame of fire.[6]

The Sibyl also identifies the leader of opposition to God as Beliar, the ultimate, Nero-like embodiment of evil mentioned in other writings of the late Second Temple period (3:63–74).

> Then Beliar will come from the Sebastenoi [the dynasty of Augustus]
> and he will raise up the height of mountains, he will raise up the sea,
> the great fiery sun and shining moon,
> and he will raise up the dead, and perform many signs
> for men. . . . But he will, indeed, also lead men astray, and he will lead astray
> many faithful, chosen Hebrews, and also other lawless men
> who have not yet listened to the word of God.
> But whenever the threats of the great God draw nigh
> and a burning power comes through the sea to land
> it will also burn Beliar and all overbearing men,
> as many as put faith in him.[7]

These and other predictions of a future deceiver and tyrant of the end time in ancient Jewish texts may not establish conclusively that Christianity inherited its idea of Antichrist exclusively, or even primarily, from Judaism. Yet they do suggest that the expectation of an eschatological villain was not at all alien to the Jewish milieu in which early Christianity took shape. Furthermore, as New Testament scholar Elaine Pagels has argued, the portrayal of satanic figures in that milieu characterized a process of self-definition, whereby sectarian Jews asserted their own superiority/election by contrasting themselves with demonic others. This was a manner of "othering," of self-assertion through the distinction between "us and them," that focused not on alien enemies that had threatened the earlier Israelite commonwealth from without but on an "intimate enemy" closer to home, on fellow Jews whose beliefs and values appeared diametrically opposed to their own. Jewish dissidents, she proposes, "often came to denounce their Jewish opponents, one and all, as apostates, and so to accuse them of having been seduced by the power of evil, called by many names: Satan, Belial, Mastema, Prince of Darkness." In a word, this "figure of Satan correlates with intra-Jewish conflict," while "conversely, the figure of Satan does not appear in the work of Jewish writers of the same period who identified with the majority of Jews and who continued to maintain the traditional identification of Israel versus 'the nations.'"[8]

Most important, after surveying Jewish biblical and apocryphal texts of the Second Temple period, Pagels demonstrates the central importance of the contrast between self and intimate enemy in the identity construction of early Christians, in the Gospels and other works of the New Testament in particular.

While the New Testament gospels *never* identify Satan with the Romans, they *consistently* identify him with Jesus' *Jewish* enemies. This research has led me to conclude that, by casting the story of Jesus into the context of cosmic war, the gospel writers express in varying ways their identification with an embattled minority against what each sees as the apostasy of the majority of Jesus' (and, of course, by extension, their own) Jewish contemporaries.[9]

Pagels never mentions Antichrist among the diabolical figures that the New Testament associates with the enemies of Jesus. Nonetheless, her conclusions do allow us to appreciate forecasts of the final cosmic struggle as befitting the conflict between those who had faith in the crucified Jesus and the majority of Jews who did not. Whether or not the authorial voices of the New Testament canon regularly intended such an association—and in some cases they may have—their audiences and subsequent readers could have readily made the connection in their aftermath.

In a vision alternatively dubbed the Eschatological Discourse or the Little— or Synoptic—Apocalypse, the Gospels of Matthew, Mark, and Luke anticipate a final, cosmic battle between enemies and supporters of Christ that would follow the destruction of the temple in Jerusalem. Drawing heavily on earlier Jewish texts and motifs, the versions of this prophecy in Mark and Matthew highlight the violent, destructive role of those who purport to be the savior but are not. Mark's Jesus first tells his disciples:

> Beware that no one leads you astray. Many will come in my name and say, "I am he!" and they will lead many astray. . . . As for yourselves, beware; for they will hand you over to councils; and you will be beaten in synagogues; and you will stand before governors and kings because of me, as a testimony to them. . . . Brother will betray brother to death, and a father his child, and children will rise against parents and have them put to death; and you will be hated by all because of my name. But the one who endures to the end will be saved. . . . And if anyone says to you at that time, "Look! Here is the Messiah!" or "Look! There he is!"—do not believe it. False messiahs and false prophets will appear and produce signs and omens, to lead astray, if possible, the elect. (Mark 13:5–6, 9, 12–13, 21–22)

While Jesus offers no details as to the identity of the villainous imposters or the historical circumstances in which they will appear, the internecine dimension of this eschatological struggle looms prominently: "Brother will betray brother to death, and a father his child, and children will rise against parents and have them put to death." Furthermore, the key motifs of the Synoptic Apocalypse could find their way into an apocalyptic vision that did react to specific historical events. As New Testament scholars have shown, the second-century Apocalypse of Peter (2:7–12) draws on Matthew's Gospel to offer an apocalyptic understanding of Jesus's parable of the fig tree.

> Were you unaware that Israel is the fig tree? I have used it to tell you that when its leaves shoot out for the last time men will come impersonating the messiah. They will give assurances by claiming, "I am the Christ who came into the world." When the people see *what evil he has done* they will leave *to follow them.* They will deny the one that our fathers worshipped, the first Christ who[m] they sinned against monstrously when they crucified him. But that imposter was not the Christ. When they reject him he will turn violent, killing, and making many martyrs. . . . Enoch and Elijah will be sent to inform people that he is the seducer decreed to enter the world in order to lure people away by performing miracles.[10]

The text is admittedly problematic, but it does move from the false prophets and messiahs of the Synoptic Gospels to one particular messianic imposter who performs miracles, appeals to those who had sinned by crucifying Christ, deceives many among the house of Israel, and brings many others to a martyr's death.[11] Might the apocryphal writer have alluded to the second-century Jewish messianic pretender Simeon bar Kokhba (or Bar Koziba), who waged a rebellion against Rome during the years 132–135 and whom some Jews, the renowned Rabbi Akiba ben Joseph included, proclaimed the messiah? Some historians have argued that he did have Bar Kokhba in mind, while others have disagreed. Yet, in any case, the description of the malicious deceiver and counterfeit messiah of the much-anticipated end hovers close to the Jews: in the motifs that depict him, in his own personal origins, and in those who deem him the messiah and rally to his cause. Scholars who give credence to Christian accounts that Bar Kokhba persecuted believers in Jesus generally identify the targets of that persecution as Jewish Christians who refused to acknowledge Bar Kokhba as their savior and to enlist in his rebellion against Rome. Some consider this the direct stimulus for the composition of the Apocalypse of Peter during the years of the Bar Kokhba rebellion.[12]

The only New Testament works containing the term "antichrist" are the first two letters of John, which warn the faithful of the impending perils of the end of time. In the first letter we read:

> Children, it is the last hour! As you have heard that antichrist is coming, so now many antichrists have come. From this we know that it is the

last hour. They went out from us, but they did not belong to us; for if they had belonged to us, they would have remained with us. But by going out they made it plain that none of them belongs to us. But you have been anointed by the Holy One, and all of you have knowledge. I write to you, not because you do not know the truth, but because you know it, and you know that no lie comes from the truth. Who is the liar but the one who denies that Jesus is the Christ? This is the antichrist, the one who denies the Father and the Son. (1 John 2:18–22)

And the second letter similarly warns its recipients: "Many deceivers have gone out into world, those who do not confess that Jesus Christ has come in the flesh; any such person is the deceiver and the antichrist!" (2 John 7). The term "antichrist" in these passages appears in a generic sense, rather than as a proper noun designating one eschatological figure in particular, and it immediately raises intriguing questions. Who constitutes the community, the "us," from among whom the dissenting, lying, deceptive antichrists have seceded? Scholars have weighed various possibilities, which include those in a community of Jewish Christians who revert to a non-Christian or anti-Christian strain of first-century Judaism.[13]

Although this is not the prevalent view of modern investigators, the possibility of reading 1 and 2 John as deriving from conflict within the Jewish community remains, whether in the actual historical context of the epistles (generally dated around 100) or, more likely, in the way that subsequent readers construed its meaning and message.[14] In the minds of second-century Christians reading the letters, one can again suggest a possible association with Bar Kokhba, whom some of the early church fathers remembered as a false messiah and persecutor of believers in Christ. One finds the following in the *First Apology* of Bar Kokhba's contemporary, Justin Martyr: "For in the Jewish war which lately raged, Barcochebas, the leader of the revolt of the Jews, gave orders that Christians alone should be led away to cruel punishments, unless they would deny that Jesus is the messiah and blaspheme."[15] As one investigator has recently written, "It is striking to note how nearly identical are 1 John's job description for antichrists on the one hand—'denying that Jesus is the messiah'—and Justin's report of Bar Kokhba's mandate for Levantine Christians on the other hand—'denying that Jesus is the messiah.'"[16] For Justin, among other early Christian writers, the linkage between Antichrist and Jews who opposed belief in Jesus may well have seemed obvious.

In a description of the eschaton that reverberates with apocalyptic motifs of the Hebrew Bible and later Jewish texts of the intertestamental period, Second Thessalonians (2:1–12) likewise anticipates the ultimate coming of the "lawless one," dispatched by Satan to sit in the Temple, declare himself to be God, and delude the unfaithful. While the powers that be now work to put off the tribulations of his arrival and ascendancy, his time will invariably come, and some readers likewise associated him with the deception and error of the Jews.[17] And although the eschatological villain of the Book of Revelation appears more a Roman imperial foe of Christians and Christianity—again, perhaps on the model of the notoriously anti-Christian emperor Nero—it blends much of earlier Jewish reflections on the coming archenemy of the messiah. As New Testament scholar Raymond Brown summarizes instructively,[18]

> The great dragon of Rev 12 who tries to destroy the Messiah is Satan the ancient serpent. . . . Its first cohort is the beast from the sea (13:1–10), which gets men to worship the dragon. Making war on the saints and blaspheming against God, this beast with ten horns is clearly modeled upon the description of Antiochus Epiphanes in Dan 7. . . . The second cohort is the beast from the land (Rev 13:11–18); specifically called the false prophet (16:13; 19:20; 20:10), it works signs to deceive.

Revelation then recasts the account of these beasts in a distinctively Christian guise.

> The first of these beasts was mortally wounded but healed; the second beast has horns like a lamb; they are, then, a blasphemous parody of Christ the Lamb that was slain but lives. Afterward Jesus comes from heaven as a warrior and destroys the two beasts and the kings whom they have gathered to make war (19:11–21); he binds the ancient serpent for one thousand years; but when finally loosed, Satan gathers Gog and Magog against Jerusalem, only to be defeated and thrown into hell (20:1–10).

Brown has concluded, "Almost every piece in the Jewish picture of future evil has been put into the mosaic." Even when these early Christian texts do not explicitly link the Antichrist-like villain with the Jews, this very tendency to envision him with motifs drawn from Jewish imaginings of an adversarial other nourished an inclination to associate him with the Jews. For if Jewish apocalyptic accentuated the essential conflict between that villain and God's faithful elect, if it appeared to manifest the chiliasm (the hope for an earthly messianic kingdom) that aroused suspicion among some Christian teachers, and if the Jews rejected Christians' claims to election—as well as their own savior—then who might better represent the agents of evil envisioned in their books than they themselves? Such Jewish background to constructions of Antichrist invariably contributed to increasingly confident identifications of the ultimate villain and his cohorts with the Jews—as writings of the early church fathers illustrate well.

Early Church Fathers

By the middle of the second century, progressively more Christians took the expectation of an eschatological enemy for granted,[19] and, in working to systematize the beliefs of their communities, patristic theologians developed the Jewish profile of Antichrist in Christian tradition. One key player in this patristic process of theological systematization was Irenaeus, bishop of Lyons, among the first to weave notions of Antichrist into "a full-blown legendary narrative,"[20] the first author to identify Antichrist with the ultimate enemy destined to rise up over everything.[21]

Irenaeus's predictions for the final battle between God, Satan, and their respective agents gave expression to his notion of recapitulation, whereby the careers of Christ and Antichrist bespoke a correspondence between past and future, such that the end of salvation history restores that situation intended for its beginning. Moreover, Christ and Antichrist culminate the workings of good and evil throughout that history, embodying their final expression.[22] Especially in the fifth and final book of his monumental *Adversus Haereses*, Irenaeus blends motifs and prophecies from both the Hebrew Bible (primarily Daniel) and the New Testament in his description of Antichrist. Antichrist brings Daniel's "abomination of desolation" into God's Temple; he is "the other" that Jesus (John 5:43) tells the Jews they accept instead of the true redeemer, the wicked one sitting in the Temple of God in 2 Thessalonians, the Beast who fights the Lamb to the finish in the Book of Revelation, and more.

> By means of the events which shall occur in the time of *Antichrist* is it shown that he, being an *apostate* and a robber, is anxious to be adored as *God*; and that, although a mere slave, he wishes himself to be proclaimed as a king. For he (*Antichrist*), being endowed with all the power of the *devil*, shall come, not as a righteous king, nor as a legitimate king, [i.e., one] in subjection to *God*, but an impious, *unjust*, and lawless one; as an *apostate*, iniquitous and murderous; as a robber, concentrating in himself [all] satanic *apostasy*, and setting aside *idols* to persuade [men] that he himself is *God*, raising up himself as the only idol, having in himself the multifarious *errors* of the other *idols*. This he does, in order that they who do [now] worship the *devil* by means of many abominations, may serve himself by this one idol.[23]

Referring to the prophecy of Jeremiah 8:16, Irenaeus establishes without hesitation that Antichrist will be a Jew, an Israelite from the tribe of Dan.

> And Jeremiah does not merely point out his sudden coming, but he even indicates the tribe from which he shall come, where he says, "We shall hear the voice of his swift horses from Dan; the whole earth shall be moved by the voice of the neighing of his galloping horses: he shall also come and devour the earth, and the fullness thereof, the city also, and they that dwell therein." This, too, is the reason that this tribe is not reckoned in the Apocalypse along with those which are saved.[24]

Irenaeus did not belabor the implications of Antichrist's origins in the Israelite tribe of Dan, nor did he dwell extensively on his career.[25] Yet his student Hippolytus of Rome did both, and his early third-century works signal a key development in the history of Christian Antichristology. Hippolytus may have viewed the cataclysmic expectations for the end time as less imminent than Irenaeus and others had viewed them, but he inherited much from his predecessors and anticipated many of the directions in which churchmen eventually came to link Antichrist with the Jews and Judaism. Both in his *De Christo et Antichristo* and in his commentary on Daniel, perhaps the oldest surviving patristic commentary on an entire book of Hebrew Scripture, Hippolytus outlined the course of salvation history—past, present, and future.[26]

Notable exegete and eschatologist, Hippolytus elaborates his vision of the end with reference to biblical prophecies that include not only those of Daniel and Revelation, but extend all the way back to the patriarch Jacob and the blessings he gave his twelve sons on his deathbed, anticipating what would befall them at the end of days (*be-acharit ha-yamim*, Genesis 49:1). As Jacob then foresaw that the savior would spring from the tribe of Judah, whom he called "a lion's whelp," so too did Scripture forecast the coming of Antichrist in similar terms, although, just as Irenaeus had taught, he would arise from the tribe of Dan.

> And in like manner also we find it written regarding Antichrist. For Moses speaks thus: "Dan is a lion's whelp, and he shall leap from Bashan." But that no one may err by supposing that this is said of the Savior, let him attend carefully to the matter. "Dan," he says, "is a lion's whelp"; and in naming the tribe of Dan, he declared clearly the tribe from which Antichrist is destined to spring. For as Christ springs from the tribe of Judah, so Antichrist is to spring from the tribe of Dan. And that the case stands thus, we see also from the words of Jacob: "Let Dan be a serpent, lying upon the ground, biting the horse's heel."

What, then, is meant by the serpent but Antichrist, that deceiver who is mentioned in Genesis, who deceived Eve and supplanted Adam (*pternisas*, bruised Adam's heel) . . .? That it is in reality out of the tribe of Dan, then, that that tyrant and king, that dread judge, that son of the devil, is destined to spring and arise, the prophet testifies when he says, "Dan shall judge his people, as (he is) also one tribe in Israel."[27]

Hippolytus proceeds to cite prophecies of Isaiah and Ezekiel concerning Antichrist, but he focuses most extensively on the visions of Daniel (7:20–22), from the fourth of whose apocalyptic beasts grew ten horns, and then another horn, "the horn that had eyes and a mouth that spoke arrogantly, and that seemed greater than the others. . . . This horn made war with the holy ones and was prevailing over them, until the Ancient One came." By this, explains Hippolytus, "was signified none other than Antichrist, who is also to raise the kingdom of the Jews."[28]

Born of the Jews, foretold by the prophets of Israel, acclaimed and encouraged by the Jews whose cause he would adopt and whose kingdom he would reinstate, Antichrist will gather the Jews from their exile and firmly ensconce himself in Jerusalem.

He, being lifted up over every king and every god, shall build the city of Jerusalem and he shall raise the toppled temple. He shall restore both all the land and its borders to the Jews. And, having summoned their people from the slavery of the nations, he shall exhibit himself to them as king, and at this the faithless shall worship him as God and shall bend the knee to him, considering him to be the Christ, not apprehending what was spoken by the prophet, how he is a deceiver and not truth.[29]

Antichrist will appeal directly to the long-standing messianic hopes of the Jews: "He will call together all the people to himself, out of every country of the dispersion, making them his own, as though they were his own children, and promising to restore their country, and establish again their kingdom and nation, in order that he may be worshipped by them as God."[30] In all, Antichrist is "a son of the devil and a vessel of Satan,"[31] with special bonds to the Jews, their temple in Jerusalem, and their messianic aspirations. Perhaps most compelling of all, Antichrist must be a Jew who offers to redeem the Jews and their kingdom, because as such he presents a mirror image, albeit perverted, of the truly divine and messianic Jesus.

Now, as our Lord Jesus Christ, who is also God, was prophesied of under the figure of a lion, on account of His royalty and glory, in the same way have the Scriptures also aforetime spoken of Antichrist as a lion, on account of his tyranny and violence. For the deceiver seeks to liken himself in all things to the Son of God. Christ is a lion, so Antichrist is also a lion; Christ is a king, so Antichrist is also a king. The Savior was manifested as a lamb; so he too, in like manner, will appear as a lamb, though within he is a wolf. The Savior came into the world in the circumcision, and he will come in the same manner. The Lord sent apostles among all the nations, and he in like manner will send false apostles. The Savior gathered together the sheep that were scattered abroad, and he in like manner will bring together a people that is scattered abroad. The Lord gave a seal to those who believed in Him, and he will give one in like manner. The Savior appeared in the form of man, and he too will come in the form of a man. The Savior raised up and showed His holy flesh like a temple, and he will raise a temple of stone in Jerusalem.[32]

Also writing in Rome and in Greek, the early third-century author of the *Refutation of All Heresies*—long attributed to Hippolytus of Rome himself—similarly linked the misguided messianic hopes of the Jews to their rejection of Jesus, although his Jews await a messiah from the descendants of David, not the tribe of Dan.

All Jews alike expect the Christ. The Law and the Prophets preached that he would come, but the Jews did not recognize the time of his arrival, persisting in their supposition that the things said about his coming do not seem to be fulfilled. They still expect the Christ to come, because they did not recognize the one who was present. And since they see that the signs of the times indicate that he has already come, they are disturbed. Still, they are ashamed to confess that he has already come, because they were his murderers. They are distressed as those refuted by him, because they did not obey their laws.

The Jewish preference for Antichrist becomes almost a foregone conclusion.

Thus they affirm that the one thus sent by God is not the Christ, but that another will come, who is not yet present. They confess that by him the signs that the Law and the Prophets declared will be partially fulfilled. Some things they believe in error. For one, they say that his birth will be from the lineage of David—not from a virgin and Holy Spirit, but from a woman and a man (as is the rule for all those born from seed). They claim that this one will come to them as their king and as a man powerful in war. He will make war upon the nations and gather the entire race of Jews. Then he will raise up Jerusalem for them as his royal city, into which he will gather the whole nation of Jews. He will again restore the ancient customs, reigning and serving as priest and dwelling in confidence for a long time.[33]

And perhaps with Hippolytus's treatise in mind, the unknown author of the Apocalypse of Elijah expressed the same idea more pointedly.

> The Lawless One will again begin to stand in the holy places.
> He will say to the sun, "Fall," and it will fall.
> He will say, "Shine!"—it does so.
> He will say, "Darken!"—it does so.
> He will say to the moon, "Become blood!"—it does so.
> He will accompany them through the sky.
> He will walk upon the sea and rivers as if on land.
> He will make the lame walk.
> He will make the deaf hear.
> He will make the dumb speak.
> He will make the blind see.
> Lepers he will purify,
> The sick he will heal,
> The demons he will cast out.
> He will multiply his signs and his wonders in the presence of everyone.
> He will do the things which the Christ did, except only for raising a
>   corpse—
> by this you will know that he is the Lawless One: he has no power to
>   give life. (3:5–13)[34]

What led Irenaeus, Hippolytus, and others to take a concerted interest in Antichrist: earlier Jewish or apostolic traditions that they inherited, their polemic against Gnosticism and Marcionism, or their opposition to Jewish eschatology? Scholars have advanced conflicting viewpoints, but in this case the results far outweigh the causes in their importance for our story. Christians continued to associate Antichrist with Jews and Judaism, and the two centuries following Hippolytus gave rise to interesting developments along those lines.

Alongside the Jewish aspects of Antichrist's profile, many Christians understandably linked him with imperial Rome and the emperor himself. As the emperor Nero had himself persecuted first-century Christians, perhaps Antichrist would be a Nero reincarnate (*Nero redivivus*)—or perhaps an imperial champion of the Jews like the fourth-century Julian the Apostate, who allegedly planned to restore their temple in Jerusalem—who would come to function as the Jews' counterfeit messiah.[35] So the third-century Victorinus of Pettau explained in his commentary on Revelation. He would be sent by God to those who deserved him, "to the Jews and to the persecutors of Christ, such a Christ as the persecutors and Jews have deserved."[36] While, for Victorinus, Nero would return as the Jewish Antichrist, some wrote about two Antichrists, a Nero-like Roman one and the Antichrist of the Jews, who would appear in successive stages of the drama of the end time. Very likely a contemporary of Victorinus, the patristic poet Commodian made the following prediction in his *Carmen apologeticum*:

> Cyrus shall arise. It shall be his will to terrorize his enemies and liberate the nobility. . . . It has already been revealed to us that this is Nero, who had flogged Peter and Paul in the city. From hidden places at the very end of the world shall he return, since he was reserved for these things. The nobility shall marvel that he is hated: for when he appears they will think that he is almost like a god. . . . And when Nero has completed his time, the Unspeakable One shall succeed him. Him shall both the Jews and Romans worship.[37]

After elaborating the violence and havoc that Nero will wreak on earth, Commodian returns to this second eschatological villain, to rise from the East, quash the forces of Nero and his allies, and continue on his way toward the Holy Land.

> With the downfall of Nero, a king will again arise from the East with four other nations. As many nations, moreover, as are willing to bring him assistance shall he thus invite into the city with him. And thus he shall be exceptionally powerful. . . . And if anyone shall go against him, that one shall be cut down with the sword.[38]

Having conquered Tyre, Sidon, and their environs, "the victor shall continue on to Judea, he whom the Judeans had observed conquering Rome. He shall make many signs so that they can believe in him. For he was iniquitously sent to seduce them."[39] Thus Commodian summarizes concerning the pair of eschatological enemies, the first the Antichrist of the Romans, the second that of the Jews: "A man from Persia will call himself immortal; as Nero was Antichrist for us, so shall this one be for the Jews. These are the two of whom there have been prophecies throughout the generations, who shall appear in the final age. Nero is the destroyer of the city, but this latter shall lay waste to the entire earth."[40]

Curiously, Commodian does not relate to the Jewish origins of this Antichrist or even mention the tribe of Dan. He does indeed indicate that Antichrist shall win the faith of the Jews with his miracles and stresses the rationale for these wonders: "For he was iniquitously sent to seduce them."[41] Nevertheless, the alliance between Antichrist and the Jews of Judea will endure for a limited time only. The Jews will regret their error; they will seek the help of God; and God will come to their rescue.

> Meanwhile he will displease the Jews . . . and they will murmur amongst themselves that he fraudulently deceived them. With wailing voices they will cry as one to the heavens, that the true God will come to their aid from on high. Then the almighty God . . . will lead forth a populace that had been hidden for a long time. They had been Jews, hidden on the further side of the Persian river [Euphrates?], whom God had wished to tarry there until the end.

Notably, Commodian had nothing but praise for these long-confined Jews, who will enter the eschatological drama as the end draws near.

> There is no dishonesty amongst them, nor any hatred. The child does not die before the parents; there is no bewailing over the dead, nor any mourning, as there customarily is amongst us. There they await the life to come. . . . They exist with their bodies intact, the course of their lives dictated by justice. Impious powers are not engendered in them, nor do illnesses of any kind ever draw near to them. For they are sincerely obedient to the universal precepts of the pristine law which both we and they follow in order to live in purity. Only death and toil can be found amongst them, but other afflictions are absent.[42]

Here Commodian anticipates two Christian ideas concerning the Jews and Antichrist that would receive full expression only centuries later—and more extensive treatment in later chapters of this book. First, he foretells that the Jews will rise up in opposition to Antichrist and lead in the fight against him.[43] Second, he mentions the tribes of Israelites hidden beyond the river in Persia who will arise to play a leading role in the cosmic struggle of the eschaton, as we shall see in chapter 6. And yet, while later medieval Christians came to identify these Jewish tribes with the forces of Gog and Magog that would wage the battles of Antichrist,[44] Commodian describes them in exemplary, nearly utopian terms. Most impressive, he makes no mention of their conversion to Christianity, casting them, perhaps, as the sole non-Christians on God's side of the eschatological battlefield. Still, in describing the final cataclysm of the end time, Commodian reverts to a more traditional posture concerning the plight of the Jews on the day of judgment.

> Whatever is marked by corruption will be carried by Hell's savage guardians into the abyss. Here there will be living Jews: and He shall lift them up that they might see the glory of Him Whom they crucified. But at last he shall arise from the depths that He might be a witness of those miserable ones, He Who was killed by them.

Jews who stubbornly refuse to accept Jesus will be damned to the fires of hell. Those Jews who accept him will join with believing Gentiles in "one holy multitude from the two peoples."[45] This Antichrist of the Jews would soon overshadow the Neronic Antichrist in patristic and medieval tradition.

While the Danite origins of Antichrist and his alliance with the Jews appear in many patristic writings, we conclude this chapter with reference to Jerome, the illustrious theologian, exegete, translator of Scripture into Latin. Jerome's discussion of Antichrist appears in his commentary on Daniel, where he vehemently attacked the interpretations of the third-century Neoplatonic philosopher Porphyry, who had (correctly) identified the villain in Daniel's visions of the end as Antiochus Epiphanes. Asserting that the villain would be none other than the future Antichrist, Jerome, as in his comments on Daniel 11:24, succinctly expressed ideas that we have encountered among his predecessors.

> But the scholars of our viewpoint have made a better and more correct emended interpretation, stating that the deeds are to be performed by the Antichrist at the end of the world. It is he who is destined to arise from a small nation, that is from the Jewish people, and shall be so lowly and despised that kingly honor will not be granted him. But by means of intrigue and deception he shall secure the government and by him shall the arms of the fighting nation of Rome be overcome and broken. He is to effect this result by pretending to be the prince of the covenant, that is, of the Law and Testament of God. And he shall enter into the richest of cities and shall do what his fathers never did, nor his fathers' fathers. For none of the Jews except the Antichrist has ever ruled over the whole world. And he shall form a design against the firmest resolves of the saints and shall do everything [he wishes] for a time, for as long as God's will shall have permitted him to do these things.[46]

Regarding Daniel 7:25, Jerome briefly echoed the idea of 2 Thessalonians (2:11–12) that in the lawless villain yet to come God would send those who refused to believe in Jesus "a powerful delusion, leading them to believe what is false, so that all who have not believed the truth but took pleasure in unrighteousness will be condemned." Only Jerome unambiguously identified these unfaithful as the Jews: "During this period the saints are to be given over to the power of the Antichrist, in order that those Jews who did not believe the truth but supported a lie might be condemned."

Yet in his letter (121) to Algasia, an educated Christian woman who had asked him to explain several difficult biblical passages, Jerome elevated the anti-Jewish elements of his Antichristology to new heights. Algasia inquired concerning the description of the satanic lawless one and his deceptive wonders in 2 Thessalonians, and, in the final paragraph of his reply, Jerome sought to reveal the underlying sense of the scriptural passage.

> Because an unmentioned question could be raised—Why did God permit him to have all the power to work wonders and miracles, through which even God's chosen might be misled, if that were possible?—he [the apostle] introduced the question with its answer and resolved what could have been objected before it was objected. He will do all these things, he says, not with his own power but with God's permission, *on account of the Jews*. . . . Those who did not receive the gift and the truth, so that, having acknowledged the savior, they might be saved—to them God sends not a worker of errors, but the error itself, that is the source of all error, so that they may believe in the lie, "for he is a liar and the father of lies" [John 8:44]. Had Antichrist been born of a virgin and come first into the world, the Jews could have had an excuse to say that they deemed him the truth, and therefore that they adopted falsehood as truth. Now, however, they must be judged, condemned without any hesitation, since, having rejected the true Christ they will then accept the lie, namely, Antichrist.[47]

For Jerome, the advent, rise, and fall of Antichrist have an overriding purpose: the punishment of the Jews. They first spurned Christ. Ultimately, they will champion Antichrist and be condemned.

CHAPTER 5

Jews and the Many Faces of Antichrist in the Middle Ages

Expectations of Antichrist varied widely, and this survey naturally highlights those with interesting, pronounced, and colorful sentiments concerning the Jews. Turning now toward the Middle Ages, we find that most Christian theologians during the several centuries that followed Jerome generally depicted Antichrist's Jewish connections less passionately than he did. One can cautiously formulate a "mainline" or consensus view—or, more helpfully still, a range of opinions—that can serve us as a point of reference for appreciating conforming and nonconforming views of the ensuing centuries.[1]

Early Medieval Foundations

Augustine wrote of the last judgment rather sparingly in *On the City of God*.

And so in that judgment, or in connection with it, we have learned that the following events are to occur: Elijah the Tishbite will come; the Jews will believe; Antichrist will persecute; Christ will judge; the dead will rise again; the good and the wicked will be sorted out; the world will be burned in flames and will be renewed. Now all these events, we must believe, will come to pass; but how or in what order, the experience of the future will teach us with a completeness that our human understanding cannot now attain. Yet I think that they will occur in the order in which I have just listed them.[2]

Augustine, to whose doctrine on the *present* role of the Jewish people in the divine economy of salvation we have alluded above, writes neither of Antichrist's Jewish origins (his birth to the tribe of Dan) nor of the Jews' support for Antichrist in his rise to power. Moreover, relying on the hermeneutical rules and the Apocalypse commentary of his contemporary Tyconius, Augustine adopted a thoroughly anti-millenarian reading of salvation history that eliminated much of the drama and upheaval expected to accompany the impending end of the world in this earthly sphere. Notwithstanding their pro forma acknowledgment in the passage just quoted, the events of the millennium properly belonged not to the last days but to the present age of the church in human history. Augustine focused much more on the collective human antichrists of the First Epistle of John, discussed above in the previous chapter, than he did on the satanic villain of the end time yet to come. As Paula Fredriksen has written, "These end-time events and more—Antichrist, Gog and Magog, the sea giving up its dead [Revelation 20:13]—Augustine, through Tyconius, can consistently deeschatologize, transposing them back into the present, where they serve to describe typologically the current experience of the Church."[3]

Augustinian eschatology invariably detracted from the prominence of any distinctive Jewish role in the drama of the end time, and it exerted a profound influence on subsequent generations. Among the many voices that offer confirmation, the English scholar the Venerable Bede (672–735) echoes Augustine's nearly perfunctory formulation of the traditional view in his *The Reckoning of Time*—in a passage to which we alluded at the very outset of our discussion.

> We have two very certain indicators of the approach of the Day of Judgement, namely the conversion of the Jewish people, and the reign and persecution of Antichrist, which persecution the Church believes will last three and a half years. But lest this [persecution] come unexpectedly and involve everyone whom it finds unprepared, [the Church believes] that Enoch and Elijah, great prophets and teachers, will come into the world before [Antichrist's] arrival, and will convert the Jewish people to the grace of faith.[4]

Although he considered the arrival of Antichrist imminent, the eighth-century Spanish monk Beatus of Liebana, in a lengthy commentary on Revelation best known for its later manuscript illuminations, likewise relied considerably on Tyconius and Augustine and barely referred to the Jews in his forecasts for the end time. Where he did, he generally understood the Jews as a *typos* representing Christians—and evil Jews as unfaithful Christians.[5] For her part, the Synagogue symbolized a community including "the devil, the Antichrist, the heretic, the hypocrite, the schismatic, superstition, the Beast, the Dragon, the locusts, the horses, and the women sitting on the Beast"—with no mention of the Jews.[6]

But the distinguishing, more colorful, and often more pernicious role of the Jews in the eschatogical drama did not disappear altogether from Christian thought in the Middle Ages. Even beyond Antichrist's origins in the Israelite tribe of Dan and his identification with Christianity's quintessentially Jewish other, the satanic duplicity and hypocrisy in his overtures to the Jews knew no limits. Pope Gregory the Great (d. 604), who shared Augustine's anti-millenarian inclination, wrote that Antichrist will observe the Sabbath on two consecutive days of every week. Because he "feigns his death and resurrection from the grave, he wishes Sunday to be kept holy; and, because he compels the people to Judaize—in order to restore the exterior observance of the law and subordinate the perfidy of the Jews to himself—he wishes Saturday to be observed."[7] A generation after Gregory, Isidore of Seville warned of the dangers that the Jews of the end time posed to Christendom: "Synagoga will rage against the church more violently at the time of Antichrist than it persecuted Christians upon the [first] advent of the savior."[8] And in his acerbic treatise sent to King Louis the Pious, *On the Superstitions of the Jews*, the ninth-century bishop Agobard of Lyons grouped the Jews among the antichrists mentioned in the First Epistle of John and then compared the Jews to *the* ultimate Antichrist himself. Citing 1 John 2:22, Agobard elaborates:

> From just this it becomes painfully evident that the Jews are not only false—they are antichrists too, since they deny the Son and in vain confess the Father. But since they do not confess the Son, they do not merit to have the Father. Above all, in denying that Jesus, born to the Virgin Mary, is the Christ, they have acquired for themselves the name and designation of the Antichrist. For what will the Antichrist say other than that Jesus was not the Christ . . .? The Antichrist exceeds the blasphemy of the Jews in this alone that he presumes to pronounce himself the Christ. Yet the Jews match the evil of the Antichrist in that they dare to deny that Jesus was the Christ. They are antichrists inasmuch as their blasphemies match those of the Antichrist.[9]

Although Augustine's defusing of millenarian expectations exerted a profound influence among his successors in the Latin West, not all of them followed suit, and millenarian and chiliastic hopes continued to flourish.[10] The Byzantine East, where Augustine's predilections exerted far less influence and where, from the seventh century onward, Islam posed a constant threat of cosmic proportion—and where Jews, in greater numbers, nurtured their own eschatological hopes—proved especially fertile ground for apocalyptic speculation and millenarian hopes.[11] Like their Western counterparts, Eastern writers of the early Middle Ages transmitted the ideas of Irenaeus, Hippolytus, and other fathers concerning Antichrist and his links to the Jews; some downplayed those Jewish connections, while others embellished them. But even when one finds the Jews largely missing from the events of the eschaton, Byzantine writers of this period developed the Antichrist narrative in ways that bore significantly on the eschatological Jew, once their works and ideas began to circulate in Christian Europe.

A late ancient or early medieval work spuriously attributed to Hippolytus of Rome offers an instructive example of how far the Jewish role in the Antichrist legend could develop. Highlighting the presumably necessary correspondence between Christ and Antichrist, Pseudo-Hippolytus's *On the End of the World* emphasizes that Antichrist will spring from the tribe of Dan. Appropriately so, for "Christ rose from among the Hebrews, and he [Antichrist] will spring from among the Jews."[12] Just as Jesus descended from the lionlike Judah whose tribe ruled in Israel, Antichrist will spring from Dan, similarly destined to judge his people and also likened to a lion's cub. And as Jesus "was born of the immaculate and virgin Mary . . ., in the same manner also will the accuser come forth from an impure woman upon the earth, but shall be born of a Virgin spuriously."[13] And as Pseudo-Hippolytus explains at greater length, ties between Antichrist and his Jewish kinsmen will initially only strengthen as he rises to power. Above all, "he will love the nation of the Jews. And with all these he will work signs and terrible wonders, false wonders and not true, in order to deceive his impious equals" as he leads a seemingly pious life. Yet, in fact,

all this he will do corruptly and deceitfully, and with the purpose of deluding all to make him king. For when the peoples and tribes see so great virtues and so great powers in him, they will all with one mind meet together to make him king. And above all others shall the nation of the Hebrews be dear to the tyrant himself, while they say one to another, "Is there found indeed in our generation such a man, so good and just?" That shall be the way with the race of the Jews preeminently, as I said before, who, thinking, as they do, that they shall behold the king himself in such power, will approach him to say, "We all confide in you, and acknowledge you to be just upon the whole earth; we all hope to be saved by you; and by your mouth we have received just and incorruptible judgment."[14]

All this, however, is a hoax, contrived to allow Antichrist to rise to power. Once enthroned, with the support of "the nation of the Hebrews" above all, Antichrist will reveal his true colors. War, pestilence, famine, and misery will become the norm. Ultimately the Jews will themselves realize their fateful mistake, although their prayers and supplications will then most likely prove to be too little and too late. In the end, even when Christ comes again and appears to them, "no one will come to their aid or have mercy on them; for they did not do penance, nor did they abandon their evil way. Thus will they leave for their eternal punishment together with demons and the devil."[15]

New elements in the Antichrist legend appear in imaginative Byzantine apocalyptic works of the following centuries, of which I mention three that have reached us in often markedly different Syriac, Greek, and/or Latin versions. First is the Tiburtine Sibyl, which may originally stem from the fourth century but whose extant Greek version, the "Oracle of Baalbek," dates from the early sixth century and whose Latin translations date from the eleventh century. Next, Pseudo-Ephrem's "Sermon on the End," a work mistakenly attributed to the great Syriac church father of that name, survives in versions from the mid-seventh century, though it too drew on versions from before the Arab conquest of the Near East. And best known of all, the *Revelations* of Pseudo-Methodius likewise reflects the threat that seventh-century Islam posed to Eastern Christendom; it too eventually circulated in Latin translation and contributed roundly to Western apocalyptic visions from the tenth century at least. Rather than struggle with the complex problems of the chronology, provenance, and interrelationship of these works' various recensions, problems that scholars have not resolved conclusively, we will highlight several noteworthy motifs that these and other Byzantine works of this period bequeathed to posterity and came to have importance in our story.[16]

Particularly as the threat of Islam reared its head during the seventh century, the legend of the Last World Emperor crystallized and assumed meaning in the Byzantine world. Visionaries imagined that this virtuous Caesar, sometimes depicted in almost Christ-like imagery, would ultimately overcome the enemies of the Roman world both within and without and bring its terrestrial history to a glorious climax, prior to the cataclysms of the end. As the Middle Ages wore on, numerous versions of the legend differed regarding the telling characteristics of this emperor, his origins and the events of his career, the timetable of his own eventual abdication and the ensuing rise of Antichrist, and the identities of his enemies.[17] Even before the appearance of the Last World Emperor, early Byzantine eschatology revived and embellished the ancient legend of Alexander the Great's confinement of ferocious, warlike tribes behind a wall in the Caucasus of central Asia.[18] Byzantine writers now identified these tribes as the warriors of Gog and Magog, the apocalyptic villains of Ezekiel 38–39, expected to unleash their fury against the people of God at the end time but ultimately to be defeated by God and his supporters. As Pseudo-Methodius recounted in his *Revelations*, Alexander took extensive measures to insure his prisoners' confinement.

> Issuing commands he gathered all of them together, and their wives and their children and all of their camps. And driving them out of the land of the dawn he pursued close behind them, until they were brought into the lands beyond the north, and there is neither way in nor way out from east to west, through which one could go over or come in to them. . . . And he prepared brazen gates and covered them with asyncite, so that if they should want to open them with iron or to dissolve them with fire they would not prevail.[19]

At the end of days, however, these gates will open, and, preparing the world for the rule of Antichrist, Gog and Magog will inflict a reign of terror on the world: "The whole earth will reel from their face, and men will cry aloud and flee and hide themselves in the mountains and in the caves and among the gravestones. And they will be deadened with fear and many will perish and there will be no one to bury the bodies. For the nations coming from the North will eat the flesh of men and will drink the blood of beasts like water."[20] Once their work is completed, Antichrist, the "Son of Perdition," will appear. As the identification of Gog and Magog as these storm troopers of Antichrist became commonplace, we shall see that later Christian writers began to link them with the ten lost tribes of Israel, themselves enclosed (by Alexander the Great himself?) by natural barriers in a remote Asian venue until the end time.[21]

For the time being, however, Byzantine apocalyptic writers generally retained a more modest role for the Jews in the drama of the last days. (Curiously, so too did they frequently refrain from calling Antichrist by that name, preferring allusive descriptors, as in the Tiburtine Sibyl's discussion of the "prince of iniquity, son of perdition, head of pride, master of error, fullness of wickedness."[22] The Oracle of Baalbek works the Jews' original rejection of Jesus into its eschatological narrative; the Latin Tiburtine Sibyl, Pseudo-Ephrem, and Pseudo-Methodius follow well-established tradition both in predicting Antichrist's origins in the tribe of Dan and in envisioning him holding court in the temple of the Jews.[23] The Syriac Pseudo-Ephrem expands on the affinities between the Jews and Antichrist slightly more in noting that upon Antichrist's entry into Jerusalem and the temple, "the Jews will take pride in him; they will prepare themselves and come to him." But immediately, upon hearing Antichrist blaspheme and declare his own divinity, many Jews will see the light and recant:

> At that time ten thousand Jews will denounce him:
> They will answer him in truth:
> "You are a deceiver for (all) creatures!
> For the one whom our ancestors restrained
> At the top of the wood(en cross) on Golgotha
> Is (actually) the redeemer of (all) creatures,
> And he was raised up to the One Who sent him!"[24]

In the sources considered thus far, we find the rudiments of most subsequent Antichristologies, enabling us to appreciate medieval compositions in which the Jews figure instructively, whether in a manner that decisively affirms earlier tradition or that departs significantly from it—or, as in many instances, both.

The Greek Apocalypse of Daniel

The biblical book of Daniel has understandably nourished much apocalyptic speculation, from its composition in ancient times down to the present. The Greek Apocalypse of Daniel (*Digesis Danielis*) probably dates from the first years of the ninth century and reflects the vagaries of the ongoing Byzantine-Muslim conflict, including the Arab siege of Constantinople in 717–718, the Iconoclast Controversy, and relations between the Byzantine East and Latin West. Throughout its second half, devoted to the career of Antichrist, the text takes pains to highlight his ties to the Jews and their cooperation with him. If the Ishmaelites constitute the enemies of Byzantium in the first half of the work, the Jews fill that role in the second. At the very beginning of this latter half of the Apocalypse one reads:[25]

> And another great scepter will arise from Judea. And his name (is) Dan. And then the Jews, the implacable Hebrew race, who are dispersed into cities and countries, will be gathered together. And they will be gathered together there. And they will come into Jerusalem toward their king. And they will afflict the Christian race in all the earth. Woe, woe, good people. (8:1–7)

In the next chapter the narrative progresses. Antichrist will soon emerge from hell and enter a small "garidion fish."

And he will be caught by twelve fishermen. And the fishermen will become maddened toward each other. One will prevail over them, whose name (is) Judas. And he takes that fish for his inheritance and comes into a place named Gouzeth and there sells the fish for thirty silver pieces. And a virgin girl will buy the fish. Her name (is) Injustice because the son of injustice will be born from her. And her surname will be Perdition. For by touching the head of the fish she will become pregnant and will conceive the Antichrist himself. (9:1–12)

The scepter arising from Judea clearly alludes to the biblical patriarch Jacob's blessing of Judah: "The scepter shall not depart from Judah, nor the ruler's staff from between his feet, until Shiloh comes and the obedience of the peoples is his" (Genesis 49:10). Jews and Christians almost universally understood this verse as rife with eschatological meaning. The royal House of David, from which the messiah would arise, descended from the tribe of Judah, and the genealogies of Jesus in the Gospels accordingly stress Jesus's own descent from that tribe. Christians and Jews over the course of late antiquity and the Middle Ages debated whether Judah had lost its royal dominion and, if so, when, in which case one might have to conclude that Shiloh, understood to denote the messiah, had come. Christians, of course, claimed that he had come. Jews tended to argue either that the tribe of Judah had lost its authority long before Jesus, or that it somehow still retained it (among the exilarchs in Babylonia, for example), even as they hoped for the speedy arrival of the Davidic messiah among Judah's descendants. Curiously, the Apocalypse of Daniel envisions that a king will yet arise from Judea, from the Jews, a king who will anticipate the arrival of Antichrist, and as such will bear the name Dan. Why did our author veer away from the common view that Antichrist would himself come from the tribe of Dan? Did he understand that Dan numbered among the ten lost tribes of Israel and no longer constituted part of the Jewish community? For whatever reason, the novelty of his account maintained the linkage between Antichrist, the Jews, and Dan, even as it allowed for his birth to a virgin. He will be a Jew by association, if not in his genes, though he too, like Jesus, will be sold by Judas for thirty pieces of silver.

As we have read, the Jews will anticipate the birth and program of Antichrist, flocking to their king Dan in Jerusalem, whence "they will afflict the Christian race in all the earth." When Antichrist does arrive on the scene, "the Jewish nation and the Jerusalemites will take counsel saying, 'Come, let us make this admirable man king.' And they make him king and crown him (after) three days. And he will reign (for) three years" (11:1–4). Famine, plague, and disaster will ensue, and evil spirits and demons will themselves adhere to Antichrist, much to the joy and exultation of the Jews and then to the dismay, affliction, and oppression of the Roman Christians.

> And then the Antichrist will lift up a stone in his hands and say, "Believe in me and I will make these stones (into) bread."' And then (the) Jews will worship (him), who are saying, "You are Christ for whom we pray and on account of you the Christian race has grieved us greatly." And then the Antichrist will boast, saying to the Jews, "Do not be grieved thus. A little (while and) the Christian race will see and will realize who I am." (13:1–7)

At the critically decisive moment, Antichrist will make his final move, blending motifs from the miracles worked by Moses and Jesus and suggestively claiming no less than to be the divine Christ himself. "And the Antichrist lifts up (his) voice toward the flinty rock, saying, 'Become bread before the Jews.'" Instead of bread, however, the rock becomes a dragon, who proceeds to shame Antichrist in front of his Jewish henchmen (13:9–13). Soon three preachers (presumably Enoch, Elijah, and John the Evangelist) come to preach to Christians against Antichrist, who eventually slays them. One must note that despite the efforts of these preachers, the Jews in this apocalyptic vision continue to resist the truth. But time marches on: "With the Antichrist reigning and with the demons persecuting, the Jews contriving vanities against the Christians, the great day of the Lord draws near. And there will be judgment and recompense. And the deception of the devil will fall. And the light of the world, Christ our Lord and king of glory, will flower, to whom is due all glory and honor and dominion forever" (14:13–16).[26]

The Apocalypse of Daniel holds out no hope for the final redemption of the Jews. Associated by the author, no doubt, with the Arabs who threatened the empire from without, and perhaps with its internal foes as well, they anticipate Antichrist, they support him, and they presumably share his ultimate fate. Yet Western churchmen rarely cast their eschatological Jews in such uncompromising terms. The Jews' bonds with Antichrist notwithstanding, at some point in his career at least some of them would see the light and join the forces of good. This expectation found expression in numerous variations, each with its own story to tell and ideology to advance.

Adso's Biography of Antichrist and Its Legacy

Its brevity notwithstanding, one medieval work more than any other proved critically influential in the history of Antichrist's literary career—and in the elaboration of his associations with the Jews.

Adso's "Libellus de Antichristo"

In the middle of the tenth century, the French abbot Adso of Montier-en-Der (ca. 910–992) composed his *De ortu et tempore Antichristi* (On the Birth and Time of Antichrist), often dubbed his "little book" on Antichrist ("Libellus de Antichristo"), in the form of a letter to the queen and (for several years) regent of France, Gerberga of Saxony. Adso blended the teaching on the Last World Emperor and Antichrist that he found in various patristic, Carolingian, and Byzantine writings—including Jerome's commentary on Daniel, Pseudo-Methodius, and Haymo of Auxerre's commentary on 2 Thessalonians—into a brief, running, readable account of the origins, life, and demise of Christianity's eschatological villain. Hundreds of extant manuscripts and dozens of different versions testify to the wide circulation and the immense popularity of Adso's work, which enshrined a basic set of traditional ideas and motifs in Western Antichristology. For centuries to come, what one knew about Antichrist typically began—and often ended—with what one read in Adso's pamphlet, which continues to serve historians as a benchmark for comparison and classification. One regularly looks back at writers on Antichrist subsequent to Adso either as reaffirming his expectations or as departing from them—or both in differing measures—but ever so rarely with total disregard for Adso.

As modern investigators have observed repeatedly, the content of Adso's work on Antichrist includes little that is original, but it innovates in its integration of earlier ideas into a single, sufficiently (though not entirely) coherent narrative. It offers a biography, like a hagiographic vita of "Christ's alter ego" or an "anti-saint," as Bernard McGinn and Richard Emmerson have aptly suggested, in a story mirroring that of Jesus himself, a story that has a beginning, a middle, and an end. Antichrist's Jewish connections that Adso imported from the works of his predecessors thus became part of the most popular Antichrist narrative of the Middle Ages.[27] We can helpfully review them as the medieval reader would have encountered them: in the progressive stages of Antichrist's career that Adso envisioned.

ANTICHRIST'S CONCEPTION AND BIRTH

Adso opens the biography of Antichrist by explaining that he bears his name "because he will be contrary to Christ in all things and will do things that are against Christ." And he soon proceeds to elaborate regarding Antichrist's origins, as noted earlier: "Our authors say, the Antichrist will be born from the Jewish people, that is, from the tribe of Dan. . . . He will sit in the wayside like a serpent and will be on the path in order to wound those who walk in the paths of justice and kill them with the poison of his wickedness."

What of Antichrist's parents, his conception, and his birth?

> He will be born from the union of a mother and father, like other men, not, as some say, from a virgin alone. Still, he will be conceived wholly in sin. At the very beginning of his conception the devil will enter his mother's womb at the same moment. The devil's power will foster and protect him in his mother's womb and it will always be with him. Just as the Holy Spirit came into the mother of Our Lord Jesus Christ and overshadowed her with his power and filled her with divinity so that she conceived of the Holy Spirit and what was born of her was divine and holy, so too the devil will descend into the Antichrist's mother, will completely fill her, completely encompass her, completely master her, completely possess her within and without, so that with the devil's cooperation she will conceive through a man and what will be born from her will be totally wicked, totally evil, totally lost.

Thus Adso concludes: "For this reason that man is called the 'Son of Perdition,' because he will destroy the human race as far as he can and will himself be destroyed at the last day."[28]

Antichrist will be born to Jews of the tribe of Dan, but this entails more than a simple ethnic association. For in keeping with the patriarch Jacob's eschatological prophecy in Genesis 49, Antichrist will bear the venomous, murderous, and malicious tendencies of his Jewish tribal progenitors. Moreover, although Antichrist will be human and not divine, the devil will participate in his conception in a manner corresponding to the Holy Spirit's impregnation of the Virgin Mary; just as the Holy Spirit engendered divinity in the fruit of Mary's womb, so, too, Antichrist's mother "with the devil's cooperation . . . will conceive through a man and what will be born from her will be totally wicked, totally evil, totally lost." With his Jewish parents, the child of this union will share their affinity with the devil, exemplifying the Jews' allegiance to evil and their rejection of God, God's mother, and God's son.

The Place of Antichrist's Birth

Antichrist will be born in Babylonia, and from there he will make his way, again in Jesus's footsteps, to fishing towns in the Galilee and finally to Jerusalem.

> You have heard how he is to be born; now hear the place where he will be born. Just as Our Lord and Redeemer foresaw Bethlehem for himself as the place to assume humanity and to be born for us, so too the

devil knew a place fit for that lost man who is called Antichrist, a place from which the root of all evil ought to come, namely the city of Babylon. Antichrist will be born in that city, which once was a celebrated and glorious pagan centre and the capital of the Persian Empire. It says that he will be brought up and protected in the cities of Bethsaida and Corozain, the cities that the Lord reproaches in the Gospel when he says, "Woe to you, Bethsaida, woe to you Corozain!"[29]

Antichrist's birthplace recalls the whore and beast of Babylon in the Book of Revelation, but his Eastern, Persian provenance also reminds us of the pair of Antichrists envisioned by patristic writers like Commodian, who, as seen in the previous chapter, anticipated a pagan, Nero-like Antichrist to be followed by a Jewish one: "A man from Persia will call himself immortal as Nero for us, so shall this one be for the Jews."[30] Why will Antichrist find the towns of Chorazin and Bethsaida so inviting? Jesus cursed them because of their refusal to repent when they encountered his preaching and his miracles—a stubbornness emblematic of the Pharisees and scribes in the Synoptic Gospels, and of the Jews in general in later Christian tradition.[31]

The Rise and Fall of Antichrist

Like Jesus, Antichrist will ascend from the Galilee to Judea, its holy city, and the temple of the Jews.

> Then he will come to Jerusalem and with various tortures will slay all the Christians he cannot convert to his cause. He will erect his throne in the Holy Temple, for the Temple that Solomon built to God that had been destroyed he will raise up to its former state. He will circumcise himself and will pretend that he is the son of Almighty God.[32]

Here one begins to encounter some confusion in the progression of Adso's narrative, but in the sequence of events that follow the Jews clearly have a significant role to play. Antichrist, we read, will terrorize the world for a period of three and a half years. Amassing support among the wicked and persecuting the good, he will find unusually supportive allies among the Jews, as Adso elaborates with reference to 2 Thessalonians.

> "He will exalt himself in such a way that he will be enthroned in God's Temple, displaying himself as if he were God." As we said above, he will be born in the city of Babylon, will come to Jerusalem, and will circumcise himself and say to the Jews: "I am the Christ promised to you who has come to save you, so that I can gather together and defend

you who are the Diaspora." At that time all the Jews will flock to him, in the belief that they are receiving God, but rather they will receive the devil.[33]

Now the narrative backtracks, as it were, and in advance of Antichrist, Enoch and Elijah appear on the scene, sent to defend the faithful and prepare them for the imminent reign of terror. They too will preach and teach over the course of three and a half years and, in so doing, will convert Jews to Christianity: "These two very great prophets and teachers will convert the sons of Israel who will live in that time to the faith, and they will make their belief unconquerable among the elect in the face of the affliction of so great a storm. At that time what scripture says will be fulfilled: 'If the number of sons of Israel be like the sand of the sea, their remnant will be saved.'"[34] According to Adso, Elijah and Enoch will convert the surviving Jews—the remnant of Israel foreseen by Isaiah and then by Paul—before Antichrist slays them. But what of those, including the Jews, whom they first converted? Antichrist will, in fact, persecute the faithful, "either by making them glorious martyrs or by rendering them apostates."[35] Will the Jews die as martyrs or number among those of the elect whom Antichrist will seduce (and whom God will give forty days to repent after the slaying of Antichrist)? Adso does not say.[36]

Adso died in 992, and while the centuries that followed him brought an array of new, creative, and highly influential developments in the medieval idea of Antichrist, his "little book" retained its impact and importance. The anticipation and the aftermath of the millennial year 1000 brought apocalyptic tensions to the forefront of Christian cultural discourse, stimulating creative thought and spilling over into everyday lives and interactions. Many saw evidence of Antichrist, his agents, and his imminent arrival in numerous quarters, ranging from raiders from beyond the frontiers of Western Christendom to heretics within them and from a marked increase in Western pilgrimage to the Holy Land to rumors that French Jews had conspired with a Muslim caliph to destroy the Holy Sepulcher in Jerusalem.[37] The papal reform movement in the eleventh century and the Investiture Controversy that it precipitated heightened the sense that cosmic forces of good and evil were at work (and at war!) within God's church itself. The Crusades to the Holy Land that began at the end of the century contributed further to this apocalyptic awareness. In the instructive words of one present-day historian, "The expedition that captured Jerusalem in 1099 became a template, a model for subsequent Christian action both at home and abroad when self-proclaimed members of the Western Church confronted heresy and unbelief, saw themselves as threatened, and, in certain circumstances, desired to propagate the faith."[38] The twelfth century, which brought medieval European civilization to unprecedented heights in its growth, saw continued, variegated development in the realms of ecclesiastical reform, crusading, campaigns against the enemies of Christ and his church—and notions of the ultimate eschatological villain soon to arrive. When, as I have suggested elsewhere, expansion gave way to entrenchment and contraction beginning in the thirteenth century,[39] speculation concerning Antichrist only increased. As we shall see below in this chapter and in the chapters that follow, Christianity's eschatological Jews continued to reflect the changing realities in which they were perennially constructed and reconstructed.[40]

The Adsonian Antichrist of the Twelfth and Thirteenth Centuries

As interest in Antichrist mushroomed during the twelfth and thirteenth centuries, his links to the Jews as portrayed by Adso proved durable and well ensconced in the Western mindset. Clerical writers drew directly on Adso's biography even as they struggled to accommodate the teaching of Jerome, Augustine, Bede, and others among their forerunners, although recent historical developments heightened the urgency in their preoccupation with Antichrist. With variations in the details and timetable of the events of the end time, many reiterated the origins of Antichrist in the Israelite tribe of Dan, his overtures to the Jews that will win him their support, and their ultimate conversion, owing to the preaching of Elijah and Enoch, either before or after his death. Among the versions of the Adsonian narrative that circulated, one even recorded that the Jews' persisting loyalty to Antichrist would lead them to visit his grave three days after his death, assuming that he had been resurrected; but they will find only a fetid corpse instead.[41] Recent scholarship has investigated the high medieval idea of Antichrist at length, especially in Germany, and historians have offered instructive suggestions (rather than unbending rules) for comparison and classification even within the Adsonian "camp." Some writers, from Rupert of Deutz at the beginning of the twelfth century to Berthold von Regensburg in the middle of the thirteenth, generally inclined away from applying apocalyptic symbolism to contemporary politics and events, persisting in the spiritualizing, nonmillenarian orientation of Tyconius and Augustine. Others, including the twelfth-century Honorius Augustodunensis in his earlier works (his *Elucidarium* above all)[42] and the thirteenth-century Hugo Ripelin,[43] picked up on the personal, more vital Antichrist of Adso's biography and contributed to a more specific set of expectations for the end of days that many considered imminent. Still others, like the French theologian William of Saint-Amour, retained the basic Adsonian narrative but proved more intent on portraying their contemporary enemies—in William's case, the mendicant friars—as the false preachers and supporters of Antichrist than on condemning the Jews.[44] I refrain from a laborious, comprehensive, and invariably repetitive review of the sources, offering several examples that, for different reasons, stand out as interesting and illuminating.[45]

THE PLAY OF ANTICHRIST

In the middle of the twelfth century, a Bavarian monk of Tegernsee composed the *Ludus de Antichristo*, a Latin drama evidently meant to be sung, complete with extensive stage directions, that stands alone among other theatrical works of the High and later Middle Ages. Scholars have belabored its distinctiveness. It drew from no known prior dramatic works, and it had no documentable influence on any that followed it. Yet as Horst Dieter Rauh has asserted,

> The most impressive, aesthetically convincing picture of Antichrist in German Symbolism does not come from an exegete or historian, but from a poet: it is found in the so-called *Ludus de Antichristo*. Strictly formed linguistic art, richness in rhythm, and sovereign mastery of tradition make this dramatic poetry the most important play of the Middle Ages.[46]

The play opens at the Lord's temple in Jerusalem, surrounded by seven royal seats. After the king of Babylon and Gentilitas enter declaring their outright rejection of biblical monotheism, Synagoga and the Jews enter affirming their belief in God but their rejection of Jesus and Christianity. Their song serves as a refrain repeated at various stages in the presentation.[47]

> O Lord, in you alone our safety lies!
> From human life no true hope can arise.
> The wrongs done in Christ's name we must despise!
>
> In him no hope of safety we can see.
> How strange that he should happen to be slain who raised the dead and made them live again:
> No man's salvation can a man ordain who cannot save himself from misery!
>
> This man is not the Lord's Emmanuel, the One to be adored by Israel.
> This Jesus, like the gods of Ishamel, I order you to banish utterly![48]

Eventually, after the emperor of the Romans has abdicated his throne Antichrist arrives, accompanied by Hypocrisy and Heresy, and seeks to rally support for himself among the rulers of the world. Once he succeeds in seducing them or overcoming their opposition, he directs Hypocrisy to Synagoga:

[ANTICHRIST]
Go to the Jews and say to them that their Messiah's come, that all the peoples of the world pay tribute and succumb. . . . Go to the Jews and say to them: Messiah—look, it's me! I am the One who's promised you by ancient prophecy!

Then the Hypocrites [go] to Synagoga:

[HYPOCRITES]
A royal people set apart: you are the chosen race. As faithful people you have been proclaimed in every place. For keeping to the law you've long been exiled, slain, pariahs—far from your fatherland, you wait the coming of Messiah. This waiting will be recompensed to your posterity: a new and joyful time will heal your old adversity! Behold, redemption is at hand, behold the mystery: a king is born to lead your faith in full authority! This king is the Emmanuel as witnessed by Scripture and through his grace you'll reign with him and always be secure. He raises up the humble, the proud he will defeat. With power, everything is cast down underneath his feet. Arise, Jerusalem! Arise and shine! Rejoice, O captive Synagogue! It's time!
[SYNAGOGA]
This is the consolation of God's generosity, rewarding us for all the years of our captivity. Let's go, therefore, and meet him now—the savior promised us! It's right to offer praise to the redeemer glorious!

We then watch as Synagoga and Anichrist forge their fateful alliance.

[SYNAGOGA]
You come, Emmanuel—whom we have waited for, whom we will always glorify and whom we all adore.
Then, when Synagoga comes, Antichrist receives her and, signing her [with his mark], sings:
[ANTICHRIST]
Through me, the end of darkness is at hand. To you I will restore the promised land. Your light will all the people's way make plain. In peace, and by your laws, all kings will reign.[49]

At last Elijah and Enoch come to reveal the truth to the Jews and expose Antichrist for the impostor that he is. They remove the veil that has blinded

Synagoga, so that she can then proclaim her acceptance of Christianity and its triune deity:

> Truly, we were led astray and this is Antichrist who lied to us and said he was the Jews' own promised Christ! Now here are the authentic proofs of our new liberty: Elijah, Enoch—prophets who have spoken truthfully! To you we give our grateful thanks, O Adonai, our King: a Trinity of Persons but in essence One Being. Truly, God the Father, from Whom issues God the Son, and from both come the Spirit so that God is Three in One.[50]

Infuriated, Antichrist threatens Elijah, Enoch, and Synagoga with death, but the Jews hold fast to their newly found faith: "Our many errors we repent, for now our faith is sure. Whatever persecution comes to us we will endure." Antichrist then slaughters them.[51]

Scholars have termed the depiction of Synagoga in the *Ludus* a sympathetic one. As John Wright observed, our playwright "in his treatment of the Jews . . . showed a broadly based, tolerant humanity which for his time, and in fact for most periods in history, is unfortunately very rare."[52] Recalling her character in many works of early medieval Christian iconography, Synagoga in the *Ludus* retains her nobility throughout. She and the Jews fall prey to the wiles of Antichrist after all the other characters on stage, most notably the rulers of Christendom, emperor of the Romans included. At the end of the drama, in the wake of the preaching of Elijah and Enoch, only Synagoga and the Jews return to God and confess their belief in his truth. Most telling, as they die as martyrs at the hands of Antichrist, they are baptized in their blood, not in water.[53]

Nevertheless, for all of the relatively gentle treatment they receive in the *Ludus*, the Jews have a role to play on stage, and play it they do. Their allegiance to Antichrist, much like their fulfillment of Paul's prophecy concerning the salvation of Israel, appears more principled than it does opportunistic—more than one can say about many of the Christians whom Antichrist seduces. Synagoga first enters the temple in Jerusalem proclaiming her belief in the one God so as categorically to reject acceptance of Jesus. She thereby gives expression to the basic Christian conception that if the Jews do not accept Christ as their messiah, then the savior whom they await must necessarily be Antichrist. Curiously, she, and only she, of all the characters in the play, identifies Antichrist for who he is: "This is Antichrist." Scholars have discussed, and debated, the degree of "political tendentiousness" that one ought rightly to attribute to the *Ludus*.[54] Yet I agree with Richard Emmerson's conclusion that "the play is more concerned with accurately dramatizing specific expectations of the tradition" than it is "with portraying realistic political situations."[55] Like Synagoga at the foot of the cross in Christian art,[56] Synagoga in the *Ludus* is a construction—not only inasmuch as the artist/playwright conceives and characterizes her, but also in her presentation to the audience as such. Unlike the Jews in Adso's biography, Synagoga in the *Ludus* has no connection to Antichrist's birth or to his upbringing, and the depiction of Jewish support for and ultimate rejection of Antichrist lacks feeling, drama, and suspense. These are not Jews that Christians might ever have imagined encountering, but the symbolic embodiment of the Old Law, as opposed to the New. Synagoga thus enthusiastically embraces Antichrist and what he represents before she recants, as her role requires her to do.[57]

THE GARDEN OF DELIGHTS

Alongside the *Ludus de Antichristo*, we turn to the *Hortus deliciarum*, an encyclopedia blending text, visual illumination, and even music compiled by the late twelfth-century German abbess Herrad of Hohenburg for the Augustinian canonesses in her community. Whereas the *Ludus* demonstrated the potential of the stage for conveying ideas of Antichrist, the *Hortus* marked a milestone in the visual representation of Antichrist, and we shall return to both the dramatic and visual representation of Antichrist in the next chapter of this book. Yet in her own fashion, the author of the *Hortus* wrestled with the challenges of conveying the teachings of her predecessors, those that she found in Adso and those that she encountered in the works of other recent writers, most notably Honorius Augustodunensis. While fire consumed the sole surviving twelfth-century manuscript some 150 years ago, scholarly reconstructions of the *Hortus* still prove valuable for our study of portrayals of Antichrist in the High Middle Ages.[58]

Herrad's text adheres rather faithfully to a twelfth-century rendition of Adso's biography attributed only in later centuries to Anselm of Canterbury, though she did reword and reorder, in order to clarify what she encountered there. She expanded the earlier narrative so as to simplify it and heighten its effect. In view of confusion (mentioned above) that she too encountered in the Adsonian account, she placed the work of Elijah and Enoch before Antichrist's rise to power. And, drawing from other sources, she referred to the armies of Gog and Magog and the resurrection of the slain Enoch and Elijah, details not found in Adso.[59] In the illustrations and their inscriptions, however, the *Hortus* assumes its truly distinctive character. Preceding the textual account of Antichrist, the pictures and their captions control the reception of Antichrist's story. Filling folio pages that exceeded fifty centimeters in height and thirty-five centimeters in width, "leaves bursting with imagery, text, and song,"[60] they communicate more directly with readers, and they give us a better sense of the lasting impressions that Herrad wished to impart.[61] These pictures highlight the Jews, disproportionately in relation to attention accorded them in the text, on the one hand emphasizing their support for Antichrist and on the other hand anticipating their conversion after his death.

The Antichrist cycle opens with a picture of the mystical winepress (fig. 2) that symbolizes the church of Christ.[62] In the bottom right Enoch and Elijah preach to an audience of Jews, or at least to a group dominated by two Jews wearing tall conical hats. At the top of the next page (fig. 3), Antichrist, having entered Jerusalem with the army of Gog and Magog, slays the two prophets, and in the bottom register all the Jews of the world flock to Antichrist, convinced by his miracles that he is God when in fact he is the devil.[63]

Fol. 241r (Pl. 133)

307

FIGURE 2.   Mystical winepress. Herrad of Hohenbourg, *Hortus deliciarum*, ed. Rosalie Green et al. (London, 1979), 2:241r. Credit: Warburg Institute.

FIGURE 3.   Jews flock to Antichrist. Herrad of Hohenbourg. *Hortus deliciarum*, ed. Rosalie Green et al. (London, 1979), 2:241v. Credit: Warburg Institute.

Curiously, perhaps owing to her adjustment of the sequence of events in Adso's account but allowing nonetheless for a markedly harsh judgment of the Jews, Herrad depicts their enthusiastic support for Antichrist even after they have heard the teaching of Enoch and Elijah. Then, after a page full of illustrations of Antichrist's oppression of the faithful, the *Hortus* accords the Jews a striking prominence in the events that follow: having witnessed his violent end, "the Jews, who persisted in the error of the Antichrist, will be baptized, heeding the preaching of Elijah and Enoch," at last acknowledging its truth.[64] Finally, at the bottom of the page, in an illustration that echoes the *Elucidarium* of Honorius Augustodunensis more than Adso's biography, we see the baptism of Synagoga—rendered here not as a female, but a male Jew!—who shall convert to the faith in Christ at the end of days.[65]

While the *Ludus de Antichristo* portrayed Synagoga almost in statuesque fashion, as a player in a drama of cosmic proportion having little connection to the sociocultural context of the playwright, the *Hortus* illustrator localizes and personalizes the Jews. At least some of them appear clothed in the hats, hair, and clothing emblematic of twelfth-century German Jewry, both in their support of Antichrist and in their responsiveness to the preaching of Elijah and Enoch. Was this a kind of "artistic shorthand"? While the canonesses presented with these illustrations could thereby visualize the Jews of the end time, for better and for worse, as having a place in—and an impact on—their own immediate surroundings, they could also recognize diversity in medieval Jewish communities; or perhaps they might view the Jews who follow Antichrist as representing unbelievers and doubters in general.

Hugo Ripelin's *Theological Compendium*

Unlike the *Hortus deliciarum*, whose one known manuscript was destroyed in the Franco-Prussian War, the theological encyclopedia compiled by the thirteenth-century Dominican Hugo Ripelin of Strasbourg survived the Middle Ages in numerous copies.[66] Hugo's *Compendium theologiae*, one of the most popular and influential medieval digests of Christian belief and doctrine, falls squarely in the Adsonian tradition in its treatment of Antichrist. Owing to its reception and impact, and on account of its significant conflation of several eschatological motifs, Hugo's discussion of Antichrist serves here to exemplify Adso's continued influence through the thirteenth century and beyond. Like Adso and so many others, Hugo wrote that the Jews would first support Antichrist but then respond to the preaching of Elijah and Enoch and convert to Christianity.[67] More notably, as Andrew Gow has shown in his important book, *The Red Jews*, Hugo followed Peter Comestor and others in building upon the linkage between the fierce tribes enclosed by Alexander the Great in Asia with Gog and Magog of Ezekiel. Proceeding in the wake of earlier Byzantine writers, Peter Comestor had linked those confined by Alexander to the ten lost tribes of Israel, Matthew Paris identified them as the forebears of the Mongols threatening thirteenth-century Christendom, and Hugo Ripelin now connected the proverbial dots and made that identification still more explicit.[68]

> Some say of Gog and Magog that they are the ten tribes shut in beyond the Caspian mountains, such that they could emerge if they were permitted, but they are not so permitted by the queen of the Amazons under whose rule and authority they live. The Jews say that at the end of the present era (*saeculum*) they will emerge and come to Jerusalem, and with their messiah they will destroy the church. Others say that by Gog and Magog one means the army of the Antichrist who at the end of the world will come to attack the church. According to the Gloss we understand "Gog" as those through whom the devil secretly persecutes the faithful, "Magog" those through whom . . . he now openly persecutes the church.[69]

Gog and Magog imprisoned by Alexander, the ten lost tribes of Israel, the Jews' longing for their messiah, Antichrist and his army bent on destroying the church, the devil, the persecution of the faithful—Hugo's juxtaposition of all these motifs in just a few lines renders explicit associations that had crystallized over time in Christian thought and would develop further still as the Middle Ages wore on.

JOACHIM AND JOACHIMITES

Writing at nearly the same time as Herrad of Hohenburg, the late twelfth-century "Calabrian abbot" Joachim of Fiore (d. 1202) left an exceedingly profound mark on medieval imaginings of the end of time. In the daring and the color of his eschatological visions, in the radical originality of his exposition of Scripture, in his readiness to depart from tradition and challenge authority, "in his apocalyptic optimism, and in the fecundity of the new symbols and myths he introduced into the apocalyptic scenario,"[70] Joachim and his followers earned a singular place in the history of Western spirituality. Historians of the last generations have studied Joachim's life, the corpus of his writings, his ideas, and his legacy, and the ongoing publication of his works in new, critical editions continues to nourish these investigations, in which the Jews and Judaism have commanded considerable attention. Most scholars discount the old reports that Joachim was of Jewish descent, but those reports continue to evoke curiosity. Beyond the question of his origins, what contacts did Joachim have with contemporary Jews? How, if at all, did Jewish traditions and ideas inspire him? Did Joachim's teachings concerning the Jews and Judaism leave any lasting mark on Christianity and on Christian-Jewish relations? Some have recently viewed Joachim's thought as remarkably "philo-Semitic," embodying the basis for a radically congenial mode of reconciliation between Judaism, Christianity, and their communities of believers.[71]

How do the Jews figure in Joachim's eschatology? The purview of this book allows only for a few broad strokes. Joachim reevaluated God's plan for human history and redemption, a plan that he interpreted in terms of overlapping numerical patterns—above all patterns of twos, threes, and sevens. On one hand, at the heart of Joachite doctrine lay the notion of *concordia*, a foundational correspondence ("a likeness of equal proportion"—*similitudinem eque proportionis*) between the ages of Old and New Testaments, each divided into seven stages, that far exceeded the typological exegesis popular among the church fathers in its depth and detail.[72] On the other hand, Joachim understood the course of salvation history as the progression of three statuses, corresponding to the three members of the Trinity: (1) that of God the Father, the status of the old covenant struck by God the Father with the Jews; (2) the status of the Son, that of the new covenant brought by Jesus's apostles to the Gentiles in the wake of the Jews' betrayal of God; and (3) the status of the Holy Spirit that would mark the climax of God's plan, a synthesis of the two earlier statuses and their respective elect communities. Joachim did not refrain from viewing contemporary and recent events in Christendom through the prism of this Trinitarian reading of history. The second status, he believed, would soon draw to a close with the coming of Antichrist, the preaching of Enoch and Elijah, and the conversion of the Jews (barring those recalcitrant ones doomed to eternal punishment).[73] In keeping with the prophecy of Romans 11, the plenitude of the Gentiles would join the community of the faithful, "and then at the end of the present age there will follow the whole of Israel, which had formerly understood the word of God in a carnal sense."[74] These events would give way to the third status, a probably short-lived millennial Sabbath on earth, in which contemplative, truly spiritual men would achieve the fullest human apprehension of God and his revealed word. Notably, even this third age would transpire within the framework of terrestrial history, before the eventual onslaught of the final Antichrist—Gog and Magog—the second coming of Christ, the last judgment, and the end of time.[75]

Joachim elaborated the symmetries and mysteries of salvation history with reference to numerous themes, motifs, stories, and images in Scripture, from the early chapters of Genesis through the end of Revelation. For example, Shem and Japheth, the sons of Noah and forebears of Israelites and

Greeks, respectively, typified the Jews and Gentiles comprising the peoples of God's elect during the first two statuses.[76] Joachim found deep significance in the travels of the biblical patriarch Jacob, heir to God's covenant with Abraham, who first fled his father Isaac's home to his uncle Laban in Haran and subsequently left Laban to return to his ancestral homeland. Jacob prefigured both the transferral of divine election from the Jews to Gentiles and its ultimate return to the Jews, as well as the fate of true Christian monks now suffering under—but soon to be freed from—the domination of less spiritual, more worldly oriented clergy.[77] For Joachim, the Apocryphal tale of the elderly Tobit, cured of his blindness by his son of the same name who had traveled to Media and returned home with the help of the angel Raphael and the curative organs of a strange fish, allegorized the blinding and ultimate restoration of the people of Israel.[78] And of course, Joachim found fertile ground for his eschatological exegesis in the visions, numbers, and images of the Book of Revelation, whose concluding chapters foretold the third millennial status, the ensuing onslaught of Gog and Magog, and the second coming to follow.

In expounding these interpretations Joachim repeatedly cited Paul's prophecy in Romans 11, *omnis Israel salvus fiet*, "all Israel shall be saved."[79] At first glance, Joachim's vision of the Jews of the end time might thus appear rather conformist. Admittedly, many historians concur that Joachim broke with Augustine in linking apocalyptic expectations to contemporary political and ecclesiastical developments, and in his chiliastic expectation of Antichrist's arrival, the conversion of the Jews, and a millennial age *between the present era and the advent of the final Antichrist, his ultimate destruction, and the second coming of Christ.* Still, there was patristic and early medieval precedent for expecting a period of peace between the destruction of Antichrist and the last judgment (as in the writings of Victorinus of Pettau, Jerome, Bede, and Haimo of Auxerre, among others), and for the notion of two distinct Antichrists (as in the work of Commodian). And Joachim followed Adso in predicting that the Jews of the world will at first rally in support of Antichrist and then, hearkening to the preaching of Elijah and Enoch, convert to Christianity and be saved.[80]

Nevertheless, as scholars of Joachim have demonstrated, the role allotted the Jews in Joachim's eschatology far exceeds the seemingly perfunctory acknowledgment of their future conversion that one encounters among many other Christian writers.[81] Hope for the restoration of the Jews lies at the bedrock of Joachim's understanding of salvation history, the *concordia* between Old and New Testaments, the Trinitarian progression of three statuses, and the extent of Jewish support for Antichrist. It pervades his reading of Scripture, from Genesis through Revelation, as in the biblical stories mentioned just above. The Jews to be converted by the spiritual men of the near future will regain their elect standing; the preaching of the Gospel will be restored to them;[82] and the devil, hitherto allowed to dwell amid the Jews, will be banished from among them and imprisoned among barbaric peoples ("those immune to all humanity").[83] Together with the Gentiles the Jews will constitute a spiritually enlightened population. Their conversion will facilitate what Robert Lerner has termed "the apotheosis of history, wherein a merged populace would be endowed with the fullest spiritual understanding."[84] When, as foreseen in Romans 11, all Israel will be saved, the elect elders of the Jews (recalling the biblical patriarchs) will join those of the Gentiles (recalling Jesus's apostles) in building the eschatological Jerusalem of Revelation 21 in its final phase: the status of the Holy Spirit.[85] As Alexander Patschovsky has observed, the difference between Augustine's hermeneutical construction of a fossilized Jew who had remained "stationary in useless antiquity" and Joachim's eschatological Jew "could not have been greater."[86]

The weight that Joachim accorded the Jews and their Scripture in his eschatology finds expression in the diagrams, tables, and charts that comprise an integral part of his corpus. Some investigators have asserted that these *figurae* actually take priority over the textual elaboration of Joachim's ideas in the crystallization of his thought and in their importance. Of the

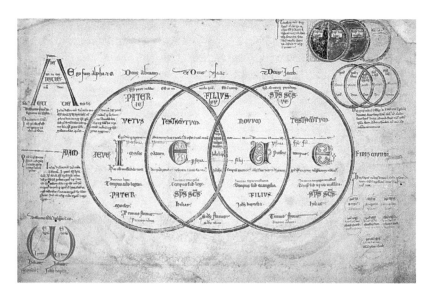

FIGURE 4.   Trinitarian circles of salvation history. Joachim of Fiore, *Liber figurarum*. Oxford, Corpus Christi College MS 255A, fol. 7v. By permission of the President and Fellows of Corpus Christi College, Oxford.

many illustrations that speak to our concerns, several of Joachim's works include sets of Trinitarian circles representing the three progressive statuses of salvation history, as one can see in the illustration from the *Concordia novi ac veteris testamenti* (fig. 4).[87]

FIGURE 5.   Vine of salvation history. Joachim of Fiore, *Liber figurarum*. Oxford, Corpus Christi College MS 255A, fol. 12v. By permission of the President and Fellows of Corpus Christi College, Oxford.

Immediately after Joachim underscores the future conversion of the Jews during (or immediately prior to) the third status[88] and the necessity that the preaching of the Gospel "return to this hitherto unbelieving people from whom it arose,"[89] one finds the adjacent (elsewhere Joachim has overlapping) circles representing the three statuses. The first denotes the status of God the Father, the "age of circumcision"; the second the status of the Word, the "age of the Cross"; and the third the status of the Holy Spirit, the "age of rest and peace."[90] In the third (or, in some cases of the diagram, the second) of the three smaller circles within the larger circle of the third status, Joachim wrote: "Those who believe in the spiritual men enter into that quietude foretold by the prophets." These, as we have seen, will include the Jews.

Similar circles appear not in a horizontal line but in a vertical stack—perhaps to convey a sense of growth and progressive development—in the Trinitarian image of a vine or tree in Joachim's *Liber figurarum* (fig. 5).[91]

At the bottom of the image, we see Noah, and immediately above him a stump bearing no fruit representing his accursed son Ham. During the status of God the Father, the branch of Noah's son Shem, ancestor of the *populus judaicus*, extending up from the left side (our right) of Noah's head and immediately curving leftward, is in somewhat fuller bloom than that of Japheth, forebear of the *populus gentilis*, extending up from Noah's right side (our left) and then curving to the right. During the status of the Son, in the second circle, the branch of the Gentiles produces much more fruit than that of the Jews, though this is not denuded entirely. In the third status of the Holy Spirit, the two branches join at the top of a full circle, producing the lush, abundant bloom that befits the ultimate spiritual union of Jews and Gentiles. As one recent study of this image has aptly concluded: "The figure of the vine diagram does not portray history as an abstract substrate with a given numerical pattern, for it makes the shifting relations between the Jews and the Gentiles themselves constitute history and its pattern. . . . What brings about the *status* of the Holy Spirit is the unification of the peoples of the first and the second *status*, into a 'spiritual Church' which immeasurably surpasses the whole preceding course of history of both the Jews and the Gentiles."[92]

As noted, Joachim reiterated the standard view that Jews will lend Antichrist their support, but in all he minimized the role of the Jews in the career of Antichrist and rarely mentioned them in this regard. Along with several other twelfth-century churchmen preceding him—Honorius Augustodunensis in his Song of Songs commentary, to whom we shall return below in chapter 7, and Gerhoh of Reichersburg in his *De investigatione Antichristi*[93]—Joachim did not teach that Antichrist would arise from the tribe of Dan, or at all from among the Jews.[94] This comports with the lack of the acerbic rancor and emotive expression that characterized much Christian anti-Jewish polemic in his work aimed at convincing the Jews to convert, entitled *Exhortatorium Iudeorum* (Exhortation of the Jews) but recalled by the elderly Joachim himself as *Contra Iudeos*. For all its novelty, deriving chiefly from the eschatological expectations that nourished all of Joachim's writing, the *Exhortatorium* proffered well-known arguments and biblical proof texts in elaborating the errors of the Jews.[95] As anti-Jewish polemic, his work broke little new ground—neither in its substance nor in any urgent call for concerted ecclesiastical efforts to missionize among the Jews. Such missionary efforts would still have been ahead of their time in the twelfth century,[96] and, when they did first appear in the thirteenth century, they generally were fueled by the new indictment of contemporary Judaism as a postbiblical, Talmudic heresy[97]—an outlook quite foreign to Joachim's approach to the Jews. As Anna Sapir Abulafia reminds us in concluding her appraisal of the *Exhortatorium*,

> Joachim's *Adversus Iudeos* is a tangible reminder that although the work of many twelfth-century polemicists implied that the Jews should be excised from Christian society, Jews did continue to play a vital role in Christian theology. And for all the negative policies which medieval Christian ecclesiastical and lay powers eventually did enact against Jews by seizing their property or life, forcing them to convert or expelling them, the institutional church as a whole did not abandon Paul's vision of the conversion of the Jews at the end of time.[98]

Was Joachim pro-Jewish? Hardly. Was he anti-Jewish?[99] In his unhesitating condemnations of the Jews, their observance, their spiritual blindness, and their error—he was, most certainly, much like virtually every other churchman of the day. But I believe that such questions miss their mark. The significance that Joachim attributed to the Jews, their place in the first status of salvation history, their conversion to Christianity, and their ensuing role in the drama of the eschaton, singles him out for well-deserved attention among his contemporaries and in the legacy of his ideas for centuries after his death.

Bearers of Joachim's Legacy

Although Joachim's distinctive ideas concerning the Jews hardly came to dominate late medieval thought, they did prove unusually attractive for some,[100] and we turn to two of the Calabrian abbot's most important disciples in this regard.

Peter Olivi

The controversial theologian, exegete, and Spiritual Franciscan Peter John Olivi (1248–1298), whose massive commentary on the Apocalypse was censured, condemned, and burned during the fourteenth century, exerted considerable influence in both his own and subsequent generations and followed Joachim in allotting the Jews a noteworthy and positive function in his expectations for the end. As the recent editor and translator of the commentary has proposed, "Olivi wrote as though he believed that he verily had discovered the eschatological Jews whom John of Patmos had foreseen. These flesh-and-blood Jews, moreover, were to become the Apocalyptic 'Order of St. Elijah' (not precisely Olivi's phrase), the shield and protector of the Spiritual Church against the forces of evil during the seventh stage."[101] Given that Olivi, in the same writer's words, "was riding the crest of a tsunami of Christian biblical hermeneutics"[102] and drew from Jewish, Greco-Roman, patristic, and more recent Catholic sources in his own exegesis, his largely Joachite forecast for the Jews of the eschaton stands out among other late medieval readings of the Apocalypse.

Throughout his Apocalypse commentary, Olivi affirms consistently that Paul's prediction (in Romans 11) for the salvation of all Israel applies to all of the Jews, and he repeatedly notes that Revelation shares such expectations for their full, general, final, and perfect conversion.[103] While Olivi acknowledges the difficulties in unraveling the complexities of Pauline eschatology and admits that one might understand Israel symbolically to mean the elect of God, whether Jew or Gentile,[104] he insists that the sealing of the 144,000 righteous in Revelation 7 refers to Jews, 12,000 from each of the tribes of Israel. For although the Epistle to the Romans clarifies that the elect from among the Gentiles who "see God by faith" descend from Abraham and number among Israelites of the spirit,

> it is necessary according to the predestination of God to be fulfilled at last that *all Israel* turn to Christ, and the Apostle proves this through statements of the Prophets. So, therefore, however many sealed ones there are of spiritual Israel from the gentiles who come before, this scripture will by no means be fulfilled until the sealing described here takes place out of the Tribes that were propagated naturally from Israel or from Jacob.[105]

As such, the conversion of the Jews will realize the ultimate destiny of God's church. If the conversion of the Gentiles once led to "a wondrous renewal of the whole world . . ., no less appropriately should the whole world again be wondrously renewed in the universal conversion of Israel." Given that

Jesus and his mother were Jews, and given that God conveyed his promises of Israel's salvation to the fathers and prophets of the Jews,

> in the most unchangeable covenants, so much the more was it necessary that this nation may be wonderfully magnified by Christ and in Christ. For this reason, it was not unfitting that the end of the age and of the church be reserved for the Jews, such that the beginning and the end of the church of Christ may be in the Jewish nation.[106]

Can one say more about the role of the Jews in the drama of the eschaton? Faithful to the teaching of Joachim, Olivi emphatically denied that Antichrist would arise from the Israelite tribe of Dan, breaking with patristic and Adsonian tradition on the matter of Antichrist's Jewish origins and identity. While the "mystical" Antichrist—the first of two Antichrists—in Olivi's eschatological forecast might call himself the "messiah of the Jews,"[107] his Apocalypse commentary does not label the Jews collectively as the supporters of Antichrist, identify them with Gog and Magog, or portray them as conspiring against the better welfare of Christendom.[108] Among the criticisms of Olivi's reading of Revelation that underlay his commentary's condemnation, he held that the widespread conversion of the Jews will at least begin before the death of Antichrist (and his slaying of Elijah and Enoch and their subsequent resurrection), likewise militating against the linkage between Antichrist and Jews.[109]

While Robert Lerner has written that Joachim foresaw a much more active role for eschatological Jewry than did Olivi, who reduced their role to "passive recipients of salvation rather than active participants in a new way of life,"[110] one hardly comes away from Olivi's Apocalypse commentary sensing that this role is a negligible one. As David Burr and others have observed,[111] Olivi underscores the importance of the Jews' conversion from the very beginning of his lengthy treatise,[112] even more than that of the Gentiles. In the opening of the sixth seal on the scroll delivered to the lamb in Revelation 5–6, we read, for example, that *all Israel* shall be converted to him and the whole world with Israel," although the Israelites shall be sealed ahead of others.[113] Whereas Revelation 7 "greatly extols the virtue and glory of those who are to be converted from among the gentiles and the whole world," in Revelation 14 "the virtue and glory of the elect of Israel are greatly extolled, and the virtue of the others is woven in" secondarily.[114] Olivi ranks the Jews sealed for salvation higher than Gentiles in the army of those faithful sealed for salvation.

> Just as in the one army of a single king, one may distinguish knights from foot soldiers, and barons or dukes or centurions and decurions from simple soldiers, likewise here, those sealed from the Twelve

Tribes are seen to be distinguished from the innumerable throng of the faithful mentioned later. By this sealing, then, is designated a special reception of them into the profession of evangelical perfection and of the higher rank of the Christian militia and to a greater configuration and transformation of them into Christ crucified.[115]

And, as the commentary neared its end and considered the dimensions of the new Jerusalem envisioned in Revelation 21, Olivi cited Joachim to the effect that the city's length and width, each measuring 12,000 stadia, designate "the twelve squadrons of holy martyrs who are designated by the 12,000 sealed from each of the Twelve Tribes of Israel." Olivi, as we have already seen, believed firmly that these Tribes of Israel denoted ethnic Israelites, Jews converted at the end time, and their perfection "designates the highest *concordia* of the blessed in the Kingdom of God."[116] More impressive still, Olivi envisioned that the center of Christian worship will return, literally, to Mt. Zion in Jerusalem following the death of Antichrist, maybe even sooner: "Nor would it be surprising if the place of our redemption should be exalted over all other places at that time, especially in view of the fact that the highest rulers of the world will find that place more suitable for the conversion and later the governance of the whole world, since it is the geographical center of the habitable world."[117]

John of Rupescissa

If Olivi had put the Jews and Jerusalem at center stage in his apocalyptic predictions, the Southern French Franciscan John of Rupescissa (d. 1366) expanded the Jews' eschatological role, added tension and excitement to the dramatic events of the end time, and elaborated an apocalyptic timetable that anticipated the career of Antichrist in the immediate future. John spent most of his clerical career in prison, where, despite horrific conditions and serious illness, he wrote numerous books on a range of subjects (including alchemy) at unimaginable speed. These included his *Liber secretorum eventuum* (Book of Secret Events) in 1349, and, in the mid-1350s, his *Vade mecum in tribulatione* (Pocket Guide for the Tribulation) and lengthy *Liber ostensor* (Book Showing That the Times Are Rushing to an End), all three of which interest us here.[118]

Like Joachim of Fiore and Peter Olivi—but as opposed to the tradition of the Red Jews considered in the next chapter—John did not identify Antichrist as a Jew from the tribe of Dan, or Gog and Magog as the ten lost tribes of Israel.[119] Yet he did, repeatedly and emphatically—especially in the *Liber ostensor*, citing John 5:43 and an otherwise unknown apocalyptic oracle *Cum necatur flos ursi*—view contemporary Jews (*hodierni Judei*) as ardent supporters of Antichrist. They will follow Antichrist, dubbed the "pseudo-messiah of the Jews,"[120] to Jerusalem, whence they will "distinguish themselves as his disciples throughout the world, disseminating lies, conveying false doctrine, miracles, and signs."[121] The vehemence of the Jews' support for Antichrist, however, underscores the wondrous nature of their conversion soon to follow. Like Olivi and some of the church fathers before him, Rupescissa anticipated the coming of two Antichrists, one in the East, the false messiah of the Jews, and one, the final Antichrist, in the West.[122] Drawing from prophecies attributed to the legendary monk Sergius,[123] who reportedly lived around the time of Muhammad, John writes that the Eastern Antichrist will contrive his own blend of Jewish, Christian, and Muslim law, ultimately alienating all three communities, the Jews above all. For he

> will say that he has been sent by God to lead the world back to a single law. He will therefore compel Jews, Saracens, Christians, and others of various sects and religions to abandon their respective laws. And since Jews and Christians have holy laws given to them by the holy God—since the law of the Jews is holy and its mandate holy, just, and good, even if it was revoked by Christ as far as the ceremonies were concerned—Jews and Christians will resist him and his false law more strenuously and accordingly will suffer more than the others. For the Jews too think that Antichrist, their false messiah, ought not to give them a new law different from the law of Moses, and for this reason many Jews will oppose him and many will be killed by him.[124]

In this passage, the Jews will come to oppose Antichrist when he seeks to draw them away from their God-given, albeit old, law, for whose sake many will suffer and die as martyrs. Elsewhere in his treatise, however, John foresees that the restorer (*reparator*) and reformer (*reformator*) of the broken world, a devout Spiritual Franciscan pope, will attack and destroy the final (Western) Antichrist, overcome the Saracens and schismatics, and convert the Jews in Jerusalem. "The Jews, seeing Jesus Christ in heaven in terrifying majesty and their false messiah that he consigned to hell," will recognize their sin and bewail their fate, as prophesied in Zachariah 12.

> The Jews will perceive in Christ apparent the one whom they affixed to the cross, and they will recognize on his body the signs of the nails and the wound in his side, and they shall see clearly that he was the true God and the true man promised to them in the law and the prophets. . . .

> Thus, according to the Old and the New Testament, in this manner will the Jews assembled in Jerusalem be converted by the appearance of Jesus Christ in person (*presencialem aparitionem Jhesu Christi*).[125]

And what of the Jews not in Jerusalem? Evidently word will travel, and they too will convert to Christianity. John expands at some length on how these events will fulfill the Pauline prophecy of all Israel's salvation in Romans 11, as well as the vision of the tribes of Israel sealed for salvation in Revelation 7.[126]

But the drama of the Jews' conversion has yet to reach its conclusion. Writing in the 1350s, Rupescissa foresaw that the death of Antichrist in 1365 would inaugurate the thousand-year-long millennial Sabbath: "On the same day will begin the conversion of the blinded people of the Jews and of the world and the conversion of all the unbelievers and the illumination of the world."[127] What would now be the role of the Jews? Nothing less than rulers of the world! During the decades immediately following that fateful day, converted Jews would join Christians in fighting the tyrants loyal to Antichrist (labeled *feces tyrranorum antichristianorum*), and rulership and imperial authority (*imperium et dominium*) will be bestowed upon the Jews: "For there will be one emperor from the people of the Jews converted to Christ ruling the whole world."[128] The seat of the Christian empire will transfer from Rome to a glorious new Jerusalem, and an Augustus born of the seed of Abraham will thus bring the destiny of the Christian empire to its perfect conclusion.[129]

Robert Lerner has labeled Rupescissa's prophecies concerning the Jews "probably the most concrete philo-Judaic predictions issued by any Christian until his time," and he has noted that John's "understanding that the Jews would be the imperial nation of the millennium" parted company with the Joachimite anticipation of balance between converted Jews and Gentile Christians at the end time.[130] While Lerner has shown how such ideas did live on in the writings of a small number of Franciscans and other Joachimites during the generations after his death, they hardly assumed popularity among Christians of the later Middle Ages and Reformation periods. Yet they still demand a place on the spectrum of possibilities that Christendom imagined for eschatological Jewry. We shall encounter some of these ideas yet again in the concluding chapter of this book, devoted to the Puritans of seventeenth-century England and New England. When these ideas did find expression among them, nearly everyone—most modern scholars who have studied them included—remained oblivious to their medieval precedents.

CHAPTER 6

Antichrist and Jews in Literature, Drama, and Visual Arts

As the Middle Ages wore on, the cultural horizons of Christian Europe broadened extensively. New avenues of literary and artistic creativity developed alongside more established ones, allowing diverse sectors of medieval society opportunities for religious expression in a world that now questioned tradition with sensitivity and sophistication. Antichrist and expectations of the end continued to exercise the late medieval imagination, generating new, variegated ideas concerning the eschaton, which many continued to anticipate with considerable urgency. Examining a few select works of vernacular literature, religious iconography, and more popular art, we shall see that while established precedent still dictated the basic parameters of the discussion, authors, dramatists, and artists portrayed the eschatological Jew in diverse ways, often with increased ambivalence, hesitation, and nuance.

Gog and Magog, the Ten Lost Tribes, and the Red Jews

We have already encountered the coalescing association of the apocalyptic villains Gog and Magog, the ten lost tribes of Israel confined beyond the river Sambatyon, and the unclean, ferocious warriors reportedly imprisoned by Alexander the Great by the shores of the Caspian Sea who would return to wreak havoc in Christendom among the supporters of Antichrist. As Andrew Gow has documented in his invaluable discussion, twelfth- and thirteenth-century writers including Peter Comestor, Matthew Paris, and Hugo Ripelin—albeit not without the disagreement of others—contributed to the resilience of this linkage in the later Middle Ages, when it flowered in the German vernacular depictions of the Red Jews.[1] The fourteenth-century German version of the antiheretical *Passauer Anonymous* draws the connections explicitly.

> As concerns the countless peoples, who are called Gog and Magog in Holy Scripture, they are twelve tribes,[2] whom the mighty king Alexander long ago enclosed with the help of almighty God behind great and horrible mountains, so that they cannot come forth until the time of the Antichrist. Then God will allow them to march against Christendom, which they want to destroy. They will cause the Christians great suffering and terror.

Eventually, a pious God-fearing king will lead in conquering these Red Jews, obliterating them all without exception.[3]

Once their story became well ensconced in the popular lore and imagination, the Red Jews grew more horrific still. The early fifteenth-century armorial handbook the *Uffenbachsche Wappenbuch* offers a horrific illustration of these "roten Juden" confined against their will beyond mountains, water, and manmade fortifications (fig. 6).[4]

Decades later, a midcentury rendition of a Zurich chronicle reports the popular conviction not only that Jews poisoned the waters of Christendom in 1349, thus facilitating the onset of the Black Death, but that the source of the poison was, in fact, the Red Jews.[5] And one particularly graphic description appears in a fourteenth-century account of the life of Alexander, which projects onto the Red Jews the long-standing attribution of cannibalism to Gog, Magog, and company. When Alexander traversed the mountains,

> he found a terrifyingly wild people that was foul, unnatural and disgusting, and frighteningly good with the bow. They were constantly engaged in magic and necromancy and all forms of wickedness. They were evil and entirely lacking in virtue and modesty. They ate dogs and all manner of animals, not caring whether they were healthy or sick, raw or cooked; they ate vipers and frogs. Nothing was disgusting to them; they found everything good and pleasant . . .,

and they even ate their own dead. Beyond such dreadful traits, these Jews have a terrifying role to play at the end of time. Until the final day of judgment,

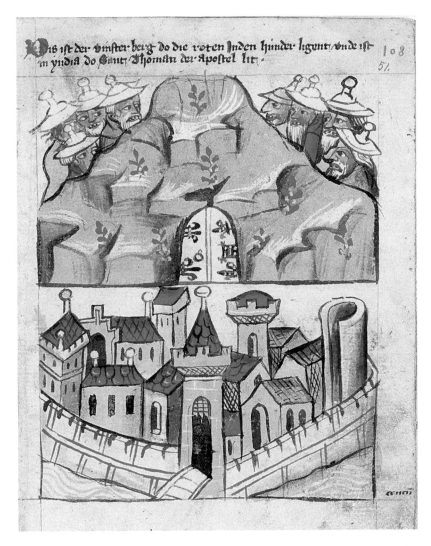

FIGURE 6. Red Jews confined. *Uffenbachsche Wappenbuch*. SUB Hamburg: Cod. in scrin., fol. 51v.

they have no escape from their confinement. But, at the end time, they will break out and join Antichrist in his onslaught on the Christian world. "Whosoever lives through that will wish that he had not!"[6]

As Gow has concluded, this conspiracy theory depended on the more popular, personalized construction of Antichrist—a wicked individual, representing the devil rather than God, perhaps the very one whom the Jews expected as their messiah—that prevailed over more theological, allegorical, and symbolic ideas, especially in the vernacular literature of the late medieval period.[7] In the last of the texts we have quoted here, one sees that it allowed more readily for the tantalizing and sensational, circulating (in today's parlance) virally, especially with the onset of printing. It easily accommodated the view that we have seen just above, that the Last World Emperor and his allies will eventually vanquish Antichrist and his Jewish associates: "They will conquer these Jews, who are also called the Red Jews, and smash them so thoroughly that not one of them is left alive."

Mandeville's *Travels*

Albeit without explicit mention of the Red Jews, the ten tribes/Gog and Magog/Antichrist legend traveled beyond Germany, surfacing and resurfacing throughout Europe, occasionally with interesting variations in content, tone, and ramifications. Perhaps its most widely disseminated version appeared in the immensely popular *Travels of John Mandeville*, a work of unknown authorship that first appeared in French and English versions in the fourteenth century but has circulated most widely in its fifteenth-century recensions. The work purports to recount the voyages of one Sir John Mandeville, an English knight who traveled from Europe into the Middle East, central Asia, China, and the Far East of Prester John. Notwithstanding its own assertions to the contrary, the book is a contrived tapestry of tradition, contemporary knowledge, folklore, and imagination. Its most recent translator into English has called it "part travelogue, part fantasy, part scholarly treatise, part pilgrimage of both body and soul, part record of ethnographic desire, wit, and whimsy," as it "explores and interrogates ideas of fantasy, good society, the human body, sexuality, magic, language, and belief."[8]

When the narrator turns his sights from lands on this, the Middle Eastern side of Cathay to those of central Asia beyond it, he reports of the Caspian Mountains:

> Jews from the Ten Tribes are locked in these mountains, and people call them Gog and Magog, and these Jews cannot leave on any side. . . . King Alexander chased them there because he thought he could lock them in through his men's labor. When he saw that he was not able, he prayed to God that he might fulfil that which he had begun. God heard his prayer and locked together the mountains, which are so high and massive that nobody can cross them, so the Jews live there as if locked and fastened within.

For the time being, these otherwise homeless Jews must pay tribute to the queen of Armenia for their residence in these mountains, but the world will hear from them yet again.

> People of the neighboring region say that in the era of Antichrist these Jews will do much harm to Christians. Therefore all the Jews who live in other parts of the world have learned to speak Hebrew, because they believe that the Jews living amongst the mountains will emerge and speak nothing but Hebrew.

Jews elsewhere will therefore address them in Hebrew, and lead them to ravage the Christian world. For "these Jews say that they know through their prophecies that the Jews who are within these Caspian Mountains will emerge and Christians will be subject to them as they have been subject to Christians."[9]

Mandeville had already condemned the Jews for their role in Jesus's crucifixion, for their abuse of Jesus before his death, for hiding his cross thereafter, and, in at least one version of the work, for plotting to contaminate the waters of Christendom with an exotic poison secured from Java.[10] Here, in Mandeville's linking of the Jews with Gog, Magog, and Antichrist, one beholds a myth of a full-blown worldwide Jewish conspiracy. Precisely for the purpose of colluding with their brethren Gog and Magog at the end of days do Jews still preserve their Hebrew language!

Mandeville's *Travels* has been labeled "the most important single work for the study of the European conception of the Other in the late medieval-early modern period,"[11] and scholars have long highlighted its interest in, tolerance of, and respect and even admiration for exotic, non-European peoples and their lifestyles.[12] Yet more recent investigators have followed Benjamin Braude in recognizing that as opposed to Christian Europe's struggle with Muslims, Mongols, and most other others,

> there was another struggle, far more difficult and more frightening than mortal combat, because it was against an adversary who was not natural, an enemy who had been vanquished, but had not disappeared, an enemy whose re-emergence at some future date was prophesized by the potent and portentous story of Gog and Magog's return to Palestine. It was an enemy whose innate evil needed to be constantly revealed and reviled so that all good Christian men be ever on their guard. That enemy was the once and future claimant to the land, the Jew.

Allied with Antichrist, the Jews would break out of their Caspian confinement, and, in reestablishing their own kingdom in Jerusalem, impose their rule over Christians, at least until Christ's ultimate defeat of Antichrist and his cohorts.[13]

Braude likewise calls attention to these next sentences in Mandeville's report, which beckons Christendom to stand on guard.

> If you want to know how they're going to find a way out, I'll tell you. . . . In the era of Antichrist a fox . . . will burrow into the earth so far until he surfaces amongst these Jews. When they see this fox . . ., they'll chase him and pursue him until he has run again into the fox-hole he came from. So then they'll dig after him so deeply until they reach those sturdily made gates which Alexander had made with great bricks and mortar, and they'll break these gates down and so they'll have found a passage out.[14]

For Braude, the motif of the fox renders the Jews' Gog and Magog connection more damning.

> Antichrist eventually frees the Jews—as Mandeville's readers had known would happen all along, but the method of their breakout is frighteningly mundane: no thunderbolts smashing the locked gates, no miraculous sundering of the rocks, no cataclysmic crash of waves, nothing but a fox, the stuff of folktales . . .—the *deus ex machina* is nothing more than a common creature of the field and forest. The message Mandeville thus sends is all the worse, for the Jews need hardly wait for Antichrist if their escape routes are so many and simple.[15]

Known for its stealth, cunning, and insidiousness, did the fox perhaps suggest something more? Even if the creator(s) of Mandeville's *Travels* did not realize this, the fox figured centrally in a well-known rabbinic homily on the imminence of Jewish national redemption. The Talmud recounts how the famed Rabbi Akiva and several of his colleagues walked around the ruins of the temple in Jerusalem destroyed by the Romans.[16] "When they arrived at Mount Scopus and saw the site of the Temple, they rent their garments in mourning, in keeping with halakhic practice. When they arrived at the Temple Mount, they saw a fox that emerged from the site of the Holy of Holies [the temple's inner sanctum]. They began weeping, and Rabbi Akiva was laughing. They said to him: 'For what reason are you laughing?' Rabbi Akiva said to them: 'For what reason are you weeping?'" Akiva elaborated how only after the biblical prophecies of the Temple's destruction had been fulfilled could the prophecies of Israel's renewal materialize. The fox, recalling Lamentations 5:18 (following the Douay-Rheims translation of the Vulgate)—"For mount Sion, because it is destroyed, foxes have walked upon it"—paradoxically encourages the Jews to appreciate that their national restoration could not be long in arriving. Had the image of the fox in the Jews' own messianic expectations somehow filtered into Christian estimations of the Jewish messianism that they deemed perfidious and threatening?

Braude's appraisal of Mandeville has had well-deserved impact.[17] None-theless, while acknowledging Mandeville's harsh words for the Jews, some investigators of the last decade have proposed to qualify Braude's appraisal in their readings of Mandeville's narrative. Miriamne Krummel suggests that for all of its denigration of the Jews, Mandeville's fable of Gog and Magog "does encourage moments of empathy." The Armenian / Amazonian queen's exacting tribute from the imprisoned Jews, even in their land of confine-ment, echoes the "monarchical extortion of Jewish communities in England" prior to their expulsion. Their plight of having no other land to call home derives from such expulsions from England and elsewhere. In all, Krummel argues, one can detect a sense of comradery, or at least an understanding that the Jews' need for vengeance stems from a supersessionist narrative and oppressive policies imposed upon them, rather than anything of their own making.[18] In a similar vein, Theresa Tinkle discerns that Mandeville's *Travels* seeks to disengage from the supersessionism at the foundation of medieval Christianity's attitudes toward Jews and Judaism. The description of Gog and Magog deprives the Jews of that covenant that Christianity claimed to have superseded, the covenant of Hebrew Scripture.

> In the valley of Gog and Magog, that prestigious [biblical] language undergoes a symbolic abjection, becoming only the speech of murder-ous conspiracy, by which in the end days Jews will be able to communi-cate with each other so as to destroy Christians. Jews are thereby denied what is arguably their most meaningful role in Christian origins: their command of Scripture. In other words, the narrative represses the his-tory of Jews as privileged recipients and preservers of God's word.

Linked to Gog and Magog, the Jews find themselves dispossessed of the promised land, their once superior learning, and their erstwhile covenant with God, "tendentiously simplifying" the Jewish-Christian encounter to that between good and evil.[19]

Yet at the same time, Tinkle argues, as the narrative moves further east-ward, it raises the subtlety of Christian ambivalence toward the Jews to a new level. For Mandeville detects the characteristics of a pure, pristine biblical religion among peoples that Christian Europe never encountered or even heard of, evincing a perhaps even jealous respect for the simplicity of their ways.

> Mandeville displaces crucial elements of Biblical Judaism onto idealized peoples in the east, bringing back into the narrative the faith supposedly superseded in the holy land, and then expelled in Gog and Magog. The symbolic expulsion of "the Jews" in Gog and Magog is clearly not the end of the story. Mandeville here reintegrates Judaism (though not named so) as a legitimate Biblical faith, not as a superseded past, not as a spectral presence, but as contemporary, very much alive, and admirable.[20]

Tinkle encapsulates Mandeville's objective: to demonstrate, in the end, that "supersession has been superseded. As Mandeville travels further east, Christian-Jewish relations grow increasingly unstable, unmoored from a coherent supersessionary model, and suggestive at best of divine inscrutability." Would such a reading mitigate the cataclysmic end forecast for the Jews at the end of time?[21]

Suzanne Conklin Akbari, for one, has offered a fascinating analysis of the ambivalence, or dissonance, between two models of Jewish alterity implicit in this fable. On one hand, one beholds the Jews of the present age, "Jews who live in other parts of the world" and particularly the Jews of Jerusalem, the very "wellspring of Christianity," on whom Christian supersessionism has imposed subjection as well as its Pauline yearning for their ultimate salvation (as Christians!). A "kind of 'fifth column' located in the vulnerable heart" of Christendom, they induce both fear and hope for reedification. On the other hand, the Jewish Gog and Magog belong to apocalyptic time, evoking terror and apprehension as the moment of their eruption into the Christian world, the onslaught of Antichrist, approaches.[22] This tension elaborated by Akbari goes to the core of the ambivalence at the heart of this book: Shall the Jews of the eschaton be saved, or will they be vanquished along with the forces of evil in the final battle between God and the devil?

Vernacular Biographies of Antichrist

As opposed to most other versions of Mandeville's *Travels*, which adhered more faithfully to their French and English predecessors, one of the German recensions does mention the Red Jews,[23] testifying to the persistence of the myth in its particularly German context. It still appears in the inordinately popular Antichrist block books of the fifteenth and early sixteenth centuries, which from the late fifteenth century enjoyed circulation in print as well as in manuscript. Known primarily for their woodcut illustrations of Antichrist's conception, life, and death—some of which we shall consider below—these books indicate just how the narrative of Adso's tenth-century biography of Antichrist had been transmitted, via works like the *Elucidarium* of Honorius Augustodunensis and *Compendium theologiae* of Hugo Ripelin, had developed, and had come to fascinate its readers. As Andrew Gow has observed, the German Antichrist-book was a popular exegetical composition intended for a lay audience. It summarized common knowledge, established tradition, and popular consensus, at the expense of exactitude in summarizing biblical and patristic sources.[24] *The Antichrist* appeared in a series of printed (or partially printed) editions between 1450 and 1500, with largely similar texts and illustrations. Only several of these have survived, but one can safely assume that they were in great demand and, as one book historian put it, were literally "read to pieces."[25]

In elaborating the relationship between the Jews and Antichrist, the book portrays various milestones in his career: the impregnation of his Jewish mother by her Jewish father of the tribe of Dan, his birth by Caesarean section, his circumcision and appeals to the Jews, their belief in him as their messiah and their efforts to rebuild their temple in Jerusalem, his bonding with the Queen of the Amazons and the Red Jews/Gog and Magog, his conflict with Elijah and Enoch, and his ultimate defeat and damnation.[26] As in the case of Mandeville's *Travels*, such vernacular lives of Antichrist appeared in various European lands, allowing for variation in substance and tone in their depiction of the Jews.[27] The Spanish *Libro del Anticristo*, published in Zaragoza during the decade when the Iberian kingdoms of Castile, Aragon, and Portugal expelled their Jews, follows the text and illustrations of the 1480–1482 Strasbourg block book rather closely and casts the Jews in an unsurprisingly negative light.[28] Yet the English *The Byrthe and Lyfe of the Moost False and Deceytfull Antechryst*, published in London by Wynkyn de Worde in 1520, has actually elicited praise for the "charitable spirit" in which it addresses the Jewish-Christian conflict.[29]

Though I might question the appropriateness of the term "charitable" in this regard, Wynkyn de Worde's departures from the German and Spanish block books do evoke curiosity. *The Byrthe and Lyfe* does depict the sexual union resulting in Antichrist's conception as incestuous and his birth—in Babylon—as unusually violent, but its text nowhere explicitly identifies his parents as Jewish (or from the tribe of Dan), nor do its woodcut illustrations.[30] Only during his childhood does the alliance between Antichrist and Jews develop.

> The Jewes shall take that chylde Antechryst and brynge hym into the Cyte of Jherusalem, and shewe unto hym the same temple that was dystroyed by the Emperour Tytus and Vespasyan. And they shall saye unto that chylde that they wyll take hym for a veray messyas yf he can gyve them counseyll how the temple might be made agayne. And thereupon he shall gyve answere agayne veray sadly and dyscretly. And after his counseyl, the sayd temple shal be edyfyed agayn.[31]

The text briefly describes how the exceedingly malicious warriors of Gog and Magog will come from the Caspian hills and help enthrone Antichrist as the "one Emperour over all the worlde"[32]—but again, with no mention of the tribes of Israel, of the Hebrew language, or of the Jews. Only later do the Jews reappear, when the text "speketh how Antechryst shall cyrcumcyse hymself in the presence of the Jewes in the temple of Jherusalem."[33] Thus the story proceeds:

> The Jewes, which have ben dystroyed and separate by all the world, in that tyme shalle come togyder agayne. Thenne shall Antechryst come into Jherusalem and shall sytte in his mageste and have grete power. And than shall he cyrcumcyse hymselfe and shal say to the Jewes that he is the veray messyas that was promised unto theym in theyr lawe. And he wyll say that our lorde Jhesu Cryst, with his dyscryples, hath ben a nygromancyer, or one that hath knowen the arte magycke. And whan the Jewes shall se that he hath so good fortune, and dooth to them so grete worshyp, and he hymself and his dyscyples do so so [*sic!*] many myracles, and that he hath subdued alle the kynges of the worlde and brought them under his subyectyon, they shalle be ryght Joyous. Thenne shall Antechryst drawe and styre the Jewes to hym with grete gyftes and dowayres. And they shall fall in a grete wanhope and dyspayre, and receyve Antechryst for the ryghtwyse messyas that was promysed and graunted to them in the lawe. And they shall praye to hym and do hym worshyp as unto God.[34]

This, the text then specifies, fulfills the scriptural forecast that "they shall praye to the beest, that is Antechryst, and theyr names shall not be wryten in the boke of lyfe" (Revelation 13:4–8). And it accords with Jesus's rebuke of the Jews in John 5:43: "I am comen to you in the name of my fader, and ye have not be wyllynge to receive me. But another, that is Antechryst, shall come in his owne name, and hym ye shall receyve as the ryghtwyse Messyas."[35] Eventually, Antichrist destroys the very temple that he had built in his youth, but, in the wake of the Jews' sorrowful entreaties, he rebuilds it with the collaboration of the devil in just a single hour.

The partnership between Antichrist and the Jews might well be lamentable, but a careful reading reveals that apart from mistaking him for the righteous messiah promised them in Scripture, the Jews commit no truly horrific acts. Maligning Jesus as a necromancer, Antichrist is the one who blasphemes. He deceitfully procures the loyalty of the Jews with money, gifts, promises, and the temple above all. He fights and subdues all the righteous kings of Christendom. All the while he works the will of the devil. For their part, the Jews do not—as they notably do in Mandeville's *Travels*—conspire against the people and institutions of Christendom. To be sure, they shall be duped and, along with others, won over by Antichrist "for fere of his cruel and tyrannous tourmentes."[36] Yet upon the ultimate destruction of Antichrist, "thenne the Jewes shall well apperceyve that they have ben begyled, and shall be sore ashamed of Antechryst. And than they shall torne to the crysten fayth and beleve. And than shall be accomplysshed the prophecy of Jheremye. . . . In those dayes shall be saved the generacyon of Juda and shall abyde stedfastly."[37]

Antichrist and the Jews on the Late Medieval Stage

Testifying further to his power to captivate the popular imagination and perhaps to the imminence of his expected arrival, Antichrist figured prominently on the late medieval stage, where he appeared more colorful and less stilted than in the *Ludus de Antichristo* of the twelfth century already considered. Playwrights and actors dramatized the legend of Antichrist as it figured in the works of the church fathers, Adso, and more recent writers as well. And, as they depicted Antichrist's conception, birth, rise to power, miracles, conquests, persecution of the righteous, his enlistment of the Red Jews, his conflict with Enoch and Elijah, and his ultimate demise—his Jewish progenitors, supporters, and henchmen assumed important, memorable roles, often quite different from their presentation in the *Ludus* and other earlier sources. Scholars have suggested that, over time, the late medieval Antichrist plays grew increasingly more condemnatory in their attitude toward the Jews, and these plays occasionally resounded with anti-Jewish libels that had nothing to do with the Jews' role at the end time. Yet much like the vernacular texts discussed above, dramatic works allowed for a range of differences and degrees of hostility.[38]

Composed during the years prior to the expulsion of the Jews from Nuremberg in 1499, Hans Folz's *Play of the Duke of Burgundy* stands out in this regard. It portrays the deception of the Jews by Antichrist claiming to be their redeemer, his exposure as an impostor, and his eventual admission to the formidable Sibyl, on the Jews' behalf, to a long list of heinous crimes. He explained that for fourteen hundred years Jews have suffered in Christendom. As for their Christian oppressors,

> if only they knew what great curses, what hatred and envy we have always harbored for them, how many whose lives we have spoiled of those to whom we were physicians; how many young children we have stolen from them and killed and stained red with their innocent blood. We stole from you Christians as well to dishonor the yearly birth of Jesus, which you always celebrate, whose hatred and envy is with us so constantly that it drives away all our pleasures, and the Messiah is so long in coming and does nothing to comfort us.[39]

Theft, blasphemy, ritual murder, and more—all these derive from the (allegedly deserved) suffering of the Jews in captivity, their bloodthirsty need for revenge, and their devious plot to subject all peoples unto themselves. Against the background of contemporary eschatological tensions, these are embodied in the personage of the deceitful Antichrist,[40] identified axiomatically with him for whom the Jews long as their messiah. The Jews suffer horrifically gruesome torture, execution, and bodily mutilation.

While the Red Jews remained an almost exclusively German literary motif, Antichrist plays appeared throughout Western Christendom, and, besides the works of Hans Folz and the *Ludus de Antichristo*, we turn to two noteworthy plays from elsewhere in Christian Europe. The first of these, the sole surviving medieval Antichrist play in French, the anonymous *Jour du Jugement* dates from around 1330. Its length, the size of its cast (including seven Jews, who have a presence on stage throughout much of the play), and the intricacy of its production, including music,[41] far exceed those of the *Ludus* less than two centuries earlier, as do what one scholar has termed its "fixation on the eschatological role of the Jews" and its "unrelenting anti-Semitism."[42]

Soon after the play opens, Satan acknowledges the imminence of the last judgment and its dire implications for him and his cohorts. He proposes accordingly:

> Before the judgment arrives, one of us [devils] should become a man and go straight to Babylon, making sure that, without any delay, he manages to bed a woman full of every type of disgrace, one who has lived all her days in a brothel, winter and summer. She will be of the lineage of Dan and will conceive a son. He will call himself Antichrist.[43]

The devil Engignart undertakes the mission and asks a young woman whom he presently encounters, "Are you a Christian or a Jew?" She replies without hesitation: "Dear sir, whatever kind of life I lead, I am a Jew, and I was born under the Law that God gave to Moses and to the rest of us; but I hate the Christians, all of them. . . . Let there be no doubt, I am of the lineage of Dan."[44] She accepts his advances; he impregnates her; and then, in response to her query, he admits that he is "one of the preeminent devils of Hell."[45] Once she overcomes the shock of that revelation, she admits: "It was an astonishingly senseless thing to do, and yet I do not regret it in the slightest, for I am secure in my knowledge that my son is destined to be more powerful than any man yet born or to be born. . . . Christianity will expire because of him, and the Jews will once again be elevated."[46]

Satan and company proceed to nurture Antichrist after his birth, and, once he becomes their vassal, the Jew Annes assumes a leading role in promoting him, convincing him to mint coins so that people will venerate his image.[47] After Antichrist wins the support of the maimed, the ill, the kings of the world, and the poor, a group of Jews conspires against Elijah and Enoch, who have begun to preach against Antichrist, and vying with each other over who will strike the deadly blows, these Jews assault and murder them. That done, Antichrist, his Jewish henchmen, and his armed knights turn against the pope, his cardinals, and the church, demanding that they adopt him as their lord and renounce Jesus. "Go and get me the Pope," he commands, "that man who snares and then steals away my people from me, as I am told. He is the one who opposes me more than anyone in the world. I feel like destroying both him and his entire Church."[48] Antichrist imprisons the pope who remains steadfast in is faith, but he succeeds in winning over the cardinals.

Then the tide begins to turn. Much to the Jews' dismay, Enoch and Elijah come back to life. And although Antichrist deceptively claims that he engineered their reappearance for the sake of identifying truly believing Christians, St. John mobilizes the angels of wrath, who, as in the Book of Revelation, pour out their vials and inflict brutal punishment on Antichrist and his supporters, bringing them to a ruinous end. Significantly, while the blind man, the leper, and the kings of the earth repent their error and return to God, the Jews, among others, do not, and God and his saints sentence them to eternal damnation and suffering in hell. Early on in this lengthy scene of the last judgment, the Jew Caiaphas understands what fate awaits him.

Our days of high living are over. May he who created everything be damned! I can see now the terrible power of those Ten Commandments that we violated: we will forever more burn in Hell, with no possibility of redemption. This everyone must believe and know, that necessarily will come to such an end.[49]

An angel bearing a lance subsequently pronounces to the Jews:

> Treacherous Jews, now you may know how he was mutilated by you and fastened with these three nails to that cross and hanged high above, and how his side was pierced for your sake by this mighty lance. Here present is the crown with which you crowned the gentle King and the vessel in which you gave . . . [him] bitter poison and sour wine to drink. He will give you your recompense for it.[50]

Curiously, the last living human to speak during the play is the patently Jewish usurer. Just before the final words of Saints John, Luke, and Paul conclude the performance, this moneylender cries out: "Alas! What sorrow! Alas! Alas! I have been dispatched to the eternal presence of the king of every iniquity and shall be toasted on every side."[51]

While the Jews, as we have seen, played a role in the traditional Antichrist narrative going back to Adso and the church fathers before him, the *Jour du Jugement* intensifies and incorporates popular anti-Jewish motifs into its cosmic, even supernatural drama of the eschaton, much as the story of the Red Jews did in German literature and lore. While Adso explained that "with the devil's cooperation" Antichrist's Jewish mother "will conceive through a man," the French play has a devil impregnate her himself, only fortifying Adso's conclusion that "what will be born from her will be totally wicked, totally evil, totally lost."[52] The Jewish mother is a whore from Babylon, suggesting—and promoting—her identification with the whore of Babylon riding the seven-headed abominable beast in Revelation 17. The telltale mark of the Jewish Antichrist that his supporters must display is here minted on a coin at the behest of the Jew Annes. Not only does this singular detail play on the popular association of the sinful Jew with money and monetary greed— as does the usurer in the closing lines of the play—but the names of Annes and Caiaphas, who sadly acknowledges his evil role, recall the chief priests Annas and Caiaphas of the passion narrative, those who plot Jesus's death. The Jews of Jesus's day who reportedly conspired against him and murdered him and the Jews of the end time are cut of the same cloth. They are the enemies of Christ who killed him upon his first coming; they will seek to do so again upon his second coming; and they strive constantly to inflict harm on God, his church, and his faithful. Unlike other eschatological forecasts that we have encountered, here the prophets Enoch and Elijah have no success in converting the Jews. To the contrary, the Jews kill them, with malice and enthusiasm, and these Jews have no hope for salvation as the drama of the eschaton unfolds. The same Jew Annes thus bemoans his fate in the face of the angels of wrath.

> I don't even have the time to repent, for that God who tells no lies has already sentenced us. Cursed be his great power, his great renown, his great force, cursed be winter and summer, and the overwhelming might of God! I am the most miserable of all; my tongue is already shriveled and charred.[53]

The play unreservedly transmits a dire message: the Jewish Antichrist is the offspring of the devil. In supporting their kinsman, the Jews as a group enlist in the camp of Satan. Appropriately, Antichrist and the Jews, condemned to eternal damnation in hell, rejoin Satan as the play concludes, returning to the point of origin whence they began.

Simpler, shorter, without illumination in its earliest surviving manuscripts, but no less profound, the *Coming of Antichrist* in the Chester mystery cycle—the only surviving Antichrist play from late medieval England—likewise preserves the basic Adsonian narrative that we have encountered repeatedly in different guises. Unlike the *Jour du Jugement*, the Chester play and cycle were definitely performed in public, and they assumed an important, perhaps even unifying role in the cultural and religious life of the local population. In a play less than one-third as long as the *Jour du Jugement*, one follows Antichrist in his claim to be the true savior and fulfillment of biblical messianic prophecy, his delusion of kings who rally to his support, his ostensive miracles (including his own resurrection), his deadly opposition to Enoch and Elijah, his punishment and death at the hands of the archangel Michael, and his eternal damnation to the company of the devils.[54]

The Jews figure in the Chester play insofar as they figure in the traditional narrative, but not as the target of virulent popular hostility that the play expresses. In stark opposition to the earlier French drama, only after Antichrist's death as the play nears its end does one learn of the satanic role in his creation, when one of the devils declares:

> This body was begotten by mine assent in pure lechery, truly. Of mother's womb before he went, I was with him within and taught him ever with mine intent to sin, by which he shall be shent [*destroyed*]. Because he did my commandment, his soul shall never blin [*find rest*].[55]

Apart from the oblique allusion to "pure lechery," we find no reference to the devil's role in Antichrist's conception, to a Jewish prostitute who bore him, to his descent from the tribe of Dan. Antichrist himself must inform us of his ties to the Jews, as he insists that he himself is the savior and Jesus the impostor.

> My people the Jews he did twin [*disperse*] that their land they cannot come in. Then on them now I must have min [*mind*] and restore them again. To build this temple will I not blin [*cease*] as God honoured be therein and endless joy I shall them win, all that to me are bain [*obedient*].[56]

Similarly, the four kings whose support Antichrist first seeks and then wins merely hint at their Jewish ethnicity *obiter dictum*.

> 1ST KING: We believe, lord, without let [*truly*] that Christ is not come yet. . . .
>
> 2ND KING: If thou be Christ, call-ed "Messy", that from our torment shall us buy. . . .
>
> 3RD KING: Then will I believe that it is so. If thou do wonders before you go so that thou save us from our woe. . . .
>
> 4TH KING: Wrongly we have believed many a year and of our expectation been in were [*doubt*].[57]

Unlike the *Jour du Jugement* but as in the *Ludus de Antichristo*, in the Chester *Antichrist* Enoch and Elijah succeed in converting the kings—who again reference their Jewishness by noting that these prophets are "of our blood" and that they appear "in books of our Law"[58]—to Christianity, so that Antichrist proceeds to slay both kings and prophets.

The Jews of the Chester *Antichrist* duly play their role in the divine economy of salvation. Blind and ignorant, they fall prey to the arguments and ruses of Antichrist, who personifies theological error. Yet they see the light in the preaching of Enoch and Elijah and even die as martyrs for their faith. Apart from Antichrist himself, they display no malice or grudge against Jesus and his church. The play does not remind us of their complicity in the crucifixion. They do not seek to destroy Christendom. Had the passage of two centuries since Edward I expelled the Jews from England in 1290 lessened the sense that the Jews constituted less of a threat? The expulsions of the Jews from France began only in the early fourteenth century, and a comparison of the Chester *Antichrist* with the *Jour du Jugement* might therefore induce one toward such a conclusion. Yet the negative portrayal of Jews in English literature and lore in the postexpulsion period should militate against a simplistic explanation.[59] The traditional Christian Antichrist narrative offered a range of possible variants, and, within limitations, the Jews could fare differently in the substance and manner of their presentation.

Manuscript Illumination/Book Illustration

The received narratives made their mark on Christian visual art, and the role of the Jews in those narratives found noteworthy artistic expression as well, especially during the second half of the Middle Ages and particularly in manuscript—and, eventually, early printed book—illustration. Not surprisingly, from the twelfth century onward, as both the lot of the Jews and Christian estimations of the Jews worsened considerably in western Europe, their visual representation grew more hostile and even abusive. Matters eschatological proved no exception, as one can already sense in the late twelfth-century *Hortus deliciarum* encountered in the previous chapter, a work that highlighted Jewish support for Antichrist. Granted, it echoes the traditional prediction that the Jews will ultimately convert to Christianity, heeding the preaching of Enoch and Elijah. In its strikingly impressive illustration of the tiers of hell, however, the *Hortus* conveys a more horrific prediction for the Jews of the eschaton, allocating them the third of hell's four levels, the lowest, innermost level of the inferno save for that of Antichrist, seated in the lap of the devil himself (fig. 7).[60]

The lavishly illuminated French *Bibles moralisées* of the early thirteenth century, which blend Scripture and commentary in both textual and visual modes, similarly manifest an intensification of hostility toward the Jews of the end of days. As Sara Lipton and Debra Higgs Strickland have demonstrated in their important studies, although these Bibles may not explicitly label Antichrist as Jewish, the Jews appear as his staunch supporters and allies, in a manner that incorporated their reputed greed, love of money, and involvement in the usurious moneylending that the church deemed so despicable.[61] The Jewish devotees of Antichrist stand out among others in their conical hats, they present Antichrist with money and a crown, and, in illustrations of the Apocalypse, they number among the worshippers of the dragon/Satan and the beast that he empowered. These Bibles take a pessimistic, condemnatory stance regarding the ultimate destiny of the Jews much more than they express hope for their eventual salvation. Admittedly, such hope is not entirely lacking; in the visual commentary on the blind Tobias's regaining of his sight that figured so significantly in Joachim's eschatology, the Jews are liberated from the malice of the devil and Antichrist, and Antichrist himself suffers a violent end.[62] Nonetheless, expectations of hopelessness, death, and damnation seem to predominate, and multiple roundels depict the final condemnation of the Jews in imagery bespeaking the

FIGURE 7.   Tiers of hell. Herrad of Landsberg (1125–1195), *Hortus deliciarum*, 1180.
Source: Wikimedia Commons.

appropriateness of physical violence against them, both by sword and by fire. Here, as elsewhere, the *Bibles moralisées* tend to depict nonspecific eschatological villains as Jews, some of them bearing money and purses. In so doing, Lipton observes perceptively, they are "not absolving Christians of sin and perdition"— two bishops are banished to hell along with these Jews—"but essentializing all sinful and damned figures as Jewish,"[63] an interpretive strategy that we encounter in other manuscripts as well. As Strickland has keenly observed concerning

FIGURE 8.   Jews, Antichrist, Satan. *Bible moralisée* (Revelation 13), Oxford Bible. London, British Library MS Harley 1527, fol. 136v. © The British Library Board.

the roundels on the left side of the page printed here, presenting the dragon and beast of Revelation 13, Antichrist's headgear, facial hair, and multiple heads do much to accentuate the likeness between him and his Jewish followers (fig. 8).[64]

The thirteenth century also saw the emergence of illuminated manuscripts of the book of the Apocalypse, above all in England and France, another exegetical genre that depicted eschatological Jews in equally, or perhaps even more pronounced, negative imagery.[65] One centrally important family of these illuminated Apocalypses featured glosses of Berengaudus, a Benedictine monk believed to have lived in the ninth century, although the commentary attributed to him probably dates from the late eleventh or early twelfth century.[66] Scholars have underscored the Berengaudus Apocalypse commentary's attitude toward the Jews, terming it "notoriously" and "stridently anti-Jewish."[67] Where other late medieval commentaries did not,[68] the Berengaudus gloss repeatedly envisioned the eschatological supporters of the devil, dragon, beasts, and Antichrist as Jews, often exclusively so. More ominously still, the gloss expressed "arguments for divinely sanctioned violence against the Jews,"[69] as it anticipates their ultimate destruction, decimation, and punishment, and even those of the land of Israel. Art historian Suzanne Lewis, whose *Reading Images: Narrative Discourse and Reception in the Thirteenth-Century Illuminated Apocalypse* stands among the foundational studies of these Gothic Apocalypses, has argued that the Berengaudus glosses excerpted in the manuscripts express thirteenth-century Christian Europe's new focus on—and hostility toward—contemporary, postbiblical Jews. While the Berengaudus commentary itself still may have reflected more traditional, Augustinian eschatological doctrine, its glosses' presentation reflects novelty as well. They represented contemporary Jews and Judaism not merely as embodying the Old Law and carnal Israel that Christianity and the church had superseded, but as living threats to the welfare of Christendom that called for harsh, often violent modes of opposition.[70]

The precise relation between textual commentary and illustration of the Apocalypse in the planning and production of these manuscripts remains unclear, and Lewis and others have noted how the pictorial programs of many manuscripts do not reflect the newly harsh anti-Jewish hostility manifested in the gloss. Yet several late medieval Gothic Apocalypses—most notably the thirteenth-century Gulbenkian and Abingdon Apocalypses—do prove exceptional in this regard. Their illustrations display an anti-Jewish interpretation of Revelation that often exceeds that of the *Bibles moralisées*, and even that of Berengaudus, in their enmity toward Jews of the present and future. They consistently represent the villains of the apocalypse in graphically Jewish terms—noses, hats, hair—like the supporters of the devil who receive the mark of the beast in Revelation 13 (fig. 9)[71] and the Gog and Magog enlisted by the Satanic Antichrist to deceive the nations of the world in Revelation 20 (fig. 10),[72] although Berengaudus makes no mention of the Jews here.[73]

According to Lewis, these images suggest that postbiblical Jews should now be deemed heretics cognizant of the truth, not simply infidels ignorant

FIGURE 9. Supporters of the devil receive the mark of the beast. Wellcome Apocalypse (13:16–17). Credit: London Wellcome Apocalypse. Wellcome Collection, MS 49, fol. 17.

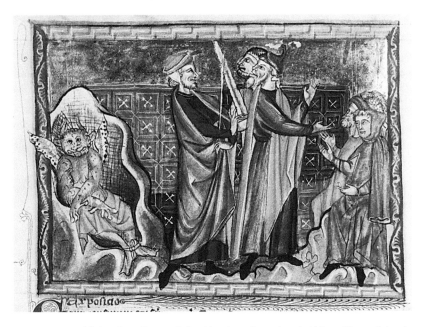

FIGURE 10. Antichrist, Gog, Magog. Gulbenkian Apocalypse (20:7). Lisbon, Museu Calouste Gulbenkian MS L.A. 139, fol. 70v. Credit line: Conway Library, Courtauld Institute of Art, London. Distributed under a Creative Commons BY NC ND 4.0 license.

of that truth. In its illustration of the beast from the earth in Revelation 13:11, the Gulbenkian Apocalypse thus distinguishes between Jews of the Old Testament, destined to believe in Jesus, receiving instruction from their prophet Elijah on our right, and medieval Jews who spurn him and follow the horned beast on the left (fig. 11).[74]

FIGURE 11. Biblical (right) and modern Jews (left). Gulbenkian Apocalypse (13:11). Lisbon, Museu Calouste Gulbenkian MS L.A. 139, fol. 38v. Credit line: Conway Library, Courtauld Institute of Art, London. Distributed under a Creative Commons BY NC ND 4.0 license.

FIGURE 12. Jews and Antichrist. Gulbenkian Apocalypse (13:5). Lisbon, Museu Calouste Gulbenkian MS L.A. 139, fol. 36v. Credit line: Conway Library, Courtauld Institute of Art, London. Distributed under a Creative Commons BY NC ND 4.0 license.

FIGURE 13.   Slaughter of Jews. Abingdon Apocalypse (6:12–17). London, British Library Add. MS 42555, fol. 17r. © The British Library Board.

In the Gulbenkian illustration of Revelation 13:5 (fig. 12) such Jews have rejected the newly launched missionary efforts of the Franciscans, whose friar preaches at center stage, and have turned to Antichrist on the left.[75] The Gulbenkian's pictorial gloss on Revelation 6:15 highlights bishops who assault medieval Jews,[76] and illustrations in this and other manuscripts threateningly portray their ultimate destruction, whether by human slaughter (fig. 13, where the Jew to the left impaled on a sword wears a moneybag)[77] or by natural disaster, as where a mountain of fire falling into the sea crushes a party of Jews.[78] In either case, the destiny that ultimately awaits them is clear: in the Gulbenkian illustration of Revelation 6:7 (fig. 14) the Jewish victims of sword, beast, famine, and fire are driven into the mouth of hell, along with their promised land of Israel.

FIGURE 14. Jews driven into hell. Gulbenkian Apocalypse (6:7). Lisbon, Museu Calouste Gulbenkian MS L.A. 139, fol. 11r. Credit line: Conway Library, Courtauld Institute of Art, London. Distributed under a Creative Commons BY NC ND 4.0 license.

As Lewis explains instructively, "The illustration depicts Israel as an isolated land mass cut off from the rest of the earth, being swallowed up by a Hellmouth at the right. Some people are being killed by the sword and wild beasts, while others gnaw at one another's legs and feet to demonstrate the desperation of famine." Curiously, the text of the commentary here makes no mention of the fire above the island in the upper right-hand corner of the image. Rather, it evokes a different passage in the commentary that cites a reference in Deuteronomy to the unrelenting fire of divine wrath.

> The fire kindled by God's wrath against Israel also appears in the flaming bowl held by the veiled horseman in the Apocalypse illustration on the facing page, so that the images of hell, death, and the consuming fire of God's anger dominate the fulfillment of Old Testament prophecy

for those who ignore his call for their conversion at the end of days.[79]

Adso wrote his most popular biography of Antichrist in the tenth century, and the monastic *Hortus deliciarum* with its illustrated Antichrist cycle dated from the twelfth. Yet illustrated lives of Antichrist in the vernacular, works that removed their subject from the genre of biblical exegesis and thereby interested and influenced a wider lay audience, first assumed prominence in

German block books of the fifteenth century considered above. Transition points during the fourteenth century include the richly illuminated Prague Velislaus Bible,[80] the German historiated Bibles,[81] and the *Jour du Jugement*, already discussed for its markedly anti-Jewish dramatization of the Antichrist narrative. In keeping with its elaborate staging of its story, the illuminations in the *Jour du Jugement*'s sole surviving Besançon manuscript are, in Richard Emmerson's words, "the largest and most developed cycle of Antichrist images in art, in any medium and from any period."[82] They help render the work much more than a mere theatrical script, but rather, as another investigator has suggested, a visualized performance, a "play within-a-book," whose "visual program works toward the creation of a spiritually profitable book, defined through the marriage of text, illuminations, and the theatrical form."[83] Just as Jews appear on stage throughout much of the play, so too do they command attention in the manuscript's illuminations (even in some scenes where the Jews have no explicitly stated role). As such, they figure impressively among those supporting Antichrist as he preaches (fig. 15),[84] those who encourage him to mint coins with his image (fig. 16),[85] and those who slay the prophets Elijah and Enoch.[86]

FIGURE 15.   Antichrist and his Jewish henchmen. *Jour du jugement.* © Bibliothèque municipale de Besançon, MS 579, fol. 10v.

FIGURE 16.   Minting coins in the image of Antichrist. *Jour du jugement.* © Bibliothèque municipale de Besançon, MS 579, fol. 9v.

The Antichrist block books of late fifteenth-century Germany, which, as
we noted, share remarkably similar texts and pictorial programs, likewise
feature illustrations that transmit pointed messages concerning the dangers
posed by Jews to Christendom owing to their ties to Antichrist. Early on
we see the patriarch Jacob gathering his sons in Genesis 49 in order to bless
them and reveal their destiny for the end of days—including the unique and
ominous empowerment of Dan (fig. 17).[87] The text quotes from Genesis
49:16–18:

> Jacob foretells the future to his son Dan with these words: Dan will
> judge his people like another tribe from Jerusalem. Dan will be a con-
> strictor on the road, a viper by the wayside, as has already been written.
> And after these words he said: "Lord, I seek your salvation."[88]

Immediately below, the devil presides over the incestuous impregnation
of Antichrist's Jewish mother by her very own father, who bears a striking

FIGURE 17. Jacob's prophecy of the end. *Von dem Endkrist*, fol. 3r. Strasbourg, 1482. Call number *KB+ 1482 (Antichrist. Legend. Von dem Endkrist). Rare Book Collection. The New York Public Library. Astor, Lenox, and Tilden Foundations.

FIGURE 18. Antichrist, Queen of the Amazons, Red Jews. *Von dem Endkrist*, fol. 8r. Strasbourg, 1482. Call number *KB+ 1482 (Antichrist. Legend. Von dem Endkrist). Rare Book Collection. The New York Public Library. Astor, Lenox, and Tilden Foundations.

resemblance to his biblical forefather Jacob (fig. 1). As we follow Antichrist from his birth to his ritual circumcision to his bonding with his Jewish supporters, we again encounter the devil.[89] We soon behold an appeal on Antichrist's behalf to the Queen of the Amazons and the Red Jews (fig. 18),[90] themselves the ten tribes of Israel—including the tribe of Dan—which reminds us yet again that the Jews as a people come by their eschatological role genetically; they have long been destined to inflict pain and suffering on the world of the end time. Nonetheless, the block books do depict Jews listening to the sermons of Elijah and Enoch; presumably, after the death and punishment of Antichrist, they will number among the saved.

Various art historians of the past generation or two have presented the iconography of Antichrist as a window to—and an expression of—themes and complexities in Christian attitudes toward Jews and their eschatological role. Building on the basic premises in her reading of the Anglo-French illuminated Apocalypse manuscripts, Suzanne Lewis has proposed:

> The new thirteenth-century apocalyptic experience can be seen as operating within an ideological construction of western European hegemony locked in battle against the alien Other—against heterodoxy, Judaism, and Islam. As an ideological construction itself, the pictured Apocalypse served as a powerful metaphorical frame within which later medieval Latin Christian identity was collectively defined on the level of allegory. Thus, the medieval reader was initiated to comprehend the allusive prophetic text as a mandate for a global strategy of appropriation, a divine command toward a series on interconnected movements—Church reform, anti-Judaism, and the Crusades, calculated to insulate the Christian West from the danger of internal collapse and heterodoxy.[91]

With regard to images that we have considered here, one can then raise the question and warning "Is it possible to see too much in a single work of art? The risk is highest when the goal of interpretation, conscious or not, is recovery of what was intended by the artist and understood by early observers."[92] Lewis believes—and argues compellingly—that the illuminations of Antichrist in the Apocalypse testify to the increasingly hostile treatment and perceptions of Jews in later medieval Europe.

One must recall, however, that the messages conveyed by representations of a Jewish Antichrist were not all devoid of ambivalence and equivocality. The oldest known anti-Jewish cartoon anywhere, from a royal British treasury document of 1233, portrays the Jewish banker Isaac of Norwich with

FIGURE 19.   Isaac the Jew of Norwich and associates. Exchequer Receipt Roll, Hilary and Easter terms, 1233. The National Archives, London, E 401/1565 M1.

three faces and a crown, as Gothic artists were prone to depict Antichrist, along with two of his Jewish associates, Mosse and Avegaye (fig. 19).

Yet in a painstakingly erudite and contextualized analysis, Sara Lipton has shown that this caricature originated in the complexity of tensions between various English barons and their king, whom the rebels associated with the Jews, moneylenders, and heinously sinful usury. Without ignoring or discounting the anti-Jewish imagery so blatant in the caricature, one should not overlook that, for the doodler, the conflation of Isaac and Antichrist served to discredit the Jews' royal patron and protector no less than the Jews themselves.

We need to modify what has become received wisdom regarding medieval Christian assumptions of Jewish Otherness. It is common to define the Other as 'that which I am not'. So, we are frequently told, Jews, as the stereotypical Other, are rendered dark, ugly, caricatured, devilish, bestial, etc., simply because they were not Christian and so were assumed to be the opposite of the Christian ideal. The caricatures of Isaac as Antichrist, and of Mosse and Avegaye as demonically hook-nosed, seem to be in accord with that usual formulation.

But additional reflection leads to a more nuanced conclusion.

The cartoon concedes instead that Jews, for all their undoubted distinctness, were not in fact completely different from, much less opposite to, Christians. They dressed like elite Christians, they frequented Westminster, they did business with Christians, their moral failings (avarice and hypocrisy, in particular) were shared by some very powerful Christians, and, to the clerk's evident disgust, they had come to be associated in people's minds with the royal court and perhaps the king himself.

FIGURE 20.   Adoration of Magi (detail). Hieronymus Bosch, "Prado Epiphany" triptych (detail). Museo del Prado.
Source: Wikimedia Commons.

Perhaps "the iconography of infamy and the discourse of Jewish perfidy," applied in this cartoon to three English Jews, had the paradoxical effect of reducing "the radical 'Otherness' of Jewish identity."[93]

Our brief survey concludes with another work that raises similar questions: the triptych of Hieronymus Bosch depicting the Adoration of the Magi, commonly known as Bosch's *Prado Epiphany*. In the background of the central panel, just inside the doorway, stands a figure (fig. 20) whose identity and purpose have intrigued viewers for some time.[94]

In a fascinating book devoted entirely to Bosch's triptych, Debra Higgs Strickland has recently argued strenuously that the figure is Antichrist—and, owing to the man's beard, ruddy facial complexion, otherwise pale skin, accentuated nose, and the sore on his leg, the Jewish Antichrist at that.[95] Strickland uses the triptych and its Antichrist-like figure above all as a kaleidoscopic reflection of virtually all major aspects of Christian anti-Judaism in the Middle Ages: from a preoccupation with alleged Jewish deicide (witness the crown of thorns), ritual murder and cannibalism, host desecration, and, of course, an alliance with Satan that leads to a villainous role at the end of days. In her words, "late medieval fears of a Jewish-led conspiracy against Christendom expected to culminate at the end of time" nourish their depiction as the followers of Antichrist.

> In this not-so-"secret plot", three kings are once again the first to pay homage—this time not to Christ, but to Antichrist. Relevant here is the late medieval eschatological belief that after seducing the world's Jews, Antichrist will gain the allegiance of the kings of Libya, Egypt, and Ethipoia and their respective nations. As part of an attempt to present the story of Antichrist as an antithetical version of the life of Christ, the episode of the three kings who arrive on the scene to pledge their unholy alliance was obviously modeled on the story of the three magi.[96]

While readers have both applauded and criticized the daring and extent of Strickland's interpretation, few critics, if any, have entirely denied the anti-Jewish side to the "notoriously inscrutable Bosch . . ., a master of hybridity, enigmatic detail, and inversion of accepted form, perhaps as a form of satire or even a method to develop religious ideas poetically, rendering legible intentionality dubious."[97] At the end of the day, as another reviewer has concluded, readers might "resist some of the specific associations she proposes, but will find it difficult to dismiss their viability for many sixteenth-century minds."[98] For the late medieval/early modern European Christian, frequently preoccupied with apocalyptic yearning and fear, the eschatological Jew remained a formidable presence.

PART III

At the Forefront of the Redemption

Most of the Christian exegetes, theologians, playwrights, and even artists whom we have encountered in the earlier parts of this book maneuvered between the two opposing alternatives for characterizing the eschatological Jew. Unless all Jews were doomed to eternal damnation for rejecting Jesus and the ultimate redemption that he offered, the Jewish origins, affiliation, and supporters of Antichrist did not preclude the inclusion of some (perhaps many, most, or even all?) Jews in the Israel to be saved once the fullness of the Gentiles would enter the community of Christian faithful.

Yet not every Christian eschatologist found a place on this spectrum. Some parted company with the mainstream by giving Jews a trailblazing role in the drama of salvation, generally at the end of days but conceivably at earlier stages of salvation history as well. These voices severed the ties between the Jews and Antichrist completely, or nearly so: his origins in the Israelite tribe of Dan, his courting of the Synagogue, and the Jews' attraction to him.

In chapter 7, we shall see how the twelfth-century German theologian Honorius Augustodunensis envisioned converted Jews as shock troops in the final battle against Antichrist and the campaign to convert the peoples of the world to Christianity. Chapter 8 considers how in early fifteenth-century Burgos, the formerly Jewish bishop Pablo de Santa María discerned the Jews at the forefront of Christian missionary efforts: at the time of the first coming of Christ, again upon his second coming, and along the course of history between the two advents. For some seventeenth-century Puritans in England and New England, like those discussed in chapter 9, not only will converted Jews contribute indispensably to the victory of Christ over Antichrist (imagined as pope, Turk, or other enemy of God's faithful), but they will reestablish a commonwealth in their ancestral holy land and rise to dominion over much, if not all, of Christendom.

All of these preachers and writers preserved a notion of the Jews' distinctive peoplehood and affiliation, one that withstands their conversion to Christianity and affords them a crucial eschatological role in the progression of salvation history.

CHAPTER 7

Honorius Augustodunensis, the Song of Songs, and *Synagoga Conversa*

The twelfth century, as medievalists well know, brought European interest in Jews and Judaism to an unprecedented high. The anti-Jewish violence that had accompanied the First Crusade in 1096, the full-scale encounter with the Muslim world sparked by the church's call to holy war, the attempts of Western princes to bolster their political power, and the intellectual awakening of the twelfth-century renaissance all led scholars, prelates, and princes to reevaluate and refine their attitudes toward the Jew. Many investigators have studied the significant developments that ensued in the interreligious polemic of the period. Others have focused on avenues of extensive cultural exchange and interaction between Christians and Jews: biblical exegesis; the translation and importation of works of classical philosophy; shared patterns of thought and expression in matters of dialectic, jurisprudence, mysticism, and martyrology. I have argued at length that the climate of the times precipitated a reclassification of the Jew in Christian thought, one that ultimately—and profoundly—altered the nature of the Jew as constructed in the Western mentality.

This chapter considers the astoundingly novel construction of the eschatological Jew elaborated in the Song of Songs commentary of Honorius Augustodunensis.[1] Here Honorius ventured far beyond the traditional Pauline prediction that at the end time "all Israel should be saved"; for unlike Paul, Honorius described the conversion of Israel as occurring before that of the plenitude of the Gentiles, rather than in its wake. He transformed converted Jewry into the veritable vanguard of Christ's church in its struggle against Antichrist and the forces of evil. As we shall see, one cannot discount the possibility that Honorius's new vision of *Synagoga conversa* resulted, at least in part, from a skillful exegete's genuine efforts to reconstruct the essential meaning of the biblical text, rather than a primary intention to promote any new eschatological vision. Nevertheless, his predictions for the end of the world shed interesting light on twelfth-century Christian longings for the final redemption, on the history of Christian perceptions of the Jew—albeit here, primarily, Jews who shall have converted to Christianity—and on the context of Jewish-Christian interaction within which Honorius wrote.

His long and impressive list of writings notwithstanding, we know distressingly little concerning the details of Honorius's biography. Modern scholars have wavered between continental, English, and Irish alternatives for his birthplace. Various proposals for his dates range from ca. 1070 to the 1150s. Even his forename (Heinricus or Honorius?), his appellation Augustodunensis, and his personal identity have raised serious questions and only the most tentative of answers. Recent research would suggest that Honorius lived and wrote in England over a considerable period of time, that before 1130 he relocated to Regensburg as a regular canon, and that there he joined the Benedictine order, affiliating with circles of reformers like that of Rupert of Deutz. His résumé lists reformist, polemical, liturgical, cosmological, didactic, and exegetical treatises that rendered him among the more prolific, widely read, and important monastic scholars of the early and mid-twelfth century.[2]

Honorius devoted two exegetical works exclusively to the Song of Songs. The liturgically grounded *Sigillum Beatae Mariae*, composed in the first years of the twelfth century, very likely in England, offers an allegorical interpretation of the Song expounding the relationship between God and the Virgin Mary. Sometime after 1132, perhaps as late as the mid-1150s, Honorius wrote his longer and more innovative *Expositio in Cantica Canticorum*, which he himself observed "expounded the Song of Songs such that it seems never to have been expounded before";[3] and it is his *Expositio* that will concern us here.[4] Together with his other works, these commentaries help to place Honorius in the tradition of conservative monastic historical theology that scholars of the twentieth century dubbed "German Symbolism." This is, admittedly, a problematic term, especially when applied to an individual of unknown origins who presumably reached Germany relatively late in his career. For Honorius spent many of his formative years in

England, where he presumably came under the lasting influence of Anselm of Canterbury, Italian by birth and later a longtime resident—and eventually abbot—of the French monastery of Bec. Yet the term can still prove useful, insofar as it highlights some of the affinities linking Honorius with the spiritual and intellectual climate exemplified in the works of Rupert of Deutz, Anselm of Havelberg, Otto of Freising, the author of the *Ludus de Antichristo*, Gerhoh of Reichersberg, and Hildegard of Bingen. In pithy terms that shed light on Honorius among these others, Horst Dieter Rauh explains:

> Much like scholastic metaphysics, [German] symbolism aspires to the knowledge of God, though differently, through nature and history. . . . The concrete revelation in the word of the Bible joins the visible world; the firm letter, ready for tasting as it were, is the foundation of symbolism. . . . The allegorical and tropological exegesis of Scripture is reflected in a cosmography that interprets nature, too, in a spiritual sense. . . . History also forms part of the world of creation; it begins and ends in God as salvation history; Genesis and Eschaton are one in Him who is the Alpha and Omega. Christ, the incarnate word, the God-man who participates in both natures, is the pivot of salvation history. The one who suffered and rose, he is the inalienable pledge of creation's transfiguration, and symbolism turns towards him anagogically.[5]

A Quaternary Reading of the Song of Songs

The first of the two prologues to Honorius's *Expositio in Cantica Canticorum* comprises a wonderful example of an early Scholastic literary introduction, an *accessus ad auctores*.[6] At the outset Honorius provides three pieces of information that he deems crucial for the beginning of any book. First, he identifies the author (*auctor*) of the Song of Songs as the Holy Spirit, speaking through the agency of Solomon, the wisest of Israelite kings and a prophet. Second, Honorius labels the subject or substance (*materia*) of his text as that of groom and bride (*sponsus et sponsa*), who are Christ and his church. The book thus concerns their marriage, which is transacted in four senses (historical, allegorical, tropological, and anagogical), and in each sense in two distinct fashions: either through the commingling of their flesh or solely through the contract of their betrothal. And third, Honorius specifies that the purpose (*intentio*) of the Song is for the church to conjoin in love with Christ, her groom.

Honorius also situates the Song of Songs within the entirety of Holy Scripture, which contains two testaments, old and new, both the expression of the Holy Spirit. Conflating the tripartite division of the Masoretic Text of the Hebrew Bible (*TaNa"Kh: Torah-Nevi'im-Ketuvim*) with the generically accepted quadripartite structure of the Christian Old Testament canon, he divides Hebrew Scripture into history, prophecy, and holy writing (*agiographia*). The law as such receives no mention, and the *agiographia* corresponds to the wisdom and poetry section of the Latin Vulgate: Job, Psalms, Proverbs, Ecclesiastes, Song of Songs, the Wisdom of Solomon, and Ecclesiasticus. Honorius explains that history treats matters of the past, prophecy those of the future, and the holy writings matters eternal.[7] The seven books of the *agiographia* thus comprise the capstone of Hebrew Scripture, and the Song of Songs ranks high on the list, inasmuch as it includes "the knowledge (*scientia*) of all of Scripture."[8]

Individual books of the Bible also have their distinctive divisions and numerical patterns, and those of the Song of Songs revolve around the number four. The Song of Songs, notes Honorius, divides neatly into four parts, corresponding to the four geographical directions, whence the church is gathered into the marriage bed of her groom by means of the four Gospels; these, in turn, represent four key stages and events in the divine plan for human salvation.[9]

> The bride was led out of the east, when the multitude of those chosen before the law was gathered[10] into the faith of the patriarchs, who believed this promise [Genesis 22:18]: "in thy seed shall all the nations of the earth be blessed," that is, in Christ. The bride was led out of the south, when a multitude of the peoples at the time of the law was gathered into the faith of the prophets, who believed in this prophecy [Isaiah 7:14]: "Behold a virgin shall conceive and bear a son, and his name shall be called Emmanuel," that is, God is with us, inasmuch as Christ the man was God. The bride was led out of the west at the time of grace when a multitude of the nations was drawn by the apostles to the religion of Christ. The bride is led from the north, when at the time of Antichrist the multitude of unbelievers will be converted to the faith.

The four winds and stages of salvation history correspond, in turn, to four proverbial ages in the life of the world: the east to childhood, the south to youth, the west to old age, and the north to infirmity. Honorius's commentary itself contains four treatises, wherein, as we have noted, the author proposes to expound the meaning of the Song in its four scriptural senses.

Yet the most striking dimension of the quaternity underlying the Song of Songs lies in the character of the bride, Ecclesia or the Church, that includes not just one but four *personae*, two of whom existed in fact and two exist in a symbolic sense:

(1) the daughter of Pharaoh (cf. 1 Kings 3:1, Song 1:8), who came from the east in a chariot, representing the Hebrew nation that turned from the observance of God's law to idolatry;

(2) the daughter of the king of Babylon—that is, of the devil—who was led out of the south (cf. Song 4:16) on a camel, representing *gentilitas*, the pagan peoples of the world;

(3) the Shunamite (*Sunamitis*, Song 6:12–7:1[11]) coming from the west in the quadriga of Aminadab, representing *Synagoga conversa*, the Jewish people who will ultimately convert to Christianity;

(4) the mandrake, a headless plant, coming from the north out of the fields, representing the infidels who will turn to Christ after the death and decapitation of their lord Antichrist.

Despite her penultimate place in this progression, *Synagoga conversa*, the queen of the west, plays the most important role in the eschatological drama that Honorius Augustodunensis discerned in the Song of Songs. Honorius noted that Shunam was the home of the Shunamite woman, whose son the prophet Elisha resuscitated, after the Book of Kings reports that Elisha's servant failed to do so with help of his staff (2 Kings 4). The dying lad, Honorius explained, symbolizes the human race. The servant who placed his staff over the dead boy symbolizes Moses; for he placed the staff of the law over those who have died spiritually through their sins, but it only imposed upon them more and failed to revivify them. Elisha, called "the salvation of my God," prefigures Christ, the salvation given by God to humanity in human form, who redeems humanity from death. Honorius then expounded the implications of this interpretation for the Shunamite bride, the queen from the west, in the Song of Songs.[12]

Shunamite means captive and is Synagoga still held captive in her perfidy by the devil. She will be led[13] to the groom from the west, since at the end of the world she will revert[14] to the faith of Christ—and this in the four-wheeled chariot of Aminadab. Aminadab was the priest in whose quadriga the ark was led back into Jerusalem [2 Samuel 6:3–4], after having been captured by pagans. The ark came from Judea to the nations of the world, when Christ transferred himself from the Synagoga to Ecclesia. The ark will be led back to Jerusalem, when, through the efforts of Elijah and Enoch, he [Christ] will return to Judea upon its conversion.

Honorius then focuses directly on Aminadab's four-wheeled vehicle.

> Aminadab, which means "my people is a gift-offering," is Christ, who was sacrificed for the people in his voluntary death. His chariot is the Gospel, through which he was transported throughout the world. The wheels of this chariot are the four evangelists. The horses are the apostles, who drew this chariot when they preached the Gospel of Christ throughout the world. Hence Scripture says [Habbakuk 3:8], "Who will ride upon thy horses: and thy chariots are salvation." The Shunamite is led to her groom on this chariot, when Synagoga is received through the Gospel into the company of Christ.

Curiously, the description of the mandrake, the last of the four brides, is less than a third as long as that of the Shunamite, and the reader quickly gains the impression that the historical drama under description reaches its climax with the third of its four heroines. Where, then, lie the novelty and unprecedented significance of the Shunamite and the *Synagoga conversa* whom she represents for Honorius Augustodunensis?

The Shunamite and Synagoga

The third of the four treatises into which Honorius divided his commentary expounds Song of Songs 6:10–7:10 (6:11–7:11 in the Hebrew Masoretic Text).[15] It opens with the triumphant entry of the Shunamite riding in from the west in the quadriga of Aminadab, celebrated by her bridesmen Elijah and Enoch, by her predecessor the queen of the south and her entourage, and by her groom the king himself, as they all join in dancing and adulation.[16] The king receives his latest bride in the nut garden, where the most revealing exchange ensues between them, an exchange whose "historical sense" as understood by Honorius blends traditional interpretation with highly suggestive and innovative allegory. These singular contributions of Honorius warrant consideration against the background of his reading of the passage as a whole, encapsulated here in tabular form.

Against the backdrop of this summary, the distinctive innovations and nuances of Honorius's reading of Song 6:10–7:10 assume greater significance and clarity. First, reacting to Synagoga's reference to the chariot of Aminadab in 6:11, Honorius identifies Aminadab as Abinadab, the ancient Israelite in whose house the ark of the covenant resided after its return by the

Table 1

SONG	BIBLICAL TEXT	HONORIUS'S INTERPRETATION
6:10	I went down into the garden of nuts, to see the fruits of the valleys, and to look if the vineyard had flourished, and the pomegranates budded.	Thus will Christ receive the returning Synagoga at the end of the world, once the preaching of Elijah and Enoch leads her to embrace Christianity. Most appropriately does she now seek him in the nut garden, Christ explains, because he previously had descended to the nut garden of Judea to see if her people had matured sufficiently in their faith, ready to sacrifice their lives on its behalf. Though he had intended to set them on the proper path had they not so matured, they refused his advances, subjecting him to a disgraceful death.
6:11	I knew not; my soul troubled me for the chariots of Aminadab.	Troubled by this justified divine reproach, the bride Shunamitess/Synagoga confesses in embarrassment. She indeed behaved as the king has noted, but she did so out of ignorance. Synagoga explains that the carnal appetites of her soul made her distrustful, since the Gospel, symbolized by the chariot of Aminadab, demanded that she replace circumcision and the other ceremonial commandments that God had given her with baptism and a new set of spiritual precepts. Shame prevents the new bride from enduring the presence of Christ, whom she had condemned to the most ignominious death, and she therefore begins to draw away from him, but the chorus of queens and daughters of Jerusalem then calls her back.
6:12	Return, return, O Sunamitess; return, return that we may behold thee.	This appeal of the daughters of Jerusalem conveys the fourfold call of preachers of the gospel entreating Synagoga to return from the four corners of the world, converting from the errors of her perfidy to faith in Christ. (Alternatively, they call upon her to return to the savior that appeals to her, wishing to receive her in her belief; to return to him in love; to return to him by fulfilling his precepts; and to return by hoping for the promise of life through him.) Thus beckoned, the Shunamite returns to the king, who accepts her in his grace; and, once converted, Synagoga will immediately sing Christ's praises and everywhere lead the fight against vice. This entitles her to an ode of lavish praise and admiration from the king himself.
7:1a	What shalt thou see in the Sunamitess but the companies of camps?	*Synagoga conversa* embodies the ten orders of the just in Christian society that must wage war against Antichrist and the devil.
7:1b, c	How beautiful are thy steps in shoes . . ., the joints of thy thighs are like jewels.	(1) feet = *agricultores*, farmers; (2) juncture of thighs = *conjugati*, married people who with their offspring adorn the church;
7:2	Thy navel is like a round bowl . . ., thy belly is like a heap of wheat.	(3) navel = *delicati et molles*, delicate and gentle; (4) belly = *uxorati*, those married people who use this world well;
7:3	Thy two breasts are like two young roes.	(5) breasts = *doctores*, teachers of doctrine, who nurse Jews and Gentiles alike;
7:4	Thy neck as a tower of ivory; thy eyes like the fishpools . . ., thy nose is as the tower of Libanus.	(6) neck = *spirituales*, regular clergy; (7) eyes = *praelati*, prelates; (8) nose = *discreti*, the wise;

(Continued)

Table 1   (Continued)

SONG	BIBLICAL TEXT	HONORIUS'S INTERPRETATION
7:5	Thy head is like Carmel: and the hairs of thy head as the purple clothing of the king bound together in the channels.	(9) head = *summi pontifices*; (10) hair = *principes*, the princes who defend the priesthood. A listing of the ten orders gives way to that of ten ages in the history of salvation, from the sole unwritten law of primeval paradise to the final age of Antichrist, five before the coming of Christ and five thereafter. Honorius then discusses the allegorical, tropological, and anagogical senses of 6:10–7:5, yet more briefly and less systematically than the historical sense.
7:6	How beautiful art thou, and how comely, my dearest, in delights!	Synagoga . . . now merits exaltation in her entirety, both for the exterior beauty of her works and for the inner beauty of her virtues.
7:9	thy throat like the best wine. . . .	Synagoga deserves to communicate the word of God, and her sages to expound it.
7:10	I to my beloved, and he has turned towards me.	The Shunamite explains to the disbelieving nations of the world that she has turned from the devil to Christ; and, he, who had previously rejected her in her perfidy, has now reciprocated in his grace.

Philistines and before its entry into Jerusalem (1 Samuel 7:1, 2 Samuel 6:3–4). He then reiterates the significance of his four-wheeled chariot that he had begun to explain in the prologue.[17]

> The quadriga is the Gospel of Christ; the four wheels are the four evangelists who at the end of time[18] travel throughout the entire world. The ark is the humanity of Christ; the manna in the ark [cf. Exodus 16:33, Hebrews 9:3–4] is the divinity of Christ. The ark was brought to the pagans, and Christ was brought to the nations by the apostles. The ark was returned to Judea on four-wheeled chariots, and Christ will be restored to Synagoga by means of the Gospels at the end time. From the house of Aminadab the ark was conveyed by David to Jerusalem. Aminadab means "the gift-offering of my people," and he is Christ, sacrificed of his own free will to atone for the sins of the people. His [Christ's] home was Jerusalem, from which his father conveyed him to the heavenly Jerusalem. As noted, the four-wheeled chariot of this Aminadab is the four Gospels, on whose account the spirit of Synagoga was confused, when her carnal understanding was greatly upset by hearing the Gospel of Christ preached throughout the world. But she now is conveyed[19] in this very quadriga, when she is brought by the teachings of the Gospels to faith in Christ.

Transported to Christ and the gospel in Aminadab's quadriga, the converted Synagoga will make a singular contribution to the drama of the culmination of terrestrial history: "As for the Jews converted at the end time, their conversion will be such that the Church will admire it and have the benefit of its example. . . . Hungry for the word of God, they will roam like dogs around the Church, the city of God, to hear the word of the Lord from the Christians; and they will live according the very practices of the church of old at the time of the apostles."[20] While Honorius might have introduced the Shunamite bride with a rather dutiful affirmation of Paul's expectation that the Jews will convert after the plenitude of the Gentiles enters the church of Christ,[21] the import of *Synagoga conversa*'s description indicates otherwise. Not only will Israel acknowledge the sins of her past and express the requisite contrition, but she will do so before the reign and ultimate demise of Antichrist, prior to the conversion of the infidels that will follow his defeat. More impressive still, not only will Christ restore Honorius's Synagoga to her former elect status, but she will serve as a model for the rest of Christendom to admire and emulate, leading the struggle against the forces of evil, working strenuously to convert the infidels, exemplifying a willingness to die a martyr's death on Christ's behalf. Newly converted Jews will serve as trailblazers, not merely as followers, in realizing the vision of Christian eschatology.

Second, such a valuation of eschatological Jewry accorded well with the crux of Honorius's novel reading of Song 7:1 and the verses that follow, where he understood that Christ (the king) sings the praises of *Synagoga conversa* (the converted Jews of the end time) to Ecclesia (his church), *rather than serenading Ecclesia herself.*[22] "O my[23] Ecclesia, in Synagoga converted to me you will see nothing but a chorus of those singing my praise, and the army of those fighting for the truth." In the coming era of persecution, tribulation, and error such as the world has never known, when pseudo-prophets will arise to perform signs and wonders so great that even the most learned will be led into error, Antichrist will arise and proclaim himself to be God. He will test the elect with every manner of false miracle and torment those who do not accept him with every manner of punishment. At this critical juncture in time, the Shunamite, the converted Synagoga, will lead the spiritually armed struggle against evil. As such, *she* embodies the ten orders of the just in Christian society[24] that must battle Antichrist. The ensuing verses of chapter 7 thus sing the praises of her limbs and beauty, not those of Ecclesia.

And third, in keeping with his likening of converted Jewry of the end time to the apostolic church, Honorius beheld in *Synagoga conversa* the veritable perfection of eschatological Christianity. In all, "just as the Church produced ten orders of the just, ten legions,[25] as it were, against Haman, chief of the devils and persecutors, so will Synagoga advance ten orders of the just in a tenfold line of battle, as it were, against Antichrist, prince of the evil."[26] With the vital participation of eschatological Jewry in the victory of the cross (7:8), "the preachers of Synagoga will be incorporated into the suffering of the passion, and their sermons into the sermons of the apostles, since they will be so perfect that no torments can turn them away from Christ."[27] In *Synagoga conversa* Honorius thus finds the shock troops of the church in her final struggle against Antichrist, those who will serve as leaders and provide inspiration for all the faithful. Just as the gospel compares the church to five virgins (Matthew 25), Honorius notes that the Song of Songs contains five odes of praise to Ecclesia, where each corresponds to the body of the faithful in a different stage of salvation history: the primitive church (Song 1:14), the church of the nations (*Ecclesia gentium*, Song 4:1), the church suffering persecution (*Ecclesia in persecutione sudans*, Song 4:10), the church living in peace (*Ecclesia in pace degens*, Song 6:3), and Synagoga converted to the faith (*Synagoga ad fidem conversa*, Song 7:6). *Synagoga conversa* marks the climax in this series; it is *this* church that "glows in its perfection."[28] As rich in allegory as the primary truth of Scripture may have been, the essential allegorical message of this part of the Song belonged to what Honorius labeled its "historical sense":[29] that one of the four senses that Christianity instinctively linked with the Jews.[30]

The fourth treatise in this Song of Songs commentary,[31] where one might have expected to find the ultimate resolution in Honorius's eschatological drama, bears out our reading of the third. Here enters the last of Christ's four brides, Mandragora, about whom Honorius explains:

> The mandrake is a plant having the shape of a person without a head and is understood as the multitude of infidels, she whose head *will then be* Antichrist, who is the head of all the evil. But the head of the mandrake *will be cut off*, when Antichrist *will be killed*. Thereafter [lit., after the slaying of Antichrist] the converted Synagoga, beholding the multitude of the infidels [or: Synagoga, beholding the converted multitude of the infidels]—now without Antichrist as their head but still without Christ as their head—prays for Mandragora to be associated with her in the religion of Christ and to be exalted with Christ as her head. She says to her bridegroom: "Come, my beloved, let us go out into the field, let us abide in the villages."[32]

One should emphasize that the verbs I have italicized here appear in the future tense, not in the past tense as has been suggested elsewhere.[33]

Moreover, before *Synagoga conversa* addresses her groom in the last sentence, the bridegroom does not appear in these lines. Rather, in the final sentence here, Synagoga beholds the infidels, and the twelfth-century manuscripts I have consulted read accordingly: "videns Synagoga conversa[m] multitudinem infidelium," as opposed to the old printed text of the *Patrologia Latina*, "videns Synagoga conversionem infidelium." As such, the text leaves little room for misunderstanding: The Shumamite/Synagoga beholds the multitude of infidels in the process of accepting Christianity. It is these infidels signified by Mandragora who bear and then lose the head of Antichrist, soon to be replaced with the head of Christ, owing to Synagoga's efforts. And then, in the closing verses of chapter 7 (11–12) of the Song, Synagoga— not the bridegroom—says to her spouse: "Come, my beloved, let us go out into the field, let us abide in the villages. Let us get up early to the vineyards, let us see if the vineyard flourish, if the flowers be ready to bring forth fruits, if the pomegranates flourish." The vineyards, Honorius explains, represent Synagoga, who proposes to her groom concerning the pagan infidels mentioned just above: "Through the efforts of preachers let us make them see if [or perhaps: how] the vine, that is Synagoga, has blossomed in faith, so that they may emulate her in her faith."[34]

If Israel once facilitated the salvation of the Gentiles, albeit unwittingly, in her rejection of Jesus and his gospel, she reassumes this role in her restoration, though now with the noblest of intentions. Honorius might have strayed from the order in which Paul foresaw the future conversion of Jews and Gentiles, respectively, but he surely upheld the underlying spirit of that Pauline prophecy, expressed rhetorically in Romans 11:15: "For if the loss of them be the reconciliation of the world, what shall the receiving of them be, but life from the dead?"

Synagoga conversa thus remains at center stage even during the final section of the Song (7:11–8:14) that should, we would have supposed, move on to focus on Mandragora. The believing Synagoga (*fidelis Synagoga*) continues to address her groom in the next verses (7:11–8:3), once more bemoaning the errors of her ancient progenitrix (*mater sua Synagoga*), while the reader must work harder to find Mandragora (in all mentioned less than one-third the number of times as Synagoga). The groom responds (8:4), adjuring the daughters of Jerusalem not to disturb the newly converted Synagoga as she sleeps, now that she has retired from the pursuit of worldly gain to a life of spiritual contemplation. Here again Honorius asserts that *Synagoga conversa* manifests the perfect concord of the two testaments. For this verse recurs three times in the Song of Songs, referring to different stages in the evolution of the church: first (2:7) to the primitive church of the Jews, second (3:5) to the church of the Gentiles, and now to *Synagoga conversa*, who facilitates the universal *concordia* of the end time. Mandragora returns to our attention only in 8:5 ("Who is this that cometh up from the desert . . .?"), as Synagoga rests; but by the end of Honorius's exposition of the verse, we again learn that of the three times that its refrain appears in the Song ("Who is this . . .?"; cf. 3:6, 6:9), this third instance refers to the eschatological communion of Jew and Gentile to be facilitated by *Synagoga conversa*.

In a word, Shunamite/Synagoga dominates her successor, instead of gracefully bowing out of the picture as her predecessors did for her. As he repeatedly blends his historical and allegorical senses of the Song, Honorius at times even conflates the two brides, such that Mandragora essentially loses her distinctive identity. Upon reaching the concluding lines of the Song (8:8–8:14), Honorius declares outright: "What has been said concerning Mandragora can also be understood as applying to the Shunamite,"[35] but nothing indicates that the reverse is also true. Fortified in Christian doctrine, the bride Synagoga grows from her companions' little sister without breasts (8:8) to become a wall whose breasts are like towers (8:10). She brings forth the most perfect fruit (8:11–12), none other than "the glorious blood of the martyrs."[36] Although her ancient infidelity and call for Jesus's crucifixion once rendered her miserable, Christ now accepts her back, assuring her that all will seek her peace. Mention of a garden in the second to last verse of the Song (8:13) induces Honorius to take stock of the four gardens inhabited by the church over the course of its history. The fourth, the nut garden (6:10), is that of *Synagoga conversa*; Mandragora, curiously, has none.

Honorius and Jews of the End Time

I believe that Honorius's portrayal of the Shunamite bride and *Synagoga conversa* bears evaluation from a number of different perspectives; only thus can we situate his ideas in their proper context and appreciate their broader ramifications.

Christian Exegesis on the Song of Songs

Modern scholars have long recognized many of the important contributions and novelties of Honorius's commentary on the Song of Songs: the four brides and the corresponding fourfold patterns so basic to its exegesis; its demonstration of the virtually limitless potential of Christian allegory in general, and that of the Song in particular; and the added visual dimension to biblical interpretation provided in some of its earliest manuscripts. Noting

that "Honorius opened up the cryptic poems of the Song of Songs as a narrative pulsing with life," and that no other medieval commentary on the Song
of Songs surpasses the seriousness and complexity of his, Ann Matter has
summarized the tour de force of Honorius's historical/allegorical exegesis
adeptly, and with elegance.

> Rhetorical and thematic devices by which Honorius interpreted the
> Song of Songs in this treatise demonstrate the multivocality which crit-
> ics describe as the heart and soul of medieval allegorical interpreta-
> tion. . . . Yet the basic insight into the Song of Songs, the perception of
> four Brides from the four ages of the world, is superimposed on the
> text because of an imaginative insight that is uniquely the author's.
> This flash of Honorius's imagination was transposed into representa-
> tional images through a series of illustrations which defied logic and
> perspective.[37]

Yet notwithstanding such tribute that Honorius and his commentary have
deservedly received, their novel representation of the Shunamite and the
converted Synagoga for a long time remained unappreciated. The figure of
Synagoga conversa, one should note, had made earlier appearances in Latin
commentaries on the Song of Songs, as well as in other exegetical contexts.
Gregory the Great, followed by Angelom of Luxeuil, identified her with the
black and beautiful bride of Song 1:4, and Angelom understood "My soul
troubled me for the chariots of Aminadab" (6:11) to express the awakening
of Synagoga, who for so long had remained ignorant, to the truth of Christianity.[38] Bede explained that in "Return, return, O Sulamitess" (6:12), Ecclesia pleaded with Synagoga to confess her faith in Christ,[39] and Haimo of
Auxerre noted that the "companies of camps" to be seen in the Shunamite
(7:1a) indicated that "the converted Synagoga will harmoniously preach of
Christ together with the Church and will fight until death on behalf of the
religion of Christ."[40] For whatever reason, however, Honorius parted company with these and other Christian commentators—Bede, Haimo, and even
the German Williram of Ebersberg—in his exposition of the Song's ensuing
praises of the bride's beautiful body: "How beautiful are thy steps in shoes"
(7:1b–9). Where his predecessors typically beheld Christ serenading Ecclesia
in these verses,[41] Honorius understood the body and beauty under discussion
as those of Synagoga.

Why? What precipitated Honorius's novel explanation? Did he capitalize
on an opportunity to advance his own distinctive eschatological ideas, glori-
fying the Jewish people of the end time, their conversion to Christianity, and
their decisive role in the battle against Antichrist and the conversion of the

Gentiles? Or did he present his candid interpretation of this passage simply and forthrightly, expounding the biblical text as he truly understood it? Upon reflection, and given the general framework of a Christian allegorical interpretation of the Song, either Honorius's or the traditional reading of these transitional verses makes sense. One might assume, as Bede, Haimo, and many others agreed, that Synagoga declares that "my soul troubled me for the chariots of Aminadab" (6:11), and that Ecclesia offers her the encouraging reply of "Return, return, O Sunamitess" (6:12). If, in the next verse, the groom first asks, "What shalt thou see in the Sunamitess but the companies of camps?" (7:1a), presumably addressing Ecclesia and speaking of the Shunamite/Synagoga in the third person, to whom does he proceed to exclaim in the second person, "How beautiful are thy steps in shoes" (7:1b), if not to Ecclesia herself? Nevertheless, one might reason just as cogently—as Honorius evidently did—that if Ecclesia calls the Shunamite to return so "that we may behold thee" (6:12), the bodily description that begins in 7:1b simply follows through on this intention and refers to her that is beheld.

Honorius, to be sure, rarely presented his theology in revolutionary or iconoclastic fashion. Typically conservative and noncontroversial in their tone, his other writings relate to the Jews and Judaism in a manner that has understandably evoked little scholarly attention.[42] Perhaps genuinely exegetical considerations yielded his fascinating portrait of the Shunamite bride. Still, Honorius developed this portrait in a thorough, generally unhesitating fashion. Whatever his initial intention may have been, one has difficulty imagining that so learned a scholar and so sensitive an exegete could not appreciate the implications of his biblical commentary.

Twelfth-Century Christian Attitudes toward Jews and Judaism

The tone of Honorius's reformulation of Israel's role at the end of days contrasts sharply with the increasingly harsh tenor of Christian *Adversus Judaeos* texts of the twelfth century, just as his exegesis of the Song of Songs parted company with that of his predecessors.[43] Let there be no misunderstanding. When the commentary of Honorius bestows praise on Synagoga and the Jews of the end time, he speaks specifically of *Synagoga conversa*, of the Jews who shall have affiliated with the community of the Christian faithful. Honorius offers no anachronistically ecumenical blueprint for religious pluralism at the end of days; the only Jews to be saved will be baptized Jews. And yet, Honorius's eschatological program casts the Jews in a truly singular fashion, such that his commentary on the Song stands out among the flurry of twelfth-century Christian texts that take up the problematic status of the Jews in a properly ordered Christian world.

First, in its content and in its terminology, Honorius's commentary itself emphasizes the distinctly Jewish character of *Synagoga conversa*. Notwithstanding her conversion to Christianity, symbolized in her marriage to Christ, Honorius portrays Synagoga as a separate entity; she retains her own identity, and she functions beside Ecclesia in the drama of the end time. Readers know that she now has accepted Jesus, but they never forget that she still embodies the Jewish people, as she helps to lead the forces of good to victory over Antichrist and the forces of evil. Honorius reinforces this impression by using the terms *Synagoga conversa* and *Synagoga* interchangeably: of the seventy instances in which he refers to *Synagoga* in her eschatological role in the third and fourth treatises of his commentary, only twenty times does he denote her specifically as *conversa*. Despite the rebirth that conversion to Christ entails, the eschatological Jews of Honorius's commentary remain *Jews*, albeit not *Jewish* in a confessional sense. As we have seen, embodied in Synagoga, they proceed to perform critically important tasks in the culmination and resolution of salvation history.

Second, while the volume and the hostility of Christian anti-Jewish polemic increased over the course of the twelfth century, Honorius's commentary on the Song of Songs generally avoids such tendencies. Despite the presumed interaction between Anselm of Canterbury and Honorius Augustodunensis during the latter's sojourn in England, Honorius's commentary does not betray the influence of Anselm's *Cur Deus homo* or of the anti-Jewish polemics of Anselm's disciples, like Gilbert Crispin, Odo of Cambrai, and Guibert of Nogent. Neither does it challenge Judaism on rational grounds, nor does it group the Jews along with other communities of infidels, thereby undermining, however subtly, the unique role and status that they had previously enjoyed in Christian schemes of salvation history. This Song of Songs commentary hardly depicts the Jews as irrational, questionably human deviants from the self-evident truth of Christianity, as, for example, Honorius's Benedictine confrere Peter the Venerable did in his lengthy anti-Jewish treatise, *Adversus Iudaeorum inveteratam duritiem* (Against the Inveterate Obstinacy of the Jews, 1144–1147). While Honorius makes no blatant use of Jewish exegetical tradition in his commentary, as Andrew of St. Victor, Herbert of Bosham, and some other progressive Christian scholars of the twelfth century began to do, he also did not attack the aggadic lore of the Talmud, as both Peter Alfonsi and Peter the Venerable did in their anti-Jewish polemical treatises.[44]

On the contrary, Honorius's commentary reaffirms and even glorifies the importance of Israel in Christian salvation history, as elaborated. And though one can hardly label Honorius or his exegesis pro-Jewish or philo-Semitic, terminology that makes little sense in the medieval Christian context, the tone of his portrayal of the Jewish people, embodied in the figure of Synagoga, is moderate indeed. In keeping with long-standing Augustinian precedent, Honorius's Synagoga once rejected and crucified Jesus not out of any malicious intention but simply out of blind ignorance.[45]

> When I saw you living among men as a man, I did not know that you were God. When I saw you hanging between thieves, I did not know [cf. 1 Corinthians 2:8] that you were the savior of the world.[46] But you blinded me, so facilitating the salvation of the human race through me, and therefore I did not know what I did.

Synagoga's infamous ancient cry, "his blood be upon us and upon our children" (Matthew 27:25), similarly testifies to the miserable legacy that the Jews who crucified Christ bequeathed to their descendants, not to the extent of their responsibility for deicide.[47] The emphasis on her return to God and reacceptance by him overshadow whatever criticism of the Jews one might find in Honorius's treatise. Confronted with the mandate of "Return, return, O Sunamitess" (6.12), Synagoga responds with exemplary will, determination, and success, worthy of emulation by all.

Third, and perhaps most revealing of all for the present book, while Honorius's commentary on the Song of Songs may not have manifested the twelfth century's distinctive contributions to Christian anti-Jewish polemic, it certainly broke new ground in the development of Christian conceptions of Jews and Judaism at the end of days. Beyond its uncharacteristically effusive praise of eschatological Israel, it did not echo the conventional wisdom on both constitutive elements of the typical Christian ambivalence concerning the eschatological function of the Jews: belief in the ultimate salvation of Israel, and the linkage between the Jews and cosmic forces of evil.

On the one hand, the eschatological scenario elaborated in Honorius's exegesis of chapters 7–8 of the Song depicted the Jews as converting in advance of the final battle against Antichrist and the ensuing conversion of "the multitude of the infidels" symbolized in Mandragora, a conversion that Synagoga herself helped to facilitate. Yet Paul's forecast that "blindness in part has happened in Israel, until the fullness of the Gentiles should come in," but that then "all Israel should be saved," indicated that the Jews would convert only after the plenitude of the Gentiles, and thus did the mainstream of medieval Christian exegesis interpret Romans 11:25–26. Looking back to the commentaries discussed above in part 1 of this book, Christian exegetes before the twelfth century did not reverse the order of the events anticipated by Paul. As noted in chapter 3, the overwhelming consensus (which included Origen, Jerome, Ambrosiaster, Augustine, Gregory the Great, Isidore of Seville, and Bede, along with others)[48] found concurrence and expression in the words of the ninth-century Haimo of Auxerre, who reflected that this ordering—first Gentiles, then Jews—made good sense. For when Paul had noted (1 Corinthians 15:46) with regard to the ultimate resurrection of the dead that "that was not first which is spiritual, but that which is natural, [and only] afterwards that which is spiritual," he meant to convey precisely that first the Gentiles should come to believe, and only then Synagoga.[49]

On the other hand, Honorius in his commentary on the Song also departed from the increasingly accepted picture of the interaction between Jews and Antichrist, discussed above in part 2, that would transpire at the end of days. Honorius's commentary on the Song steers a different course altogether. Although his earlier and popular theological dialogue, the *Elucidarium*, perfunctorily affirms the widely held notion of Antichrist's Jewish parentage,[50] his Song of Songs commentary contains no hint of it. Eschatological Israel does not spawn, support, or maintain any special ties with Antichrist but leads the fight against him. Very significantly, the conversion of Synagoga occurs in the third of the commentary's four treatises, representing the *penultimate* age in the divine historical plan, and not in the very last days, as many had previously envisioned.

One can focus more sharply on these unique expectations by contrasting them with several other works commonly grouped along with Honorius's opus in the tradition of twelfth-century German Symbolism. In the eighth book of his *Chronicon*, Honorius's junior contemporary Otto of Freising faithfully adhered to the traditional scenario.

> While Antichrist shall himself be preaching and leading astray the human race—and particularly the Jewish people—Enoch and Elijah, who still survive, will come, it is believed, in order that by the authority of these men . . . the world which has been deceived by error may return to "the knowledge of the truth. . . ." The time of the persecution is to continue for three years and a half. . . . When the head of the impious city shall be smitten, the Jews, that unbelieving people, seeing that they have been deceived will, it is believed, be converted.[51]

Equally instructive is the scene depicted in the *Ludus de Antichristo*, discussed in the previous chapter, written in Tegernsee, not too far away, within a decade or two after Honorius completed his *Expositio* on the Song of Songs in Regensburg. In memorable form and at considerable length, as we have seen, the playwright dramatizes Antichrist's dispatching of the Hypocrites to Synagoga, the acquiescence of the Jews to their call, and the adoption of the Jews by Antichrist as his stalwart advocates.[52] The midcentury German abbess Hildegard of Bingen, well known for her remarkable image of Antichrist emerging from the womb of Ecclesia and noted for the mildness of her references to the Jews, also remained committed to the notion of their ultimate salvation. Unlike Honorius, however, Hildegard essentially read the Jews out of the drama of Antichrist, according them no significant role (beyond that of Elijah and Enoch) in the final struggle between good and evil.[53] And, as discussed above, the late twelfth-century German *Hortus deliciarum* (Garden of Delights) by Herrad of Hohenbourg similarly envisions the Jews—personified by a male Synagoga—first as duped by Antichrist, then as baptized only after his death.[54]

Yet the informative and striking contrast lies not merely between the penitent Synagoga in the *Ludus* whom Antichrist kills, Synagoga in Otto's *Chronicon* and Herrad's *Hortus* who converts only after the smoke has cleared, and Honorius's *Synagoga conversa*, who wages war against Antichrist, emerges victorious, and exults in the ensuing age of glory. Rather, one must also underscore the difference in the timing of Synagoga's conversion: in Honorius's treatise on the Song, Synagoga converts *before* the appearance of Antichrist, such that she never succumbs to his fraud or numbers among his followers. In this, Honorius broke not only with Adso but also with the large majority of Catholic writers on Antichrist who preceded him. In his interpretation of the romance between God and his faithful church, a drama played out over the various stages of history, he never portrays Synagoga among the agents of the final enemy. In view of the watershed in the history of Christian apocalypticism that followed quickly upon the career of Honorius, can one discern a connection between the ideas of his commentary and those of Joachim and his disciples that would subsequently precipitate a revolution in the religious mentality of medieval Europe?

Our appreciation of Honorius's reading of the Song of Songs hardly lessens the importance of Joachim and the Joachimites discussed above in chapter 5, but it does detract somewhat from their novelty and uniqueness. Recalling Robert Lerner's assessment that Joachim's "proposition that at the end of time the world will be transformed in a mutually beneficial union of Christians and Jews" constituted an "unprecedentedly irenic vision,"[55] we should note that several key elements of the Joachite vision do appear to have a precedent in Honorius's portrayal of *Synagoga conversa*: the timing of the conversion of the Jews in the drama of the end of days; the relationship between the Jews and Antichrist; and the millennial synthesis of Jewish and Gentile peoples, reflecting the *concordia* of Old and New Testaments.[56]

First, for Joachim, even if some Jews will convert before the advent of Antichrist, most will convert following the destruction of Antichrist—in whose support they had previously rallied—but prior to the last judgment. In Honorius's interpretation of the Song of Songs, Antichrist belongs to the age of the fourth and final bride, Mandragora, who appears on the scene following the nuptials of the Shunamite. Although one can find airtight consistency neither in the writings of Joachim nor in the commentary of Honorius, the latter's Synagoga converts before the arrival, reign, and demise of Antichrist. Synagoga leads the faithful in their battle against his tyranny, and, in order for her to do so, the conversion of Israel must already have occurred. Second, Honorius—like Gerhoh of Reichersburg—preceded Joachim in breaking with patristic and Adsonian teaching on Antichrist's Jewish origins; for them he was not born into the Israelite tribe of Dan. Lerner observes that Joachim "had such an unusual view of the place of the Jews at the culmination of earthly history that he broke with a thousand-year-old Christian tradition that Antichrist would be born of the lost Jewish tribe of Dan." Even if Antichrist would have a considerable number of Jewish followers, Lerner insists that "the standard medieval view . . . that Antichrist would be born of the tribe of Dan" was "never contradicted until Joachim."[57] Yet Honorius, as we have seen, pits the converted Synagoga squarely against Antichrist and his followers. He mentions no Jews among Antichrist's followers, and not once does his Song of Songs commentary allude to any Jewish lineage in Antichrist's pedigree, as Honorius had done in his earlier *Elucidarium*.[58] And third, replete with its numerical lists and recurring division of the annals of the world—and the church—into different stages, Honorius's interpretation of the Song even adumbrates Joachim's use of biblical typology to delineate the largely Trinitarian symmetries of salvation history. For Honorius understood the description of the Shunamite/Synagoga's various limbs and organs to include all ten orders of a righteous Christian society. In this vein, the joints of her thighs that are like jewels "made by the hand of a skillful workman" (7:1) refer to *conjugati*, married people who, with their offspring, adorn the church with their faith and good works. But then Honorius proposes a second exegesis that resonates with the gist of Joachite ideas to come: "Alternatively, the juncture of the thighs is the concord of the two peoples—the Jewish people and the Gentile people—whom the Christian sacraments join in one religion of Christ and bring forth as spiritual offspring."[59] No less suggestively, Honorius explained why the groom's adjuration of the daughters of Jerusalem not to rouse the bride from her slumber appears three times in the Song (2:7, 3:5, 8:4): "The first time it refers to the primitive [Jewish] church, the second time to the church of the Gentiles, and the third time to *Synagoga conversa*; altogether it denotes the concord of them all[60] in the one faith of the Trinity."[61]

Synagoga and Aminadab in Contemporary Christian Imagery

Honorius's strikingly innovative portrayal of Synagoga at the end time appears not only in the text of his commentary but also in the illuminations in six of its earliest extant manuscripts. These illuminations depict the various brides described by Honorius in his work, and both the details of the illustrations and their southern German, mid-twelfth-century provenance have led investigators to posit a close link between them and the commentator himself. One cannot assuredly ascribe any of the artwork to the hand of Honorius, and, from an iconographic point of view, the differences between the various illuminated manuscripts are hardly insignificant. Yet the consensus points to a geographic, religious, and cultural context that commentator and illuminators shared, such that the illuminations offer insight both into our author's ideas and into the responses that they evoked among their earliest readers. Michael Curschmann, for one, has argued that Honorius himself devised a set of illustrations, that illumination may have begun even before he completed the text, that the earliest illuminated manuscripts display an impressive uniformity in their pictorial execution of Honorius's program, and that the extant illustrations themselves testify to the open-ended, multivalent nature of the biblical exegesis in question. In Curschmann's words, "We are fortunate indeed to be able to reconstruct in such detail the ways in which a loosely defined group of illustrators struggled to meet the demands of a new text of a very special kind. . . . What the surviving manuscripts reveal are reflexes, emanations of a situation very close to the author, where, nevertheless, the response to his text remained tentative, open-ended, experimental in a number of ways."[62]

Here we cannot review all the illustrations, but one can fairly conclude that, of the three brides depicted in all six twelfth-century illuminated manuscripts (the daughter of Babylon, the Shunamite, and Mandragora), the Shunamite surpasses the daughter of Babylon and the mandrake in her majestic presentation. Only the Shunamite enters on a chariot, while the daughter of Babylon rides a camel and the decapitated Mandragora must stand on her own two feet. Only the Shunamite holds a regal banner as she enters, and, while the philosophers usher in the daughter of Babylon toward her groom, it is the apostles, in most instances accompanied by Aminadab himself, who escort the Shunamite in her procession.

The illustration reproduced here (fig. 21) depicts the Shunamite on the quadriga of Aminadab. Interestingly, the original, now obsolete Roman quadriga, a two-wheeled chariot drawn by a team of four horses, has here given way to the contemporary medieval cart with four wheels and only two horses.[63] As such, the conveyance accommodates identification with the wagon of Abinadab (2 Samuel 6:3) on which the ark of the covenant returned to Jerusalem in the days of King David and, by extension, with the chariot that Plato, Ambrose, and others had likened to the human soul.[64] The bride appears holding her pennant, led by the apostles and Aminadab himself, and followed by the Jews on their return to Christ. The figure in the upper right-hand corner of the illustration reminds us that the Shunamite has come from the west. The wheels of her chariot encircle figures of a man, an eagle, an ox (or calf), and a lion, recalling the creatures and cherubs envisioned by Ezekiel (chs. 1, 10). In the patristic tradition first enunciated by Irenaeus of Lyons and then developed by Jerome and others, these represent the evangelists Matthew, Mark, Luke, and John, respectively.[65] Along the border of the illustration one reads: "Quae fuit inmitis mansueta redit Sunamitis. Haec prius abiecta regnat captiva revecta." The Shunamite who was unruly returns after having become

FIGURE 21. Shunamite on the quadriga of Aminadab. Honorius Augustodunensis, *Expositio in Cantica Canticorum*. Munich, Bayerische Staatsbibliothek, MS Clm 4550, fol. 77r.

tame. She who was previously deprived of her power now rules, a captive restored to her freedom.

Underscoring her prominence further still, the illuminator of this twelfth-century manuscript included a frontispiece (fig. 22) depicting the bride (*sponsa*), presumably Ecclesia, to our left, the groom (*sponsus*), Jesus, sitting next to her on the throne with his right arm over her shoulders, and a kneeling woman to the lower right. Christ extends his left arm to her through

FIGURE 22.   Ecclesia, Jesus, Shunamite-Synagoga. Honorius Augustodunensis, *Expositio in Cantica Canticorum*. Munich, Bayerische Staatsbibliothek, MS Clm 4550, fol. 1v (frontispiece).

an open window and lovingly cradles her cheek, and art historians Suzanne Lewis and Elizabeth Monroe have identified her as Synagoga in the person of the Shunamite. Next to the two women appear both halves of the verse (Song 2:6, 8:3), "His left hand is under my head [next to Synagoga], and his right hand shall embrace me [next to Ecclesia]," suggesting that these two females are somehow the same. The kneeling woman holds a scroll quoting Song 5:4, "My beloved put his hand through the key hole." And, on the tree behind her, we read from Song 8:5, "Under the tree I raised thee up," which, Honorius suggests, can be understood as Christ speaking to *Synagoga conversa* of the cross, whose saving power she has now recognized and in which she has found new life.[66] Telling indeed is the illuminator's choice for a frontispiece that portrays the heavenly marriage of Christ and Ecclesia as that with the converted Synagoga.[67]

One finds a potentially instructive parallel to Honorius's representation of *Synagoga conversa* in the famed anagogical window of the royal abbey of Saint-Denis, created and installed in its church during Abbot Suger's renovations of the 1140s, no more than a few years before or after Honorius wrote his exposition of the Song. Suger himself left us details of the program for the window (fig. 23), which contained five roundels, all of them scenes expressing Paul's allegorical framework for establishing the harmony between Old and New Testaments (in their original ascending order): Paul turning the mill to grind out the true meaning of Old Testament prophecy; the unveiling of Moses; the quadriga of Aminadab bearing the ark of the covenant and the cross; the unsealing of the book by the lion and the lamb; and the unveiling of Synagoga at the end of time.

Only two of the original twelfth-century roundels remain, but, fortunately, these two bear most directly on our discussion.[68] Drawing on references to the ark of the covenant, Abinadab, and Aminadab in Exodus, 2 Samuel, the Song of Songs, and Hebrews, the Aminadab roundel (fig. 24) stands in striking similarity to the verbal and pictorial portrayal of the Shunamite encountered in Honorius's commentary.

Jacqueline Frank offers a helpful description of the scene at Saint-Denis.

A rectangular flat-bedded floral decorated car occupies the center of the roundel, surrounded by four winged, nimbed, half-figure Evangelist symbols. A cross in the form of a tree of life bearing the image of Christ against a yellow veil, and supported by God the Father, protrudes from the car. Four wheel-shapes, each decorated with eight spokes are attached to the four corners of the cart. Those on the near side are placed in the lower corners, while those on the far side abut the upper corners of the vehicle.

FIGURE 23. Anagogical Window, Abbey of Saint-Denis. https://www.medart.pitt.edu/image/France/St-denis/windows/Anagogical/mo541esds.jpg © Alison Stones.

FIGURE 24.   Aminadab roundel. Anagogical window, Abbey of Saint-Denis. https://www.medart.pitt.edu/image/France/St-denis/windows/Anagogical/anag8jvs.jpg © Alison Stones.

Drawings of the window prior to its restoration depict the tablets of the Law and the staff of Moses's brother Aaron beside the cross. The inscription reads: "On the Ark of the Covenant is established the altar with the Cross of Christ; here life wishes to die under a greater covenant." The wagon is labeled *Quadrige Aminadab.*[69]

Frank rightly dwells on the differences between the Saint-Denis quadriga and that in the Honorius manuscripts, but I believe that precisely in these details the symbolism of the former can prove useful in "unpacking" the significance of the latter. First, one must appreciate that the Saint-Denis roundel appears in a window devoted to the concord between Old Testament and New. Second, the Saint-Denis roundel juxtaposes the representative emblems of the two covenants—the rod of Aaron and the tablets of the law on the one hand, the cross on the other hand—and thus offers an emphatic declaration of the harmonious continuity between them. Third, the Saint-Denis image of the divine *maiestas Domini* riding Aminadab's chariot proclaims the essential identity of the old law and the new. The one is embodied in the ark of the covenant that this quadriga returned to Jerusalem; the other disseminated throughout the world by the four evangelists, depicted here beside the cart's four wheels. God's upholding of the crucified Jesus against the backdrop of the yellow veil, itself denoting the curtain of the biblical temple, decisively resolves any residual tension between the two. What impression, then, does the Saint-Denis quadriga communicate? Labeling it a harmoniously and felicitously proportioned "work of genius," Louis Grodecki has summarized its message thus: "The crucified Christ rests in the Ark of the Covenant; God the Father supports the Cross before a veil that is the veil of the Temple; the whole Church, represented by the four Evangelists, surrounds this symbolic vision, at once Jewish and Christian, since the Ark of the Covenant symbolizes the Altar of Christ."[70]

The progression of the roundels in Suger's anagogical window clarifies the import of the quadriga of Aminadab further still. To paraphrase very simply from Suger's own description of the program: Pauline allegorical exegesis allows for unveiling the doctrine of Christ embedded in the law of Moses; the new covenant of Christ is established on the foundation of the ark of the old covenant, facilitating the fulfillment of God's salvific plan by the lion of Judah, who is himself the sacrificial lamb of God.[71] Curiously, Suger's extant notes make no explicit mention of the fifth roundel at the top of the window (fig. 25), which brings the entire series to its climactic conclusion: the unveiling of Synagoga, fulfilling the prophecy of Exodus 34:34 (as allegorized in 2 Corinthians 3:15ff.) in the final conversion of Israel.

The dominant tendencies in twelfth-century Christian iconography exhibited increasing hostility toward Synagoga: blindfolded, deprived of her crown, holding a now broken staff, and at times even juxtaposed with the devil, she begins to lose her place under the outstretched arms of the crucified Jesus, prodded offstage by zealous angels of the Lord.[72] But Suger's anagogical window, Honorius's Song of Songs commentary, and several other contemporary representations offered an alternative. Instead of focusing on the perfidy of the Jew of the present, they could look forward to his ultimate redemption. Synagoga would have her veil removed (Saint-Denis); Ecclesia might even offer Synagoga her chalice filled with Christ's saving blood

FIGURE 25. Unveiling of the Synagoga roundel. Anagogical Window, Abbey of Saint-Denis.
https://www.medart.pitt.edu/image/France/St-denis/windows/Anagogical/sdaga-ecsyns.jpg
© Alison Stones.

(a twelfth-century sacramentary from Tours[73]); the quadriga of Aminadab
might transport *Synagoga conversa* to the marriage bed of Christ her groom
(Honorius's *Expositio*).

In her now classic study of thirteenth-century illuminated manuscripts
of the Apocalypse, Suzanne Lewis has shown how eschatological texts of
the later Middle Ages appropriated these and other images, drawing repeatedly on Honorius and his Song of Songs commentary, as they continued
to develop this alternative emphasis on the conversion and reconciliation
of Israel—with no apparent link to Joachim and his Franciscan heirs.[74]
Lewis draws the connection from Honorius to Suger but moves beyond the
French abbot to the thirteenth-century *Bible moralisée*,[75] and to the illuminated French Burckhardt-Wildt Apocalypse, which thus contrasts with the
Gulbenkian and Abingdon Apocalypses mentioned in the previous chapter.
In particular, she turns to the Burckhardt-Wildt Apocalypse illustration that

regrettably, owing to steep fees demanded by its owners, could not be reproduced here. The image portrays a woman representing faithless Israel, lying naked in a bed with the devil pulling a rope around her neck. Outside the devil's abode stands Jesus who calls inside to his ensnared, but still beloved, Israel, with his cry written on an unfurled scroll: "Return, return, O Sunamitess; return, return that we may behold thee." As Lewis maintains, "It is the bridal figure of the Shulamite introduced and expounded by Honorius Augustodunensis that dominates the discourse of the image, for she personifies the soul's yearning for God (*sub gratia*) in a tropological reading that transcends allegory as it reaches into the affective regions of the reader's inner world."[76] Put more concisely, "For Honorius the Shulamite is Judaism converted; she becomes the Church who now carries the banner of Faith."[77]

Neither did the German Honorius Augustodunensis preach with the prophetic inspiration of the Calabrian abbot Joachim, nor did he pursue his idea of *Synagoga conversa* to the daring and controversial conclusions of Joachite millennialism. Nevertheless, his commentary on the Song of Songs attributes to the character of *Synagoga conversa* much of the central importance and positive nature that strike one as so noteworthy in the works of Joachim. The parallels noted here appear to substantiate Horst Dieter Rauh's observation of continuity between the hermeneutical methods and mentality of twelfth-century German Symbolism and those of Joachim.[78] Alongside the intensification of Christian anti-Jewish polemic, perhaps the twelfth century also gave rise to new hopes for Synagoga's reconciliation with Ecclesia, hopes that blended no less well with the ideology of crusading and the growth of missionary theology.[79] In other words, the spirit of Honorius's commentary on the Song may well reflect a more pervasive phenomenon—not a general trend, to be sure, but an alternative for situating the "eschatological Jew" in a Christian plan for salvation history. Whether or not one ought to credit Honorius and his commentary with bequeathing such ideas to posterity, these ideas did return in later centuries, in contexts and among writers with no patent links to the legacy of Joachim.

CHAPTER 8

Jewish Converts and Christian Salvation

Pablo de Santa María, Bishop of Burgos

Solomon ben Isaac Halevi of Burgos, a promi-
nent, well-educated Jewish intellectual and courtier in late fourteenth-
century Castile, became a Christian in 1390 or 1391, immediately prior to or
perhaps in an early phase of the massive wave of conversions remembered
in Jewish history as the persecutions of 5151 (Anno Mundi, or 1391 C.E.).
Unlike many of the other *conversos*, Solomon, who assumed the name of
Pablo (Paul), evidently converted of his own free will, convinced that his
destiny lay in the church. He converted with his sons and some of his siblings
and was followed several years later by his wife, and he then rose to become
bishop of Burgos, a close confidant of the Avignonese pope Benedict XIII,
a respected Catholic theologian, and one of the most important Christian
biblical scholars of the later Middle Ages. Pablo's 1090 critical notes (*Additiones*) to the famed Nicholas of Lyra's monumental biblical commentaries
(*Postillae*) circulated in several dozen manuscripts and appeared in nearly
as many early printed editions of the Scriptures, typically alongside the
Glossa ordinaria, the *Postillae*, and the ensuing defense of Lyra in Matthias
Döring's *Replica* or *Defensorium* of Lyra's exegesis. Later in his career, Pablo
authored his massive anti-Jewish polemic, *Scrutinium Scripturarum*, in the
form of a dialogue, first between Saul the Jew and Paul the Christian and
then between a Christian master and his disciple—perhaps the longest such

anti-Jewish polemical dialogue ever written, spanning some five hundred pages in its early printings.[1]

Additiones

Where Honorius Augustodunensis (as seen in the previous chapter) looked forward to *Synagoga conversa*'s centrally important, leading role in the final redemption to come, Pablo de Santa María looked back in time, maintaining that Jewish converts to Christianity were the key players in the ongoing drama of salvation that began with the first coming of Christ.[2] Pablo developed this idea with repeated reference to Paul's Epistle to the Romans, in both his *Additiones* and his *Scrutinium Scripturarum*.[3] Although he fell in line with many of his predecessors in affirming that all Jews, even those still obstinate in their rejection of Christianity, will be saved at the end time, and although he hints that they will be saved after severing their ties with Antichrist, the futuristic, eschatological emphasis in his work is markedly subdued. Pablo has considerably more interest in the Jewish converts who became Jesus's apostles and those who later joined the church. When Paul cited Isaiah in Romans 9:27 to the effect that a remnant of Israel would be saved, and again in 9:29 that this seed served the Gentiles as the source of their salvation— "Unless the Lord of Sabaoth had left us a seed, we had been made as Sodom and we had been like unto Gomorrha"—Pablo understood that he referred to the Jewish apostles of Jesus who first established the church. And when he came to Paul's famous parable of the olive tree in Romans 11, Pablo parted company with most Christian commentators before him. He identified the holy root of the tree (*radix sancta*) not as the Hebrew patriarchs, as most had done before him, but as those very Jewish apostles who, together with subsequent Jewish converts who followed their example, remained the source of blessing and salvation for Gentile Christians.[4]

Teaching that Isaiah's remnant of Israel worthy of salvation already found salvation, and in identifying this remnant with the root of Paul's olive tree, Pablo reminds one of Pelagius, who (as noted above in chapter 2) had understood the hope of Romans 11:26 (*omnis Israhel salvus fieret*) to have materialized: "All Israel *was* saved," not "*will be* saved." Admittedly, Pablo believed that the salvation of the currently recalcitrant portions of Israel still awaited the ultimate conversion of the fullness of the Gentiles, but the events of the first coming had, in terms of their redemption, leveled the distinction between Jews and Gentiles. Among both, one can now distinguish between those already saved and those at present unsaved; all had equal access to salvation. And, although he makes no mention of Pelagius, Pablo likewise contended that the salvation of the Gentiles in the Christian church did not disenfranchise Israel. Since the birth of Christianity Israel has been a "bifurcated" Israel[5] but still a Jewish Israel, not merely a new symbolic or allegorized collective of Abraham's spiritual descendants. Both those Jews who had converted and those who remained outside the church contributed roundly to the ongoing process of salvation in Christ. Through their conversion, the former facilitated the fulfillment of the divine covenant with biblical Israel within the church; their function as root of the olive tree constituted "great praise or blessing for the people of Israel" (*magnam laudem seu benedictionem populi Israelitici*).[6] As branches of the cultivated olive tree chopped off to allow for grafting of wild branches onto it, the still unconverted Jews also worked to implement the divine plan, bearing the books of the law and their latent promise of redemption throughout the world. Even rejected Israel has not forfeited its singular status in the divine economy of salvation. In this way, one scholar has noted, Pablo "rejected Thomistic views that Judaism became a conscious evil choice of infidelity following the arrival of Christ."[7]

In his doctoral dissertation and forthcoming book on Pablo, Yosi Yisraeli has carefully tracked the exposition of these ideas. The *Additiones* to Deuteronomy 32–33, comprising the Song of Moses and Moses's final blessing to the twelve tribes of Israel before they entered the promised land without him, use Romans 9–11 to read these final chapters of the Pentateuch as envisioning the fulfillment of God's covenant with Israel, in the establishment of Christianity and the calling of the Gentiles. Both the provocation of sinful Israel by the Gentiles ("a non-people," Deuteronomy 32:21) and the call of the nations (32:43), to "praise his people . . ., for he will revenge the blood of his servants and will render vengeance to their enemies, and he will be merciful to the land of his people," accord with Pablo's understanding of Romans. The promises of Hebrew Scripture bore fruit in the new covenant of grace begun at Calvary, in the (Jewish) apostles' role in preaching it, and in the Gentiles' replacement of those Jews who rejected Jesus and his gospel. Like Moses in this concluding verse of his song, Paul reiterated the primacy of Israel in the new church as his epistle neared its conclusion.

> For I tell you that Christ has become a servant of the circumcised on behalf of the truth of God in order that he might confirm the promises given to the patriarchs, and in order that the Gentiles might glorify God for his mercy. As it is written, "Therefore I will confess you among the Gentiles, and sing praises to your name"; and again he says, "Rejoice, O Gentiles, with his people." (Romans 15:8–10)

Pablo developed these ideas as he proceeded to expound Moses's prophetic blessings of the Israelites in Deuteronomy 33, and Yisraeli has effectively summarized Pablo's message as follows:

> In the *additiones* to Deuteronomy 32–33, Pablo portrayed the establishment of the Church as the final materialization of God's covenant with Israel. In his terms, the promises made to biblical Israel were realized in the Jewish followers of Jesus who became the nourishing root of the Church on which all the nations had been feeding spiritually. Notably, these first followers of Jesus were still considered by Pablo as the historical Israel, and they were identified as such even inside the new universal congregation of the Church.

Such an understanding had far-ranging implications for Christian ideas of the Jews and their role in the divine economy of salvation.

> For Pablo, it is thus clear that the Church and the new covenant by no means signaled the annulment or the replacement of the old covenant with Israel. Nevertheless, Pablo did acknowledge that the larger part of Israel, that denied the messiah, was severed from the new congregation. . . . However, did that mean that the Israel that did not join the Church was cast away by God and ostracized from His covenant with the chosen people? Has this part of Israel ceased to play any productive role in God's eschatological plan and been completely excluded from the future of human salvation?[8]

As much as Pablo emphasized Paul's instruction in Romans, and the mystery that intertwined the destinies of the Gentiles and Israel in Romans 11:25 in particular—"For I would not have you ignorant, brethren, of this mystery . . . that blindness in part has happened in Israel, until the fullness of the Gentiles should come in"—Pablo's focus remains strikingly noneschatological. Surprisingly, Romans 11:26—"And so all Israel should be saved"—receives no mention here, and, in a manner suggestive of Pelagius, the discussion centers on the birth of Christianity in the wake of Jesus's first coming, not the final, complete redemption of Israel at the time of the second coming.

Medieval European Christians characteristically based their understanding of the ongoing role that the Jews played—or at least were supposed to play—in Christian history on Augustine's acclaimed doctrine of Jewish witness. Pending his ultimate salvation of Israel, which included those Jews and those Gentiles destined for salvation, God preserved the Jewish people, who in turn preserved their Old Testament, to testify to the roots of Christianity.

The Jews, their books, and their observance of the law survived as fossils of biblical antiquity, bearing witness to the truth of Christianity that had superseded them, even though the Jews failed to acknowledge the Christian truth that their very own books proclaimed. Oblivious to developments in Judaism that had transpired since the first century, Augustine constructed a "hermeneutical" Jew embodying an obsolete understanding of Scripture that nevertheless served Christian purposes. As we have seen, he found biblical support for his ideas in Psalm 59:11–13 (Psalm 58 in the Vulgate), which, he believed, addressed their proper place in Christendom: "God shall let me see over my enemies: slay them not, lest at any time my people forget. Scatter them by thy power; and bring them down, O Lord, my protector." Until the final redemption, this Jew's place remained outside the church; otherwise, they could not fulfill their role.[9]

Pablo's views concerning the Jewish converts at the root of Christianity—as the mechanism whereby God's promises to Israel found and continued to find fulfillment among the Christian faithful—entailed a unique role for the Jews in facilitating salvation, a role that lay within the church just as much as outside it. Given the doctrine of Jewish witness that Augustine found embedded in Psalm 59, in his own *additio* on Psalm 59[10] Pablo incorporated that doctrine into his notion of a "bifurcated Israel" and his quasi-Pelagian view that the faith of the Jewish apostles in Jesus constituted the salvation of the "remnant of Israel." After its opening verses deal with the conflict between David and Saul, Pablo writes that the psalm proceeds to address the Jews in the divine economy of salvation in three ways.

First, in those that "shall return (*convertentur*) at evening, and shall suffer hunger like dogs: and shall go round about the city" (v. 7), Pablo referred to those Jews who converted following the crucifixion, resurrection, and ascension of Jesus, late in the day, as it were—not when Jesus himself first offered redemption to the Jews. Yet, like Paul, Stephen, and the other apostles, they were and still are hungry to convert others to their new faith; roaming the world, they make an uproar in reproving the infidels, "just as dogs bark at robbers and thieves at night."[11] "They shall return at evening," Pablo continues, also denotes the many Jews who have converted since and continue to convert daily, converted Jews who have done much to fight against Jewish error and heresy. And here Pablo offers examples of such illustrious Jewish converts, above all in Spain, among them (the seventh-century bishop) Julian Pomerius, Peter Alfonsi, and Abner of Burgos.

Second, Pablo turns to the Jews at the heart of Augustine's witness doctrine, those who have rejected Christianity, stubbornly clinging to their blindness and error. As Augustine did before him, Pablo explains that the magnitude of their crimes against Jesus warranted the total and immediate obliteration of these Jews from the face of the earth, but that divine wisdom ordained otherwise, and this for several reasons. Some of these Jews, too, convert and are saved over the course of time. From those who spurn Christianity "the church receives testimonies of the old law. For they are, as the *Glossa* notes, our librarians, the keepers of our scriptures, from whom testimony is received more reliably the more avidly they oppose us."[12] Their opposition to Christianity notwithstanding,

> divine vengeance / punishment shines forth in them more when their suffering and hatred are evidenced in diverse times and places than if they had been consumed quickly in specific areas. Thus the Psalmist prayed appropriately, saying: "Slay them not, lest my people forget." That is, lest they forget your mercy, so that they might be induced to convert. Similarly, lest they forget your holy letters, which reside among them naturally (owing to their birth / origin—*originaliter*). Likewise, lest they forget your justice, seeing them afflicted daily and subdued in punishment for the crime of Christ's murder. For all these could be forgotten, if they had been destroyed speedily.

God took care in ordaining otherwise.

> If they had remained to be punished in one place or region, the benefits we have mentioned would not have accrued throughout the entire world. Thus he says: "Scatter them by your power," so that they might be dispersed among all the peoples, and the evidence of holy scripture that they constitute among us, as well as the evidence of divine vengeance, might be demonstrated everywhere. "And bring them down," that is, let them be the despised of all people. And so those perfidious ones, even if they can no longer disobey in action, they still do not stop blaspheming him in their words.[13]

Pablo leaves no room for doubt that the Augustinian doctrine of Jewish witness and its mandate of "Slay them not lest my people forget"— considered above in part 1—have not lost their relevance. Their force and importance endure, still applying directly to contemporary Jews. Significantly, as Yisraeli emphasizes,[14] this means that Pablo did not uphold an outright distinction between ancient biblical and contemporary rabbinic Jews in this regard. While he too may have denounced the absurdities in various Talmudic homilies, Pablo parted company with those of his medieval predecessors and contemporaries (like his student Gerónimo de Santa

Fe at the Disputation of Tortosa[15]) who condemned the Talmudic sages for forsaking the God-given law of Moses, for replacing the biblical covenant with a new fabricated law of their own. Augustine's preservationist mandate applied equally to both ancient and contemporary Judaism. For Pablo held that traditions of rabbinic Judaism furnished the church with testimony to Christianity's Jewish roots; alongside Hebrew Scripture, they too gave expression to authentic Judaism. Although guilt and opprobrium persisted among contemporary Jews, Pablo did not view them as heretics vis-à-vis their Judaism, heretics who now stood outside the divine economy of salvation.

Third, Pablo writes that as Psalm 59 approaches its conclusion (vv. 14–16), it now relates to the Jews of the eschaton.

> When they are consumed by thy wrath, and they shall be no more. And they shall know that God will rule Jacob, and all the ends of the earth. They shall return at evening and shall suffer hunger like dogs: and shall go round about the city. They shall be scattered abroad to eat, and shall murmur (Hebrew *vayyalinu*) if they be not filled.

As a result of their prolonged and nearly ubiquitous suffering, the Jews will admit their error and acknowledge the truth of Christianity. Reiterating its earlier words (v. 7), "They shall return (*convertentur*) at evening," as a refrain in verse 15, the Psalm now closes the circle and forecasts the salvation of Israel at the ultimate evening or end of days. Pablo explains: "When those Jews will know that God rules over Jacob and over the ends of the world with the true faith, then they will convert . . ., and they will be scattered abroad to eat, namely, so that they can win over others." But Pablo understood the Hebrew *vayyalinu* to mean not that they "shall murmur" (as the Vulgate understood) but that they "shall rest." Even if they do not succeed in converting all infidels, they will still find peace in their conversion.[16]

As opposed to Augustine's understanding of these final verses, in which Jews and Gentiles consolidate and lose their respective differences in an ideal eschatological union, Pablo continues to accord the Jews a distinctive character and function. If one discerns any conjunction of identities, one might say that Pablo finds it in the fusion of Augustine's "hermeneutical Jew" with Paul's "eschatological Jew." Throughout all three phases of salvation history since the birth of Christianity, the Jews contribute to the redemption of humanity by enabling others to apprehend the truth: in the first and final phases as converts who proceed to proselytize others; in the second phase as those who promote the Christian faith even in their denial but eventually—in many cases even before the end time—see the light. The remnant of Israel that converted at the time of Jesus or soon thereafter continued to bear fruit in the proverbial olive tree of Romans 11, and the Jews who bore witness to Christianity in their steadfast allegiance to the old law did so as well. For Pablo, the eschatological process began long ago; rather than break radically with the salvation history of Israel that had already passed, its conclusion will bring that process to completion and perfection.

Scrutinium Scripturarum

The more thematically organized *Scrutinium scripturarum* allowed Pablo to elaborate these ideas further and more succinctly. As Claude Stuczynski and Yosi Yisraeli have shown, Pablo's exegetical method led him to link prophecies of the Hebrew Bible with the salvation-historical scheme outlined by Paul in Romans in elucidating the eschatological role of historic (that is, Jewish) Israel. Pablo understood the particular status, the privileges, and the benefits that Paul accorded Israel in Romans 11 as applying above all to those Jews who have converted to Christianity and have found—and will find—their place within the church. Isaiah 29:22–23 ("Jacob shall not now be confounded, neither shall his countenance now be ashamed . . . when he shall see his children, the work of my hands in the midst of him sanctifying my name") underlay Pablo's assertion that the merits of the apostles will counterbalance the sins of the Pharisees in overcoming any collective guilt that resided in Israel: "In the establishment of the Church, the prime movers were those who descended from the lineage of Jacob, so much so that shame was thereby removed from Jacob and the faithful descending from him."[17] Isaiah had also prophesied (17:4–6): "And it shall come to pass in that day, that the glory of Jacob shall be made thin, and the fatness of his flesh shall grow lean, and it shall be . . . as the shaking of the olive tree, two or three berries in the top of a bough, or four or five upon the top of the tree." Here Pablo found further support for his interpretation of Paul's parabolic olive tree in Romans 11 and its implications for the present historical era. Although most Jews may have been cut off from the olive tree, some, those who converted to Christianity, remained on the tree and rooted in its apostolic origins. As he did in the *Additiones*, Pablo mentioned some of the noteworthy converts who had campaigned and written important works on behalf of the church.[18] And, after relating Isaiah 4:3 ("It shall come to pass, that every one that shall be left in Sion, and that shall remain in Jerusalem, shall be called holy") to the first coming of Christ, Pablo turned to the second coming, drawing on the

Targum to find confirmation of Romans 11:26—that all Israel will eventually be saved—in Hosea 3:4–5.

> Upon the second coming of Christ, which will be witnessed near the end of the world, those same people who at the first coming of Christ played leading roles ought to play leading roles upon this second coming, as it is said, "concerning the rest" [Isaiah 4:2–3], namely the Jews, who shall remain at that time. It is commonly held that, having discarded the falsehood of the Antichrist, they will adhere most loyally to Christ, so much so that for his faith they will endure great persecutions, even to the extent of martyrdom, and they will persevere in the faith of Christ most devotedly. Concerning these one understands what the Apostle wrote in Romans 11, "All Israel shall be saved." Here the Doctors understand what is read properly and clearly in Hosea 3, where he says: "For the children of Israel shall sit many days without king, and without prince, and without sacrifice, and without altar, and without ephod, and without theraphim. And after this the children of Israel shall return and shall seek the Lord, their God, and David, their king"—where in the Aramaic translation it says: "and they shall serve the Messiah, the son of David their king, having fear of the Lord."[19]

Pablo opted to cite Hosea, Stuczynski suggests,[20] rather than the verse from Isaiah (59:20) quoted by Paul himself in Romans 11:26, because the Hosea prophecy befits Jewish converts to Christianity in stressing that the Jews themselves would seek out their God and their savior.

Jewish conversion to Christianity afforded Christian salvation history its dynamic, the key to its momentum and fulfillment, and a coherent framework incorporating its past, present, and future stages.

> If you should carefully study the scriptures, you will find that both at the origination of the Church and at the end time—which are the more important phases in the entire history of Christ's church and in which Christ's presence in his church is deemed more pronounced—the believers in Christ who descend biologically (*carnaliter*) from the Israelite people were and will be his leading associates. For at his first advent the Apostles, who were for the most part Israelites among some others, were chosen by Christ to cultivate the fruit of redemption in the world. . . . Likewise, in the second coming, these very ones will appear more important.[21]

As we have seen, the process of Jewish acceptance of Christ brings the world to redemption. This process began long ago at the time of the apostles, and its completion at the time of the second coming will proceed on the model of what transpired upon his first coming.

The Next Generation

While the concern of this chapter lies chiefly with Pablo de Santa María, we might better appreciate the substance and impact of his teaching by turning briefly to the writings of two of his foremost disciples. Pablo's son Alonso de Cartagena, who succeeded his father as bishop of Burgos, vehemently opposed the hostility toward the Jewish *conversos* in fifteenth-century Spain, especially in his work *Defensorium unitatis christianae* (The Defense of Christian Unity). Like Pablo, Alonso positioned the Jews at the epicenter of God's plan for the salvation of humanity. They facilitated the illumination of the new faith at the time of the apostles, they will do so yet again at the end time—leading the Gentiles along the way to Christ—and their present-day conversions invariably indicate the approach of the last judgment.[22] As it did for his father, Romans 11 offered Alonso ample support for his ideas. The Jews never strayed far from the heart of the divine economy of salvation. Their covenant with God had never lost its force and given way to another one. Owing to their God-given laws and prophecies, whose literal sense at no time lost its value, they have retained their singularity as the people of God even in their diaspora.[23]

> For there are many senses in the sacred scriptures that may be understood to be true, useful, and conducive to our salvation. Moreover, the literal sense is primary, more solid, and more memorable. The others proceed from it as if from a sort of root. It is not false to speak of "faithful Israelites" since these are the true Israelites who have joined the Catholic faith to their upright and pious traits of character.[24]

Jews need not give up their identity as Jews in order to find salvation in Christ. In Bruce Rosenstock's words, they "have no distance to traverse to achieve redemption; they have only to receive a fuller illumination from the meridian sun of divine love." They will bring the true covenant to the Gentiles, not the reverse.[25]

Alonso de Cartagena's contemporary Cardinal Juan de Torquemada, whose mother may, perhaps, have hailed from a Jewish home,[26] likewise rallied in support of Iberian Jewish converts to Christianity. In his *Tractatus contra madianitas et ismaelitas* (Treatise against the Pagans and Muslims), Torquemada similarly followed Pablo de Santa María in arguing from Romans 11 that the salvation of the Gentiles depended upon the Jews, and that the covenant between God and the (Jewish) people of Israel remained intact.[27] Torquemada marshals a dozen elements in the message of Romans 11 in order to drive his point home, so that Gentile Christians should not cast aspersions on Jewish converts to the faith owing to their ancestors' lack of belief and fall from divine favor.

1. As demonstrated by Paul himself and the seven thousand who God assured Elijah remained faithful with him, not all Jews had fallen.
2. The fall of the Jews proved useful for the Gentiles, inasmuch as the apostles turned their sights from the Jews toward them when the Jews proved obstinate in rejecting the new faith.
3. If the conversion of the *conversos'* ancestors, the apostles, proved so beneficial, then how much more must one value the contemporary and future conversion of multitudes of Jews?
4. The fall of the Jews hardly lacked a remedy.
5. The conversion of the Jews suits the needs of the church, as Paul himself notes that it will ultimately result in the resurrection of the dead.
6. Those descended from the Jews have a propensity for the good and therefore are reparable for salvation.
7. "All the glory and advancement of those very Gentile converts derives from their assumption into the worthiness of the Jewish people and ingrafting into their roots."
8. "The salvation of the nations somehow proceeds from among the Jews."
9. The steadfastness of the *conversos* in their faith in Christ, given the fall and failure of many other Jews, derives not from their own doing but the gift of God.
10. "The Jews will not remain in their disbelief but are already embracing Christianity."
11. The blindness that has come about among the Jews will come to an end and, as the apostle himself prophesied, "All Israel will be saved."
12. The blindness of disbelief was in fact common to both, namely to Gentiles as well as Jews, so that it is not appropriate for one to malign or insult the other for disbelief.[28]

As Pablo de Santa María had contended before him, Torquemada believed that the conversion of the Jews underlying Christian salvation history was an ongoing process, begun at the time of the apostles and continuing ever since, gaining momentum in the present, and soon to reach completion in the near future. He brought the optimistic exegesis of the eschatology elaborated in

Romans 9–11, whose origins and history we discussed in part 1 of this book, to one of its ultimate expressions. As Rosenstock has concluded, "No earlier commentator provided such an unambiguously positive interpretation of Romans 11 as does Torquemada, bringing together from scattered sources as much traditional exegesis of the passage as he can in order to amass a case for the significance of the Jews for the salvation of gentiles." To Torquemada's mind, only a few Jews had forever forfeited the promise of salvation made by God to their ancestors. In Rosenstock's words, his scheme of the future "seems to make the salvation of the gentiles ancillary to the salvation of the Jews." In the campaigns of both Cartagena and Torquemada to defend the *conversos* in fifteenth-century Spain, "their ultimate line of defence is to agree that Jews cannot, in fact, convert: they have never really been expelled from their covenant with God."[29]

To underscore the novelty in the ideas of Pablo de Santa María and his disciples concerning the Jews in the process of Christian salvation, one can compare them to the views of Alonso de Espina, a contemporary of Alonso de Cartagena and Juan de Torquemada known for his pronounced hatred and mistrust of Jews, *conversos* among them. The harshness of the polemic in his *Fortalitium fidei* (Fortress of the Faith) and his program for discriminating against Jews in Christian society notwithstanding, his expectations for the Jews of the eschaton fell squarely within the mainstream of medieval Christian eschatology.[30] Espina subscribed to none of the Joachimite tendencies that we find among some of his Franciscan confreres on the margins of their order, tendencies discussed above in chapter 5. And, in sharp contrast to Pablo de Santa María, Cartagena, and Torquemada, Espina believed that the Jews and their old law posed a clear and present danger to contemporary Christendom, aggravated by the blasphemous, absurd rabbinic *aggadot* of their Talmud and midrash. Simply put, the Jews, their Mosaic law, and their Talmud impeded the salvation of Christendom; they hardly advanced or facilitated it. As Steven McMichael has summarized, "On one hand, the Jews were in league with heretics, demons, and Muslims; and on the other hand, they were viewed as the main internal enemy of church reform."[31]

Nevertheless, against the backdrop of the Christian traditions we have reviewed in this book, Espina's expectations for the Jews of the approaching end of days hardly deviated from the consensus of most medieval theologians. Granted he linked Antichrist with the tribe of Dan, as many had done before him, but he never identified Antichrist's parents as Jews. Antichrist will release the lost tribes of Israel once confined by Alexander between the fortresses of Gog and Magog and now protected by the Queen of the Amazons. The Jews, surely, will thus number among Antichrist's most adamant supporters, and Antichrist will court their loyalty by circumcising himself, and perhaps by rebuilding the temple in Jerusalem. These and other deeds will identify him as the "man of lawlessness" or "man of sin" in 2 Thessalonians 2:3–4. And yet, eventually Elijah and Enoch will preach and help bring the Jews to acknowledge their error. They will convert to Christianity, and many will die as martyrs in the final rampage of Antichrist and his cohorts.

Like Pablo de Santa María, Espina also quoted Hosea 3 to establish that the Jews will ultimately convert to Christianity. But the similarities between the eschatologies of these two Spanish churchmen do not extend much further. Contrasting Espina and the Joachimite Franciscans, McMichael writes that "in the *Fortalitium Fidei* of Alonso de Espina, the Jews and Judaism find their place in an apocalyptic of devastating consequence."[32] In view of Espina's subscription to the mainstream in medieval Christian apocalyptic thought, these last words might overstate the case, but they certainly accentuate the difference between his ideas and those of Pablo de Santa María, Alonso de Cartagena, and Juan de Torquemada. For Espina, the Jews were the villains of the drama of Christian salvation history; for Pablo and those who followed him, they were the heroes of that drama. Or as Yosi Yisraeli has concluded concerning Pablo,

> For the converted Bishop of Burgos, the story of human salvation was the story of Israel, both prior to and after the establishment of the Church and the calling to the nations. In that sense, the historical Israel never ceased to be a relevant category of spiritual identity, inside or outside the Church, and the spiritual status of converts was determined, among other things, by the bond of their ancestral merits that stretched from the biblical fathers, through the Pharisees and the Apostles and up to their own days.[33]

For Pablo, converts were the key. Curiously, he never indicated that the elite status deriving from their singular role, importance, and status extended to their descendants. Ironically, his descendants actually worked hard to have their ancestor's pedigree cleansed of his Jewish lineage, tracing his roots to the Virgin Mary instead, and in 1604 the king of Spain and the pope endorsed their request. Still, Pablo's books circulated in many more manuscripts and early printed editions than the writings of his son Alonso—or those of Juan de Torquemada. If, in general, he believed that "the story of human salvation was the story of Israel," perhaps, more specifically, his own conversion and career exemplified that story better than anything else.[34]

Chapter 9

Puritans, Jews, and the End of Days

This concluding chapter ventures out of the premodern purview of my book thus far, jumping from Europe of the later Middle Ages to England and New England in the late sixteenth and seventeenth centuries. In so doing, I bypass much of the volatile religious history of the Reformation, some of whose main characters have received little more than passing mention in earlier chapters. And yet, notwithstanding my original intention to restrict this investigation to ancient and medieval sources, the select Puritan preachers considered below proved nothing less than irresistible. Without admitting to any dependence upon—or even acquaintance with—Honorius Augustodunensis or Pablo de Santa María and his disciples, their voices blend many of the distinctive, novel ideas of those medieval theologians, giving the Jews a centrally important and constructive eschatological role more developed and fascinating than any we have already discussed. As a link between the earlier traditions we have reviewed and concern with Jews of the end time in present-day Evangelical Christianity, the Puritans assume lasting prominence in the history of the eschatological Jew.

Puritan Apocalyptic Thought and Judeo-Centrism

Apocalyptic thought and millennial expectation served as driving forces in Protestant Christianity in general and in English Puritanism, from its birth in the sixteenth century, in particular. As one historian has recently proposed concerning their formative impact on a distinctly western European worldview,

> The sixteenth-century Protestant apocalypse created the first genuinely historical vision of Europe. Its devisers based it on institutional development, and, if it incorporated allegory and the manipulation of mystical numbers, it became increasingly independent of them. We need to see the new apocalypse as part of a broader cultural shift, the temporalization of Western thought and outlook. The world increasingly assumed meaning not through its underlying structure, but through its development. Integral to this shift, and hugely strengthening to the Protestant vision, was the relatively new phenomenon of humanism.

Instead of blending the divine word of Scripture and ecclesiastical tradition "into a single, coherent statement of religious truth," as medieval Catholic Scholastics had done, Protestant humanists focused on contemporary Europe in their apprehension of divine revelation as a dynamic temporal process.[1] Previous chapters in this book surely demonstrated that the Middle Ages cultivated a Christian sense of temporality and temporal change[2]—and, for our purposes, with regard to Jews of the past, present, and future. Yet the Puritans developed this concern of their medieval predecessors further. They grounded their theology in the literal meaning of the biblical text, its historical context, its original languages, and its grammar and lexicography; and the apocalypse offered them a most illuminating case in point.

Many have looked to John Bale's *The Image of Both Churches* (1545–1550) as a milestone in the process whereby proto-Puritan and Puritan reformers critiqued and broke with both the Catholic Church and the Church of England. Bale interpreted the Book of Revelation as forecasting an ongoing conflict between "the proud painted church"—namely, the false church of Antichrist (which included the Church of Rome and overly "established" Protestant churches like the Church of England)—and "the poor persecuted church" of God's true saints. This struggle would soon entail the eschatological fulfillment of Paul's prophecies in Romans 11: the entry of the fullness of the Gentiles and the conversion of the Jews. But alongside his vehement critique of the false church and its identification with Antichrist, mentioned no less than 165 times in its twenty-two chapters, Bale's work recalls the structure and eschatology of Augustine's *City of God* (and the rules of Tyconius on which Augustine had relied) and adds little to Christian expectations for the Jew of the end time.[3] Similar yearning for the conversion of the Jews interwoven with a historicist understanding of Revelation appears in the writings of John Foxe (as in his *A Sermon preached at the Christening of a certaine Iew, at London, Conteining an exposition of the xi. Chapter of S. Paul to the Romanes*, 1578)[4] and John Napier (in *A plaine discovery of the whole revelation of Saint John*, 1594),[5] although they too, like Bale, retained traditional medieval, largely Augustinian, and notably negative ideas concerning Jews and Judaism.

Yet from the last decades of the sixteenth century, and for several generations thereafter, there emerged an increasingly prominent current of Judeo-centrism in Puritan eschatology. The Jews as a people would convert and would play a critically central and leading role in the events of the impending millennium. As Catholics and Turks assumed the role of Antichrist in Protestant and Puritan imaginations, the linkage between Antichrist and the Jews dissipated in large measure, if not entirely. The Jews were the Israel whose salvation Paul predicted in Romans 11:26. They constituted the Israel promised redemption, restoration to the Holy Land, and dominion over other nations in the messianic prophecies of Hebrew Scripture. Historians have identified and debated the relative importance of various factors that contributed to this Judeo-centrism: the Puritan commitment to Hebraic scholarship and a literalist reading of the Old Testament; vehement opposition to the Catholic Church and its theology; and political and social developments in seventeenth-century England that prompted connections between eschatological Israel and England in the forthcoming final redemption. One encounters numerous variations on these themes.[6] Some have questioned the degree of their preponderance and impact in contemporary English preaching and theology; and others have argued that Puritan primitivism and a commitment to reliving a golden apostolic age of Christian purity outweighed Puritan millennialism. At the end of the day, however, primitivism and apocalyptic yearning or millennialism hardly precluded each other, even as one can attribute varying measures of significance to either one. As Richard Cogley concludes his defense of a composite, generalizing summary of Puritan Judeo-centrism,

> The idea of a restoration to Palestine is better understood as part of the larger "primitivist dimension in Puritanism." Judeo-centrists understood the millennium as the re-creation of the apostolic church in all its original grandeur. This restoration was to occur in Jerusalem, the city where the apostolic church first existed, and it was to take place among the first Christians, Jewish converts to the religion of Jesus. After its reestablishment in Jerusalem, the apostolic or millennial church would spread among the Gentiles.

The earthly, political dimensions of this restoration of Israel took on a critical importance in this eschatological worldview.

> For Judeo-centric millenarians, the Jews had to reoccupy Palestine so that Christian history could start anew. The lost tribes of Israel were also to repatriate even though they had not been part of the apostolic church. Judeo-centrists assumed that God would right the wayward course of ancient Israelite history by restoring the union of Judah and Israel that had existed during the time of Saul, David, and Solomon. Thus, the millennium involved the restoration of an institution (the apostolic church), a place (Jerusalem), and a people (the Jews and the lost tribes).[7]

Beginning in 1608 with his *The Worldes resurrection, or The generall calling of the Iewes: A familiar commentary upon the eleuenth chapter of Saint Paul to the Romaines*, Thomas Draxe (d. 1618–1619) published a series of works anticipating the conversion of the Jews. His expectations assumed an increasingly political, terrestrial dimension, and in his *Alarum to the Last Judgement* (1615), he wrote that the Jews would return to their homeland, suffer from Turkish aggression, and then find salvation in Christ. In keeping with the teachings of Paul in Romans, "the Iewes being once conuerted, shall bee a most famous, reformed, and *Exemplary Church* of all the world, and all Nations shall flow vnto it, and it shall bee, as it were, a visible heauen vpon earth."[8] Draxe found support for his views in the conversion of Jews throughout the entire course of Christian history, a pattern that would soon reach its climax at the end time: "The calling and conuersion of some Iewes to the *Christian Faith* in all ages, doth conclude that the Iewes are not wholy forsaken, but are rather the first fruites of a greater *Haruest*, and the Fore-runners of a reater *Conuersion*."[9] Significantly, Draxe identifies the Antichrist neither as a Jew nor as hailing from the tribe of Dan, but as the "Bishop, or Pope of Rome."[10]

In 1621, Henry Finch, lawyer, member of Parliament, and sergeant at arms at the court of King James I, published *The World's Great Restauration, or, The Calling of the Jewes*, which he prefaced by reaching out to the Jews in both Hebrew and English. Finch's book reviews a large number of biblical prophecies concerning the future redemption of Israel, Judah, Zion, and Jerusalem—in all of which, he asserts categorically,

> the Holy Ghost meaneth not the spirituall Israel, or Church of God, or Church of God collected of the Gentiles, nor of the Iewes and Gentiles both (for each of these haue their promises seuerally and apart) but Israel properly descended out of *Iacobs* loynes.

The same iudgement is to bee made of their returning to their land and ancient seates, the conquest of their foes, the fruitfulnes of their soile, the glorious Church they shall erect in the land it selfe of Iudah, their bearing rule farre and neere. These and such like are not Allegories, setting forth in terrene similitudes or deliuerance through Christ (whereof those were types and figures) but meant really and literally of the Iewes.[11]

The calling and conversion of the Jews will result in the destruction of their enemies, the glorious restoration of their Davidic kingdom in the Jews' national homeland and its supremacy over the Gentiles, divinely wrought miracles that will induce other nations to submit to Jewish sovereignty, and more. Not even once does Finch include the Jews among the supporters of Antichrist. To the contrary, as he elaborates with regard to the Gog-Magog prophecies in Ezekiel 37–39 and again concerning the concluding chapters of Revelation, the realization of these apocalyptic prophecies will proceed in stages: (1) "the Jewes' first conversion"; (2) "a further progresse of their conversion" including that of the ten lost tribes, the unification of the tribes of Judah and Israel into one, "the bringing of them to their owne country from all the places where they were scattered, their making of one entire kingdome"; (3) their role in the destruction of God's enemies, especially "Gog, out of the land of Magog"; and (4) the establishment of the "Christian Jewish Church."[12] Ultimately, the promise of the millennium will be fulfilled in the supremacy of Israel restored and in "the flourishing felicitie of the Jewish Christian Church."[13] Understandably, Finch recognized the radical, iconoclastic nature of his doctrine and published his work anonymously. Still, he was soon identified as its author and imprisoned for several months, and his book, which aroused considerable controversy, was condemned.[14]

As the seventeenth century ensued, the noteworthy currents of Puritan eschatology made their way from England to New England, where the youthful enthusiasm of the colonial enterprise coupled with the religious convictions of the Puritans led preachers to focus repeatedly on Romans 11 and the ultimate conversion of Israel in a distinctly North American fashion.[15] As one recent study has observed,

The New England Puritans translated these prophecies into their own local and historical reality as part of a millenarian typology. . . . In the colonial transfer of millenarian ideas from Europe to North America, and from the Old Testament into the wilderness of New England (now made an eschatological location), ethnological and theological knowledge converged with constructs of apocalyptic promise. . . .

Without the conversion of the Jews, the millenarians thought, the rule of Christ could not come to pass.[16]

Some reformulated the earlier Iberian identification of the American Indians with the lost tribes of Israel, while others argued that Israel—and the ultimate salvation of Israel—typified the Puritan community in New England. Yet here too we encounter Judeo-centrism in its full-blown expression. In his own treatise on Romans 11, published in 1669, the influential Salem preacher and Harvard College president Increase Mather encapsulated his conclusions at the very top of his title page:

THE MYSTERY OF Israel's Salvation, EXPLAINED and APPLYED: OR, A DISCOURSE Concerning the General Conversion of the ISRAELITISH NATION.
  Wherein is Shewed,

1. *That the Twelve Tribes shall be saved.*
2. *When this is to be expected.*
3. *Why this must be.*
4. *What kind of Salvation the Tribes of* Israel *shall partake of* (viz.) A Glorious, Wonderful, Spiritual, Temporal *Salvation*[17]

In the opening chapter, Mather reviews various interpretations of "all Israel" whose salvation Paul promised in Romans. Of these he rejects several: "that by all Israel is meant some very Few of all *Israel*"; "that by all *Israel* is meant all the elect of God"; and that by all Israel one can "understand, all and every one of the natural posterity of *Jacob*." He then proceeds to explain how he cannot accept figurative readings of apocalyptic prophecies like Daniel 12:2: many of those who sleep in the dust of the earth shall awake, some to everlasting life, and some to shame and everlasting contempt.

I am slow to embrace a metaphorical sence of that Scripture. . . . Why may not the true meaning of the place be this? *viz.* After the *Iews* are brought into their own Land again, and there disturbed with *Gog* and *Magog* (not *Iohn's*, but *Ezekiel's Gog* and *Magog*, at the battel of *Armageddon*) who shall think with great fury to destroy the converted *Israelites*. After this shall begin the resurrection of the dead, some of which, namely, the Saints of the first resurrection, shall be to everlasting life; but other some, *i.e.* the wicked, after the time belonging to the first resurrection is expired, shall be raised to everlasting shame.[18]

Finally Mather interprets the Pauline promise as he deems correct.

> Others think, that by *all Israel*, is meant the body of the *Israelitish* Nation. And that seemeth to be the genuine interpretation of the words; for in other Scriptures, *all* is used to signifie many. . . . So when it is said, *All Israel shall be saved, h.e.* [that is] very many *Israelites* shall be saved. Yea, *all* here noteth, not only many, but most; it signifieth not only a *Majority*, but a very full and large *Generality*. . . . Now as when the fulness of the *Gentiles* shall be brought in, that must not be extended to every particular person, nor yet to a few only, but to the body of *Gentile* Nations, whom that prophesie doth concern; so may we say concerning this *fulness of Israel*. Moreover, such was *Israels rejection*, such must their *re-assumption* into divine favour be. . . . But their rejection was not of every particular person, nor yet of a few only, but of the body of the Nation; so shall their *salvation* be *National*.[19]

The conversion of Jewish Israel stood at the center of Mather's eschatological drama, conversion that would facilitate salvation at once "Glorious, Wonderful, Spiritual, Temporal."[20] Mather's elaborate and lengthy forecast defies any brief summary, but a brief, exemplary quote concerning the ultimate nature of the Jews' salvation must suffice here.

> Justly how long this glorious day shall continue, is not for us to say, for therein the Scripture is silent; Only it is evident, that it will be for Generations one after another. If you look into that place in the Prophet, from whence the Apostle taketh the words of my Text (*viz. Isa.* 59.20, 21.) you will see that *the saved state of Israel* must continue at least for three Generations. See also *Ezek.* 37.25. yea this glory will continue for many Generations, *Isa.* 60.15. Hence *the new heavens and the new earth*, which God will create when the salvation of all *Israel* shall be consummate, is said (not to be for a while, and so to pass away, but) *to remain* before him, *Isa.* 66.22. Yea this glorious state and condition of *Israel* is said *to last for ever*, partly because they shall never more be brought into the hands of any oppressors, and partly because this their glory will be of very long continuance, *Ioel* 3.20.[21]

Rather than proceed in strict chronological order, we now focus on several Puritan writers, in England and in New England, whose noteworthy ideas offer a fitting conclusion to this book.

Thomas Brightman

Thomas Draxe, Henry Finch, Increase Mather, and numerous other Puritans of the seventeenth century shared a debt to the ideas of one writer, who exerted a profound impact upon them. Even most of those historians who question the preponderance and impact of Judeo-centrist millennialism among the Puritans of seventeenth-century England acknowledge that its most influential spokesperson was the preacher and exegete Thomas Brightman (1562–1607).[22] Owing to charges of prophesying and nonconformity, Brightman was suspended from his parish in Bedfordshire in 1604–1605, and books began to circulate only in the wake of his premature death. His three eschatologically focused biblical commentaries appeared first in Latin in Basel and several years thereafter in English translation: on Revelation in 1609 and then in English in 1611 (in Amsterdam); on the last two chapters of Daniel in Latin in 1611 and in English in 1635 (in Amsterdam); and on the Song of Songs in 1614 and in English (in London) in 1644. Despite their printing in England only after the relaxation of restrictions on publications in 1640, Brightman's works had already begun to command attention and alter the conceptual map of Puritan eschatology. Brightman himself underscored the eschatological importance of these three biblical books, observing that their authors—Solomon, Daniel, and John of Patmos—served as three witnesses testifying to the truth of "the happie and longed for vocation of the Iewes."[23]

Modern students of Brightman's exegetical opus consider his commentary on the Apocalypse, *A Revelation of the Revelation*, a veritable blockbuster in the development of Protestant expectations of the end. In a word, one historian has posited, Brightman here "immersed the millennium in the realm of history." His "exegesis of Revelation constituted a unique and influential philosophy of redemptive history in which the millennium, or the advent of the Kingdom of God, was considered to be within time and history."[24] The millennial drama of the end of days prophesied in Revelation had begun to unfold several centuries ago and would soon near its culmination. As time progressed, the respective roles of England, the Puritans, and the saints of God on the one hand, and Rome, the papacy, the Turks, and the forces of Antichrist on the other hand, grew clearer and more concrete. Among the leading players in this drama stood the Jews, whose promised conversion to Christianity would begin within decades and would conclude by the end of the seventeenth century. As another investigator has commented, "The destiny of the world was dependent on the destiny of the Jews and, more specifically, on their restoration to Israel. . . . Thomas Brightman may rightly be seen as the founder of the British tradition of Philo-semitism, and particularly of their [the Jews'] restoration to Jerusalem prior to the second coming of Christ and thus within time and history."[25]

The opening chapter of Revelation proclaims: "Look! He is coming with the clouds; every eye will see him, even those that pierced him; and on his account all the tribes of the earth will wail" (1:7). Brightman identifies "those that pierced him" as the Jews who crucified Jesus upon his first coming; the tribes of the earth he identifies as "the whole nations of the Iews," who now "with abundance of tears bewaile the lewdnesse of their fore-fathers in putting Christ to death." The wailing of the Jews attests to their repentance, and as such demonstrates that John here speaks not of the last judgment, when repentance would be too late, "but rather of that exceeding glory, which shall be made manifest to the world in the calling of the Iews." Lest someone confuse the glory of their calling with that of the last judgment, Brightman emphasizes that "this Booke of the Revelation staieth his discourse in the conversion of these Iews."[26] And, before this opening chapter concludes, he offers additional evidence. All of the seven golden candelabra or lampstands envisioned by John several verses hence and understood as the seven churches "come forth of that one Church of the Iews, as it were out of the shaft [of the menorah], which shaft was more beautiful then [sic] the rest of the branches . . . because, as it seemeth, the Church of the Iewes is to be at length more abundantly filled with the gifts of the holy Ghost, then this of ours that be Gentiles."[27]

Brightman returns to these ideas repeatedly over the course of his commentary, and I offer several examples. Regarding the 144,000 souls sealed for salvation (Revelation 7:4), 12,000 from each of the twelve tribes, he affirms that these include both Jews and Gentiles, in keeping with the predictions of Romans 11. Yet he emphatically rejects the tradition that the tribe of Dan does not appear because the Jewish Antichrist will originate from within it. Rather, the Jews especially will suffer from but "shall revive out the tyranny of Antichrist,"[28] whom Brightman identified as the pope of Rome.[29] Perhaps most significant of all, from the renowned vision of the angels' pouring out "the seven bowls of the wrath of God" in Revelation 16, Brightman accords particular attention to the sixth angel, who "poured his bowl on the great river Euphrates, and its water was dried up in order to prepare the way for the kings from the east" (16:12).[30] The drying of the waters recalls the Israelites' exodus from Egypt, and, inasmuch as "this miracle is proper to this people alone," making way for the kings of the East thus refers to nothing other than the redemption and restoration of the Jews.

> It is no marvell therefore that a peculiar note and cognizance of this people alone, is here put for the men themselves. But what need have they to have a way prepared for them? What, shall they return to Jerusalem againe? There is nothing more certaine, the Prophets do every where directly confirm it and beat upon it.

This restoration of the Jews will hardly entail the renewal of their obser-vance of the ceremonial laws, and of the sacrificial cult of the temple in particular; on the contrary, "they shall worship Christ purely, and sincerely, according to his wil & Commandment alone." Returning to the bowl or vial and the drying up of the river—a miracle that, as noted, pertains exclusively to the Jews—Brightman explains the urgency of his interpretation.

> I do not rashly and on a sudden suppose that this thing onely is treated of in this place, which must either finde a place here, or else it must be wholly concealed in this Book without speaking of it. Wherefore after that Rome shall be thrown down and destroyed, there shall be spread every where a rumor touching this new Christian people, at the hear-ing whereof the Gentiles shall be astonished.

Yet one question remains concerning Revelation's prophecy of the kings of the East.

> But what, are the Iewes Kings?, why not . . .? the Holy Ghost gives the Iewes this magnificall name, because it shall be an honourable thing for them in a special manner, to return again at last to this truth, to which they had been like dead men before, as also to love and honour that truth with very great godlinesse, holinesse and reverent homage, having their unbelieving and obstinate hearts subdued and mollified, and all this after so many ages and after such obdurate contumacy of that Nation.

Not least important, the restoration of the Jews will include political trans-formations: "And besides all this, the whole East shall be in obedience and subjection unto them; so that this people are not called Kings unworthily, in regard to their large and wise Jurisdiction and Empire."

The Jews, Brightman argued, would never number among the citizens in the kingdom of Antichrist.[31] The sacrilegious apostasy of Antichrist proph-esied in 2 Thessalonians could apply only to Gentiles, not at all to Jews. Contrary to traditional Catholic teaching, reaffirmed most recently by Jesuit commentators like Robert Bellarmine, Antichrist will be destroyed, and Rome will fall upon the calling and conversion of the Jews.[32] This calling of the Jews would transpire in stages, the first around 1650, although Bright-man could not predict the precise date of Rome's fall, which he expected soon, with any precision.[33] Revelation 20 prophesied a restoration and resur-rection of the Jews foreshadowing the general resurrection of the dead at the time of the last judgment. Furthermore, despite the common understanding of Romans 11:25–26 that the final salvation of the fullness of the Gentiles would precede that of the Jews, Revelation, Brightman contended, taught otherwise: "Namely, that the Gentiles which shall be saved, shall walk in the light of the Church of the Jews, and that the Kings of the earth shall bring their glory and honour to this new Jerusalem."[34] Indeed, the foundations of the new holy city, the apocalyptic Jerusalem, described in Revelation 21 would not be the apostles, as many of his predecessors had taught, but teachers from among the Jews who "excel above other men."[35] This ultimate, exemplary perfection of the Jews will endure. "The glory of the Iewes shall remain as well intire, and undefiled: as it shall be secure, and free from the fear of the enemies."[36]

One investigator has written that whereas another British Protestant exegete, Brightman's contemporary Hugh Broughton, had dubbed Revelation an elaboration of the apocalyptic forecasts of Daniel for the Gentiles, Brightman considered Daniel a condensed rendition of the prophecies of Revelation written especially for the Jews.[37] As he did in the case of Revelation 20, Brightman insisted that Daniel 11–12 predicted specifically the resurrection of the Jews and not merely the general resurrection of souls that would accompany the second coming of Christ; otherwise, the work would lose its rationale: "That truly is of great weight that Daniels prophecie is deputed and appointed for the Iewes, to whom notwithstanding he bringeth no comfort, if that resurrection spoke of [at] 12.2 be understood of the last and general resurrection."[38] After the kings of Daniel 11:36–40—representing the end-time enemies of the Jews who will bring them much grief and suffering (Rome, the Saracens of the south, and the Turks of the north)—will be overthrown, God will restore the Jews to their land, their glory, and their promised salvation.

> Behold I saie, a plaine and cleere portraiture of the Iewes vocation, not only undertaken and begun ([11:]44.45) but consummate and perfect (ch. 12. 1.2.3) where it shall bee made manifest (I think) without obscuritie. That the resurrection there, is the full restoring of the Iewish nation out of the dust of destruction and their calling to the faith in Christ, whereby those that are dead in sinne are truly raised up againe according to that of the Apostle, If the casting away of them be the reconciling of the world, what shall the receiving of them be, but life from the dead. Rom. 11.15.[39]

Daniel's concluding prophecy encapsulates the history of the Jews, their sufferings, and their restoration from Second Temple times until the end of days: "I trow it shall evidently appeere to any man embracing the truth without contention, that it is the purpose of the spirit in this place to comprise in a short abridgement the whole estate of the people of the Iewes in a continuall orderly succession even to the second coming of Christ."[40] Curiously, Brightman takes care to indicate that not each and every Jew will share in this restoration. Rather, "there shall bee also a choice and difference in this people: Theire deliverannce shal not be so confused to bring all to eternall life, but those onely which together with this outward safetie from these great dangers shall bee by saving faith adopted for sonnes."[41] Yet some of the Jews will "hold so obstinately their legall rites and institutions," that they will refuse the salvation offered them and remain obstinate in their superstition.[42] Brightman begins his count of the 1,290 days symbolizing years in Daniel 12:11—"from the time that the regular burnt offering is taken away and the abomination that desolates is set up"—with the rule of Julian the Apostate, such that the present age will end in 1650. Then the Euphrates will dry, preparing the way for the Jewish kings of the East, as in Revelation 16. Then will the power of the king of the north—not Antiochus as some earlier commentators had understood, but the Turks—begin to decline, and after an additional forty-five years it will collapse entirely, as forecast in the very next verse (Daniel 12:12): "Happy are those who persevere and attain the thousand three hundred thirty-five days." Referring to the restoration of the Jews, Brightman concludes:

> And then indeed shall all the Saincts be blessed, who shall have a glorious resurrection, and be raised out of the dust of destruction, and every one of them shining like the firmament and stares: for this is the time and limit of that resurrection.[43]

"The Church of the Iewes": Brightman and Beyond

Published after his works on Revelation and Daniel, Brightman's commentary on the Song of Songs, the third of his three scriptural witnesses testifying to the Jews' impending restoration, took its place amid an unprecedented wave of exegetical interest in this small but captivating biblical work. Seventeenth-century England saw the publication of over five hundred commentaries on the Song of Songs—perhaps more than all the Christian commentaries composed previously.[44] The charm and passion of its erotic poems, the yearning for renewal and fulfillment in the exchanges between the lovers, and the consensus among Christians that this biblical work necessarily concerned the love between God and his chosen people—all these fueled the burgeoning interest in the Song and resulted in a wide range of interpretations.

As one expert on early modern English culture has aptly noted, "The freedom of interpretation guaranteed by the allegorical status of the Song of Songs allowed the assignations of radically different meanings to the textual metaphors."[45] Of the triad of Brightman's apocalyptic-exegetical works before us, his *Commentary on the Canticles or the Song of Salomon Wherein the Text Is Analised, the Native Signification of the Words Declared, the Allegories Explained, and the Order of the Times Whereunto They Relate Observed* might prove the most intriguing and interesting.

Brightman's commentary boldly veered away from the allegorical consensus still predominant among Catholic exegetes of his day and rehistoricized the symbolic interpretation of the romantic relationship between God and his beloved. Granted, some earlier Christian commentators had taken a historicizing route before Brightman. Nicholas of Lyra, whose commentary on the Song of Songs had appeared in over forty printed editions by the end of the sixteenth century, had understood the Song as a historical allegory depicting the history of the church until the reign of Constantine. And Martin Luther had focused on the reign of the historical King Solomon, while acknowledging that one could implement the lessons of the Song in any proper Christian kingdom with a truly believing ruler. Yet Brightman's interpretation carried the story forward to his own day, and even beyond. Albeit in terms different from those in which Honorius Augustodunensis had imagined her, Brightman likewise restored the newly rehabilitated *Synagoga conversa*, her lavish anatomical beauty vividly elaborated in Song of Songs 7, to center stage and to the front lines of the battle against God's enemies in the drama of the eschaton.[46]

According to Brightman's historical-eschatological reading, Song of Songs first (1:1–4:6) concerns the period of the Old Testament ("the Legall Church"[47]); it then (4:6–6:8) elaborates the history of the Christian church from its foundations until its renewal with the crowning of Queen Elizabeth; the remainder (6:10–8:14) pertains to the final redemption. In the character of the bride depicted in these last chapters of the Song, Brightman distinguished between three sisters. The first and most important of these, represented from Song 6:10–8:5, he identified as "the Church of the Iewes," of more grandeur and greater stature than any other church, the princess whom God will call imminently, and in the wake of whose calling the throne of Antichrist in Rome will be utterly destroyed. This calling of the Jews will itself transpire in two stages: the first depicted through Song 7:6, and the second in the ensuing verses. At the outset, Brightman portrays Christ's calling of the Jews and their ultimate accession to it—as opposed to their previous refusal to recognize their savior.

"I went down to the nut orchard . . ., to see whether the vines had bud-
ded." (Song 6:11)

Such then shall Christ finde the Iewes, when he shall visit them, like
Nuts covered with a hard shell. . . . The hard winter as yet keepeth back
the buds, but at length in fit time, the Sun of righteousnesse shall thaw
that frozen earth, and shall afford a more gentle aire whereby they may
breake forth freely.[48]

"Return, return, O Shulammite! Return, return, that we may look
upon you." (Song 6:13, 7:1 in the Masoretic Text)

These words yeeld two arguments, whereby they may appear properly to belong to the Church of the *Iews*. First, because the exhortation or incouragement is expressed in a word of returning: wherby he
granteth that the Nation which he now calleth, had bin before turned
away: which cannot properly take place in any other, but in the *Iew-
ish* Nation. Secondly, of set purpose for difference sake he calleth her
by her countrey name, of the *Old Salem*: Whereas before confessedly
through the whole Song, he had notified all the citizens of the Church
gathered together as well of the Gentiles as of the Iewes, by the name
of daughters of *Ierusalem*. [Thirdly:] That is to say, by this difference it
might plainly appeare, that he now turned his speech to the old Countrey breed, letting alone the new inhabitants which are free in the City
by Christ. Fourthly, after the Conversion he sheweth the *Shulamite*, by
the similitude of Tents, that she shall deliver her self by Armes from
the power of her enemies, whom she now serveth.[49]

"How graceful are your feet. . . ." (Song 7:1ff.). In the limbs of the
Shulamite admired in this verse and those that follow, Brightman finds
expressions of the future glory of the Church of the Jews, her wonderful
attributes and those of her leaders, the fecundity promised her, her power
and victory over her enemies, her dominion in her land and even over the
remainder of Christendom, and the esteem accorded her by the nations
of the world. Brightman links the details of this description to prophecies
of redemption in the Hebrew Bible—from Isaiah above all, and also from
Jeremiah, Ezekiel, and Zachariah—soon to materialize.[50] And Brightman
understood the verse "Your eyes are pools in Heshbon, by the gate of Bath-
rabbim, your nose is like a tower of Lebanon, overlooking Damascus,"
(7:4) to map out the territories and borders of the land that the Jews, now
faithful to Christ and redeemed from their exile, will ultimately regain as
their inheritance. But here Brightman took care to clarify his rejection of
traditional Jewish messianic hope: "I dreame not of that returne, which

as yet they do, That they may renew the Temple, restore the Ceremonies, and possesse the land in times past promised and given as an earnest of the heavenly. (These things are eternally buried, not worne out by time, but utterly abolished by Christ.)." Perhaps he thus sought to dispel criticism that his radical eschatological expectations for the Jews as a people somehow manifested a preference for Judaism over Christianity. Only then did he offer clarification.

> But I speak of a restoring to their Country, wherin they shall worship Christ according to his Ordinances: which is not contrary to Religion every one knoweth, and all the Prophets seeme to foretell it with one consent. When I think hereof, it seemeth no light Argument, that untill this day that people remaine (although dispersed through the whole world) divided and separated from the Nations with whom they live. A thing truly wonderfull marvellous, but that it appeares plainely to be God's doing.

Brightman proposed an instructive comparison with other nations and ethnic groups of the past.

> We know the *Gothes, Vandals, Hunnes,* and very many other Nations, forsaking their Countries, have also changed their speech, names, and natures. So that (were it not for letters) they cannot be discerned from the people of the Country with whom they live. But the *Iewes* . . . suffer none of our customes to be fastned on them, but in the midst of us, keepe their old name and Ordinance: would we know the cause? First God would have them, for the sale of his despised Sonne, be a spectacle to the world: then also to advise us, lest the people commonly accounted superstitious, should perhaps make saving doctrine suspected by their consenting. Lastly, that he might make plaine his infinite and unmeasurable favour and truth at length, in restoring this people.[51]

As scholars have noted, Brightman emphatically and repeatedly distinguishes between Judaism, rejected by God, and the Jews, who never ceased to play a leading role in the divine plan for the salvation of the world. Why has God had the Jewish people, unlike any other, preserve its ancient name, language, and way of life, retaining its exalted national identity? First, they are to serve as an example, an instructive "spectacle" for the rest of the world; second, to preempt Christian doctrine from arousing any suspicion should the Jews espouse it before the eschaton; and third, to underscore the wonders of their ultimate restoration. God works in strange ways indeed.

What follows in Song 7 affirms that despite God's singular praise, the calling of the Jews has yet to reach completion. In her call (Song 7:11–13), "Come, my beloved, let us go forth into the fields . . ."—that is, outside the cities—the Church of the Jews beckons her savior to join her in returning the many Jews still in the fields, who have yet to convert to Christianity. And with reference to the apocalyptic visions of Daniel, Brightman explains:

> She therefore goeth a hunting, not to catch wilde beasts, but men; very many *Iewes* were yet busied in the countrey without the holy City, for whom all this watching and trouble shall be undertaken; that they may be gathered into one sheepfold, and fitted into one body of Christ with their brethren. This vocation shall so much exceed the former, as the open fields exceed the city, or the whole multitude a small company.[52]

Precisely in these latecomers Brightman discerns the mandrakes mentioned in 7:13, that at long last will emit their pleasant fragrance and heed the call of their elders to assume their places in the community of Christian faithful. And this leads Brightman to underscore the world of difference between the Jews of old, before their entry into the church, and those perfected at the end of days.

> Everything now at length fully perfected, and all the faithfull Iewes fitted into one body of Christ, their affection is wonderfull, made clear by the *Antithesis* of the former Iewes, with whom Christ in times past had to do in the earth, that with wondrous skill, with one and the same labour, he setteth forth as well the accursed hatred of these, as the willing and ready love of those new citizens. The old Iewes despised and refused Christ coming in the flesh and shewing himself a brother: but there shall be nothing better to those [Jews of the end time], nothing that they shall more desire, then that they may enjoy the favour of his presence whereby that horrible wickednesse of despising the Son of God by their elders, may be recompenced by their faith and diligence in holy duties. . . . These later people altogether unlike to those their wicked elders; *Salomon* hath most divinely comprised in these words, as well the wickednesse of those former in refusing Christas, the pietie of those later in imbracing him.[53]

When will all this come about? Brightman, who died in 1607, predicted that the first stage in the Jews' return to Jesus "it is to be expected about the yeer 1650,"[54] and the mass conversion of the remaining Jews to Christianity by the end of the seventeenth century.[55]

Echoes of Brightman's Judeo-centrist and apocalyptic reading of the Song of Songs resound in the works of many other seventeenth-century English exegetes: Nathanael Homes, John Davenport, George Wither, and Thomas Beverley among others. Homes, for example, followed Brightman in understanding that Song 6:10–8:4 forecasts the "general call of the Jews." Admittedly, many have trouble appreciating this, for various reasons. "Some say, there is no Jew to be converted, but what is within us"—meaning that the prophesied salvation of Israel refers not to ethnic Jews but to Christian constituents of a new, spiritual Israel. "Others, that there is no conversion of them, but such as has been in all ages since the Apostles, viz. now and then a sprinkling of two or three in an age. And the Jews themselves, though they expect their restauration, believe not at all *their conversion to our Faith*, but our conversion to theirs."[56] Reviewing the evidence in the Song for such collective Jewish conversion to Christianity, Homes advances four doctrinal observations.[57]

- First, "that certainly there shall be in due time an effectual general call and conversion of the Jews." What Homes termed the "sprinkling" of prior Jewish conversion could not possibly fulfill the promise of Israel's salvation in Romans 11:25–26. "For the Apostle tells us no Mystery, if he tells us only of what is visible before every mans eyes, that ever and anon one or two of the Jews in an age are converted."
- Second, "the conversion of the *Jews* shall be such, and so suddain when their time is come, as shall be little expected by most, and much admired by all."
- Third, the Jews will ultimately illuminate the truths of biblical prophecy and glories of eshcatological Christianity. *"The converted Jews shall have a triple spiritual light above that they had afore conversion, viz. a MORNING light, a MOON light, and a SUN light."*
- And fourth, "the Jews at their general call, lifting up ther formidable Banners, shall be the great smighters of the grand enemies of the Church": Turks, Saracens, and the emperor of Rome.

Like Brightman and Honorius Augustodunensis long before him, Homes interpreted the ensuing description of the bride's body in Song 7 as referring to "the Church (if I may so call it) or the Synagogues of the Jews."[58]

We find one of the most instructive and interesting examples of Brightman's legacy in the Song of Songs exegesis of John Cotton (1585–1652), whose daughter eventually married Increase Mather, whom we considered briefly earlier in this chapter. Cotton served as minister and preacher of Boston in Lincolnshire (England), until political and ecclesiastical pressure—he was deemed a Puritan "nonconformist"—induced him to emigrate to New England. There he distinguished himself as a leading churchman, scholar, and polemicist in the Massachusetts Bay Colony and its capital of Boston. His commentary on the Song of Songs first appeared in 1642, attesting to his familiarity with Brightman's work in its Latin original, and again in a second edition after his death, in 1655. Yet while Brightman took a predominantly theological and eschatological interest in the Song, Cotton's sermons assumed a decisively sociological and pastoral dimension, within the context of the leadership roles and conflicts that occupied him in his Bostonian congregations—first in Lincolnshire and then in Massachusetts. His expectations for the Jews in his postmillennialist rendition of the drama of the end of days closely resembled those of Brightman, meriting explicit reference in the very title of his book: *A BRIEF EXPOSITION Of the whole Book of CANTICLES, OR, SONG OF SOLOMON; Lively describing the Estate of the Church in all the Ages thereof, both Jewish and Christian, to this day: And Modestly pointing at the Gloriousnesse of the restored Estate of the Church of the Iewes, and the happy accesse of the Gentiles, in the approaching daies of Reformation, when the Wall of Partition shall bee taken away.*[59] The Jews will repent and express contrition for their ancestors' refusal to believe in Jesus and join his church; they will glow in the praises of the Shulamite in Song 7; they will take a leading role in the perfection of the world and will fight against the enemies of God's true church: Turks, Tartars, papists. "The Armies of the Jewes shall bee terrible to the Turkes and Tartars, and to the false Prophet then driven from Rome by ten Christian Princes, and associating himselfe to the Turke for succour."[60] But more than Brightman did, Cotton interpreted the Song of Songs as speaking directly to Christian communities, from their part in bringing the Jews into the church to the ways in which the redemption of the Jews will serve their needs.[61]

Cotton depicts the Protestant clergy as wholeheartedly committed to proselytizing among the Jews. He identifies the nut garden where the bridegroom descended in Song 6:11 with the Jewish synagogues; and Christ's "Ministers, that in his Name shall goe into the Garden of Nuts," will facilitate the salvation of Israel. These ministers

shall finde the Jewes as Charets of willing people, ready to march with them, whethersoever in Christs Name they shall call; their soule should no sooner desire it, but they should bee set in all readinesse; where also is intimated the willing readinesse of a willing people among the Gentiles, to convey the Jewes into their owne Countrie, with Charets, and horses, and Dromedaries.

Returne, returne, O Shulamite: returne, returne, that we may looke upon thee. . . . *Returne, returne, O Shulamite, returne.* This call so often repeated, doth imply. First, the earnestnesse of the Ministers that shall call them. Secondly, the haste that they would have them to make in going through with their conversion.

That we may looke upon thee, or behold thee. It is the desire of the Ministers, and of all the Faithfull, to behold this glorious Church when shee shall be called.[62]

Like Brightman, Cotton describes at length how the graphic description of the bride's body in Song 7 pertains to the "Jewish Church"; simply put, "the Iewes converted shall be of much glory and authority, even as the Kings of the Earth."[63] Once the Jews become Christian, as Cotton underscores in his exposition of Song 8, one will behold the miraculous transformation in their character, the astounding contrast between them and their ancestors of old who rejected Jesus.

The Church of the Jewes, both in City and Country thus gathered, doe here expresse her ardent affection to Christ, and due respect of him . . . : she therefore to shew her affection, desireth that he were now amongst them conversant in their streets againe in bodily presence, shee would not doe then as the old Synagogue did, be ashamed of him, or come to him by night; but she would kisse him, and embrace him in the open streets, and yet no man should then despise her for her so doing as they did; but every one should encourage her in her obsequiousnesse to him: She would not reject him, and thrust him out of the Synagogue, as her old Ancestors had done; but if she found him without, she would lead him, and invite him into their Synagogue, or Temple, there to instruct her, and teach her the will of her father; shee would not give him gall to eat, and Vinegar to drink, as her forefathers had done; but she would cause him to drink of the best delicate spiced wine, and the juice of her Pomegranat.[64]

Cotton presented the three sisters that Brightman had distinguished in the concluding verses of the Song of Songs as three churches, the Jewish Church most exemplary among them. "Who is that coming up from the wilderness, leaning upon her beloved?" (8:5). Cotton explained: "In these words the holy Ghost setteth out the calling and estate of two other Churches after the calling of the Jewes."[65] The example set by the Jewish Church, the admiration she enjoyed in the eyes of the others, and the "the water of Gods Spirit" that would flow from her restored, now spiritual temple would facilitate the entry of these other churches into the community of the faithful.[66]

What advantages, then, will the conversion of the Jews bring to Christendom in general and Cotton's Christian communities in particular? Cotton offered several lists of these advantages, like that of the following six distinct benefits or "uses."

- The first Use of this is for discerning a different estate of all Christian Churches and Congregations, and triall of our owne parishes. . . .
- A second Use is for a discerning of a different estate of all Christian souls, and triall of our owne estates before God. . . .
- A third Use to direct and instruct Ministers and people how to approve themselves and their Congregations in best sort unto Christ. . . .
- A fourth Use may be to encourage men to wayes of spotlesse Innocency; they are not disgracefull, but blessed of the Faithfull, and praised, even of them that are without. . . .
- Fifthly, to reprove the children of the separation, who reproach the Church in stead of blessing, or praising them. . . .
- Sixthly, this may teach us to expect a powerfull and glorious calling of the Jewes in all the particulars before described: say, they bee now, as *Gideons* Fleece, dry; when the Gentiles are moystned with heavenly dew, they shall againe be moystened, when we shall seeme dry in comparison of them. Though *Leah* step first into *Iacobs* Bed, and so the lesse comely Church of the Gentiles into the fellowship with Christ; yet the Church of the Iewes, as beautifull as *Rachel*, shall in the end finde fellowship with Christ.[67]

Curiously, five of the six benefits to accrue from the return of the Jewish Shulamite will materialize in the spiritual awakening and ecclesiastical renewal that Cotton expected—and demanded—in his communities: among members of the clergy, congregational leaders, and the body of the faithful en masse. Geopolitically, the eschatological destiny of the Jews will play out above all in the lands of the Mediterranean. But prophecies concerning the eschatological Jew will eventually bear their true fruit not only in the political ascendancy and dominion of the Jewish people, as Brightman and others contended, but in the flourishing of reformed churches in Britain, Europe, and even North America. Cotton's Judeo-centrism extended far beyond the theoretical and the remote. It functioned as a means for preparing the sheep, whom Cotton served as their shepherd, for the second coming of their savior.

Thomas Beverley's *An Exposition of the Divinely Prophetick Song of Songs Which Is Solomons, Beginning with the Reign of David and Solomon Ending in the Glorious Kingdom of our Lord Jesus Christ*, published in 1687, may have been the last English Puritan commentary on the Song to follow Brightman's line of interpretation. In Puritan New England, John Cotton's grandson and Increase Mather's son Cotton Mather (1663–1728) penned two commentaries on the Song of Songs, the second one completed during the first decades of the eighteenth century. Over the course of his career, the younger Mather veered away from the postmillennialist eschatology of his grandfather and father. As one historian has noted, "For a long time, Cotton agreed with his father that a regeneration of the church and the Christianisation of the Jews was to be expected before the Second Coming.' In the years that followed, however, he began to question the imminence of the Jews' conversion," and his visions became "increasingly less corporate, more individualistic, pietistic, and ecumenical," such that the faith of the individual mattered far more than any collective "eschatological significance to the New England Way."[68]

As a result, Brightman's focus on eschatological Jewry fell out of the younger Mather's reading of the Song of Songs almost altogether: "He no longer believed the diasporic Jews had to be collectively brought to Christ before His return." Curiously, like Pablo de Santa María three centuries before him, "Mather thought the prophecies concerning the saving of the 'remnant' of Israel had already found their literal *primum implementum* in the Christianisation of Jewish communities during the Apostolic Age." The true Israel of eschatological prophecy was "the New Israel of the church."[69]

Admittedly, then, the reading of Song of Songs proposed by Brightman may have waned, both in England and in North America. Still, the seeds planted by Brightman and others for attributing a glorious role to the Jewish people in the drama of the end time would continue to bear fruit in the traditions of Christian Zionism that developed in the centuries that followed and to find expression in various Evangelical churches even today. This history falls far beyond the scope of this book. Yet it demonstrates that Christianity's eschatological Jew has not ceased to evoke curiosity and interest. Constructed in the ideas of the church fathers, medieval theologians, Puritans, and others, the eschatological Jew continues to exercise the imagination, fascinating, challenging, and influencing the lives of real Christians and Jews confronted with these ideas.[70]

Afterword

A brief note spanning just several pages, published in *Studia Patristica* at the turn of our own century, observed that the subject of the Jews in "Christian eschatological scenarios" remains "untidy and uncertain, yet significant," and expressed the hope that others would investigate it more thoroughly.[1] The present book of several hundred pages reaffirms the various components of such a conclusion: untidiness, uncertainty, and significance. Qualification and reservation must lie at the core of any summary judgment. As Christians might see it, when Jews reject Jesus Christ, Son of God, as their savior, they epitomize the corruption and antithesis of much that distinguishes Christians and Christianity, pinning their hopes for redemption on Antichrist, agent of Satan and personification of evil, the false messiah par excellence. And yet, Christianity from its inception has linked the perfection of the end time to the enlightenment and repentance of the Jews, as in the prediction of the apostle Paul that, ultimately, "all Israel will be saved." As much as opposition to Christ and his church epitomized by both Jew and Antichrist must be vanquished at the end of days, Christianity's eschatological drama yearns for a happy end that entails the reinstatement of Israel within the community of God's elect. Untidiness aside, however, our subject's significance cannot be disputed. Pursuit of Christianity's "eschatological Jew" aids in unraveling a dimension of the religious imagination that has figured prominently in the history of Christianity in general and Jewish-Christian interaction in particular.

This selective history of Christianity's eschatological Jew has proceeded along three trajectories. First, it has tracked Christian understanding of Paul's prediction in Romans 11 that, in the end, following the conversion of the Gentiles, all Israel will be saved. From Paul himself through the end of the Middle Ages and beyond, ambiguity has abounded in the interpretation of this passage, allowing for different, conflicting understandings of the Israel to be saved, the extent to which this Israel will include the Jews, and just what such salvation entailed. While one can hardly discern a consensus in this exegetical history, the large majority of exegetes landed somewhere in a middle ground: "All Israel" includes neither every Jew nor no Jews at all; and the salvation of Jews mandates their conversion to Christianity. Second, this book has explored connections between the Jews and Antichrist, in his origins, his career, and his characterization. Theologians might debate whether Antichrist would himself be a Jew, would command the Jews' loyalties, and would champion their cause. Here again, few could read such an enduring association out of Christian eschatology entirely. And third, this book has highlighted exceptional instances of Christian thinking about the end time. In these instances, perhaps counterintuitively, the Jews will not merely come to accept and acknowledge Christianity, but will become leaders, perhaps even rulers, of the community of Christian faithful.

After covering the ground we have covered, I would offer several concluding observations. Beyond any Christian ideas that may have stemmed from ancient Jewish messianic thought, the role of the Jew in Christian eschatology documents the depth of Christianity's attachment to its Jewish heritage, an attachment that has never abated. Judaism fueled an identity crisis in early Christianity, before, during, and after the gradual process of separation between synagogue and church. The association of the Jews with Antichrist, the epitome of evil, coupled with the linkage of their salvation with the final redemption of Christendom, underscores the complexity of the feelings harbored by the church toward its progressively more estranged sister, the synagogue. Christianity's prophetic imagination played out the tension between conflicting tendencies in these feelings, striving ultimately toward their apocalyptic synthesis and reconciliation. Christianity's eschatological Jews thus testify to much in the collective self-consciousness of Christendom. I have here sought to identify instances in which they have exerted a profound impact on Western religion and culture, leaving a thorough review of expressions of such impact to future publications.

Additionally, Christian eschatology has contributed directly to the history of antisemitism, for all the debate and qualification concerning the use of the term in political contexts, in the press, and in historical scholarship. The mainstream of Christian eschatology has defined Jewishness as a state of corruption and alienation, temporary by definition, to be renounced as human civilization approaches a climactic conclusion to its terrestrial history. The perfection of Christendom requires that renunciation, and, as bitter experience in ancient, medieval, and modern times has demonstrated, the seekers of that perfection will at times forego no means to realize it. Furthermore, as Christians have worshipped their beneficent savior, sanctified him, and anxiously awaited his future advent, they have defined Jewish messianic expectations in starkly antithetical terms: believers yearn for Christ, the Jews for Antichrist. And as Christians have construed Antichrist individually and collectively, as readily identifiable and as concealed in the workings of society and culture, as omnipresent throughout history and as an apocalyptic beast to appear at the end of time, so has their imagination often given free rein to constructions of the sinister, evil essence of the Jewish other. As such, the story told here sheds additional light on recent studies of the racialization of Jews, Muslims, and other "others" in medieval Christendom. Geraldine Heng writes in her important book, *The Invention of Race in the European Middle Ages*, that "race is a structural relationship for the articulation and management of human differences, rather than a substantive content" essentially inherent in physiological or anatomical difference. Yet the Jews more than any other group, notes Heng, "functioned as the benchmark by which racial others were defined, measured, scaled, and assessed." Perceptions of Jewish affinity with embodiments of cosmic evil like Satan and Antichrist undoubtedly nourished the processes whereby "modalities of racial form thus worked with a near monomaniacal attention to congeal Jews as figures of absolute difference."[2]

Perhaps most important of all, like the hermeneutical Jew as crafted in the doctrine of Augustine and his medieval successors, Christianity's eschatological Jew is far from a real Jew, but rather a theological construction. As we have seen in various instances—Augustine, Joachim and his followers, Alonso de Espina, and others discussed above—the relative harshness or leniency of churchmen regarding the Jews of their own day did not necessarily correspond to the fate that they envisioned for the Jews of the eschaton. Moreover, just as eschatological Jews are not real Jews, they might well not be Jewish. For nearly all Christian exegetes, the ultimate salvation envisioned by Paul for Israel—to the extent that Israel denoted the Jewish people—presupposed their acceptance of Jesus and their conversion to Christianity.

Especially for those who allocated a centrally important role to *Synagoga conversa* in the drama of the eschaton—from Honorius Augustodunensis, to Joachim and the Joachites, to the Puritans—the gap between eschatological Jewry and the religion of Judaism appears immense. Even so, some—like Pablo de Santa María, his son Alonso de Cartagena, and his disciple Juan de Torquemada—persisted in their conviction that Jews need not give up their identity as Jews in order to find salvation in Christ. The essence of God's biblical covenant with the Jews remains intact, they believed, in a way that defies traditional Christian notions of supersessionism.

Much like eschatology in general, Christianity's eschatological Jew bespeaks a quest for perfection and resolution. The role awaiting the Jews of the end time continued—and continues still—to exercise the imagination long after the chronological purview of this book reached its outer limit. As the title of a recent collection reminds us, the end is all around us[3]—in literature, from the scholarly to the most popular, in art, on television and in film, and in messages imparted by present-day spiritual leaders to their flocks. As long as that end tarries in its arrival, definitive answers to the ultimate questions that preoccupy us will remain elusive.

Notes

Introduction

1. "Pastor at US Embassy Opening in Jerusalem Says Trump Is 'on the Right Side' of God," *Vox*, 14 May 2018, https://www.vox.com/2018/5/14/17352676/robert-jeffress-jerusalem-embassy-israel-prayer; "Robert Jeffress, Pastor Who Said Jews Are Going to Hell, Led Prayer at Jerusalem Embassy," *New York Times*, 14 May 2018, https://www.nytimes.com/2018/05/14/world/middleeast/robert-jeffress-embassy-jerusalem-us.html.

2. Bede, *De temporum ratione 69*, CCSL 123B:538; Bede, *The Reckoning of Time*, trans. Wallis, 241–42; see also Darby, *Bede and the End of Time*, and "Bede's History of the Future."

3. Cohen, *Living Letters of the Law: Ideas of the Jew in Medieval Christianity*.

1. Paul and the Mystery of Israel's Salvation

In quoting from the Bible, I have generally followed the New Revised Standard Version (NRSV) or the Douay-Rheims translation of the Vulgate.

1. Among others, see Harrill, *Paul the Apostle: His Life and Legacy in Their Roman Context*; and Fredriksen, *Paul: The Pagans' Apostle*; on Paul's developing attitudes toward the Jews and Judaism, see also the helpful studies of Boyarin, *A Radical Jew: Paul and the Politics of Identity*; and Penna, "The Evolution of Paul's Attitude toward the Jews."

2. Wagner, *Heralds of the Good News: Isaiah and Paul "in Concert" in the Letter to the Romans*, 305, 346–52.

3. Hübner, "New Testament Interpretation of the Old Testament," 1,1:345; see also Hübner, *Gottes Ich und Israel: Zum Schriftgebrauch der Psalmen in Römer 9–11*, and *Biblische Theologie des Neuen Testaments*, 2:239–58.

4. Longenecker, *The Epistle to the Romans: A Commentary on the Greek Text*, 8.

5. Hays, *Echoes of Scripture in the Letters of Paul*, 35; and *The Conversion of the Imagination: Paul as Interpreter of Israel's Scripture*. See also Aageson, "Scripture and Structure in the Development of the Argument in Romans 9–11," and "Typology, Correspondence, and the Application of Scripture in Romans 9–11"; Hofius, "Das Evangelium und Israel: Erwägungen zu Römer 9–11," and "All Israel Will Be Saved: Divine Salvation and Israel's Deliverance in Romans 9–11"; Lodge, *Romans 9–11: A Reader-Response Analysis*; Moo, "Paul's Universalizing Hermeneutic in Romans"; Kirk, "Why Does the Deliverer Come in *Ek Siōn* (Romans 11.26)?"; and Belli, *Argumentation and Use of Scriptures in Romans 9–11*, among others.

6. See the discussion in Wagner, *Heralds of the Good News*, ch. 4, esp. 238–40: "'The Remnant' and 'the Rest'"; and Heil, "From Remnant to Seed of Hope for Israel: Romans 9:27–29."

7. See these verses—embellished by Paul—as numbered in NRSV, corresponding to 2:25 and 2:1 in the Hebrew original.

8. See Piper, *The Justification of God: An Exegetical and Theological Study of Romans 9:1–23.*

9. Cook, "The Ties That Blind: An Exposition of II Corinthians 3:12–4:6 and Romans 11:7–10," 134–36; and see the comments of Sievers, "'God's Gifts and Call Are Irrevocable': The Reception of Romans 11:29 through the Centuries and Jewish-Christian Relations," cited below, in chapter 2, note 2. A prior version of this study appeared as Sievers, "A History of the Interpretation of Romans 11:29."

10. Merkle, "Romans 11 and the Future of Ethnic Israel," 709.

11. Studies of Paul, his theology, and Romans are legion, and we cannot begin to survey the pertinent literature. See the helpful overviews in Donfried, *The Romans Debate: Revised and Expanded Edition*; Talbert, "Paul, Judaism, and the Revisionists"; Westerholm, *Perspectives Old and New on Paul: The "Lutheran" Paul and His Critics*; Garlington, *Studies in the New Perspective on Paul: Essays and Reviews*; Zetterholm, *Approaches to Paul: A Student's Guide to Recent Scholarship*; and the broad range of essays collected in Wilk and Wagner, *Between Gospel and Election: Explorations in the Interpretation of Romans 9–11.*

12. See Reasoner, "Romans 9–11 Moves from Margin to Center, from Rejection to Salvation," 89: "The chapters we call Rom 9–11 are no longer a parenthesis in the letter; they are now a controlling locus for how an exegete reads the whole letter."

13. See the helpful overview of recent scholarship in Reasoner, "Romans 9–11 Moves from Margin to Center, from Rejection to Salvation," along with the studies of Campbell, *Paul's Gospel in an Intercultural Context: Jew and Gentile in the Letter to the Romans, Paul and the Creation of Christian Identity,* and "The Addressees of Paul's Letter to the Romans: Assemblies of God in House Churches and Synagogues?"; Spencer, "Metaphor, Mystery, and the Salvation of Israel in Romans 9–11: Paul's Appeal to Humility and Doxology." Older but still instructive views are argued in Refoulé, ". . . Et ainsi tout Israël sera sauvé": *Romains 11, 25–32,* and "Cohérence ou incohérence de Paul en Romains 9–11"; Getty, "Paul and the Salvation of Israel: A Perspective on Romans 9–11"; Chilton, *Studying the Historical Jesus: Evaluations of the State of Current Research.*

14. Stowers, *A Rereading of Romans: Justice, Jews, and Gentiles,* 21–41 and passim.

15. Gager, *Reinventing Paul,* ch. 4.

16. Fredriksen, *Paul,* 156–57, 247 n. 63; on the importance of this "New Perspective," see also Snyder, "Major Motifs in the Interpretation of Paul's Letter to the Romans," esp. 61–63; and other works cited below.

17. See also Cook, "The Ties That Blind," esp. 134–36, and "Paul's Argument in Romans 9–11," which incorporates Jewish readings of Paul into this subsequent interpretation history.

18. Barclay, "A Rereading of Romans: Justice, Jews, and Gentiles," 650–51. More recently, see also Barclay, *Paul and the Gift,* esp. 556–61.

19. Longenecker, *Introducing Romans: Critical Issues in Paul's Most Famous Letter,* 247–53, 409–21, and *The Epistle to the Romans,* 769–900; see also Harding, "The Salvation of Israel and the Logic of Romans 11"; and Cranford, "Election and Ethnicity: Paul's View of Israel in Romans 9.1–13."

20. Moo, *The Epistle to the Romans*, 553; and see also Moo, "Paul's Universalizing Hermeneutic in Romans."

21. Sanders, *Paul and Palestinian Judaism*; *Paul, the Law, and the Jewish People*; and *Comparing Judaism and Christianity*; Dunn, *The New Perspective on Paul: Collected Essays*. See also Snyder, "Major Motifs in the Interpretation of Paul's Letter to the Romans"; Garlington, *Studies in the New Perspective on Paul*; Zetterholm, *Approaches to Paul*, chs. 4–5.

22. Eisenbaum, *Paul Was Not a Christian: The Original Message of a Misunderstood Apostle*, 2; and see Dunn, *The New Perspective on Paul*, and "A New Perspective on the New Perspective on Paul."

23. Donaldson, "'Riches for the Gentiles' (Rom 11:12): Israel's Rejection and Paul's Gentile Mission," 81–82; cf. also Haynes, "'Recovering the Real Paul': Theology and Exegesis in Romans 9–11"; Cosgrove, "The Church with and for Israel: History of a Theological Novum before and after Barth," and *Elusive Israel: The Puzzle of Election in Romans*; Patte, "A Post-Holocaust Biblical Critic Responds," and the other essays in the same collection.

24. Above all, see the various studies of Dunn: *Paul and the Mosaic Law*; *The Theology of Paul the Apostle*; *The New Perspective on Paul*; and "A New Perspective on the New Perspective on Paul."

25. For example, Räisänen, *Paul and the Law*, "Paul, God, and Israel: Romans 9–11 in Recent Research," and "Torn between Two Loyalties: Romans 9–11 and Paul's Conflicting Convictions."

26. Westerholm, "The 'New Perspective' at Twenty-Five," 37–38.

27. Above all Westerholm, *Perspectives Old and New on Paul*. See also Westerholm, "The New Perspective on Paul in Review"; and Mason, "Paul, Classical Anti-Jewish Polemic, and the Letter to the Romans."

28. Moo, "John Barclay's Paul and the Gift and the New Perspective on Paul," 281.

29. George, "Modernizing Luther, Domesticating Paul: Another Perspective," 449, with n. 13, where he adduces support even from the writings of Dunn; and cf. Grindheim, *The Crux of Election: Paul's Critique of the Jewish Confidence in the Election of Israel*, and Thomas, "Hermeneutics of the New Perspective on Paul."

30. Mussner, "Ganz Israel wird gerettet werden (Röm 11:26)"; Gager, *The Origins of Anti-Semitism: Attitudes toward Judaism in Pagan and Christian Antiquity*, chs. 11–15, and *Reinventing Paul*; Gaston, *Paul and the Torah*; Stowers, *A Rereading of Romans*; Hogeterp, "The Mystery of Israel's Salvation: A Re-Reading of Romans 11:25–32 in Light of the Dead Sea Scrolls," and *Expectations of the End: A Comparative Traditio-Historical Study of Eschatological, Apocalyptic, and Messianic Ideas in the Dead Sea Scrolls and the New Testament*, 226–27; and others.

31. Among others, see Johnson, "The Structure and Meaning of Romans 11"; Holtz, "Das Gericht über die Juden und die Rettung ganz Israels (1 Thess 2,15f und Röm 11,25f)"; Hvalvik, "A 'Sonderweg' for Israel: A Critical Examination of a Current Interpretation of Romans 11:25–27"; Donaldson, "Jewish Christianity, Israel's Stumbling, and the Sonderweg Reading of Paul"; Gathercole, "Locating Christ and Israel in Romans 9–11."

32. For example, Beker, "Romans 9–11 in the Context of the Early Church"; Martyn, "The Covenants of Hagar and Sarah"; Boyarin, "The Subversion of the Jews: Moses's Veil and the Hermeneutics of Supersession"; Wasserberg, "Romans 9–11

and Jewish-Christian Dialogue: Prospects and Provisos"; Räisänen, "Torn between Two Loyalties."

33. Marshall, "Quasi in Figura: A Brief Reflection on Jewish Election, after Thomas Aquinas," 477.

34. Wright, "Romans 9–11 and the 'New Perspective,'" 50.

35. Vlach, *The Church as a Replacement of Israel: An Analysis of Supersessionism*, 27 (emphasis Vlach's).

36. Goodrich, "Until the Fullness of the Gentiles Comes In: A Critical Review of Recent Scholarship on the Salvation of 'All Israel' (Romans 11:26)." See also Stanley, "'The Redeemer Will Come *Ek Siōn*': Romans 11.26–27 Revisited"; Scott, "'And Then All Israel Will Be Saved' (Rom 11–26): Introduction"; Zoccali, "'And So All Israel Will Be Saved': Competing Interpretations of Romans 11.26 in Pauline Scholarship"; Johnson, "Paul and 'the Israel of God': An Exegetical and Eschatological Case-Study"; Kim, "Reading Paul's Καὶ Οὕτως Πᾶς Ἰσραὴλ Σωθήσεται (Rom. 11:26a) in the Context of Romans"; Venema, "In This Way All Israel Will Be Saved: A Study of Romans 11:26"; González Martínez, "Interdependencia entre Judíos y Gentiles en Rm 11,25–27"; Staples, "What Do the Gentiles Have to Do with 'All Israel'? A Fresh Look at Romans 11:25–27"; Garroway, *Paul's Gentile-Jews: Neither Jew nor Gentile, but Both*; du Toit, "The Salvation of 'All Israel' in Romans 11:25–27 as the Salvation of Inner-Elect, Historical Israel in Christ," esp. nn. 1–2.

37. Harding, "The Salvation of Israel and the Logic of Romans 11:11–36."

38. See Kyrychenko, "The Consistency of Romans 9–11"; Thielman, *From Plight to Solution: A Jewish Framework for Understanding Paul's View of the Law in Galatians and Romans*, 123–32; Campbell, *Paul and the Creation of Christian Identity*; Fredriksen, *Paul*; and others.

39. Pitts, "Unity and Diversity in Pauline Eschatology," 89–91.

40. See also the interesting study of Johnson Hodge, *If Sons, Then Heirs: A Study of Kinship and Ethnicity in the Letters of Paul*.

41. Reasoner, "Romans 9–11 Moves from Margin to Center, from Rejection to Salvation," 88.

42. Meeks, "On Trusting an Unpredictable God: A Hermeneutical Meditation on Romans 9–11," esp. 124; among many, many others, see also Hafemann, "Paul and His Interpreters"; Wright, "Romans 9–11 and the 'New Perspective'"; Eastman, "Israel and Divine Mercy in Galatians and Romans"; Gromacki, "Israel: Her Past, Present, and Future in Romans 9–11"; and Nanos, *Reading Paul within Judaism: Collected Essays of Mark D. Nanos*.

43. Philippe Buc's study of the formative role of Protestant anti-Catholic polemic in shaping modern social scientific categories in religious studies proves suggestive and illuminating along these lines; see Buc, *The Dangers of Ritual*, pt. 2.

2. The Pauline Legacy

1. Martin Luther, *Scholien—Epistola ad Romanos*, in *Werke* 56:436–37; Martin Luther, *Lectures on Romans*, trans. Pauck, 315.

2. For annotated lists of Romans commentaries until the early fourteenth century, see Affeldt, "Verzeichnis der Römerbriefkommentare der lateinischen Kirche bis zu Nikolaus von Lyra"; Affeldt, *Die weltliche Gewalt in der Paulus-Exegese: Rom.13,*

1–7 in den Römerbriefkommentaren der lateinischen Kirche bis zum Ende des 13. Jahrhunderts, 256–85; Froehlich, "Romans 8: Pauline Theology in Medieval Interpretation," 241–42 n. 7. See also the important surveys of Schelkle, *Paulus, Lehrer der Väter: Die altkirchliche Auslegung von Römer 1–11*; Caubet Iturbe, "Et sic omnis Israel salvus fieret, Rom 11, 26: Su interpretación por los escritores cristianos de los siglos III–XII"; Judant, *Judaïsme et Christianisme: Dossier Patristique*; Parmentier, "Greek Church Fathers on Romans 9"; Taylor, "The Freedom of God and the Hope of Israel: Theological Interpretation of Romans 9." One must, of course, acknowledge the seminal contributions of Joseph Sievers, who, more than anyone else, has carefully and thoughtfully reviewed the interpretation history of Romans 11:29–32: "For the gifts and the calling of God are irrevocable. Just as you were once disobedient to God but have now received mercy because of their disobedience, so they have now been disobedient in order that, by the mercy shown to you, they too may now receive mercy. For God has imprisoned all in disobedience so that he may be merciful to all." See Sievers, "A History of the Interpretation of Romans 11:29," and "'God's Gifts and Call Are Irrevocable': The Reception of Romans 11:29 through the Centuries and Jewish-Christian Relations"; and cf. also Nanos, "'The Gifts and the Calling of God Are Irrevocable' (Romans 11:29): If So, How Can Paul Declare That 'Not All Israelites Truly Belong to Israel' (9:6)?"

3. Heckart, "Sympathy for the Devil?," 49.

4. Among the works on Origen and his biblical exegesis that have proven helpful here, see—among very many others—Trigg, *Origen: The Bible and Philosophy in the Third-Century Church* (1983), and *Origen* (1998); Crouzel, *Origen: The Life and Thought of the First Great Theologian*; Tzamalikos, *Origen: Philosophy of History and Eschatology*. On his Romans commentary and its Latin translation by Rufinus: Hammond Bammel, *Der Römerbrieftext des Rufin und seine Origenes-Übersetzung*; Roukema, *The Diversity of Laws in Origen's Commentary on Romans*; Scheck, *Origen and the History of Justification: The Legacy of Origen's Commentary on Romans*, and "Origen's Interpretation of Romans"; Coccini, "Paul and the Destiny of Israel in Origen's Commentary on the Letter to the Romans"; Prinzivalli, "A Fresh Look at Rufinus as a Translator"; Madden, "A Rapprochement between Origen and the 'New Perspective' on Paul: Christ and the Law in Origen's Commentary on Romans"; Bagby, *Sin in Origen's Commentary on Romans*. And on his encounter with Jews and Judaism: Bietenhard, *Caesarea, Origenes und die Juden*; De Lange, *Origen and the Jews: Studies in Jewish-Christian Relations in Third-Century Palestine*; Gorday, *Principles of Patristic Exegesis: Romans 9–11 in Origen, John Chrysostom, and Augustine*, ch. 3; Hammond Bammel, "Die Juden im Römerbriefkommentar des Origenes"; McGuckin, "Origen on the Jews"; O'Leary, "The Recuperation of Judaism"; Hirshman, *A Rivalry of Genius: Jewish and Christian Biblical Interpretation in Late Antiquity*, chs. 7–8; Clark, "Origen, the Jews, and the Song of Songs: Allegory and Polemic in Christian Antiquity"; Rizzi, "Some Reflections on Origen, Celsus, and Their Views on the Jews"; Roukema, "Origen, the Jews, and the New Testament." I have here presented Origen-Rufinus simply as Origen, adopting the working assumptions of Scheck, *Origen and the History of Justification*, 3–5, though of course remaining aware that Rufinus might have modified the form, contents, and import of the commentary in no small measure.

5. Origen, *Commentaria in Epistolam ad Romanos* 7.11, in *Der Römerbriefkommentar*, ed. Hammond Bammel, 3:612. In preparing my translations, I have consulted Origen, *Commentary on the Epistle to the Romans: Books 6–10*, trans. Scheck, FOC 104.

6. Origen, *Commentaria in Epistolam ad Romanos* 8.1, 8.11, 3:644, 699–704.

7. Origen, *Commentaria in Epistolam ad Romanos* 7.12, 3:615–16.

8. On this understanding of the name Israel, see Hayward, *Interpretations of the Name Israel in Ancient Judaism and Some Early Christian Writings*, ch. 5.

9. Origen, *Commentaria in Epistolam ad Romanos* 8.6, 3:670–71.

10. Origen, *Commentaria in Epistolam ad Romanos* 8.6, 3:672.

11. Origen, *Commentaria in Epistolam ad Romanos* 8.7, 3:673.

12. Origen, *Commentaria in Epistolam ad Romanos* 7.17, 3:633–34, where the term appears repeatedly.

13. See Paul's quotation from Hosea in Romans 9:22–26; and cf. above, chapter 1, note 7.

14. Romans 9:22; Origen, *Commentaria in Epistolam ad Romanos* 7.17, 3:634; cf. 8.5, 3:659–60.

15. Origen, *Commentaria in Epistolam ad Romanos* 8.7, 3:675. Cf. 3:673: "ipse dederit oculos *residuo Israhel* quibus non videat."

16. Origen, *Commentaria in Epistolam ad Romanos* 8.8, 3:683.

17. De Lange, *Origen and the Jews*; Gorday, *Principles of Patristic Exegesis*, esp. ch. 3; Reasoner, *Romans in Full Circle: A History of Interpretation*, esp. 121–22, on the one hand; McGuckin, "Origen on the Jews"; O'Leary, "The Recuperation of Judaism", on the other hand.

18. Origen, *Commentaria in Epistolam ad Romanos* 8.8, 3:685–86.

19. In pointed rhetorical fashion, Origen preempts a putative retort to his theory by addressing his reader directly: Might not God have dealt similarly with the Gentiles and their inevitable sins, rewarding some but not others, so that such treatment would not be unique to Israel alone, but that the good, just God would treat all equally? "You, the reader, should explore this matter yourself." Origen, *Commentaria in Epistolam ad Romanos* 8.8, 3:686.

20. Origen, *Commentaria in Epistolam ad Romanos* 8.11, 3:699–700.

21. Origen, *Commentaria in Epistolam ad Romanos* 8.9, 3:691.

22. See above, note 14.

23. Origen, *Commentaria in Epistolam ad Romanos* 8.11, 3:704.

24. Origen, *Commentaria in Epistolam ad Romanos* 8.5, 3:663.

25. Origen, *Commentaria in Epistolam ad Romanos* 8.4, 3:656.

26. Origen, *Commentaria in Epistolam ad Romanos* 8.1, 3:641.

27. Origen, *Commentaria in Epistolam ad Romanos* 8.7, 3:676. For instructive insights concerning this question, see Bagby, "Volitional Sin in Origen's Commentary on Romans."

28. Origen, *Commentaria in Epistolam ad Romanos* 8.8, 3:683. Fredriksen, *Augustine and the Jews: A Christian Defense of Jews and Judaism*, 423 n. 17, has questioned: "But how significant is this . . .? Origen anticipated the final redemption of all rational beings . . . even Satan himself." Yet see Satran, "The Salvation of the Devil: Origen and Origenism in Jerome's Biblical Commentaries"; Heckart, "Sympathy for the Devil? Origen and the End"; and Holliday, "Will Satan Be Saved? Reconsidering Origen's Theory of Volition in *Peri Archon*" for a conflicting view. Cf. the recent proposal for reconciling the two interpretations in Ramelli, *The Christian Doctrine of Apokatastasis: A Critical Assessment from the New Testament to Eriugena*, 154–55, with n. 413: "Origen

thought that the devil will be saved not as devil, enemy, and death, but as a creature of God, after he has been healed and is no enemy anymore, but has returned to the Good, that is, to God. . . . In the very end, the devil himself will voluntarily submit to Christ-Logos and will thereby be saved. . . . Not even a fool would maintain that the devil is to be saved, since not even sinners will enter the Kingdom of God, clearly meaning that *until* they are sinners and have not repented they will not enter. Likewise, neither will the devil, until he repents."

29. Origen, *Commentaria in Epistolam ad Romanos* 8.8, 3:684.

30. Origen, *Commentaria in Epistolam ad Romanos* 8.11, 3:702.

31. Origen, *Commentaria in Epistolam ad Romanos* 8.11, 3:702–3; see also *In Jeremiam Homilia* 5.4, SC 232:290–93; and *Commentaria in Matthaeum* 17.5, GCS 40:590.

32. See above, note 15 and elsewhere; and for other instances of these terms, albeit with inconsistent conclusions, see Origen, *In Leviticum homilia* 3.5, 5.11, GCS 29:309, 353–54, and *In librum Iudicum homilia* 6.1, GCS 30:498.

33. Origen, *Commentaria in Epistolam ad Romanos* 8.11, 3:703.

34. Origen, *Commentaria in Epistolam ad Romanos* 8.11.

35. See Origen, *In librum Iesu Nave* 8.5, GCS 30:341; and see Gorday, *Principles of Patristic Exegesis*, 94. One wonders curiously concerning the possible link between such a posteschatological stage in Origen's thinking and his idea of continually repeating world cycles; on the latter, see Trigg, *Origen*, 108–10.

36. See, for example, Origen, *In Genesim homilia* 5.5, GCS 29:64; *In Exodum homilia* 6.9, GCS 29:199–200; *In Leviticum homilia* 3.5, 5.11, GCS 29:309, 353–54; *In Numeros homilia* 6.4, GCS 30:36.

37. Among others, see Ramelli, *The Christian Doctrine of Apokatastasis*.

38. Fredriksen, *Augustine and the Jews*, 423 n. 17; and cf. the viewpoints in the works cited above, note 28.

39. Among many others, see De Lubac, *Medieval Exegesis: The Four Senses of Scripture*, ch. 4; Scheck, *Origen and the History of Justification*; Ramelli, *The Christian Doctrine of Apokatastasis*; McClymond, *The Devil's Redemption: A New History and Interpretation of Christian Universalism*.

40. John Chrysostom, *Adversus Iudaeos homilia* 1.6, PG 48:852; trans. in Meeks and Wilken, *Jews and Christians in Antioch in the First Four Centuries of the Common Era*, 97.

41. Quasten, *Patrology*, 3:442.

42. Mitchell, "'A Variable and Many-Sorted Man': John Chrysostom's Treatment of Pauline Inconsistency," 93.

43. Mihoc, "Saint Paul and the Jews According to Saint John Chrysostom's Commentary on Romans 9–11," 125, 138.

44. Reasoner, "Romans 9–11 Moves from Margin to Center, from Rejection to Salvation," 88 n. 62. Cf. O'Leary, "The Recuperation of Judaism," 373: "Though Origen is more benign toward Judaism than any other of the fathers, the powerful recuperative dynamic of his thought, which aimed 'to appropriate the Old Testament and with it the heritage of Judaism for the Christian Church,' had a more enduring negative effect than the ill-considered vituperations of a Chrysostom." Cf. also Rémy, "Jean Chrysostome, interprète de Romains 9–11: Un regard chrétien sur les Juifs et les Gentils."

45. Gorday, *Principles of Patristic Exegesis*, 129–30.

46. John Chrysostom, *In Epistolam ad Romanos homilia* 19.6, PG 60:592. With occasional modification, I have followed the translation in *The Homilies of St. John Chrysostom*, trans. Morris et al., SLNPNF 1.11—here 493.

47. On Chrysostom, his attitudes toward the Jews, and his commentary on Romans, see also Gorday, *Principles of Patristic Exegesis*, ch. 4; Wilken, *John Chrysostom and the Jews: Rhetoric and Reality in the Late Fourth Century*; Trakatellis, "Being Transformed: Chrysostom's Exegesis of the Epistle to the Romans"; Kelly, *Golden Mouth: The Story of John Chrysostom, Ascetic, Preacher, Bishop*; Ritter, "John Chrysostom and the Jews: A Reconsideration"; Horst, "Jews and Christians in Antioch at the End of the Fourth Century"; Hall, "John Chrysostom."

48. Cf. the study of Chrysostom's comments concerning Jesus's Jewishness: Garroway, "The Law-Observant Lord: John Chrysostom's Engagement with the Jewishness of Christ."

49. Origen, *Commentaria in Epistolam ad Romanos* 7.11, 3:612.

50. John Chrysostom, *In Epistolam ad Romanos homilia* 16.1, PG 60:549; trans. 460.

51. John Chrysostom, *In Epistolam ad Romanos homilia* 16.3, PG 60:552; trans. 462.

52. John Chrysostom, *In Epistolam ad Romanos homilia* 17.1, PG 60:564; trans. 472.

53. John Chrysostom, *In Epistolam ad Romanos homilia* 18.1–2, PG 60:575–76; trans. 480–81.

54. John Chrysostom, *In Epistolam ad Romanos homilia* 19.1, PG 60:583–84; trans. 487.

55. John Chrysostom, *In Epistolam ad Romanos homilia* 19.3, PG 60:587.

56. John Chrysostom, *In Epistolam ad Romanos homilia* 19.2, PG 60:585; trans. 488.

57. John Chrysostom, *In Epistolam ad Romanos homilia* 19.7, PG 60:592; trans. 493.

58. John Chrysostom, *In Epistolam ad Romanos homilia* 8.2, PG 60:457; trans. 387–88.

59. John Chrysostom, *In Epistolam ad Romanos homilia* 9.1, PG 60:467; trans. 395.

60. John Chrysostom, *In Epistolam ad Romanos homilia* 19.7, PG 60:592; trans. 494 (with modifications).

61. The extant fragments of Theodore's commentary on Romans 9–11 appear in Staab, *Pauluskommentare aus der griechischen Kirche*, 143–59, here 143; cf. PG 66:833–60. An annotated English translation appears in "Theodore of Mopsuestia, *Commentary on Romans*: An Annotated Translation," trans. Gregory, here 82 (ad 9:1–5).

62. Theodore of Mopsuestia, *Commentary on Romans* ad 9:25–26, ed. Staab, 148, trans. 91–92.

63. See above, note 20 and chapter 1.

64. Theodore of Mopsuestia, *Commentary on Romans* ad 11:11, ed. Staab, 155–56, trans. 104 (following NRSV).

65. Theodore of Mopsuestia, *Commentary on Romans* ad 11:25–26, ed. Staab, 159, trans. 109.

66. On Ambrosiaster, his exegesis, and the possibility of his Jewish origins, see, above all, the still foundational works of Souter, *A Study of Ambrosiaster*, and *The Earliest Latin Commentaries on the Epistles of St. Paul*, ch. 2; and Speller, "Ambrosiaster and the Jews"; Hunter, "'On the Sin of Adam and Eve': A Little-Known Defense of Marriage and Childbearing by Ambrosiaster," 283–87; Bray, "Ambrosiaster."

67. Ambrosiaster, *Ad Romanos* 9.13.3, CSEL 81,1:314–15; with occasional modification, I have followed *Ambrosiaster's Commentary on the Pauline Epistles: Romans,* trans. De Bruyn, here 177.

68. Ambrosiaster, *Ad Romanos* 11.10.2–5, CSEL 81,1:368–71; trans. 206–7 (with modification).

69. Ambrosiaster, *Ad Romanos* 9.27, CSEL 81,1:332–33; trans. 186.

70. One finds similar ambiguity in the repeated observation of Hilary of Poitiers, *Tractatus in Psalmos* 59.13, 121.4, 126.10, that upon the entry of the full number of the Gentiles "relicum Israhel"—not "omnis Israhel"—will be saved; CSEL 22:201, 573, 620.

71. Ambrosiaster, *Ad Romanos* 11.1, CSEL 81,1:362–63; trans. 203 (emphasis mine).

72. Ambrosiaster, *Ad Romanos* 10.3, CSEL 81,1:342–45; trans. 193, translating *malivolentia invidiae* as "spiteful ill will," thereby avoiding the term "envy," which Ambrosiaster elsewhere associates with those who failed to believe owing to their ignorance. Cf. Ambrosiaster, *Commentaries on Romans and 1–2 Corinthians*, ed. Bray, 83: "malice or envy."

73. Ambrosiaster, *Ad Romanos* 11.22.1a, CSEL 81,1:378–79.

74. Ambrosiaster, *Ad Romanos* 11.10.5a, CSEL 81,1:371.

75. Ambrosiaster, *Ad Romanos* 10.3, CSEL 81,1:342–45; trans. 193.

76. See the sources cited in Cohen, *Living Letters of the Law: Ideas of the Jew in Medieval Christianity*, 214 n. 140.

77. See also Cohen, "The Jews as the Killers of Christ in the Latin Tradition, from Augustine to the Friars"; Cohen, *Christ Killers: The Jews and the Passion from the Bible to the Big Screen*, ch. 4.

78. Above, note 68.

79. See Ambrosiaster, *Ad Romanos* 11.28.2, CSEL 81,1:384–87; trans. 214, which does appear to leave the door open for a most welcome return of the Jews to the faith.

80. See Ambrosiaster, *Ad Romanos* 11.28.2, CSEL 81,1:384–87; trans. 214.

81. See Sievers, "'God's Gifts and Call Are Irrevocable,'" 130–35, on the mistaken rendition of the Greek adjective *ametameleita* as a noun, applying ostensibly to the beneficiary rather than the gifts (and giver), and its impact on subsequent Latin exegesis.

82. Pelagius, *Expositio in Romanos* 11.26, in Pelagius, *Expositions of Thirteen Epistles of St. Paul*, 2:91; I have followed the translation in Pelagius, *Commentary on St Paul's Epistle to the Romans*, trans. De Bruyn, 129 (with modifications).

83. On Pelagius and his doctrine concerning sin and salvation, see, among numerous others, Brown, "Pelagius and His Supporters: Aims and Environment"; Burns, "The Interpretation of Romans in the Pelagian Controversy"; Basevi, "La justificación en los comentarios de Pelagio, Lutero y Santo Tomás a La Epístola a los Romanos"; Markus, "The Legacy of Pelagius: Orthodoxy, Heresy, and Conciliation"; Johnson, "Purging the Poison: The Revision of Pelagius' Pauline Commentaries by Cassiodorus and His Students"; Rees, *Pelagius: Life and Letters*, esp. ch. 4; Scheck, "Pelagius's Interpretation of Romans"; and De Bruyn's introduction to Pelagius, *Commentary on St Paul's Epistle to the Romans*, esp. 46–49.

84. Pelagius, *Expositio in Romanos* 11.17, 2:89; trans. 127.

85. Pelagius, *Expositio in Romanos* 11.1, 2:85; trans. 124.

86. Pelagius, *Expositio in Romanos* 11.11, 2:88; trans. 126–27.

87. Pelagius, *Expositio in Romanos* 11.17, 2:86–87; trans. 125–26.

88. Pelagius, *Expositio in Romanos* 11.25, 2:91; trans. 129.

3. The Latin West

1. See Augustine's *Expositio quarundam propositionum ex Epistola ad Romanos* and *Epistolae ad Romanos inchoata expositio*, in Fredriksen, *Augustine on Romans: Propositions from the Epistle to the Romans, Unfinished Commentary on the Epistle to the Romans*. In addition to Fredriksen's introduction, see also her valuable studies linking Augustine's interpretation of Romans and his attitudes toward the Jews, especially "*Excaecati occulta justitia Dei*: Augustine on Jews and Judaism," "Divine Justice and Human Freedom: Augustine on Jews and Judaism," 392–98," "*Secundum Carnem*: History and Israel in the Theology of St Augustine," "Allegory and Reading God's Book: Paul and Augustine on the Destiny of Israel," "Augustine and Israel: *Interpretatio ad litteram*, Jews, and Judaism in Augustine's Theology of History," and *Augustine and the Jews: A Christian Defense of Jews and Judaism*, 280–81, 362–64, 422–23 n. 17. I have responded to Fredriksen's reading of Augustine's anti-Judaism in Cohen, "'Slay Them Not': Augustine and the Jews in Modern Scholarship," and "Revisiting Augustine's Doctrine of Jewish Witness"; and I presented my own interpretation in Cohen, *Living Letters of the Law: Ideas of the Jew in Medieval Christianity*, ch. 1. On Augustine's Romans exegesis in particular, see also, among others, Babcock, "Augustine's Interpretation of Romans"; Zumkeller, "Der Terminus 'sola fides' bei Augustinus"; Hammond Bammel, "Augustine, Origen, and the Exegesis of St. Paul"; Bright, "Augustine."

2. Augustine, *Epistolae* 149.18, CSEL 44.364; Augustine, *Letters*, trans. Parsons, FOC 20:253 (with modifications). See also my discussion of this theme in Cohen, *Be Fertile and Increase, Fill the Earth and Master It: The Ancient and Medieval Career of a Biblical Text*, 245–59.

3. Augustine, *Expositio quarundam propositionum ex Epistola ad Romanos* 70, in Fredriksen, *Augustine on Romans*, 40–41.

4. Augustine, *Epistolae* 149.20, CSEL 44.365–66; trans. 253–54. Jews could air similar arguments in responding to Christian charges of deicide; see Cohen, *Christ Killers: The Jews and the Passion from the Bible to the Big Screen*, 147–48.

5. Augustine, *Epistolae* 149.20, CSEL 44.365; trans. 253 (with modification). See the comments of Sievers, "'God's Gifts and Call Are Irrevocable': The Reception of Romans 11:29 through the Centuries and Jewish-Christian Relations," 135–36; and the medieval Jewish arguments cited in Cohen, *Christ Killers*, 147–48; and Ben-Shalom, "Between Official and Private Dispute: The Case of Christian Spain and Provence in the Late Middle Ages," 24–29.

6. Above, chapter 2, note 9.

7. Augustine, *Tractatus adversus Iudaeos* 5.6, PL 42:55; trans. in Augustine, *Treatises on Marriage and Other Subjects*, ed. Deferrari, FOC 27:398.

8. Augustine, *De praedestinatione sanctorum* 16.33; trans. in Augustine, *Four Anti-Pelagian Writings*, trans. Mourant and Collinge, FOC 86:258. And see Sievers, "'God's Gifts and Call Are Irrevocable.'"

9. Augustine, *De civitate Dei* 4.34, in *The City of God against the Pagans*, ed. McCracken et al., 2:128–29.

10. Augustine, *Epistolae ad Romanos inchoata expositio* 20–23, in Fredriksen, *Augustine on Romans*, 82–89.

11. Cohen, "The Jews as the Killers of Christ in the Latin Tradition, from Augustine to the Friars," esp. 8–10.

12. See Blumenkranz, "Augustin et les Juifs. Augustin et le judaïsme"; Cohen, *Living Letters of the Law*, pt. 1; and Fredriksen, *Augustine and the Jews*, pt. 3.

13. Augustine, *De civitate Dei* 20.29, 6:432–33.

14. Joachim, *De ultimis tribulationibus* 31 (ll. 310–14): "Testantur etiam hoc duo magni doctores, Augustinus et Gregorius, videlicet quod ad predicationem Helie Iudeorum populus convertetur ad Deum, secundum quod et apostolus de eorum conversione testatus et est dicens: Cum plenitudo gentium intraverit, tunc omnis Israel salvus fiet."

15. Blumenkranz, "Augustin et les Juifs. Augustin et le judaïsme," 235–36 with n. 46; Lipton, *Images of Intolerance: The Representation of Jews and Judaism in the Bible Moralisée*, 114–15, 204 nn. 6–7; Thornton, "Jews in Early Christian Eschatological Scenarios," 568; Van Liere, "Christ or Antichrist? The Jewish Messiah in Twelfth-Century Christian Eschatology"; and cf. Fredriksen, *Augustine and the Jews*, 328, 422–23 n. 17.

16. Cassiodorus (Ps.-Primasius), *In Epistolam ad Romanos commentaria*, PL 68:489.

17. Cassiodorus, *In Epistolam ad Romanos commentaria*, PL 68:492.

18. Cassiodorus, *In Epistolam ad Romanos commentaria*, PL 68:493.

19. Cassiodorus, *In Epistolam ad Romanos commentaria*, PL 68:491.

20. Cassiodorus, *In Epistolam ad Romanos commentaria*, PL 68:487.

21. Cassiodorus, *In Epistolam ad Romanos commentaria*, PL 68:472–73. On Cassiodorus's debt to Pelagius, see Johnson, "Purging the Poison."

22. John the Deacon (Ps.-Jerome), *Commentarius in Epistolam ad Romanos*, PL 30:699.

23. *Expositio Pauli Epistolae ad Romanos*, CCCM 151:77–112 nn., passim.

24. Cf. below, chapter 8.

25. See Frank's helpful dissertation, "The Unbelieving Jews in the Epistle of Paul to the Romans, Chapter 9–11: A Study of Selected Latin Commentaries from Atto of Vercelli (885–961) to Giles of Rome (1274–1316)"; and the studies of Heil, *Kompilation oder Konstruktion? Die Juden in den Pauluskommentaren des 9. Jahrhunderts*; Harris, "Enduring Covenant in the Christian Middle Ages."

26. Sedulius Scotus, *Collectanea in Epistolam ad Romanos*, PL 103:106.

27. Atto of Vercelli, *Expositio in Epistolam ad Romanos*, PL 134:244.

28. Gregory the Great, *Moralia in Iob* 30.9.32, CCSL 143B:1512–13.

29. Haymo of Auxerre, *Homilia* 139, PL 118:741.

30. Herveus of Bourg-Dieu, *Expositio in Epistolam ad Romanos* 11, PL 181:757–58. On Elijah and Enoch and their eschatological role in both Jewish and Christian traditions, see, among others, Milikowsky, "Elijah and the Messiah," and "Trajectories of Return, Restoration, and Redemption in Rabbinic Judaism: Elijah, the Messiah, the War of Gog, and the World to Come"; Petersen, *Preaching in the Last Days: The Theme of "Two Witnesses" in the Sixteenth and Seventeenth Centuries*; Weaver, *Theodoret of Cyrus on Romans 11:26: Recovering an Early Christian Elijah Redivivus Tradition*; Cazanave, "Hénoch

et Elie: 'Et c'est la fin des temps pour quoi ils sont ensemble . . .'." More recently, on the entangled relationship of Jewish and Christian traditions concerning Elijah's eschatological role, see the illuminating dissertation of Shacham-Rosby, "Elijah the Prophet in Medieval Franco-German (Ashkenazi) Jewish Culture" [Hebrew].

31. William of Saint-Thierry, *Expositio in Epistolam ad Romanos* ad 11:26, CCCM 86:156–57.

32. Peter Lombard, *Collectanea in Epistolam Pauli ad Romanos*, PL 191:1489–91.

33. *Glossa ordinaria* ad Romans 11:25–26, *Biblia latina cum glossa ordinaria*, 4:298.

34. Haymo, *Homilia 2*, PL 118:24.

35. Rabanus Maurus, *Enarrationes in Epistolam ad Romanos*, PL 111:1534.

36. Bruno the Carthusian, *Expositio in Epistolam ad Romanos*, PL 153:95, 97–98. On the attribution of this work, see Spicq, *Esquisse d'une histoire de l'exégèse latine au moyen âge*, 55; Smalley, *The Study of the Bible in the Middle Ages*, 48.

37. Peter the Venerable, *Adversus Iudaeorum inveteratam duritiem 5*, CCCM 58:127.

38. Otto of Freising, *Chronica sive historia de duabus civitatibus* 8.7, 594, refers to the future conversion of the Jews as fulfilling Isaiah's prophecy concerning the remnant of Israel, invoked by Paul in Romans 9:27.

39. See Cohen, "The Jews as the Killers of Christ in the Latin Tradition"; and the more recent studies of Watt, "Parisian Theologians and the Jews: Peter Lombard and Peter Cantor"; and Resnick, "Talmud, Talmudisti, and Albert the Great," 80–85.

40. Peter Abelard, *Expositio in Epistolam ad Romanos* ad 9:27, 3:650; trans. in his *Commentary on the Epistle to the Romans*, trans. Cartwright, 302.

41. Peter Abelard, *Expositio in Epistolam ad Romanos* ad 11:26, 3:702–4; trans., 323–26.

42. Sievers, "'God's Gifts and Call Are Irrevocable,'" 160 n. 14, writes that Abelard was the first to link the eschatological roles of Enoch and Elijah to his understanding of Romans 11:26, but see the more recent study of Weaver, *Theodoret of Cyrus on Romans 11:26*.

43. See Isidore, *De fide catholica contra Iudaeos* 2.13.3–5, PL 83:519–20; cf. also 2.5.8, cols. 509–10.

44. I have used Thomas's *Commentary on the Letter of Saint Paul to the Romans*, trans. Larcher, ed. Mortensen and Alcarón, emending the English translation as necessary. My thanks to the Aquinas Institute for allowing me to quote from this translation. Numbers in parentheses in the ensuing discussion designate paragraphs in this commentary. On Thomas's *Commentary on Romans*, see also O'Connor, "St. Thomas's Commentary on Romans"; Domanyi, *Der Römerbriefkommentar des Thomas von Aquin: Ein Beitrag zur Untersuchung seiner Auslegungsmethoden*; Ryan, "The Love of Learning and the Desire for God in Thomas Aquinas's Commentary on Romans"; and the essays in Levering and Dauphinais, *Reading Romans with St. Thomas Aquinas*.

45. Tapie, *Aquinas on Israel and the Church: The Question of Supersessionism in the Theology of Thomas Aquinas*, 99, reads: abrogated.

46. Tapie, *Aquinas on Israel and the Church*, 105, with n. 93.

47. See Cohen, "The Jews as the Killers of Christ in the Latin Tradition," and *Christ Killers*, ch. 4; and cf. Synan, "Some Medieval Perceptions of the Controversy on Jewish Law," 117–18.

48. Wisdom of Solomon 1:22; Isaiah 6:10, 29:10, 42:20.

49. In interreligious debate, medieval Jews themselves would ask Christians that if this indeed were the case, why should Christians condemn the Jews for having caused the death of Jesus. An early fourteenth-century handbook for Jewish debaters instructed them to respond to a Christian accusing them of deicide as follows: "You say that he came to die at the hands of man. If so, those who killed him fulfilled his will, and it was through them that his counsel and decree to redeem the souls from hell were carried out, while nothing at all was accomplished through those who did not touch him. Indeed, if the former had also refrained from harming him like the latter, then his entire advent would have been useless and in vain. Consequently, you should reverse your words and say that those who fulfilled his will and through whom his counsel was carried out are the righteous men, while those who did not touch him are wicked because they did not hasten to carry out his counsel so that he might redeem people from hell. Indeed, it is amazing that you call those who hanged him evil men and sinners"; Berger, *The Jewish-Christian Debate in the High Middle Ages: A Critical Edition of the Niẓẓaḥon Vetus*, 136; see also Cohen, *Christ Killers*, 147–49. Echoes of a similar Jewish argument appear already in the second-century poem of Melito of Sardis, *On Pascha*, ll. 528–29, ed. Hall, 41.

50. Above all Boguslawski, *Thomas Aquinas on the Jews: Insights into His Commentary on Romans 9–11*.

51. For instance, Commodian; see below, chapter 4.

52. See Boguslawski, *Thomas Aquinas on the Jews*; Harris, "Enduring Covenant in the Christian Middle Ages," 579–81; Tapie, *Aquinas on Israel and the Church*, 88–106 (esp. 104–5), following Soulen, "They Are Israelites: The Priority of the Present Tense for Jewish-Christian Relations," 497–504. Yet see also the more cautious analysis of Schenk, "Covenant Initiation: Thomas Aquinas and Robert Kilwardy on the Sacrament of Circumcision."

53. *Contra* Matthew Tapie's assertion, *Aquinas on Israel and the Church*, 105, that here "Aquinas explicitly states that circumcision is a *present* spiritual benefit (*praesentis spiritualis beneficii*)," Thomas groups circumcision among *beneficia figuralia, quorum tria sunt figura praesentis spiritualis beneficii*; he does not contend that spiritual benefit either derives from or inheres in the maintenance of circumcision—or any other Jewish rite—at present. Rather, that pact of circumcision *is a figure of the present spiritual benefit* residing among those spiritual men who now constitute the people of Israel. And this comports well with Thomas's explanation of how true circumcision (*circumcisio vera*) is, like true Judaism, inward, not outward, and is that of those who worship God with their hearts—that is, believers in Christ. On Paul's statement (Romans 2:29) that "he is a Jew who is one inwardly (*in abscondito*), and real circumcision is a matter of the heart, spiritual and not literal," Thomas wrote: "Then when he says but he 'who is one inwardly,' he assigns the reason why the uncircumcision of one who [truly] keeps the Law is regarded as circumcision and prevails over [lit., renders judgment over, *iudicet*] bodily circumcision. The reason is that *he is truly a Jew who is one inwardly*, i.e., whose heart is possessed by the precepts of the Law. . . . Again, true circumcision *is of the heart in the spirit*, i.e., made by one's spirit, which expels superfluous thoughts from the heart. Or *in the spirit*, i.e., through a spiritual and *not a literal* understanding of the Law. . . . Hence, inward Judaism and circumcision prevail over the outward" (244–45).

54. Thomas Aquinas, *Summa theologiae* 2–2.10.11, 32:72–73.

55. Investigators have repeatedly highlighted the wavering in Thomas's stance vis-à-vis Jews and Judaism of his day; see, for example, Hood, *Aquinas and the Jews*; Cohen, *Living Letters of the Law*, ch. 9 ("Ambiguities of Thomistic Synthesis"); Levering, *Christ's Fulfillment of Torah and Temple: Salvation According to Thomas Aquinas*; Marshall, "'Quasi in Figura': A Brief Reflection on Jewish Election, after Thomas Aquinas"; Pomplun, "'Quasi in Figura': A Cosmological Reading of the Thomistic Phrase," esp. 508–17; Harris, "Enduring Covenant in the Christian Middle Ages," 579–81; Coolman, "Romans 9–11: Rereading Aquinas on the Jews." All essentially acknowledge that for Aquinas the continued observance of Jewish law constituted mortal sin. While I attempted to demonstrate that, ambiguities notwithstanding, Thomas thereby contributed to the new intolerance toward Judaism in high medieval Christendom, Marshall, Pomplun, and Coolman seek to salvage what they term Aquinas's "unofficial," more accepting inclinations that might comport with the present-day rejection of supersessionism.

56. See Cohen, "*Synagoga Conversa*: Honorius Augustodunensis, the Song of Songs, and Christianity's 'Eschatological Jew.'" Whalen, *Dominion of God: Christendom and Apocalypse in the Middle Ages*, esp. 186–93, contextualizes these ideas most instructively.

57. See the studies cited above, notes 53, 55.

58. Boguslawski, *Thomas Aquinas on the Jews*, 28, 129.

59. *Glossa ordinaria* ad Rom. 11:7, *Biblia latina cum glossa ordinaria*, 4:297; trans. Woodward, *The Glossa Ordinaria on Romans*, 168: "They were aided in their will not to understand what is true, because they knew the truth but were saying it was false. The envy of an evil will merits this. But this is not true for those who act in ignorance."

60. Cited above, note 47.

61. Sievers, "'God's Gifts and Call Are Irrevocable,'" 144, notes that Thomas was the only medieval Christian commentators to accept Ambrosiaster's misreading of Romans 11:29—that one not need repent of one's sins in order to be saved in Christ—and link it to the salvation of the Jews at the end time. See above, chapter 2, note 81.

62. In addition to the works cited below, see Ehrensperger and Holder, *Reformation Readings of Romans*.

63. See Nicholas of Lyra, *Postilla litteralis* ad Romans 11:11, in *Biblia sacra cum glossis*, 6:25r.

64. Nicholas of Lyra, *Postilla litteralis* ad Romans 11:26, 6:26r.

65. Erasmus, *Paraphrasis in Epistolam ad Romanos* ad 10:1, in *Opera omnia*, 7:810; trans. in Erasmus, *New Testament Scholarship: Paraphrases on Romans and Galatians*, ed. Sider, 59.

66. Erasmus, *Paraphrasis in Epistolam ad Romanos* ad 11:25–26, in *Opera omnia*, 7:815, *New Testament Scholarship*, 67 (with slight modification). See also Payne, "Erasmus: Interpreter of Romans," and "Erasmus on Romans 9"; Margolin, "The Epistle to the Romans (Chapter 11) According to the Versions and/or Commentaries of Valla, Colet, Lefèvre, and Erasmus."

67. Erasmus, *Paraphrasis in Epistolam ad Romanos* ad 11:28, in *Opera omnia*, 7:816, *New Testament Scholarship*, trans. 67–68. On Erasmus's attitudes toward Jews and Judaism, see Oberman, "Three Sixteenth-Century Attitudes to Judaism: Reuchlin,

Erasmus, and Luther," esp. 339–42; Oberman, *The Roots of Anti-Semitism in the Age of Renaissance and Reformation*, ch. 4; Markish, *Erasmus and the Jews*; Pabel, "Erasmus of Rotterdam and Judaism: A Reexamination in the Light of New Evidence."

68. See Awad, "The Influence of John Chrysostom's Hermeneutics on John Calvin's Exegetical Approach to Paul's Epistle to the Romans."

69. John Calvin, *Commentarius in Epistolam Pauli ad Romanos* ad 11:26, ed. Parker and Parker, 247. See also Hesselink, "Calvin's Understanding of the Relation of the Church and Israel Based Largely on His Interpretation of Romans 9–11."

70. Martin Luther, *Scholien—Epistola ad Romanos*, in *Werke*, 56:439; trans. Luther, *Lectures on Romans*, ed. Pauck, 317.

71. See above, note 8.

72. Martin Luther, *Scholien—Epistola ad Romanos*, in *Werke*, 56:439; Luther, *Lectures on Romans*, 317. Cf. Calvin, *Commentarius* ad 11:11, 238–39, who also noted the difficulty in understanding this passage. See also Hummel, "'Wrath against the Unrighteous': The Place of Luther's Lectures on Romans in His Understanding of Judaism."

73. Martin Luther, *Scholien—Epistola ad Romanos*, 56:437–38; *Lectures on Romans*, 315.

74. Martin Luther, *Scholien—Epistola ad Romanos*, 56:434; *Lectures on Romans*, 311.

75. Martin Luther, *Vom Schem Hamphoras*, in *Werke*, 53:579–80; trans. Falk, *The Jew in Christian Theology: Martin Luther's Anti-Jewish "Vom Schem Hamphoras,"* 167.

76. Cornelius à Lapide, *Commentaria in sacram scripturam*, 18:194. On Cornelius and his exegetical opus, see McConnell, "Communis omnium patria"; Wim, "Grace, Free Will, and Predestination in the Biblical Commentaries of Cornelius a Lapide"; Luke, "Jesuit Hebrew Studies after Trent: Cornelius à Lapide (1567–1637)."

77. On the origins and development of this tradition, see below, chapters 4–6.

78. Cohen, *Living Letters of the Law*.

Part II. The Jews and Antichrist

1. "Antichrist Is Alive, and a Male Jew, Falwell Contends," *New York Times*, 16 January 1999, A8.

2. Bärsch, "Antijudaismus, Apokalyptik und Satanologie: Die religiösen Elemente des Nationalsozialistischen Antisemitismus," and "Der Jude als Antichrist in der NS-Ideologie: Die kollektive Identität der Deutschen und der Antisemitismus unter religionspolitologischer Perspektive."

3. Boveland et al., *Der Antichrist, und die fünfzehn Zeichen vor dem jüngsten Gericht: Faksimile der ersten typographischen Ausgabe eines unbekannten Strassburger Druckers, um 1480*, 2:3r.

4. *Sielen trost*, cited and translated in Gow, *The Red Jews: Antisemitism in an Apocalyptic Age, 1200–1600*, 222.

5. Adso, *Epistola de ortu et tempore Antichristi*, CCCM 45:23; in quoting from Adso, I have followed the translation of Bernard McGinn in McGinn, *Apocalyptic Spirituality: Treatises and Letters of Lactantius, Adso of Montier-en-Der, Joachim of Fiore, the Franciscan Spirituals, Savonarola*, 89–96, here 90. My thanks to the Paulist Press for permission to quote from this translation.

6. "Falwell Confidential," 22 January 1999, https://liberty.contentdm.oclc.org/digital/api/collection/p17184coll4/id/299/download.

4. Antichrist and the Jews in Early Christianity

1. Fornari, "Figures of Antichrist: The Apocalypse and Its Restraints in Contemporary Political Thought," 53.

2. Among numerous others, see the studies of Bousset, *The Antichrist Legend: A Chapter in Jewish and Christian Folklore*; Rigaux, *L'antéchrist et l'opposition au royaume messianique dans l'Ancien et le Nouveau Testament*; Arrighini, *L'anticristo: Nelle sacre scritture, nella storia, nella letteratura*; Jenks, *The Origins and Early Development of the Antichrist Myth*; Sbaffoni, *Testi sull' anticristo*; Schoeps, Schulte, and Stumpfe, "Der Antichrist"; Ford, "The Construction of the Other: The Antichrist," and "The Physical Features of the Antichrist"; Lietaert Peerbolte, *The Antecedents of Antichrist: A Traditio-historical Study of the Earliest Christian Views on Eschatological Opponents*; Horbury, "Antichrist among Jews and Gentiles," *Messianism among Jews and Christians: Twelve Biblical and Historical Studies*, and "Messianism among Jews and Christians in the Second Century"; McGinn, *Antichrist: Two Thousand Years of the Human Fascination with Evil*; Goff, "Antichrist and His Predecessors: The Incorporation of Jewish Traditions of Evil into Christian End-Time Scenarios"; Lorein, *The Antichrist Theme in the Intertestamental Period*; Potestà and Rizzi, *L'anticristo*; Bădiliță, *Métamorphoses de l'Antichrist chez les Pères de l'Église*; Vicchio, *The Legend of the Anti-Christ: A History*; the essays collected in Brandes and Schmieder, *Antichrist: Konstruktionen von Feindbildern*; Waters, "The Two Eschatological Perspectives of the Book of Daniel"; Almond, *The Antichrist: A New Biography*; along with the essays collected in Collins, McGinn, and Stein, *The Encyclopedia of Apocalypticism*. These publications, their rich notes included, have served as valuable guides to the sources considered below, although I have not always cited them in my references to every ancient or medieval writer.

3. See the thoughtful comments of Reed, "Messianism between Judaism and Christianity," along with additional studies cited in the notes to her essay.

4. Meeks, *The Prophet-King: Moses Traditions and the Johannine Christology*.

5. In addition to the works already cited, see Buitenwerf, *Book III of the Sibylline Oracles and Its Social Setting*, and "The Identity of the Prophetess Sibyl in 'Sibylline Oracles' III"; Lightfoot, *The Sibylline Oracles, with Introduction, Translation, and Commentary on the First and Second Books*; Collins, "Pre-Christian Jewish Messianism: An Overview"; Collins, *Apocalypse, Prophecy, and Pseudepigraphy: On Jewish Apocalyptic Literature*, chs. 7, 15; DiTommaso, "The Apocalyptic Other."

6. Charlesworth, *OTP*, 1:375.

7. Charlesworth, *OTP*, 1:363.

8. Pagels, "The Social History of Satan, the 'Intimate Enemy: A Preliminary Sketch,'" 108–9. Studies of the devil and Satan are legion. Among the many that have proven useful here, see Russell, *The Devil: Perceptions of Evil from Antiquity to Primitive Christianity*, *Satan: The Early Christian Tradition*, and *Lucifer: The Devil in the Middle Ages*; Forsyth, *The Old Enemy: Satan and the Combat Myth*, and *The Satanic Epic*; Uddin, "Paul, the Devil and 'Unbelief' in Israel (with Particular Reference to 2 Corinthians 3–4 and Romans 9–11)"; Kelly, *Satan: A Biography*; Almond, *The Devil: A New Biography*—along with the insightful review of Dendle.

9. Pagels, "The Social History of Satan, Part II: Satan in the New Testament Gospels," 19.

10. Buchholz, *Your Eyes Will Be Opened: A Study of the Greek (Ethiopic) Apocalypse of Peter*, 172–75 (following Buchholz's free translation, emphasis mine). See also the studies of Bauckham, "The Apocalypse of Peter: An Account of Research"; Hills, "Parables, Pretenders, and Prophecies: Translation and Interpretation in the 'Apocalypse of Peter' 2"; Frey, Dulk, and Van der Watt, *2 Peter and the Apocalypse of Peter*.

11. On the text's problematic shift of focus from multiple false messiahs to a single impersonator of Christ, see Hills, "Parables, Pretenders, and Prophecies: Translation and Interpretation in the 'Apocalypse of Peter' 2"; Hill, "Antichrist from the Tribe of Dan," 105–7; Lietaert Peerbolte, *The Antecedents of Antichrist*, 56–61, and the literature cited there.

12. For discussion of the threat to Christians, real or perceived, in the Bar Kokhba rebellion, see also the different opinions of Collins, "The Early Christian Apocalypses," 72–73; Schäfer, *Der Bar Kokhba-Aufstand: Studien zum zweiten jüdischen Krieg gegen Rom*, 60–61, and *The Bar Kokhba War Reconsidered*; Duker Fishman, "The Bar-Kokhva Rebellion in Christian Sources" [Hebrew]; Bauckham, "The Two Fig Tree Parables in the Apocalypse of Peter," "Jews and Jewish Christians in the Land of Israel at the Time of the Bar Kochba War, with Special Reference to the Apocalypse of Peter," and *The Fate of the Dead: Studies on the Jewish and Christian Apocalypses*, ch. 8; Reinhartz, "Rabbinic Perceptions of Simeon Bar Kosiba"; Van de Water, "Bar Kokhba and Patristic Interpretations of the 'Antichrist'"; Bourgel, "Jewish Christians and Other Religious Groups in Judaea from the Great Revolt to the Bar-Kokhba"; Oliver, "Jewish Followers of Jesus and the Bar Kokhba Revolt: Re-Examining the Christian Sources," among others.

13. For an array of opinions, see Brown, *The Epistles of John*; Hakola, "The Johannine Community as Jewish Christians? Some Problems in Current Scholarly Consensus," "The Reception and Development of the Johannine Tradition in 1, 2, and 3 John," and *Reconsidering Johannine Christianity: A Social Identity Approach*; Rensberger, "Conflict and Community in the Johannine Letters"; Streett, *They Went Out from Us: The Identity of the Opponents in First John*; Thatcher, "Cain the Jew the AntiChrist: Collective Memory and the Johannine Ethic of Loving and Hating"; the essays in the valuable collection of Anderson and Culpepper, *Communities in Dispute: Current Scholarship on the Johannine Epistles*; and Cirafesi, "The Johannine Community Hypothesis (1968–Present)."

14. See, for example, Bede ad 2:22, *Super epistolas catholicas expositio*, PL 93:95, and the *Glossa ordinaria* ad 2:21, *Biblia latina*, 4:537.

15. Justin Martyr, *First Apology* 31.5, SC 507:210–11; trans. ANF 1:173.

16. Novenson, *The Grammar of Messianism: An Ancient Jewish Political Idiom and Its Users*, 248 n. 113.

17. Above all, see the helpful study of Hughes, *Constructing Antichrist: Paul, Biblical Commentary, and the Development of Doctrine in the Early Middle Ages*; and see also Davies, "Eschatological Hope in the Early Christian Community"; Wills, *What Paul Meant*, 125–29; de Villiers, "The Future Existence of the Believers According to 2 Thessalonians"; Kucicki, *Eschatology of the Thessalonian Correspondence: A Comparative Study of 1 Thess 4, 13–5, 11 and 2 Thess 2, 1–12 to the Dead Sea Scrolls and the Old Testament Pseudepigrapha*; Johnson, "Paul's 'Anti-Christology' in 2 Thessalonians 2 in Canonical Context."

18. Brown, *The Epistles of John*, 335–36. More recently, see also Müller, "Der Apo-kalyptische Prophet Johannes als Judenchrist: Judenchristliche Traditionen in der Johannesoffenbarung."

19. See esp. Lietaert Peerbolte, *The Antecedents of Antichrist*, pt. 1, esp. 95, 183, 192–93, for discussion of the pertinent passages in the writings of the apostolic fathers and early church fathers, including Justin Martyr, the Didache, and the Epistle of Barnabas.

20. McGinn, *Antichrist*, 58; and cf. Almond, *The Antichrist*, 41: "a cohesive narrative whole."

21. Potestà and Rizzi, *L'anticristo*, 1:30–31.

22. In addition to the works of McGinn and others cited above, note 2, see Orbe, *Antropología de San Ireneo*, and "San Ireneo y el régimen del milenio"; Tsirpanlis, "The Antichrist and the End of the World in Irenaeus, Justin, Hippolytus, and Tertullian"; Smith, "Chiliasm and Recapitulation in the Theology of Irenaeus"; Osborn, *Irenaeus of Lyons*; Steenberg, *Irenaeus on Creation, the Cosmic Christ, and the Saga of Redemption*; Koester, "The Antichrist Theme in the Johannine Epistles and Its Role in Christian Tradition," 189; Almond, *The Antichrist*, 41–47.

23. Irenaeus, *Adversus Haereses* 5.25.1, SC 153:308–11; trans. ANF 1:553 (italic in trans.).

24. Irenaeus, *Adversus Haereses* 5.30.2, SC 153:376–79; trans. ANF 1:559.

25. On the similarities between Irenaeus's description of Antichrist and Euse-bius's subsequent description of Bar Kokhba, see the interesting comments of Hill, "Antichrist from the Tribe of Dan," 107 n. 15.

26. In addition to the works already cited, see Dunbar, "The Eschatology of Hip-polytus of Rome," "The Delay of the Parousia in Hippolytus," and "Hippolytus of Rome and the Eschatological Exegesis of the Early Church"; Weinrich, "Antichrist in the Early Church"; Hill, "Antichrist from the Tribe of Dan," and *Regnum Caelorum: Patterns of Millennial Thought in Early Christianity*; Cerrato, *Hippolytus between East and West: The Commentaries and the Provenance of the Corpus*, and "Hippolytus and Cyril of Jerusalem on the Antichrist"; Norelli, "Un 'testimonium' sur l'Antichrist (Hippolyte, *L'Antichrist* 15 et 54)"; Travassos Valdez, *Historical Interpretations of the "Fifth Empire": The Dynamics of Periodization from Daniel to António Vieira, S.J.*, ch. 5; Schmidt's introduc-tion to Hippolytus of Rome, *Commentary on Daniel and "Chronicon"*; and Rüpke, "Writ-ing the First Christian Commentary on a Biblical Book in Ancient Rome."

27. Hippolytus of Rome, *De Christo et Antichristo* 14–15, GCS 1,2:11–12; trans. ANF 5:207.

28. Hippolytus, *De Christo et Antichristo* 25, 17–18; trans. ANF 5:209.

29. Hippolytus, *In Danielem* 4.49.5, SC 14:364–65; trans. Schmidt, Hippolytus of Rome, *Commentary on Daniel and "Chronicon,"* 179–80 (with slight modification).

30. Hippolytus, *De Christo et Antichristo* 54, GCS 1,2:36; trans. ANF 5:215.

31. Hippolytus, *De Christo et Antichristo* 57, GCS 1,2:37; trans. ANF 5:216.

32. Hippolytus, *De Christo et Antichristo* 6, GCS 1,2:7–8; trans. ANF 5:206.

33. Litwa, *Refutation of All Heresies* 9.30.5–7, 692–93.

34. Trans. in Frankfurter, *Elijah in Upper Egypt: The Apocalypse of Elijah and Early Egyptian Christianity*, 313–15.

35. On Nero in early Christian Antichristology, see the helpful survey of Law-rence, "Nero Redivivus"; along with the more nuanced discussions of Trudinger,

"The 'Nero Redivivus' Rumour and the Date of the Apocalypse of John"; Kreitzer, *The New Testament in Fiction and Film: On Reversing the Hermeneutical Flow*; McGinn, *Antichrist*, 65–67; Van Henten, "Nero Redivivus Demolished: The Coherence of the Nero Traditions in the Sibylline Oracles"; Klauck, "Do They Never Come Back? Nero Redivivus and the Apocalypse of John"; Gumerlock, "Nero Antichrist: Patristic Evidence for the Use of Nero's Naming in Calculating the Number of the Beast (Rev 13:18)"; Tonstad, "Appraising the Myth of Nero Redivivus in the Interpretation of Revelation." On Julian, Antichrist, and the Jews, see also Kalleres, *City of Demons: Violence, Ritual, and Christian Power in Late Antiquity*, 189–95.

36. Victorinus of Pettau, *Commentarii in Apocalypsin* ad 13.3, CSEL 49:120–21.

37. Commodianus, *Carmen de duobus populis*, CCSL 128:103; for this and the following quotations, I have used (with occasional modification) the translation by D. M. Klein, http://christianlatin.blogspot.com/2008/08/excerpt-from-commodia nus-carmen.html, who incorporates variants from earlier editions. Unsuccessfully, I repeatedly sought permission from Mr. Klein to quote from his translation. See also Sordi, "Commodianus, *Carmen apologeticum* 892 ss.: *Rex ab oriente.*"

38. Commodianus, *Carmen de duobus populis*, CCSL 128:106; trans. D. M. Klein.

39. Commodianus, *Carmen de duobus populis*, CCSL 128:107; trans. D. M. Klein.

40. Commodianus, *Carmen de duobus populis*, CCSL 128:107; trans. D. M. Klein.

41. Commodianus, *Carmen de duobus populis*, CCSL 128:107; trans. D. M. Klein.

42. Commodianus, *Carmen de duobus populis*, CCSL 128:107–8. See the still valuable study of Martin, "Commodianus."

43. See above, chapter 3, note 51.

44. On Gog and Magog, see the studies of Manselli, "I popoli immaginari: Gog e Magog"; Westrem, "Against Gog and Magog"; Bøe, *Gog and Magog: Ezekiel 38–39 as Pre-Text for Revelation 19,17 and 20,7–10*; Scherb, "Assimilating Giants: The Appropriation of Gog and Magog in Medieval and Early Modern England"; Schmidt, "Die 'Brüste des Nordens' und Alexanders Mauer gegen Gog und Magog"; Carbó García, "La venida de Gog y Magog: Identificaciones de la prole del Anticristo entre la tradición apocalíptica, la Antigüedad tardía y el Medievo"; Franke, "Miracles and Monsters: Gog and Magog, Alexander the Great, and Antichrist in the Apocalypse of the Catalan Atlas (1375)," among others.

45. Commodianus, *Carmen de duobus populis*, CCSL 128:112–13; trans. D. M. Klein.

46. Jerome, *Commentarii in Danielem* ad 11:24, SC 602:464; trans. in Jerome, *Commentary on Daniel*, ed. Archer, 131. On the relationship of Jerome's discussion of Antichrist (his *De Antichristo*) to the rest of his commentary on Daniel and the date of its composition, see Courtray, "Nouvelles recherches sur la transmission du *De Antichristo* de Jérôme," who takes issue with the conclusions of François Glorie in the introduction to his edition of the *Commentary* in CCSL 75A. See also Courtray's introduction to the edition we have cited in SC 602, and, on the impact of Jerome's commentary during the Middle Ages, Courtray, "La réception du commentaire sur Daniel de Jérôme dans l'occident médiéval chrétien (VIIe–XIIe siècle)"; Travassos Valdez, *Historical Interpretations of the "Fifth Empire,"* ch. 6.

47. Jerome, *Epistula* 121.11, CSEL 56:55 (emphasis mine); and see the summary and partial paraphrase of the letter in Hughes, *Constructing Antichrist*, 74–79. Cf. also Theodoret of Cyrrhus, *Haereticarum fabularum compendium* 5.23, PG 83:527–28; and Bădiliță, *Métamorphoses de l'Antichrist chez les Pères de l'Église*, ch. 10.

5. Jews and the Many Faces of Antichrist in the Middle Ages

1. In the ensuing discussion, I have regularly drawn from the valuable studies of Rauh, *Das Bild des Antichrist im Mittelalter: Von Tyconius zum deutschem Symbolismus*; Emmerson, *Antichrist in the Middle Ages: A Study of Medieval Apocalypticism, Art, and Literature*; Rusconi, *Profezia e profeti alla fine del Medioevo*; McGinn, *Antichrist: Two Thousand Years of the Human Fascination with Evil*; Potestà and Rizzi, *L'anticristo*; Bădiliță, *Métamorphoses de l'Antichrist chez les Pères de l'Église*; Whalen, *Dominion of God: Christendom and Apocalypse in the Middle Ages*; and have refrained from citing them excessively. Whalen, "Joachim of Fiore, Apocalyptic Conversion, and the 'Persecuting Society,'" and "Joachim the Theorist of History and Society," also proved helpful in appreciating the ramifications of such apocalyptic speculation in their medieval context.

2. Augustine, *De civitate Dei* 20.30, *The City of God against the Pagans*, 6:450–51. Cf. also *Epistula* 199, CSEL 57:243–92; and *In Epistolam Joannis ad Parthos* 3, PL 35:1997–2005.

3. Fredriksen, "Tyconius and Augustine on the Apocalypse," 32.

4. Bede, *De temporum ratione* 69, CCSL 123B:538; trans. Wallis, in Bede, *The Reckoning of Time*, 241–42.

5. Beatus of Liebana, *Tractatus de Apocalipsin* 2.2, CCSL 107:246.

6. Beatus of Liebana, *Tractatus de Apocalipsin* 2.prol. 2, CCSL 107B:179; trans. O'Brien, in Beatus of Liebana, *Commentary on the Apocalypse*, 1:2695.

7. Gregory the Great, *Epistulae* 13.1, in Simonsohn, *The Apostolic See and the Jews—Documents: 492–1404*, 22–23.

8. Isidore of Seville, *De fide catholica contra Iudaeos* 1.25.6, PL 83:593; cf. Theodoret of Cyrrhus, *Haereticarum fabularum compendium* 5.23, PG 83:527–28.

9. Agobard of Lyon, *De iudaicis superstitionibus* 19, CCCM 52:214, largely following the translation in Stow, "Agobard of Lyons and the Origins of the Medieval Conception of the Jew," 64.

10. See Gow, "The Jewish Antichrist in Medieval and Early Modern Germany," 252 n. 11, who takes issue with the attribution of millenarian longings to the rank and file of Christian believers in particular, as (perhaps) suggested by McGinn, *Visions of the End: Apocalyptic Traditions in the Middle Ages*, 16–17; and Aichele, *Das Antichristdrama des Mittelalters der Reformation und Gegenreformation*, 15. For Gow, any "strict division between popular and learned theology is facile and does not address the significant Latin tradition in which the Antichrist appeared as a real person, nor does it take into account communication between various levels of theology: Latin "high" theology, more popular Latin theology, and vernacular exegetical works."

11. McGinn, *Antichrist*, 87–88. On Jewish apocalyptic speculation in the Byzantine Empire and its interaction with Christian tradition, see Berger, "Three Typological Themes in Jewish Messianism: Messiah Son of Joseph, Rabbinic Calculations, and the Figure of Antichrist"; Dan, "Armilus: The Jewish Antichrist and the Origins and Dating of Sefer Zerubbavel"; Latteri, "A Dialogue on Disaster: Antichrists in Jewish and Christian Apocalypses and Their Medieval Recensions"; and the recent work of Himmelfarb, *Jewish Messiahs in a Christian Empire: A History of the Book of Zerubbabel*, along with other studies cited there.

12. Pseudo-Hippolytus, *De consummatione mundi* 20, GCS 1,2:296–97; trans. ANF 5:247.

13. Pseudo-Hippolytus, *De consummatione mundi* 22, GCS 1,2:297–98; trans. ANF 5:247–48.

14. Pseudo-Hippolytus, *De consummatione mundi* 23–24, GCS 1,2:298–99; trans. ANF 5:248 (with slight modification).

15. Pseudo-Hippolytus, *De consummatione mundi* 40, GCS 1,2:305.

16. On these Eastern apocalyptic works, see Alexander, *The Byzantine Apocalyptic Tradition*; Reinink, "Pseudo-Methodius und die Legende vom römischen Endkaiser," "Pseudo-Methodius: A Concept of History in Response to the Rise of Islam," "Pseudo-Methodius and the Pseudo-Ephremian 'Sermo de Fine Mundi,'" and "From Apocalyptics to Apologetics: Early Syriac Reactions to Islam"; Hoyland, *Seeing Islam as Others Saw It: A Survey and Evaluation of Christian, Jewish, and Zoroastrian Writings on Early Islam*, esp. 260–67; Thomas, Roggema, and Monferrer Sala, *Christian-Muslim Relations: A Bibliographical History*, vol. 1, *600–900*, 160–71 (the entries of Harald Suermann and Lutz Greisiger); and Gantner, "Hoffnung in Der Apokalypse? Die Ismaeliten in den älteren lateinischen Fassungen der Revelationes des Pseudo-Methodius"—among others.

17. In addition to studies cited in the previous notes, see Alexander, *The Byzantine Apocalyptic Tradition*, 151–84; Möhring, *Der Weltkaiser der Endzeit: Entstehung, Wandel und Wirkung einer tausendjährigen Weissagung*; Potestà, "The *Vaticinium of Constans*: Genesis and Original Purposes of the Legend of the Last World Emperor"; Bonura, "When Did the Legend of the Last Emperor Originate? A New Look at the Textual Relationship between the Apocalypse of Pseudo-Methodius and the Tiburtine Sibyl," among many others.

18. See Gow, "The Jewish Antichrist in Medieval and Early Modern Germany," 254, along with the classic study of Anderson, *Alexander's Gate, Gog and Magog, and the Inclosed Nations*, still of considerable value.

19. Pseudo-Methodius, *Apocalypse* 13.19–20, 60–63. See also Garstad, "Alexander's Gate and the Unclean Nations: Translation, Textual Appropriation, and the Construction of Barriers."

20. Pseudo-Methodius, *Apocalypse* 13.19–20, 60–63. See also Garstad, "Alexander's Gate and the Unclean Nations."

21. See above, chapter 4, note 42, for the third-century Commodian's praise of the Jewish tribes confined in Persia, and cf. Bădiliţă, *Métamorphoses de l'Antichrist chez les Pères de l'Église*, 513–19.

22. Alexander, *The Byzantine Apocalyptic Tradition*, 194, with n. 7; Sackur, *Sibyllinische Texte und Forschungen: Pseudomethodius, Adso und die tiburtinische Sibylle*, 185.

23. Sackur, *Sibyllinische Texte und Forschungen*, 185; Verhelst, "Scarpsum de dictis sancti Efrem prope fine mundi," 526; Pseudo-Methodius, *Apocalypse* 14.6, 134–35.

24. Pseudo-Ephrem, "Sermon on the End," trans. Reeves, https://pages.uncc.edu/john-reeves/research-projects/trajectories-in-near-eastern-apocalyptic/pseudo-ephrem-syriac/.

25. OTP 1:767; Berger, *Die griechische Daniel-Diegese: Eine altkirchliche Apokalypse*, 15–16 (Greek text marked chs. 10–11). On the Daniel Apocalypse, see, above all, DiTommaso, *The Book of Daniel and the Apocryphal Daniel Literature*, esp. 130–41, 356–59, and "The Apocryphal Daniel Apocalypses," along with other studies cited

therein. On the linkage between such anti-Jewish currents in Byzantine eschatology and debates over imperial policy toward the Jews, including the decrees of Emperor Heraclius to convert them forcibly, see Magdalino, "'All Israel Will Be Saved'? The Forced Baptism of the Jews and Imperial Eschatology."

26. OTP 1:768–70; Berger, *Die griechische Daniel-Diegese*, 16–18 (chs. 12–14).

27. In addition to the studies cited above (note 1), see the still valuable contributions of Konrad, *De ortu et tempore Antichristi: Antichristvorstellungen und Geschichtsbild des Abtes Adso von Montier-en-Der*; Rangheri, "La Epistola ad Gerbergam Reginam *De ortu et tempore Antichristi* di Adsone di Montier-en-Der e le sue fonti"; Verhelst, "La préhistoire des conceptions d'Adson concernant l'Antéchrist," "Adso of Montier-en-Der and the Fear of the Year 1000," and his introduction in CCCM 45:1–19; Emmerson, "Antichrist as Anti-Saint: The Significance of Abbot Adso's *Libellus de Antichristo*"; McGinn, *Antichrist*, ch. 2; MacLean, "Reform, Queenship, and the End of the World in Tenth-Century France."

28. Adso, *Epistola de ortu et tempore Antichristi*, CCCM 45:23; trans. McGinn, in *Apocalyptic Spirituality: Treatises and Letters of Lactantius, Adso of Montier-en-Der, Joachim of Fiore, the Franciscan Spirituals, Savonarola*, 90.

29. Adso, *Epistola*, CCCM 45:23–24; trans. McGinn, 91.

30. See above, chapter 4, note 40.

31. Emmerson, *Antichrist in the Middle Ages*, 80–81.

32. Adso, *Epistola*, CCCM 45:24; trans. McGinn, 91. On the enduring, multifaceted legacy of Adso's circumcised, Judaized Antichrist in the Western worldview—medieval, early modern, and recent—see the interesting, suggestive ruminations of Rhoads and Lupton, "Circumcising the Antichrist: An Ethnohistorical Fantasy."

33. Adso, *Epistola*, CCCM 45:27; trans. McGinn, 94.

34. Adso, *Epistola*, CCCM 45:28; trans. McGinn, 94.

35. Adso, *Epistola*, CCCM 45:28; trans. McGinn, 96.

36. On the confusion and inconsistency in Adso's account, see McGinn, *Antichrist*, 101.

37. Landes, "Lest the Millennium Be Fulfilled: Apocalyptic Expectations and the Pattern of Western Chronography 100–800 CE," "The Fear of an Apocalyptic Year 1000: Augustinian Historiography, Medieval and Modern," and "What Happens When Jesus Doesn't Come? Jewish and Christian Relations in Apocalyptic Time"; McGinn, *Antichrist*, 99–100 (with nn.); the studies collected in Landes, Gow, and Van Meter, *The Apocalyptic Year 1000: Religious Expectation and Social Change, 950–1050*; Whalen, *Dominion of God*, 47–56; Fried, "'999 Jahre nach Christi Geburt: der Antichrist': Wie die Zerstörung des heiligen Grabes zum apokalyptischen Zeichen wurde und die denkfigur universaler Judenverfolgung hervorbrachte."

38. Whalen, *Dominion of God*, 70–71, and, more recently see the important studies of Rubenstein, *Armies of Heaven: The First Crusade and the Quest for Apocalypse*, and *Nebuchadnezzar's Dream: The Crusades, Apocalyptic Prophecy, and the End of History*.

39. Cohen, *The Friars and the Jews: The Evolution of Medieval Anti-Judaism*, ch. 10.

40. Among others, see Heimann, "Antichristvorstellungen im Wandel der mittelalterlichen Gesellschaft"; Flanagan, "Twelfth-Century Apocalyptic Imaginations and the Coming of the Antichrist"; Van Liere, "Christ or Antichrist? The Jewish Messiah in Twelfth-Century Christian Eschatology"; and the studies of Emmerson and McGinn cited above.

41. Pseudo-Methodius, "Epistola de Antichristo," included in Lambert of Saint-Omer's *Liber floridus*, CCCM 45:151–52; and Derolez, *The Making and Meaning of the Liber Floridus*, 113–14, with n. 399; "De Antichristo," published in Ivanov, "A Text on Antichrist in St. Petersburg, National Library of Russia Lat. Q.v.IV.3 and the *Liber Floridus*," 107. Rubenstein, *Nebuchadnezzar's Dream*, 38–40, attributes this departure from Adso's narrative to Lambert himself, although Ivanov (not cited by Rubenstein) tends to prefer a date slightly earlier than that of the *Liber floridus*. See also Verhelst, "Les textes eschatologiques dans *Le Liber Floridus*"; Derolez, *The Autograph Manuscript of the Liber Floridus: A Key to the Encyclopedia of Lambert of Saint-Omer*, 4:112–14.

42. See below, chapter 7.

43. Below, at notes 66–69.

44. William of Saint-Amour, *Liber de Antichristo et ejusdem ministris*, in Martène and Durand, *Veterum scriptorum et monumentorum historicorum, dogmaticorum, moralium, amplissima collectio*, 9:1273–1446, where the work is attributed to Nicholas Oresme. William elaborates his attack on the mendicants in *De periculis novissimorum temporum*. Helpful studies include Szittya, *The Antifraternal Tradition in Medieval Literature*; Traver, "The *Liber de Antichristo* and the Failure of Joachite Expectations"; Geltner, "William of St. Amour's '*De Periculis Novissimorum Temporum*': A False Start to Medieval Antifraternalism?" and *The Making of Medieval Antifraternalism: Polemic, Violence, Deviance, and Remembrance*.

45. Emmerson, *Antichrist in the Middle Ages*, offers a very manageable and instructive overview of the pertinent sources.

46. Rauh, *Das Bild des Antichrist im Mittelalter*, 365.

47. Trans. (with slight emendation) https://www.academia.edu/31354647/THE_PLAY_ABOUT_THE_ANTICHRIST_LUDUS_DE_ANTICHRISTO_TRANSLATED_FROM_THE_LATIN_BY_CAROL_SYMES, forthcoming in *The Play about the Antichrist (Ludus de Antichristo): A Historical Exegesis, Performance Dramaturgy, and Latin Edition*, ed. K. A. Thomas, quoted here with the translator's and editor's permission. I am especially grateful to Carol Symes for sending me the recently revised version of her translation and to Kyle Thomas for his annotated Latin edition.

48. Young, *The Drama of the Medieval Church*, 2:372, ll. 33–43; following Synagoga's speech, we read: "quod et ipsa cantabit in singulis temporibus."

49. Young, *The Drama of the Medieval Church*, 2:383–84, ll. 301–28.

50. Young, *The Drama of the Medieval Church*, 2:385–86, ll. 361–68.

51. Young, *The Drama of the Medieval Church*, 2:387, ll. 398–401.

52. See the introduction to Wright, *The Play of Antichrist*, 57–61 ("The Jews in the 'Play of Antichrist'").

53. See Carr, "Visual and Symbolic Imagery in the Twelfth-Century Tegernsee *Ludus de Antichristo*," 174–218, who notes that "the martyrdom of Synagoga is portrayed nowhere else in medieval imagery" (218).

54. McGinn, *Antichrist*, 135.

55. Emmerson, *Antichrist in the Middle Ages*, 170; and see also Aichele, "The Glorification of Anti-Christ in the Concluding Scenes of the Medieval 'Ludus de Antichristo.'"

56. Among many others, see the still helpful study of Seiferth, *Synagogue and Church in the Middle Ages: Two Symbols in Art and Literature*; along with Cohen, *Christ Killers: The Jews and the Passion from the Bible to the Big Screen*, 186–90; and, more

recently, the important studies of Rowe, *The Jew, the Cathedral, and the Medieval City: Synagoga and Ecclesia in the Thirteenth Century*, including extensive bibliographical references (for the *Ludus*, see 187–88), and Rubin, "Ecclesia and Synagoga: The Changing Meanings of a Powerful Pairing."

57. In addition to the studies cited previously, see also the discussions of the *Ludus* in Günther, *Der Antichrist: Der staufisches Ludus de Antichristo*; Aichele, *Das Antichristdrama des Mittelalters der Reformation und Gegenreformation*; Hempel, "Ludus Typologicus: Die allegorische Struktur des *Ludus de Antichristo*."

58. On Herrad's understanding and pictorial representation of Antichrist in its twelfth-century context, see also Lerner, "Refreshment of the Saints: The Time after Antichrist as a Station for Earthly Progress in Medieval Thought," 108–15; Curschmann, "Texte—Bilder—Strukturen der *Hortus deliciarum* und die frühmittelhochdeutsche Geistlichendichtung"; Wright, *Art and Antichrist in Medieval Europe*, 78–89; Monroe, "Dangerous Passages and Spiritual Redemption in the *Hortus Deliciarum*"; Campbell, "'Lest He Should Come Unforeseen': The Antichrist Cycle in the *Hortus Deliciarum*," (esp. 96–101 concerning Herrad's sources).

59. See Campbell, "'Lest He Should Come Unforeseen,'" 97, on Herrad's use of a revised version of Adso's *Libellus* entitled *Liber Anselmi de Antichristo*, CCCM 45:161–66.

60. Joyner, *Painting the Hortus Deliciarum: Medieval Women, Wisdom, and Time*, 1.

61. Joyner, *Painting the Hortus Deliciarum*, esp. ch. 1; Griffiths, *The Garden of Delights: Reform and Renaissance for Women in the Twelfth Century*, esp. ch. 6; and see also Phelan, "*Hortus Deliciarum/Garden of Delights*: A Somatic Interpretation."

62. Herrad of Hohenbourg, *Hortus deliciarum*, 2:241r.

63. Herrad of Hohenbourg, *Hortus deliciarum*, 2:241v.

64. Herrad of Hohenbourg, *Hortus deliciarum*, 2:213, inscr. 314.

65. Herrad of Hohenbourg, *Hortus deliciarum*, 2:213, inscr. 316.

66. Steer, *Hugo Ripelin von Strassburg: Zur Rezeptions- und Wirkungsgeschichte des "Compendium theologicae veritatis" im deutschen Spätmittelalter*, 647–60.

67. Hugo of Ripelin, *Compendium theologicae veritatis* 7.7–16, wrongly attributed to Albert the Great in his *Opera omnia*, 34:241–45.

68. Gow, *The Red Jews: Antisemitism in an Apocalyptic Age, 1200–1600*, ch. 3.

69. Hugo of Ripelin, *Compendium theologicae veritatis* 7.10, 34:243. See also the texts from Peter Comestor's *Historia scholastica* and Matthew Paris's *Chronica maior* in Gow, *The Red Jews*, 308, 318, 320.

70. McGinn, *Visions of the End*, 146; cf. also McGinn, *The Calabrian Abbot: Joachim of Fiore in the History of Western Thought*.

71. Above all Lerner, *The Feast of Saint Abraham: Medieval Millenarians and the Jews*, ch. 2 (see 137 n. 58 for the term "philo-Semitism"). On Joachim and the Jews, see also Hirsch-Reich, "Joachim von Fiore und das Judentum"; Abulafia, "The Conquest of Jerusalem: Joachim of Fiore and the Jews"; Alexander Patschovsky's invaluable introduction to his edition of Joachim of Fiore, *Exhortatorium Iudeorum*, 1–116; Daniel, *Abbot Joachim of Fiore and Joachimism: Selected Articles*; Whalen, *Dominion of God*, ch. 5; and, more recently, Whalen, "Joachim the Theorist of History and Society"; Ambrus, "The Eschatological Future of the Jews in the 'Vine Diagram' of Joachim of Fiore"; Gatto, "The Life and Works of Joachim of Fiore—An Overview," 21 n. 8. For a critique of Lerner's assessment, see below; and cf. Sara Lipton's review of

his *Feast of Saint Abraham* at https://scholarworks.iu.edu/journals/index.php/tmr/article/view/15165/21283.

72. Joachim of Fiore, *Concordia Novi ac Veteris Testamenti* 2.1.2.1, ed. Patschovsky, 2:65, along with the monumental introduction in vol. 1, and Daniel's introduction to his partial edition of Joachim's *Liber de Concordia Novi ac Veteris Testamenti*, xxii–xliii.

73. Joachim of Fiore, *Tractatus super quatuor evangelia* 3.18, ed. Santi, 325–27.

74. Joachim of Fiore, *Tractatus super quatuor evangelia* 1.6, ed. Santi, 91.

75. See, above all, the studies of Lerner, "Refreshment of the Saints," "Antichrists and Antichrist in Joachim of Fiore," and "The Medieval Return to the Thousand-Year Sabbath"; but cf. the opposing views of Daniel, "A New Understanding of Joachim: The Concords, the Exile, and the Exodus," and "Double Antichrist or Antichrists: Abbot Joachim of Fiore"; and the insightful observations of Patschovsky in Joachim, *Exhortatorium Iudeorum*, 47–62, 201–4 with nn., including his suggestions for reconciling conflicting impressions gained from different passages in Joachim's works. See also Joachim, *Tractatus super quatuor evangelia* 1.6, ed. Santi, 109–12.

76. Joachim of Fiore, *Psalterium decem cordarum*, ed. Selge, 298–302.

77. Joachim, *Concordia Novi ac Veteris Testamenti* 5.2.7.9–28, ed. Patschovsky, 3:657–73.

78. Joachim, *Concordia Novi ac Veteris Testamenti* 5.4.3, ed. Patschovsky, 3:884–902; *Exhortatorium Iudeorum*, 276–84. Several hundred years before Joachim, Bede understood the allegorical meaning of Tobit as bearing on the Jews of the eschaton. See his *In Librum Beati Patris Tobiae*, CCSL 119B:1–19; and Darby, *Bede and the End of Time*. On Joachim's adaptation of Bede's interpretation, see Arsenio Frugoni's notes to his edition of Joachim, *Adversus Iudeos*, 96–99, Hirsch-Reich, "Joachim von Fiore und das Judentum," 493–94 with nn.; Lerner, *The Feast of Saint Abraham*, 5–7, 126 n. 1; and Patschovsky's notes to *Exhortatorium Iudeorum*, 276–84.

79. See, for example, Joachim, *Concordia Novi ac Veteris Testamenti* 5.2.7.20, ed. Patschovsky, 3:667, on the patriarch Jacob; 5.4.3.1, 3:885, on Tobit; *Tractatus super quatuor evangelia* 1.6, 110, on the holy family's flight to Egypt; *Expositio in Apocalypsim* 21.21, 220ra, on the twelve pearls and gates of the new heavenly Jerusalem; and other references in *Exhortatorium Iudeorum*, 264 n. 630, 270, and *Concordia Novi ac Veteris Testamenti*, ed. Patschovsky, 2:166 n. 655. On Joachim's variant of "fiet" for the accepted "fieret" in Romans 11:26, see Patschovsky's comments on the *Exhortatorium Iudeorum*, 264 n. 630. On Joachim's *Expositio*, see, most recently, McGinn, "Apocalypticism and Mysticism in Joachim of Fiore's *Expositio in Apocalypsim*." (Alexander Patschovsky and Kurt-Victor Selge's new critical edition of Joachim's *Expositio in Apocalypsim* was not yet available to me as this book went to press.)

80. See the opposing views of Lerner and Daniel cited just above. Daniel remains steadfastly opposed to the understanding that we have mentioned here: "Joachim was a reformist apocalyptic, not a millenarian" (Daniel, "Double Antichrist or Antichrists," 4); following Augustine, Adso, and others, he expected the coming of a single Antichrist, traditionally conceived, at the very end of human history.

81. Lerner, *The Feast of Saint Abraham*, chs. 1–2; Whalen, *Dominion of God*, 101–2, notes that Joachim "was not content with the stock and somewhat colorless descriptions" of the conversion of the Jews expected at the end time, and turned it into "a vivid component of his schemes." See also Whalen, "Joachim the Theorist of History and Society."

82. Joachim, *Concordia Novi ac Veteris Testamenti* 2.2.5.6, ed. Patschovsky, 2:168.

83. Joachim, *De ultimis tribulationibus* 32 (ll. 329–31).

84. Lerner, *The Feast of Saint Abraham*, 33.

85. Joachim, *Expositio in Apocalypsim*, 220ra-rb, cited in Lerner, *The Feast of Saint Abraham*, 138–39 nn. 73–75.

86. Patschovsky's introduction to Joachim, Exhortatorium Iudeorum, 33 n. 110: "Der Kontrast zwischen den Juden Augustins . . . und dem hier entwickelten Juden-bild Joachims könnte nich größer sein"; and cf. Cohen, *Living Letters of the Law: Ideas of the Jew in Medieval Christianity*.

87. See Joachim of Fiore, *Il libro delle figure dell'abate Gioachino da Fiore*, ed. Tondelli and Reeves, 2:pl. XIa.

88. Joachim, *Concordia Novi ac Veteris Testamenti* 2.2.5.5, ed. Patschovsky, 2:166.

89. Joachim, *Concordia Novi ac Veteris Testamenti* 2.2.5.6, ed. Patschovsky, 2:168.

90. On the diagram and its different permutations, see Reeves and Hirsch-Reich, *The "Figurae" of Joachim of Fiore*, 38–58, 192–98; Joachim, *Liber de Concordia*, ed. Daniel, xxviii–xxxv, 163–72, and *Concordia Novi ac Veteris Testamenti*, ed. Patschovsky, 1:cccxlvii–cccxlix, 2:161–72 (2.2.5–6, with nn.).

91. Joachim of Fiore, *Il libro delle figure*, 2:pl. XXII.

92. Ambrus, "The Eschatological Future of the Jews in the 'Vine Diagram' of Joachim of Fiore," 190 (quotation; Ambrus's emphasis); and see the earlier studies of Reeves and Hirsch-Reich, *The "Figurae" of Joachim of Fiore*, 170–73; Lerner, *The Feast of Saint Abraham*, 36–37, 139–40 (nn. 80–81).

93. Gerhoh of Reichersberg, *De investigatione Antichristi* 1.2, Monumenta Germaniae Historica, *Libelli de lite imperatorum et pontificum* 3:309–10. On Gerhoh's Anti-christology, see Meuthen, *Kirche und Heilsgeschichte bei Gerhoh von Reichersberg*, ch. 7 esp.; Rauh, *Das Bild des Antichrist im Mittelalter*, ch. 6.

94. See the conversation between Joachim and the Cistercian Adam of Persigne in which Joachim stated that the Antichrist was already alive, a youth now living in Rome; reported in Ralph of Coggeshall, *Chronicon Anglicanum*, ed. Stevenson, 68–69, cited in Whalen, *Dominion of God*, 123.

95. See Patschovsky's introduction to Joachim's *Exhortatorium Iudeorum*, 3–6 on the work's title, and 6–34 on its structure and contents.

96. Berger, "Mission to the Jews and Jewish-Christian Contacts in the Polemical Literature in the High Middle Ages."

97. See Cohen, *The Friars and the Jews*, "Scholarship and Intolerance in the Medi-eval Academy: The Study and Evaluation of Judaism in European Christendom," and *Living Letters of the Law*, pts. 3–4.

98. Abulafia, "The Conquest of Jerusalem: Joachim of Fiore and the Jews," 146. Cf. Patschovsky's more impassioned summation in *Exhortatorium Iudeorum*, 34: "Die so oft gerühmte brüderliche Hinwendung zu den Juden ist für ihn die pure Selbstver-ständlichkeit; als Mann des Geistes kann er gar nicht anders."

99. Lerner, *The Feast of Saint Abraham*, 33, asks of Joachim: "Was he for the Jews or against them?"

100. See the studies in Lerner, *The Feast of Saint Abraham*, chs. 3–8; Potestà and Rizzi, *L'anticristo*; Whalen, *Dominion of God*, esp. ch. 8, in addition to others cited below.

101. Peter John Olivi, *Commentary on the Apocalypse*, trans. Lewis, xxxiv.

102. Peter John Olivi, *Commentary on the Apocalypse*, xi. On Olivi, his works, and his ideas, in addition to the works cited just above, see the erudite studies of Burr cited below.

103. Peter John Olivi, *Lectura super Apocalypsim* 3.20, ed. Lewis, 184.

104. Peter John Olivi, *Lectura super Apocalypsim* 12.63, 537–38.

105. Peter John Olivi, *Lectura super Apocalypsim* 7.35, 343–44; trans. *Commentary on the Apocalypse*, 251 (emphasis mine).

106. *Lectura super Apocalypsim*, prol. 155, 39–40; trans. 29–30.

107. *Lectura super Apocalypsim* 9.33, 411.

108. *Lectura super Apocalypsim* 13.24, 591; trans. 414: "After the Jews were crushed by the Romans, we have never heard at all that the Jews raised up arms against the Christians in defense of the Law." See also 13.44, 601; 20.35–48, 800–804. See also Burr, *Olivi's Peaceable Kingdom: A Reading of the Apocalypse Commentary*, ch. 6; as well as Lerner, "Antichrists and Antichrist in Joachim of Fiore"; Daniel, "Abbot Joachim of Fiore and the Conversion of the Jews"; Daniel, "Double Antichrist or Antichrists."

109. Here Olivi equivocates, ascribing his ambiguity to Scripture itself. See *Lectura super Apocalypsim* 6.102, trans. 238: "Neither the full sealing nor the conversion of the Twelve Tribes of Israel will take place until after the death of antichrist, although according to Joachim it begins before that. But these are the ones who are to "receive" the antichrist, as Christ says in John 5. Lest, moreover, they be deprived of the glorious martyrdom to be perpetrated by the antichrist, it is appropriate that a noble army first be sealed out of Israel, so that the antichrist can make martyrs of them. Both times, then, are touched on here indistinctly in the usual manner of prophetic scripture." See also Burr, "The Persecution of Peter Olivi," "Olivi's Apocalyptic Timetable," and "The Antichrist and the Jews in Four Thirteenth-Century Apocalyse Commentaries."

110. Lerner, *The Feast of Saint Abraham*, 63; Lerner, "Peter Olivi on the Conversion of the Jews."

111. See the studies cited in note 108.

112. Olivi, *Lectura super Apocalypsim*, prol. 3–4, 1–2.

113. Olivi, *Lectura super Apocalypsim* 5.37, 254–55; trans. 186 (emphasis mine).

114. Olivi, *Lectura super Apocalypsim* 14.4, 633; trans. 442.

115. Olivi, *Lectura super Apocalypsim* 7.22, 338–39; trans. 248.

116. Olivi, *Lectura super Apocalypsim* 21.49, 833–34; trans. 573.

117. Olivi, *Lectura super Apocalypsim*, cited and translated in Burr, *Olivi's Peaceable Kingdom*, 194. See also Olivi, *Lectura super Apocalypsim* 14.5, 633–34; trans. 442; and *Quaestio de altissima paupertate*, in Schlageter, *Das Heil der Armen und das Verderben der Reichen*, 34:158–60; cf. Lerner, "Peter Olivi on the Conversion of the Jews," 214 n. 1; *The Feast of Saint Abraham*, 152 nn. 50–52.

118. On John and his works, see Bignami Odier, *Jean de Roquetaillade (De Rupescissa)*; Lerner, *The Feast of Saint Abraham*, ch. 5, and his introductions to John of Rupescissa, *Liber secretorum eventuum*, ed. Lerner and Morerod-Fattebert, 1–85, and *Vade mecum in tribulatione*, ed. Tealdi, 1–35; the introduction to John of Rupescissa, *Liber ostensor quod adesse festinant tempora*, ed. Vauchez, Thévenaz Modestin, and Morerod-Fattebert, 1–104; Schmieder, "Prophetische Propaganda in der Politik des 14. Jahrhunderts: Johannes von Rupescissa"; Mesler, "John of Rupescissa's Engagement

with Prophetic Texts in the Sexdequiloquium"; Devun, *Prophecy, Alchemy, and the End of Time: John of Rupescissa in the Late Middle Ages*; Whalen, *Dominion of God*, 223–26, whose translations of the titles of John's writings I have borrowed here. Whalen dates the *Liber ostensor* in 1353, Lerner in 1356. See also Kriegel, "The Reckonings of Nahmanides and Arnold of Villanova: On the Early Contacts between Christian Millenarianism and Jewish Messianism," 18–20.

119. John of Rupescissa, *Vade mecum in tribulacione (1356): A Late Medieval Eschatological Manual for the Forthcoming Thirteen Years of Horror and Hardship*, ed. Kaup, 258–59.

120. John of Rupescissa, *Liber ostensor* 4.146–47, 232–33; and 2.2, 114; 4.112, 210; 4.137, 226–27; for the *Cum necatur flos ursi* oracle, see 948–51.

121. John of Rupescissa, *Liber ostensor* 4.52, 168.

122. John of Rupescissa, *Liber ostensor* 4.162, 244; 4.172, 252; John of Rupescissa, *Vade mecum* 30, ed. Kaup, 168–71, with nn. 106, 113.

123. John of Rupescissa, *Liber ostensor* 6.2–4, 318–19; see also 920–22.

124. John of Rupescissa, *Liber ostensor* 6.35, 337 (see also the interesting elaboration in 6.36, 337–38); and cf. *Vade mecum* 70–71, ed. Kaup, 217.

125. John of Rupescissa, *Liber ostensor* 4.194, 264.

126. John of Rupescissa, *Liber ostensor* 4.84–88, 190–92; 4.137–39, 226–27.

127. John of Rupescissa, *Vade mecum* 106, ed. Kaup, 260–61.

128. John of Rupescissa, *Liber secretorum eventuum* 106–7, 192–93.

129. John of Rupescissa, *Liber secretorum eventuum* 122, 200.

130. Lerner, *The Feast of Saint Abraham*, 79–81.

6. Antichrist and Jews in Literature, Drama, and Visual Arts

1. Gow, *The Red Jews: Antisemitism in an Apocalyptic Age, 1200–1600*; for examples of resistance to these connections, see 56–58. On the ten lost tribes in Jewish messianic hopes, cf. Benmelech, "Back to the Future: The Ten Tribes and Messianic Hopes in Jewish Society during the Early Modern Age." And see also above, chapter 4, note 42; chapter 5, notes 68–69.

2. See the Sibylline prophecy concerning the twelve Hebrew tribes in Henneke et al., *New Testament Apocrypha*, 2:713, cited in Emmerson, *Antichrist in the Middle Ages: A Study of Medieval Apocalypticism, Art, and Literature*, 86 n. 43.

3. See Gow, *The Red Jews*, 205–8, for the German text and Gow's English translation. The Latin original does not identify Gog and Magog with the twelve tribes or the Red Jews; see Patschovsky, *Der Passauer Anonymus: Ein Sammelwerk ueber Ketzer, Juden, Antichrist aus der Mitte des 13. Jahrhunderts*, 161–62; and Gow, *The Red Jews*, 75.

4. See Strickland, *Saracens, Demons & Jews: Making Monsters in Medieval Art*, 234.

5. Gow, *The Red Jews*, 225–27.

6. Gow, *The Red Jews*, 338–42. On the associations with cannibals and cannibalism, see Pseudo-Methodius, *Apocalypse*, 26–27, and the other references cited by Gow, *The Red Jews*, 45–46 with n. 38.

7. Gow, *The Red Jews*, 93–95.

8. Sir John Mandeville, *The Book of Marvels and Travel*, trans. Bale, x. On Bale's choice of version, see xxix–xxxii.

9. Sir John Mandeville, *The Book of Marvels and Travel*, 104–5; a different version reads Queen of Amazonia for Queen of Armenia (164 n. 105).

10. Sir John Mandeville, *The Book of Marvels and Travel*, 160 n. 83; see also Fleck, "Here, There, and In Between: Representing Difference in the Travels of Sir John Mandeville," esp. 395–99; Jordan, "Judaizing the Passion: The Case of the Crown of Thorns in the Middle Ages."

11. Braude, "The Sons of Noah and the Construction of Ethnic and Geographical Identities in the Medieval and Early Modern Periods," 115.

12. See the studies cited in Tinkle, "God's Chosen Peoples: Christians and Jews in *The Book of John Mandeville*," 443 n. 2.

13. Braude, "'Mandeville's' Jews among Others," 151.

14. Sir John Mandeville, *The Book of Marvels and Travel*, 105.

15. Braude, "'Mandeville's' Jews among Others," 147; see also Krummel, *Crafting Jewishness in Medieval England: Legally Absent, Virtually Present*, 84.

16. Babylonian Talmud, *Makkot* 24b, trans., https://www.sefaria.org.il/Makkot.24b?lang=en.

17. See Lomperis, "Medieval Travel Writing and the Question of Race"; Schaaf, "The Christian-Jewish Debate and the 'Catalan Atlas,'" 249–52.

18. Krummel, *Crafting Jewishness in Medieval England: Legally Absent, Virtually Present*, 80–83.

19. Tinkle, "God's Chosen Peoples," 461.

20. Tinkle, "God's Chosen Peoples," 465.

21. In addition to the studies already cited, see Kupfer, "'. . . Lectres . . . plus Vrayes': Hebrew Script and Jewish Witness in the Mandeville Manuscript of Charles V"; Mittman, "Mandeville's Jews, Colonialism, Certainty, and Art History."

22. Akbari, *Idols in the East: European Representations of Islam and the Orient, 1100–1450*, 136–40; see also Lomperis, "Medieval Travel Writing and the Question of Race"; Leshock, "Religious Geography: Designating Jews and Muslims as Foreigners in Medieval England"; Schaaf, "The Christian-Jewish Debate and the 'Catalan Atlas,'" 249–52; Tinkle, "God's Chosen Peoples," 443 n. 3 (with the additional studies cited there).

23. Higgins, *Writing East: The "Travels" of Sir John Mandeville*, 188, whose book assesses variations in attitudes toward the Jews among the different versions of the work.

24. Gow, *The Red Jews*, 118.

25. See the introduction to *Der Antichrist und die fünfzehn Zeichen: Faksimile-Ausgabe des einzigen erhaltenen chiroxylographischen Blockbuches*, ed. Musper and von Arnim: "The Chiro-Xylographic Antichrist and the Fifteen Signs," 1:1–8 (quotation on 1); Gow, *The Red Jews*, 115–16.

26. On the images depicting Antichrist's conception and birth, see Blumenfeld-Kosinski, "Illustration as Commentary in Late Medieval Images of Antichrist's Birth"; and on the inconsistencies and contradiction between various details in the biography of Antichrist—for instance, his birth in Babylon or Jerusalem despite his belonging to the "lost" tribe of Dan—see Gow, *The Red Jews*, 120 with n. 99: "Logic and system are foreign to the tradition."

27. See the citations in Gow, *The Red Jews*, 116 n. 82.

28. Martín Martínez de Ampiés, *Libro del Anticristo: Declaración . . . del sermón de San Vicente* (1496), ed. Gilbert; see also Fagan, "A Critical Edition of Martín Martínez Dampiés's 'Libro Del Antichristo', Zaragoza, 1496."

29. See Ricke, "The Antichrist 'Vita' at the End of the Middle Ages: An Edition of 'The Byrthe and Lyfe of the Moost False and Deceytfull Antechryst,'" 126–30; and Emmerson, "Wynkyn De Worde's Byrthe and Lyfe of Antechryst and Popular Eschatology on the Eve of the English Reformation."

30. Emmerson mentions no portrayal of Antichrist's Jewish or Danite origins or link to Jacob's deathbed prophecy. Ricke, "The Antichrist 'Vita,'" 126, offers the suggestion that Antichrist's "parents' names, 'Ulcas and Schalcus,' are no doubt meant to suggest Hebrew names."

31. Ricke, "The Antichrist 'Vita,'" 162–63.

32. Ricke, "The Antichrist 'Vita,'" 167.

33. Ricke, "The Antichrist 'Vita,'" 171.

34. Ricke, "The Antichrist 'Vita,'" 171–72.

35. Ricke, "The Antichrist 'Vita,'" 172.

36. Ricke, "The Antichrist 'Vita,'" 185.

37. Ricke, "The Antichrist 'Vita,'" 185–86.

38. Among others, see Enders, *The Medieval Theater of Cruelty: Rhetoric, Memory, Violence*; Evitt, "Eschatology, Millenarian Apocalypticism, and the Liturgical Anti-Judaism of the Medieval Prophet Plays"; Cockett, "Staging Antichrist and the Performance of Miracles"; Parker, *The Aesthetics of Antichrist: From Christian Drama to Christopher Marlowe*; Ridder and Barton, "Die Antichrist-Figur im mittelalterlichen Schauspiel"; Stevenson, "Poised at the Threatening Edge: Feeling the Future in Medieval Last Judgment Performances."

39. Gow, *The Red Jews*, 371–72, 375–76 (with slight modification); and see Martin, "Dramatized Disputations: Late Medieval German Dramatizations of Jewish-Christian Religious Disputations, Church Policy, and Local Social Climates," "The Depiction of Jews in the Carnival Plays and Comedies of Hans Folz and Hans Sachs in Early Modern Nuremberg," and *Representations of Jews in Late Medieval and Early Modern German Literature*, esp. 126–28 (on the ritual murder charge); Huey, *Hans Folz and Print Culture in Late Medieval Germany*, ch. 5.

40. Cf. Ragotzky, "Fastnacht und Endzeit: Zur Funktion der Antichrist-Figur im nürnberger Fastnachtspiel des 15. Jahrhunderts."

41. On music in the production, see Emmerson and Hult, *Antichrist and Judgment Day: The Middle French "Jour du jugement,"* 99–104.

42. Emmerson, "Antichrist on Page and Stage in the Later Middle Ages," 12.

43. Roy, *Le "Jour du jugement": Mystere français sur le Grand Schism*, 218, ll. 207–17; trans. Emmerson and Hult, *Antichrist and Judgment Day*, 11.

44. Roy, *Le "Jour du jugement,"* 219–20, ll. 291–300; trans. Emmerson and Hult, *Antichrist and Judgment Day*, 14.

45. Roy, *Le "Jour du jugement,"* 220, l. 332; trans. Emmerson and Hult, *Antichrist and Judgment Day*, 16. Such a report of an incestuous coupling of a father and daughter from the tribe of Dan—with Beelzebub as a participant—already appeared in Berengier's *De l'avenement Antecrist*, in Emmanuel Walberg, *Deux versions inédites de la légende de l'Antéchrist, en vers français du XIIIe siècle*, 63–64; cited and translated in Rouillard, *Medieval Considerations of Incest, Marriage, and Penance*, 83.

46. Roy, *Le "Jour du jugement,"* 221, ll. 385–91; trans. Emmerson and Hult, *Antichrist and Judgment Day*, 18.

47. On the linkage between Jews, money, and Antichrist, see Lipton, *Images of Intolerance: The Representation of Jews and Judaism in the Bible Moralisée*, 42, 49.

48. Roy, *Le "Jour du jugement,"* 235, ll. 1213–19; trans. Emmerson and Hult, *Antichrist and Judgment Day*, 46.

49. Roy, *Le "Jour du jugement,"* 241–42, ll. 1592–98; trans. Emmerson and Hult, *Antichrist and Judgment Day*, 58–59.

50. Roy, *Le "Jour du jugement,"* 252, ll. 2209–20; trans. Emmerson and Hult, *Antichrist and Judgment Day*, 80–81.

51. Roy, *Le "Jour du jugement,"* 255, ll. 2408–11; trans. Emmerson and Hult, *Antichrist and Judgment Day*, 87.

52. See above, chapter 5, note 28.

53. Roy, *Le "Jour du jugement,"* 241, ll. 1571–79; trans. Emmerson and Hult, *Antichrist and Judgment Day*, 58.

54. On the Chester cycle in general, its Antichrist play in particular, and its representation of the Jews of the end time, see Lucken, *Antichrist and the Prophets of Antichrist in the Chester Cycle*; Martin, "Comic Eschatology in the Chester Coming of Antichrist"; Clopper, "The History and Development of the Chester Cycle"; Spector, "Anti-Semitism and the English Mystery Plays"; Ovitt, "Christian Eschatology and the Chester 'Judgment'"; Emmerson, "'Nowe Ys Common This Daye': Enoch and Elias, Antichrist, and the Structure of the Chester Cycle," "Contextualizing Performance: The Reception of the Chester Antichrist," and "Antichrist on Page and Stage in the Later Middle Ages"; Walsh, "Demon or Deluded Messiah? The Characterization of Antichrist in the Chester Cycle"; Stevens, *Four Middle English Mystery Cycles: Textual, Contextual, and Critical Interpretations*, 298–322; Dox, "Representation without Referent: The Jew in Medieval English Drama"; Ruud, "The Jews in the Chester Play of Antichrist"; Kelley, "Doubt and Religious Drama across Sixteenth-Century England, or Did the Middle Ages Believe in Their Plays?"; Adams and Hanska, *The Jewish-Christian Encounter in Medieval Preaching*, 62–67; McNabb, "Night of the Living Bread: Unstable Signs in Chester's Antichrist"; McGavin and Walker, *Imagining Spectatorship: From the Mysteries to the Shakespearean Stage*, ch. 4; among others.

55. Chester Cycle 1572/2010, adapted as an acting text by Alexandra Johnston, assisted by Linda Phillips (2010), from the modernized version by David Mills, ll. 646–53, https://pls.artsci.utoronto.ca/wp-content/uploads/2015/09/chester22.pdf. My thanks to Alexandra Johnston, owner of the copyright, for directing me to this website.

56. Chester Cycle 1572/2010, ll. 33–40.

57. Chester Cycle 1572/2010, ll. 61–76.

58. Chester Cycle 1572/2010, ll. 279–81.

59. Among many others, see Despres, "Cultic Anti-Judaism and Chaucer's Litel Clergeon"; Bale, *The Jew in the Medieval Book: English Antisemitisms, 1350–1500*, and "Christian Anti-Semitism and Intermedial Experience in Late Medieval England"; Williams Boyarin, *Miracles of the Virgin in Medieval England*.

60. In understanding the depiction of hell as a prediction for the end time, I have followed Campbell, "'Lest He Should Come Unforeseen': The Antichrist Cycle in the *Hortus Deliciarum*," 107 with n. 107, who cites McGinn, "Portraying Antichrist in the

Middle Ages," 15–16; and Monroe, "Dangerous Passages and Spiritual Redemption in the *Hortus Deliciarum*."

61. Lipton, *Images of Intolerance*, esp. ch. 5; Strickland, *Saracens, Demons & Jews* ch. 5; Strickland, "Antichrist and the Jews in Medieval Art and Protestant Propaganda," 12–15.

62. Lipton, *Images of Intolerance*, 116.

63. Lipton, *Images of Intolerance*, 119–20.

64. Strickland, *Saracens, Demons & Jews*, 216–17.

65. On earlier medieval commentaries on the Apocalypse, see, among others, Lobrichon, "L'ordre de ce temps et les désordres de la fin: Apocalypse et société, du IXe à la fin du XIe siècle," and Lobrichon, "Stalking the Signs: The Apocalyptic Commentaries"; Matter, "The Apocalypse in Early Medieval Exegesis," along with other essays in Emmerson and McGinn, *The Apocalypse in the Middle Ages*; Palmer, *The Apocalypse in the Early Middle Ages*. Cf. also the studies of illuminated medieval Psalters in Belkin, "The Antichrist Legend in the Utrecht Psalter," and "Antichrist as the Embodiment of the Insipiens in Thirteenth-Century French Psalters."

66. See Lewis, "Exegesis and Illustration in Thirteenth-Century English Apocalypses," and *Reading Images: Narrative Discourse and Reception in the Thirteenth-Century Illuminated Apocalypse*, 40–48, 340–44; O'Hear, *Contrasting Images of the Book of Revelation in Late Medieval and Early Modern Art*, esp. ch. 2; Emmerson, "Medieval Illustrated Apocalypse Manuscripts," and *Apocalypse Illuminated: The Visual Exegesis of Revelation in Medieval Illuminated Manuscripts*, 112–27. For opposing views concerning the dates of Berengaudus and his work, see also Visser, *Apocalypse as Utopian Expectation (800–1500): The Apocalypse Commentary of Berengaudus of Ferrières and the Relationship between Exegesis, Liturgy, and Iconography*; Knibbs, "Berengaudus on the Apocalypse."

67. Lewis, "*Tractatus adversus Judaeos* in the Gulbenkian Apocalypse," and *Reading Images*; Strickland, *Saracens, Demons & Jews*, 220–21; O'Hear, *Picturing the Apocalypse: The Book of Revelation in the Arts over Two Millennia*, 21, 37–39.

68. Burr, "The Antichrist and the Jews in Four Thirteenth-Century Apocalypse Commentaries," esp. 36–38.

69. Lewis, *Reading Images*, 217.

70. Lewis, "*Tractatus adversus Judaeos* in the Gulbenkian Apocalypse," 554–55, notes that Berengaudus "eagerly embraced" the hope for Jewish salvation evinced in Romans 11:25–26—even if this passage is nowhere cited in commentary itself—although in *Reading Images*, 217, she states that from perspective of this commentary, there appears to be "no hope for conversion at the end of time . . ., little or no possibility for redemption or conversion" of the Jews. See also Strickland, "Antichrist and the Jews in Medieval Art and Protestant Propaganda"; O'Hear, *Contrasting Images of the Book of Revelation in Late Medieval and Early Modern Art*, esp. 37–39.

71. See Strickland, *Saracens, Demons & Jews*, 215.

72. Lewis, "*Tractatus adversus Judaeos* in the Gulbenkian Apocalypse," 557.

73. Berengaudus, *Expositio super septem visiones libri Apocalypsis*, PL 17:931–32.

74. See Lewis, *"Tractatus adversus Judaeos* in the Gulbenkian Apocalypse," 548–49; and cf. Berengaudus ad loc., PL 17:886: "Quia quamvis multi credant ex Judaeis per praedicationem Eliae in Christum; maxima tamen pars eorum Antichristum secutura est."

75. Lewis, *"Tractatus adversus Judaeos* in the Gulbenkian Apocalypse," 556 (not in Berengaudus ad loc., PL 17:884).

76. Nothing along these lines is described in Berengaudus ad loc., PL 17:841–42, though Lewis, *"Tractatus adversus Judaeos* in the Gulbenkian Apocalypse," 562–63 with n. 113, cites the *Expositio* ad 16:8–9 (the opening of the fourth seal/vial), PL 905–6: "Quartus igitur angelus phialam suam in solem effudit; quia Christus et apostoli ejus, quod impii Judaei a Romanis delendi essent, apertis vocibus praedixerunt. Nam sicut quilibet servus accipit a Domino suo gladium, non unde ipse juguletur, sed unde reum jugulet: ita et Romani effusionem phialae, in qua ira Dei continebatur, non ad hoc susceperunt, ut ipsi in ea perirent, sed ad vindicandum Christi sanguinem in Judaeos effunderent; unde et sequitur: Quia datum est illi aestu afficere homines et igni. Possumus per aestum obsidionem, per ignem autem famem et gladium, quibus Judaei pene omnes consumpti sunt, intelligere."

77. Strickland, *Saracens, Demons & Jews,* 220–21.

78. Lewis, *"Tractatus adversus Judaeos* in the Gulbenkian Apocalypse," 550–51.

79. Lewis, *"Tractatus adversus Judaeos* in the Gulbenkian Apocalypse," 560.

80. Poesch, "Antichrist Imagery in Anglo-French Apocalypse Manuscripts," 318–19; Emmerson, *Antichrist in the Middle Ages,* 124–25.

81. Gow, *The Red Jews,* 62, 385.

82. Emmerson, "Visualizing Performance: The Miniatures of the Besançon MS 579 *Jour du jugement,*" 254.

83. Kitzinger, "Judgment on Parchment: Illuminating Theater in Besançon MS 579," 49; see also Emmerson, *Antichrist in the Middle Ages,* 172–80; Emmerson, "Visualizing Performance"; Griffith, "Illustrating Antichrist and the Day of Judgment in the Eighty-Nine Miniatures of Besançon, Bibliothèque Municipale MS 579," and "Performative Reading and Receiving a Performance of the *Jour du jugement* in MS Besançon 579"; and the introduction to Emmerson and Hult, *Antichrist and Judgment Day,* ix–xxxiv.

84. Emmerson, "Visualizing Performance," 268, 283; see also Kjær, "Une lecture du mystère du *Jour du jugement* portant sur l'imagination allégorique," esp. 119.

85. Emmerson, "Visualizing Performance," 275.

86. Emmerson, "Visualizing Performance," 284.

87. *Der Antichrist,* ed. Boveland, 2:3r.

88. *Der Antichrist,* ed. Boveland, 1:7.

89. *Der Antichrist,* ed. Boveland, 2:4r.

90. *Der Antichrist,* ed. Boveland, 1:10, 2:8r.

91. Lewis, *Reading Images,* 233.

92. Al Acres, review of Strickland, *The Epiphany of Hieronymus Bosch,* https:// hnanews.org/hnar/reviews/epiphany-hieronymus-bosch-imagining-antichrist-oth ers-middle-ages-reformation/.

93. Lipton, "Isaac and Antichrist in the Archives," 42 (image on 9).

94. Philip, "The Prado 'Epiphany' by Jerome Bosch"; and other works cited in Strickland, *The Epiphany of Hieronymus Bosch: Imagining Antichrist and Others from the Middle Ages to the Reformation*, 104 n. 4.

95. Strickland, *The Epiphany of Hieronymus Bosch*, 76.

96. Strickland, *The Epiphany of Hieronymus Bosch*, 89–90.

97. Kimberlee Cloutier-Blazzard, review of Strickland, *The Epiphany of Hieronymus Bosch*, https://networks.h-net.org/node/7833/reviews/192814/cloutier-blazzard-strickland-epiphany-hieronymus-bosch-imagining.

98. Acres, review of Strickland, *The Epiphany of Hieronymus Bosch*.

7. Honorius Augustodunensis, the Song of Songs, and *Synagoga Conversa*

1. Honorius Augustodunensis, PL 172: 348–496. In addition to the Migne edition, I have also consulted six of the extant twelfth-century manuscripts: MSS Munich, Bayerische Staatsbibliothek Clm. 4550, Clm. 5118, Clm. 18125; MS UB Augsburg—Oettingen-Wallersteinsche Bibliothek, Cod.I.2.2.13; MS Vienna, Österreichische Nationalbibliothek lat. 942; MS Baltimore, Walters Art Museum 29. These and other manuscripts are listed in Curschmann, "Imagined Exegesis: Text and Picture in the Exegetical Works of Rupert of Deutz, Honorius Augustodunensis, and Gerhoch of Reichersberg," 154 n. 121; and Flint, *Honorius Augustodunensis of Regensburg*, 167–68. (In the case of the Vienna MS listed here, Flint departs from Curschmann and offers a thirteenth-century date.) All of the manuscripts consulted share the same textual tradition; while the differences between them and the printed PL text are plentiful, I have called attention to them only in the several instances where they bear on the meaning and significance of the passage under discussion. On the relationship between the texts of the printed Migne edition and a later generation of thirteenth-century manuscripts, see the intriguing comments of Menhardt, "Der Nachlass des Honorius Augustodunensis," 62–63; and see also Menhardt, "Die Mandragora im millstätter *Physiologus*, bei Honorius Augustodunensis und im St. Trudperter Hohenliede."

2. On Honorius's life and work, see Flint, *Honorius Augustodunensis of Regensburg*, which blends the findings of many of her previous essays on Honorius; and the differing reconstruction of his career proposed by Garrigues, "Qui était Honorius Augustodunensis?," "Quelques recherches sur l'oeuvre d'Honorius Augustodunensis," and "L'oeuvre d'Honorius Augustodunensis: Inventaire critique"; the more recent unpublished overview in Hannam, "The 'Inevitabile' of Honorius Augustodunensis: A Study in the Textures of Early Twelfth-Century Augustianisms," ch. 1; and, most recently, De Toro, "*Exsilium hominum ignorantia est*: Honorius Augustodunensis and Knowledge in the Twelfth Century."

3. Honorius Augustodunensis, *De luminaribus ecclesiae* 4.17, PL 172:233–34, as cited in Hannam, "The 'Inevitabile' of Honorius Augustodunensis," 5–6.

4. On Honorius's commentaries on the Song of Songs, see especially Flint, "The Commentaries of Honorius Augustodunensis on the Song of Songs"; Garrigues, "L'oeuvre d'Honorius Augustodunensis," 61–75, 123–27; Astell, *The Song of Songs in the Middle Ages*, 31–33; Matter, *The Voice of My Beloved: The Song of Songs in Western Medieval Christianity*, 58–76, 155–58; Fulton, "The Virgin Mary and the Song of Songs in the High Middle Ages," and "Mimetic Devotion, Marian Exegesis, and the

Historical Sense of the Song of Songs"; Monroe, "Images of Synagoga as Christian Discourse (1000–1215)," 126–37, and "'Fair and Friendly, Sweet and Beautiful': Hopes for Jewish Conversion in Synagoga's Song of Songs Imagery."

5. Rauh, *Das Bild des Antichrist im Mittelalter: Von Tyconius zum deutschen Symbolismus*, 166–67.

6. Honorius Augustodunensis, *Expositio in Cantica Canticorum*, PL 172:348–53; cf. the seminal study of Minnis, *Medieval Theory of Authorship: Scholastic Literary Attitudes in the Later Middle Ages*, esp. ch. 2; and see also Matter, *The Voice of My Beloved*, 60–64.

7. Honorius Augustodunensis, *Expositio in Cantica Canticorum*, PL 172:351.

8. The idea of the superiority of the Song of Songs among all the books of Scripture in general and among the books of wisdom literature ascribed to Solomon in particular finds ample grounding in the prologue to Origen, *Commentarium in Cantica Canticorum*, GCS 33:75–79. Cf. the famous Mishnaic dictum, *Yadayim* 3.5, attributed to Rabbi Akiba, that "all the *ketuvim* [=Scriptures or, perhaps, hagiographic writings] are holy, but the Song of Songs is the holy of holies."

9. Honorius Augustodunensis, *Expositio in Cantica Canticorum*, PL 172:351.

10. Following MSS "collecta," vs. PL "electa."

11. One finds Shulamite in the Hebrew Masoretic Text (שולמית), the Greek Septuagint (Σουλαμῖτις), and the Latin Vulgate (*Sulamitis*), but the reading of Shunamite (*Sunamitis*) is well attested in Latin sources: Ambrose, *Epistulae* 12.15, CSEL 82,1:100; Jerome, *Epistulae*. 121.praef., CSEL 56:3; Bede, *In Cantica Canticorum* 6.12, CCSL 119B:314; and numerous others. Cf. also the editorial note to PL 28:1290.

12. Honorius Augustodunensis, *Expositio in Cantica Canticorum*, PL 172:352–53.

13. Following MSS "adducetur," vs. PL "adducitur."

14. Following MSS "revertetur," vs. PL "convertetur."

15. Honorius Augustodunensis, *Expositio in Cantica Canticorum*, PL 172:453–72.

16. On the exegetical significance of this difficult passage, see Tournay, "Les chariots d'Aminadab (Cant. vi 12): Israël, peuple théophore"; LaCocque, "La Shulamite et les chars d'Aminadab: Un essai herméneutique sur Cantique 6,12–7,1"; Froehlich, *Sensing the Scriptures: Aminadab's Chariot and the Predicament of Biblical Interpretation*.

17. Honorius Augustodunensis, *Expositio in Cantica Canticorum*, PL 172:454–55; cf. above at note 12.

18. MSS read "saeculi" vs. PL "mundi."

19. Following MSS "vehitur," vs. PL "vehit."

20. Honorius Augustodunensis, *Expositio in Cantica Canticorum*, PL 172:455. On the significance of this allusion to Psalm 59(58):15, see also below, chapter 8, note 16 for the allusion to roaming dogs.

21. Honorius Augustodunensis, *Expositio in Cantica Canticorum*, PL 172:453; and see below, notes 50–51.

22. Honorius Augustodunensis, *Expositio in Cantica Canticorum*, PL 172:456.

23. MSS read "mea"; PL omits.

24. In keeping with earlier tradition, Honorius explained elsewhere, *Liber duodecim quaestionum* 5, PL 172:1181, that there were ten orders of angels, of which one had fallen. The remaining nine he repeatedly likened to the orders of the just in the church; cols. 1178, 1182: "in Ecclesia sint novem ordines justorum secundum

novem ordines angelorum." Previously in the *Expositio in Cantica Canticorum*, he made several comparisons to various numbers (6, 7, 10) of the *ordines electorum* in the church; cf. PL 172:403, 414, 427, 431, 444. Given the Pseudo-Dionysian connection of the context in which Honorius composed his *Expositio*, one should take note of the prominence of the celestial *ordines* in the works of Pseudo-Dionysius, their Latin translations by John Scot Eriugena, and Eriugena's own *In ierarchiam coelestem*, CCCM 31. See also Gersh, "Honorius Augustodunensis and Eriugena: Remarks on the Method and Content of the *Clavis Physicae*"; Flint, *Honorius Augustodunensis of Regensburg*, 141–43.

25. Following MSS "legiones," vs. PL "acies."

26. Honorius Augustodunensis, *Expositio in Cantica Canticorum*, PL 172:460.

27. Honorius Augustodunensis, *Expositio in Cantica Canticorum*, PL 172:468.

28. Honorius Augustodunensis, *Expositio in Cantica Canticorum*, PL 172:469. Cf. Honorius's overview of the progression of salvation history, capped with an enumeration of the four brides in the Song, in the second prologue to his *Expositio*, PL 172:353–58.

29. See Honorius Augustodunensis, *Expositio in Cantica Canticorum*, PL 172:461: "Haec de Synagoga quasi historice dicta sunt."

30. On the lines of demarcation between the senses, see, among others, De Lubac, *Medieval Exegesis*, vol. 2, chs. 7–8; and Dahan, "Genres, Forms, and Various Methods in Christian Exegesis of the Middle Ages"; and, with regard to the Song of Songs in particular, see Matter, *The Voice of My Beloved*, ch. 3; Cohen, "The Song of Songs and the Jewish Religious Mentality," 3–17; Carr, "The Song of Songs as a Microcosm of the Canonization and Decanonization Process"; Froehlich, *Sensing the Scriptures*.

31. Honorius Augustodunensis, *Expositio in Cantica Canticorum*, PL 172:471–96.

32. I have here quoted the text, not as it appears in PL 172:471, but as it appears in manuscripts that I consulted (see above, note 2): Munich, BSB Clm. 4550, fol. 89rv; Clm 5118, fols. 77v-78r; Clm 18125, fols. 77v-78r; Baltimore, Walters Art Museum MS 29, fol. 103v-104r; boldface type indicates discrepancies between this textual tradition and that in the printed edition: "Postquam totus comitatus Sunamitis in aulam regis est receptus, et regalibus nuptiis admissus; ecce ab aquilone nova sponsa cum magno apparatu, scilicet Mandragora sine capite sponso adducitur; cui ab eo aureum caput imponitur diademate redimitur, in nuptiis recipitur. Sunamitis quippe **de urbe** egressa, invenit Mandragoram regalem puellam sine capite in agro iacentem: cui nimium compassa, et ad regem regressa, obnixe supplicat ut secum eat, miserae subveniat. Rex ergo, cum Sunamite in agrum veniens et miseram miserabiliter nudam inveniens, elevat, vestit, aureum caput imponit ad nuptias introducit. Mandragora est herba formam humani corporis habens sine capite, et intelligitur multitudo infidelium; quae tunc erit, cujus caput Antichristus erit, qui est caput omnium malorum. Sed caput Mandragorae amputabitur, quando Antichristus occidetur. Post cujus occisionem videns Synagoga **conversa[m] multitudinem infidelium** sine capite Antichristo, et etiam carere capite Christo, optat eam sibi in fide Christi associari, et capite Christo sublimari, dicit sponso: 'Veni, dilecti mi, egrediamur in agrum, commoremur in villas.'" Some of the manuscripts read "videns Synagoga conversam multitudinem infidelium," at least one "videns Synagoga conversa multitudinem infidelium." But in either case, Synagoga is the subject of the sentence; *she* beholds the infidels. On

the symbolic history of the mandrake, see Menhardt, "Die Mandragora im millstätter Physiologus, bei Honorius Augustodunensis und im St. Trudperter Hohenliede,";
Engstrom, "The Voices of Plants and Flowers and the Changing Cry of the Mandrake"; Rahner, *Greek Myths and Christian Mystery*, 223–77; Zarcone, "The Myth of the
Mandrake, the 'Plant-Human,'" with additional references to primary and secondary
sources; Berg and Dircksen, "Mandrake from Antiquity to Harry Potter."

33. Matter, "The Love Song of the Millennium: Medieval Christian Apocalyptic
and the Song of Songs"; Matter, "Wandering to the End: The Medieval Christian
Context of the Wandering Jew."

34. Honorius Augustodunensis, *Expositio in Cantica Canticorum*, PL 172:472.

35. Honorius Augustodunensis, *Expositio in Cantica Canticorum*, PL 172:488.

36. Honorius Augustodunensis, *Expositio in Cantica Canticorum*, PL 172:489.

37. Matter, *The Voice of My Beloved*, 76. On patristic and medieval Christian exegesis of the Song of Songs, see also Riedlinger, *Die Makellosigkeit der Kirche in den
lateinischen Hoheliedkommentaren des Mittelalters*; Pope, *Song of Songs: A New Translation with Introduction and Commentary*, 89; Dronke, "The Song of Songs and Medieval
Love-Lyric"; Pelletier, *Lectures du Cantique des cantiques: De l'enigme du sens aux figures
du lecteur*; Astell, *The Song of Songs in the Middle Ages*; Dove, "Sex, Allegory, and Censorship: A Reconsideration of Medieval Commentaries on the Song of Songs"; Elliott,
The Song of Songs and Christology in the Early Church, 381–451; Moore, "The Song of
Songs in the History of Sexuality"; Black, "Unlikely Bedfellows: Allegorical and Feminist Readings of Song of Songs 7.1–8"; Turner, *Eros and Allegory: Medieval Exegesis of
the Song of Songs*; Birnbaum, "Sulamit und die Kirchenväter: Wer ist die Geliebte des
Hoheliedes?"—among others.

38. Gregory the Great, *Expositio in Canticum Canticorum* 36, CCSL 144:35; Angelom of Luxeuil, *Enarrationes in Cantica Canticorum* 1.5, 6.11, PL 115:573, 620.

39. Bede, *In Cantica Canticorum* 6.11–12, CCSL 119B:314f.

40. Haimo of Auxerre, *Commentarium in Cantica Canticorum* 7.1, PL 117:341.

41. Bede, *In Cantica Canticorum* 7.1, CCSL 119B:315; Haimo of Auxerre, *Commentarium in Cantica Canticorum* 7.1, PL 117:341; Williram of Ebersberg, *Expositio in Cantica Canticorum* 111–21, ed. Lähnemann and Rupp, 210–31. With Honorius's novel
interpretation in mind, one might perceive a faint gesture in such a direction in the
Glossa ordinaria on Song 7.1, CCCM 170:348–49, which notes that here the redeemer
begins to lavish his praises on *ecclesia coniuncta*, perhaps the church reconstituted by
Jews and Gentiles alike. Yet the suggestion remains implicit, with no explicit mention of Synagoga whatsoever. More explicit in anticipating Honorius's presentation
of *Synagoga conversa* is the Song of Songs commentary of Anselm of Laon; see the
recent important study of LaVere, *Out of the Cloister: Scholastic Exegesis of the Song
of Songs, 1100–1250*, esp. 46–48. On Honorius's use of earlier commentaries on the
Song, cf. also Flint, "The Commentaries of Honorius Augustodunensis on the Song
of Songs," 210–11.

42. Recounting the greatness of the Virgin in his earlier, Marian commentary on the
Song of Songs, Honorius briefly mentioned the oft-told story of the Jewish boy
thrown into the flames by his parents for partaking of the Eucharist and then saved
through the miraculous intervention of Mary; *Sigillum beatae Mariae* 1.1, PL 172:500.
Apart from the brief summary in Schreckenberg, *Die christlichen Adversus-Judaeos-
Texte (11.–13. Jh.): Mit einer Ikonographie des Judenthemas bis zum 4. Laterankonzil*,

114–16, 564–66, Honorius receives little or no attention in the works cited in the next note below.

43. The many studies of the last generation on Jews and Judaism in twelfth-century Christendom include the following: Awerbuch, *Christlich-jüdische Begegnung im Zeitalter der Frühscholastik*; Moore, "Anti-Semitism and the Birth of Europe"; Dahan, *Les intellectuels chrétiens et les juifs au Moyen Age*; Abulafia, *Christians and Jews in the Twelfth-Century Renaissance*, and *Christians and Jews in Dispute: Disputational Literature and the Rise of Anti-Judaism in the West (c. 1000–1150)*; Cohen, ed., *From Witness to Witchcraft: Jews and Judaism in Medieval Christian Thought*, and *Living Letters of the Law: Ideas of the Jew in Medieval Christianity*, pt. 3; Chazan, *Medieval Stereotypes and Modern Antisemitism*; Schreckenberg, *Die christlichen Adversus-Judaeos-Texte (11.–13. Jh.)*; Signer and Van Engen, *Jews and Christians in Twelfth-Century Europe*; Iogna-Prat, *Order & Exclusion: Cluny and Christendom Face Heresy, Judaism, and Islam, 1000–1150*; Moore, *The Formation of a Persecuting Society: Authority and Deviance in Western Europe, 950–1250*; Resnick, *Marks of Distinction: Christian Perceptions of Jews in the High Middle Ages*.

44. In addition to the various works cited in the previous note, see Geissler, "Die Juden in mittelalterlichen Texten Deutschlands: Eine Untersuchung zum Minoritätproblem anhand literarischer Quellen," 182–89, who points to the interpretation of the Song of Songs as a centrally important medium for anti-Jewish polemic in eleventh- and twelfth-century Germany.

45. Honorius Augustodunensis, *Expositio in Cantica Canticorum*, PL 172:454. Here too cf. LaVere, *Out of the Cloister*, 44 n. 134.

46. Following MSS "mundi salvatorem," vs. PL "salvatorem."

47. Among others, see the various patristic and medieval opinions surveyed in Cohen, "The Jews as the Killers of Christ in the Latin Tradition, from Augustine to the Friars," and *Christ Killers: The Jews and the Passion from the Bible to the Big Screen*; and Kampling, *Das Blut Christi und die Juden: Mt 27,25 bei den lateinischsprachigen christlichen Autoren bis zu Leo dem Grossen*.

48. See above, part 1.

49. Haimo of Auxerre, *Homilia* 139 (Dominica XXV post Pentecosten), PL 118:741.

50. Honorius Augustodunensis, *Elucidarium* 3.10, in Gottschall, *Das "Elucidarium" des Honorius Augustodunensis*, 259: "Antichristus in magna Babylonia de meretrice generis Dan nascetur. In matris utero diabolo replebitur, in Corozaim a maleficis nutrietur. Universo orbi imperabit, totum genus humanum sibi quatuor modis subjugabit." Cf. PL 172:1163.

51. Otto of Freising, *Chronica sive historia de duabus civitatibus* 8.5–7, 594–96; trans. Evans and Knapp, *The Two Cities: A Chronicle of Universal History to the Year 1146 A.D.*, 461. On Otto's expectations of the end, see Rauh, *Das Bild des Antichrist im Mittelalter*, 302–65.

52. Cf. the comments of Gow, *The Red Jews: Antisemitism in an Apocalyptic Age*, 106–13, who casts the presentation of the eschatological Jewry by Otto of Freising and in the *Ludus* as the milder of the two prevalent alternative expectations.

53. On Hildegard, the Jews, and Antichrist, see Rauh, *Das Bild des Antichrist im Mittelalter*, 454–527; Schreckenberg, *Die Christlichen Adversus-Judaeos-Texte*

(11.-13. Jh.), 225–31; Carlevaris, "Sie Kamen zu Ihr, um Sie zu Befragen: Hildegard und die Juden"; McGinn, *Antichrist: Two Thousand Years of the Human Fascination with Evil*, 128–32; Emmerson, "The Representation of Antichrist in Hildegard of Bingen's *Scivias*: Image, Word, Commentary, and Visionary Experience." While the *Expositio in Psalmos* attributed to Gerhoh of Reichersberg (PL 194:538–39), yet another exponent of twelfth-century German Symbolism, does look forward to a glorious union of Jews and Gentiles in the eschatological church to wage war against Antichrist, Glorieux, *Pour revaloriser Migne: Tables rectificatives*, 75, credits Honorius with this section of the commentary.

54. See above, chapter 5, at notes 62–65.

55. Lerner, *The Feast of Saint Abraham: Medieval Millenarians and the Jews*, 24; and, on the ultimate conversion of the infidels in Honorius's commentary, see also Lerner, "Refreshment of the Saints: The Time after Antichrist as a Station for Earthly Progress in Medieval Thought," 110–12.

56. Cf. also Rainini, *Disegni dei tempi: Il "Liber figurarum" e la teologia figurativa di Gioacchino da Fiore*, 88, 125, esp. nn. 18–19.

57. Rainini, *Disegni dei tempi*, 31, 136 n. 45; cf. also Lerner, "Antichrists and Antichrist in Joachim of Fiore," esp. 566–70.

58. Above, note 50.

59. Honorius Augustodunensis, *Expositio in Cantica Canticorum*, PL 172:457. Earlier medieval examples of this reading include the commentaries of Bede, Angelom of Luxeuil, and Haymo of Auxerre.

60. MSS "concordia omnium" vs. PL "concordia omnino."

61. Honorius Augustodunensis, *Expositio in Cantica Canticorum*, PL 172:474.

62. Curschmann, "Imagined Exegesis," esp. 158–59. On the illustrations of Honorius's commentary, see also Menhardt, "Die Mandragora im millstätter Physiologus, bei Honorius Augustodunensis und im St. Trudperter Hohenliede," 178; Matter, *The Voice of My Beloved*, 65–68. And on trends in twelfth-century iconographic representations of the Song of Songs, see Wechsler, "A Change in the Iconography of the Song of Songs in Twelfth- and Thirteenth-Century Latin Bibles"; Malaise, "L'iconographie biblique du Cantique des Cantiques au XIIe siècle"; Shalev-Enyi, "Iconography of Love: Illustrations of Bride and Bridegroom in Ashkenazi Prayerbooks of the Thirteenth and Fourteenth Century."

63. Frank, "The Quadrige Aminadab Medallion in the 'Anagogical' Window at the Royal Abbey of Saint-Denis," 220; and see also Froehlich, *Sensing the Scriptures: Aminadab's Chariot and the Predicament of Biblical Interpretation*.

64. Plato, *Phaedrus* 246A; Ambrose, *De Abraham* 2.8.54, CSEL 32,1:607; and the additional citations adduced by Mähl, *Quadriga virtutum: Die Kardinaltugenden in den Geistesgeschichte der Karolingerzeit*, pt. 1. See also the rich and helpful studies of Eismeijer, *Divina Quaternitas: A Preliminary Study in the Method and Application of Visual Exegesis*; and Jacoff, *The Horses of San Marco and the Quadriga of the Lord*, ch. 1.

65. Irenaeus of Lyons, *Adversus haereses* 3.11.8, SC 211:160–71; Jerome, *Epistula* 53.9, CSEL 54:462–63; and the studies of Eismeijer and Jacoff cited in the previous note; more recently, cf. also Ambrus, "Love, Number, Symbol: The Figure of the *Rotae Ezekiel* in Joachim of Fiore."

66. Honorius Augustodunensis, *Expositio in Cantica Canticorum*, PL 172:481.

67. See Lewis, *Reading Images: Narrative Discourse and Reception in the Thirteenth-Century Illuminated Apocalypse*, 298–303; Monroe, "'Fair and Friendly, Sweet and Beautiful,'" 44–48.

68. Suger's description of the window appears in his *De administratione* 34, in Suger, *On the Abbey Church of St.-Denis and Its Art Treasures*, ed. Panofsky and Panofsky-Soergel, 72–77. Helpful studies include Hoffmann, "Sugers 'Anagogisches Fenster'" in St. Denis"; Grodecki, "The Style of the Stained-Glass Windows of Saint-Denis," and *Études sur les Vitraux de Suger à Saint Denis (XIIe siècle)*; Caviness, "Suger's Glass at Saint-Denis: The State of Research"; Frank, "The Quadrige Aminadab Medallion in the 'Anagogical' Window at the Royal Abbey of Saint-Denis"; Rudolph, "Inventing the Exegetical Stained-Glass Window: Suger, Hugh, and a New Elite Art."

69. Frank, "The Quadrige Aminadab Medallion in the 'Anagogical' Window at the Royal Abbey of Saint-Denis," 221. On the early medieval history of the *Maiestas Domini* motif in its various forms, see the magisterial study of Kühnel, *The End of Time in the Order of Things: Science and Eschatology in Early Medieval Art*.

70. Grodecki, "The Style of the Stained-Glass Windows of Saint-Denis," 276–77.

71. See Suger, *On the Abbey Church of St.-Denis and Its Art Treasures*, 72–77, 207–17 nn.

72. On the medieval representation of Synagoga, see, among others, Blumenkranz, *Le juif médiéval au miroir de l'art chrétien*, 105–15; Seiferth, *Synagogue and Church in the Middle Ages: Two Symbols in Art and Literature*; Schreckenberg, *The Jews in Christian Art: An Illustrated History*, ch. 3; Rowe, *The Jew, the Cathedral, and the Medieval City: Synagoga and Ecclesia in the Thirteenth Century*; Rubin, "Ecclesia and Synagoga: The Changing Meanings of a Powerful Pairing."

73. Schreckenberg, *The Jews in Christian Art: An Illustrated History*, 73.

74. Lewis, *Reading Images: Narrative Discourse and Reception in the Thirteenth-Century Illuminated Apocalypse*, 215–21, 296–309, 332–36, 399–400 nn. 293–99.

75. Lewis, *Reading Images*, 328–34.

76. Lewis, *Reading Images*, 298–300.

77. Lewis, *Reading Images*, 334. On this illuminated Apocalypse, see also De Winter, "Visions of the Apocalypse in Medieval England and France {Burckhardt-Wildt Apocalypse}."

78. Rauh, *Das Bild des Antichrist im Mittelalter*, 165, 177.

79. In addition to the works cited above, see Pelikan, *The Christian Tradition: A History of the Development of Doctrine*, vol. 5, ch. 4; and Evans, *Old Arts and New Theology: The Beginnings of Theology as an Academic Discipline*, ch. 4 (where Honorius Augustodunensis receives mention); but cf. the conclusions of Berger, "Mission to the Jews and Jewish-Christian Contacts in the Polemical Literature in the High Middle Ages"; and Chazan, *Daggers of Faith: Thirteenth-Century Christian Missionizing and Jewish Response*, ch. 1.

8. Jewish Converts and Christian Salvation

1. This chapter draws extensively from the pioneering doctoral thesis of my student Yosi Yisraeli, "Between Jewish and Christian Scholarship in the Fifteenth Century: The Consolidation of a 'Converso Doctrine' in the Theological Writings of Pablo de Santa María," parts of which have been published in Yisraeli, "Constructing

and Undermining Converso Jewishness: Profiat Duran and Pablo de Santa María," "A Christianized Sephardic Critique of Rashi's 'Peshaṭ' in Pablo de Santa María's 'Additiones ad Postillam Nicolai de Lyra,'" and "From Christian Polemic to a Jewish-Converso Dialogue: Jewish Skepticism and Rabbinic-Christian Traditions in the *Scrutinium Scripturarum*." On Pablo's career and opus, see also the studies of Baer, *History of the Jews in Christian Spain*, 2:141–51; Deyermond, "Historia universal e ideología nacional en Pablo de Santa María"; Kriegel, "Autour de Pablo de Santa Maria et d'Alfonso de Cartagena: Alignement culturel et originalité 'converso,'" and "Paul de Burgos et Profiat Duran déchiffrent 1391"; Jones, "Paul of Burgos and the 'Adversus Judaeos' Tradition"; Szpiech, "Scrutinizing History: Polemic and Exegesis in Pablo de Santa María's *Siete edades del mundo*," "A Father's Bequest: Augustinian Typology and Personal Testimony in the Conversion Narrative of Solomon Halevi/Pablo de Santa María," and *Conversion and Narrative : Reading and Religious Authority in Medieval Polemic*, esp. ch. 1.

2. This contrasts impressively with Honorius Augustodunensis, *Expositio in Cantica Canticorum*, PL 172:473, where *Synagoga conversa* laments the error of her ancient forebear in rejecting and crucifying Jesus.

3. Yisraeli, "Between Jewish and Christian Scholarship," ch. 4.

4. These ideas bear an intriguing resemblance to those of Judah Halevi in his parable of the seed portraying the relationship between Judaism and the monotheistic religions (Christianity and Islam) that followed in its wake—as explained in Lasker, "Proselyte Judaism, Christianity, and Islam in the Thought of Judah Halevi," 86–87: "The religion of Moses is like a seed. The religions which came after Judaism will eventually become like Judaism, even if temporarily they appear to overwhelm their source, just as earth, water, and soil overwhelm the seed. Christianity and Islam are, in truth, a preparation for the Messiah, who is the fruit, and they will become his fruit. If they accept the Messiah, they will become one tree; then the nations will revere the root which they had previously despised. This imagery of Christianity and Islam returning to the tree of the true religion, which is Judaism, was particularly appropriate for Halevi's polemic with the competing religions since its origin is the New Testament. In the Epistle to the Romans, chapter 11, Paul compares the Jews to branches of an olive tree which have been cut off from the trunk. Onto the original trunk were then grafted new branches, namely, the Gentiles. When the Jews eventually recognize the truth of Jesus as the Messiah, they will then be grafted back unto the tree trunk from which they were removed. Halevi's point is clear: Judaism is the original tree, and the Jews were always part of it. Eventually other nations will be grafted onto this tree, but they will recognize their naturalized status and revere the original native-born part of the tree."

5. Yisraeli, "Between Jewish and Christian Scholarship," 294.

6. Pablo de Santa María, *Additio* ad Deuteronomy 33, *Biblia sacra*, 1:376, cited in Yisraeli, "Between Jewish and Christian Scholarship," 294.

7. Stuczynski, "Pro-'Converso' Apologetics and Biblical Exegesis," 169; and cf. Cohen, *Living Letters of the Law: Ideas of the Jew in Medieval Christianity*, ch. 9, and "Supersessionism, the Epistle to the Romans, Thomas Aquinas, and the Jews of the Eschaton."

8. Yisraeli, "Between Jewish and Christian Scholarship," 301–2.

9. See Cohen, *Living Letters of the Law*, among others.

10. See *Biblia sacra*, 3:168rv.

11. Cf. the previous understanding of these roaming dogs in Honorius Augustodunensis, *Expositio in Cantica Canticorum*, above, chapter 7, note 20.

12. *Biblia sacra*, 3:168r, cited in Yisraeli, "Between Jewish and Christian Scholarship," 309 n. 63.

13. *Biblia sacra*, 3:168rv, cited in Yisraeli, "Between Jewish and Christian Scholarship," 309–10, n. 64.

14. Yisraeli, "Between Jewish and Christian Scholarship," 86–89, 151–53, 167–68, and elsewhere.

15. See Cohen, "Tortosa in Retrospect: The Disputation as Reported in Solomon Ibn Verga's *Shevet Yehudah*" [Hebrew], and *A Historian in Exile: Solomon Ibn Verga, Shevet Yehudah, and the Jewish-Christian Encounter*, ch. 2, along with other studies cited there.

16. *Biblia sacra*, 3:168v.

17. Pablo de Santa María, *Scrutinium scripturarum* 2.6.13, ed. Sanctotis, 529; ed. Javier Martínez de Bedoya, "La segunda parte del *Scrutinium scripturarum*," 164; cited in Yisraeli, "Between Jewish and Christian Scholarship," 330–31 n. 95.

18. Pablo de Santa María, *Scrutinium scripturarum* 2.6.14, ed. Sanctotis, 532; ed. Martínez de Bedoya, 166–67; cited in Yisraeli, "Between Jewish and Christian Scholarship," 337 n. 110.

19. Pablo de Santa María, *Scrutinium scripturarum* 2.6.13, ed. Sanctotis, 530; ed. Martínez de Bedoya, 1; cited in Yisraeli, "Between Jewish and Christian Scholarship," 329 n. 93. Cf. Cathcart and Gordon, *The Targum of the Minor Prophets*, 35–36.

20. Stuczynski, "Pro-'Converso' Apologetics and Biblical Exegesis," 169–70.

21. Pablo de Santa María, *Scrutinium scripturarum* 2.6.13, ed. Sanctotis, 528–29; ed. Martínez de Bedoya, 163; cited in Yisraeli, "Between Jewish and Christian Scholarship," 327–28 n. 91.

22. Alonso de Cartagena, *Defensorium unitatis christianae* 2.1.2, ed. Manuel Alonso (Madrid, 1943), 99; cited in Rosenstock, *New Men: Conversos, Christian Theology, and Society in Fifteenth-Century Castile*, 41 n. 9. On Alonso and his ideas concerning Jews and Judaism, see also Kriegel, "Autour de Pablo de Santa Maria et d'Alfonso de Cartagena"; Rosenstock, "Alonso de Cartgena: Nation, Miscegenation, and the Jews in Late-Medieval Castile"; Edwards, "New Light on the Converso Debate? The Jewish Christianity of Alonso de Cartagena and Juan de Torquemada"; Harris, "Enduring Covenant in the Christian Middle Ages," 581–83.

23. See Alonso de Cartagena, *Defensorium unitatis christianae* 1.5, 75–77; cited in Rosenstock, *New Men*, 31 n. 10.

24. Alonso de Cartagena, *Defensorium unitatis christianae* 2.1.2, 98–99; cited in Rosenstock, *New Men*, 38–40, translation (here emended slightly) in n. 8.

25. Rosenstock, *New Men*, 38–40. See also Harris, "Enduring Covenant in the Christian Middle Ages," 581–83.

26. Cf. the observations and cited references in Netanyahu, *The Origins of the Inquisition in Fifteenth-Century Spain*, 421; Meyuhas Ginio, "An Appeal in Favor of the Judeoconversos: Juan de Torquemada and His *Tractatus contra Madianitas et Ismaelitas*" [Hebrew], 327–28; Izbicki, "Juan de Torquemada's Defense of the Conversos," 198–99.

27. See the studies in the previous notes.

28. Juan de Torquemada, *Tratado contra los madianitas e ismaelita* 13, ed. Eloy Benito Ruano et al., 195–206.

29. Rosenstock, *New Men*, 61–68.

30. See McMichael, "The End of the World, Antichrist, and the Final Conversion of the Jews in the *Fortalitium Fidei* of Friar Alonso de Espina (d. 1464)," which includes Alonso's *Fortalitium Fidei* 3.12.6–8 on 264–73. See also McMichael, *Was Jesus of Nazareth the Messiah? Alphonso de Espina's Argument against the Jews in the "Fortalitium Fidei"* (c.1464), "The Sources for Alfonso de Espina's Messianic Argument against the Jews in the *Fortalitium Fidei*," "Did Isaiah Foretell Jewish Blindness and Suffering for Not Accepting Jesus of Nazareth as Messiah? A Medieval Perspective," and "Alfonso de Espina on the Mosaic Law"; Echevarria, *The Fortress of Faith: The Attitude towards Muslims in Fifteenth-Century Spain*; Meyuhas Ginio, "La polémica cristiana *Adversus Judaeos* en España a fines de la Edad Media," "The Fortress of Faith—at the End of the West," and "Expectations of the End of Time in Alonso de Espina's *Fortalitium Fidei* (Castile, 1464)" [Hebrew]; Vidal Doval, *Misera Hispania: Jews and Conversos in Alonso de Espina's "Fortalitium Fidei."*

31. McMichael, "The End of the World, Antichrist, and the Final Conversion of the Jews," 237.

32. McMichael, "The End of the World, Antichrist, and the Final Conversion of the Jews," 237.

33. Yisraeli, "Between Jewish and Christian Scholarship," 344.

34. Yisraeli, "Between Jewish and Christian Scholarship," 38, 343–44, 362–63.

9. Puritans, Jews, and the End of Days

1. Williamson, *Apocalypse Then: Prophecy and the Making of the Modern World*, 65–69. On the development, impact, and importance of Puritan apocalyptic thought, see also Hill, *Antichrist in Seventeenth-Century England*; Capp, *The Fifth Monarchy Men: A Study in Seventeenth-Century English Millenarianism*, and "Transplanting the Holy Land: Diggers, Fifth Monarchists, and the New Israel"; Bauckham, *Tudor Apocalypse: Sixteenth-Century Apocalypticism, Millennarianism, and the English Reformation: From John Bale to John Foxe and Thomas Brightman*; Firth, *The Apocalyptic Tradition in Reformation Britain, 1530–1645*; Brady, *The Contribution of British Writers between 1560 and 1830 to the Interpretation of Revelation 13.16–18*; Bostick, *The Antichrist and the Lollards: Apocalypticism in Late Medieval and Reformation England*; Gribben, *The Puritan Millennium: Literature & Theology, 1550–1682*; Jue, "Puritan Millenarianism in Old and New England"; Bossert, "The Tudor Antichrists, 1485–1603"; Johnston, *Revelation Restored: The Apocalypse in Later Seventeenth-Century England*; Ward, "A Passion for God and a Passion for Jews: The Basis and Practice of Jewish Mission 1550–1850"—among others.

2. Among others, see Davis, *Periodization and Sovereignty: How Ideas of Feudalism and Secularization Govern the Politics of Time.*

3. John Bale, *The Image of Both Churches*, ed. Minton, along with Minton's helpful introduction. On Bale and his work, see also Warner, "John Bale: Bibliographer between Trithemius and the Four Horsemen of the Apocalypse," as well as the works cited in the previous note and below.

4. See Olsen, *John Foxe and the Elizabethan Church*; Achinstein, "John Foxe and the Jews"; Schmuck, "The 'Turk' as Antichrist in John Foxe's *Acts and Monuments* (1570)"; and others.

5. See also Almond, "John Napier and the Mathematics of the 'Middle Future' Apocalypse."

6. Crome, "'Shall They Return to Jerusalem Againe?' Jewish Restoration in Early Modern English Thought" offers a well-formulated, insightful survey. On Puritan primitivism and its bearing on apocalypticism, see Bozeman, *To Live Ancient Lives: The Primitivist Dimension in Puritanism*; Hutchins, *Inventing Eden: Primitivism, Millennialism, and the Making of New England*.

7. Cogley, "The Fall of the Ottoman Empire and the Restoration of Israel in the 'Judeo-Centric' Strand of Puritan Millenarianism," 330–31, who considers (for the most part) Puritan writers not discussed here. On Puritan Judeo-centrism and attitudes toward Jews and Judaism in general, see also Toon, *Puritans, the Millennium and the Future of Israel: Puritan Eschatology 1600 to 1660*; Katz, *Philo-Semitism and the Readmission of the Jews to England, 1603–1655*, chs. 3–4, and "Millenarianism, the Jews, and Biblical Criticism in Seventeenth-Century England"; Matar, "The Idea of the Restoration of the Jews in English Protestant Thought, 1661–1701"; Zakai, "The Poetics of History and the Destiny of Israel: The Role of the Jews in English Apocalyptic Thought during the 16th-Century and 17th-Century"; Glaser, *Judaism without Jews: Philosemitism and Christian Polemic in Early Modern England*; Guibbory, *Christian Identity, Jews, and Israel in Seventeenth-Century England*, esp. 61–67, 186–209; and, above all, the recent studies of Crome: "'The Proper and Naturall Meaning of the Prophets': The Hermeneutic Roots of Judeo-Centric Eschatology"; "Historical Understandings in Millennial Studies: A Case Study of Christian Zionism"; *The Restoration of the Jews: Early Modern Hermeneutics, Eschatology, and National Identity in the Works of Thomas Brightman*; *Prophecy, and Eschatology in the Transatlantic World, 1550–1800*; and "'Shall They Return to Jerusalem Againe?' Jewish Restoration in Early Modern English Thought."

8. Thomas Draxe, *An alarum to the last iudgement. Or an exact discourse of the second comming of Christ: and of the generall and remarkeable signes and fore-runners of it past, present, and to come; soundly and soberly handled, and wholesomely applyed. Wherein diuers deep mysteries are plainly expounded, and sundry curiosities are duely examined, answered and confuted*, 76–77.

9. Thomas Draxe, *An alarum to the last iudgement*, 78; see Crome, *The Restoration of the Jews*, 148–49.

10. Thomas Draxe, *An alarum to the last iudgement*, 34–41. On the recent development of the motif of the papal Antichrist, see Buck, "*Anatomia Antichristi*: Form and Content of the Papal Antichrist," and *The Roman Monster: An Icon of the Papal Antichrist in Reformation Polemics*.

11. Henry Finch, *The calling of the Iewes: A present to Iudah and the children of Israel that ioyned with him, and to Ioseph (the valiant tribe of Ephraim) and all the house of Israel that ioyned with him. The Lord giue them grace, that they may returne and seeke Iehovah their God, and Dauid their King, in these latter dayes. There is prefixed an epistle vnto them, written for their sake in the Hebrue tongue, and translated into English*, 6.

12. Finch, *The calling of the Iewes*, 50–52, 77–79.

13. Finch, *The calling of the Iewes*, 135. On the ten lost tribes in the Puritan imagination, see Cogley, "'The Most Vile and Barbarous Nation of All the World': Giles Fletcher the Elder's *The Tartars or, Ten Tribes* (ca. 1610).'"

14. On Finch's career and ideas, see Toon, *Puritans, the Millennium, and the Future of Israel*, 32–34; Prest, "The Art of Law and the Law of God: Sir Henry Finch (1558–1625)"; Crome, *The Restoration of the Jews*, 150–54. Inasmuch as Joseph Mede was not exactly Puritan, we have not made mention of his similar Judeo-centric millenarian ideas. See Crome, *The Restoration of the Jews*, 154–63; Jue, *Heaven upon Earth: Joseph Mede (1586–1638) and the Legacy of Millenarianism*, esp. ch. 7.

15. For a list of North American Puritan commentaries on Romans 11, see Smolinski, "Israel Redivivus: The Eschatological Limits of Puritan Typology in New England," 393–95.

16. Brunotte, "From Nehemia Americanus to Indianized Jews," 195.

17. Increase Mather, *The Mystery of Israel's Salvation*. On Mather and his ideas in their New England context, in addition to the studies cited above, see Middlekauff, *The Mathers: Three Generations of Puritan Intellectuals, 1596–1728*; Lowance and Waters, introduction to Increase Mather, "Increase Mather's 'New Jerusalem': Millennialism in Late Seventeenth-Century New England," 343–61; Lowance, *The Language of Canaan: Metaphor and Symbol in New England from the Puritans to the Transcendentalists*; Zakai, "Puritan Millennialism and Theocracy in Early Massachusetts," *Exile and Kingdom: History and Apocalypse in the Puritan Migration to America*, and "Theocracy in Massachusetts: The Puritan Universe of Sacred Imagination"; Hall, *The Last American Puritan: The Life of Increase Mather, 1639–1723*.

18. Mather, *The Mystery of Israel's Salvation*, 8.

19. Mather, *The Mystery of Israel's Salvation*, 9.

20. Mather, *The Mystery of Israel's Salvation*, 53; in the pages that follow (53–181), Mather elaborates the details of this magnificent eschatological drama and renewal, in which the Jews occupy center stage and will be the primary beneficiaries.

21. Mather, *The Mystery of Israel's Salvation*, 57.

22. On Brightman, his opus, and his impact, see Zakai, "Thomas Brightman and English Apocalyptic Tradition"; Almond, "Thomas Brightman and the Origins of Philo-Semitism: An Elizabethan Theologian and the Restoration of the Jews to Israel"; Crome, *The Restoration of the Jews*; and others cited above.

23. Thomas Brightman, *A most comfortable exposition: of the last and most difficult part of the prophecie of Daniel from the 26. verse of the 11. chap, to the end of the 12. chapter. Wherin the restoring of the Iewes and their callinge to the faith of Christ, after the utter overthrow of their three last enemies, is set forth in livelie coulours, by the labour and studie of that bright and worthie man of God*, 3.

24. Zakai, "Thomas Brightman and English Apocalyptic Tradition," 38, 43.

25. Almond, "Thomas Brightman and the Origins of Philo-Semitism," 4.

26. Thomas Brightman, *The revelation of St. Iohn illustrated with an analysis & scholions: wherein the sense is opened by the scripture & the euent of things fore-told shewed by histories*, 4th ed., 16–17. On the minimal differences—negligible for our purposes here—between this edition and the original English edition (Amsterdam, 1611), see Crome, *The Restoration of the Jews*, 217–20.

27. Brightman, *The revelation of St. Iohn*, 34.

28. Brightman, *The revelation of St. Iohn*, 255.

29. Brightman, *The revelation of St. Iohn*, 382; cf. also 555 and elsewhere.

30. For the quotations that follow here, Brightman, *The revelation of St. Iohn*, 543–45.

31. Brightman, *The revelation of St. Iohn*, 715.

32. See Brightman's "Confuting that Counterfeit Antichrist," interpolated in *The revelation of St. Iohn*, 612–746.

33. Brightman, *The revelation of St. Iohn*, 784.

34. Brightman, *The revelation of St. Iohn*, 847.

35. Brightman, *The revelation of St. Iohn*, 867.

36. Brightman, *The revelation of St. Iohn*, 876.

37. Firth, *The Apocalyptic Tradition in Reformation Britain, 1530–1645*, 172.

38. Thomas Brightman, *A most comfortable exposition . . . of Daniel*, 4.

39. Brightman, *A most comfortable exposition . . . of Daniel*, 5.

40. Brightman, *A most comfortable exposition . . . of Daniel*, 35–36.

41. Brightman, *A most comfortable exposition . . . of Daniel*, 62.

42. Brightman, *A most comfortable exposition . . . of Daniel*, 62–63.

43. Brightman, *A most comfortable exposition . . . of Daniel*, 102–4.

44. Scheper, "Reformation Attitudes toward Allegory and the Song of Songs," 556; Stievermann, "Reading Canticles in the Tradition of New England Millennialism: John Cotton and Cotton Mather's Commentaries on the Song of Songs," 215. See also Hill, *The English Bible and the Seventeenth-Century Revolution*, 363–70; Flinker, *The Song of Songs in English Renaissance Literature: Kisses of Their Mouths*.

45. Clarke, *Politics, Religion, and the Song of Songs in Seventeenth-Century England*, 127.

46. On the Song's interpretation history and Brightman's place within it, see also Ginsburg, *The Song of Songs; and, Coheleth (Commonly Called the Book of Ecclesiastes)*, 20–102; Hammond, "The Bride in Redemptive Time: John Cotton and the Canticles Controversy"; Kallas, "Martin Luther as Expositor of the Song of Songs"; Alexander, "The Song of Songs as Historical Allegory: Notes on the Development of an Exegetical Tradition," and his edition of *The Targum of Canticles*, esp. 27–52; Dove, "Literal Senses in the Song of Songs"; Longman, *Song of Songs*, 20–47; Almond, "Thomas Brightman and the Origins of Philo-Semitism," esp. 11–14; Crome, *The Restoration of the Jews*, 81–93; Keen, "Song of Songs in the Eyes of Rashi and Nicholas of Lyra."

47. Thomas Brightman, *A Commentary on the Canticles or the Song of Salomon*, 1022.

48. Brightman, *A Commentary on the Canticles*, 1052–53.

49. Brightman, *A Commentary on the Canticles*, 1055.

50. See the helpful tabulation in Crome, *The Restoration of the Jews*, 89–91.

51. Brightman, *A Commentary on the Canticles*, 1060.

52. Brightman, *A Commentary on the Canticles*, 1065.

53. Brightman, *A Commentary on the Canticles*, 1069.

54. Brightman, *A Commentary on the Canticles*, 1051.

55. Brightman, *A Commentary on the Canticles*, 1065; and see Crome, *The Restoration of the Jews*, 65–66, 103.

56. Homes, *A Commentary, Literal or Historical, and Mystical or Spiritual, on the Whole Book of Canticles*, 413.

57. Homes, *A Commentary, Literal or Historical, and Mystical or Spiritual, on the Whole Book of Canticles*, 413–15.

58. Homes, *A Commentary, Literal or Historical, and Mystical or Spiritual, on the Whole Book of Canticles*, 418.

59. See Rosenmeier, "Eaters and Non-Eaters: John Cotton's *A Brief Exposition of . . . Canticles* (1642) in Light of Boston's (Linc.) Religious and Civil Conflicts, 1619–22," 149; Clarke, *Politics, Religion, and the Song of Songs in Seventeenth-Century England*, 124. On Cotton's leadership, polemics, and biblical commentaries in Puritan New England, see also Smolinski, "'The Way to Lost Zion': The Cotton-Williams Debate on the Separation of Church and State in Millenarian Perspective"; Gordis, *Opening Scripture: Bible Reading and Interpretive Authority in Puritan New England*; Stievermann, "Reading Canticles in the Tradition of New England Millennialism," and *Prophecy, Piety, and the Problem of Historicity: Interpreting the Hebrew Scriptures in Cotton Mather's "Biblia Americana"*; along with the works cited above in notes 15–17.

60. John Cotton, *A Brief Exposition of the Whole Book of Canticles, or, Song of Solomon*, 195.

61. Among others, see Lowance, *The Language of Canaan*, ch. 3; Hammond, "The Bride in Redemptive Time"; and Stievermann, "Reading Canticles in the Tradition of New England Millennialism," 219–20, who points out that the second posthumous edition (London, 1655) of Cotton's commentary seeks to defuse criticism with "less controversial, practical-devotional observations."

62. Cotton, *A Brief Exposition of the Whole Book of Canticles*, 196–97.

63. Cotton, *A Brief Exposition of the Whole Book of Canticles*, 207–13 (quote on 208).

64. Cotton, *A Brief Exposition of the Whole Book of Canticles*, 237–38.

65. Cotton, *A Brief Exposition of the Whole Book of Canticles*, 243.

66. Cotton, *A Brief Exposition of the Whole Book of Canticles*, 246.

67. Cotton, *A Brief Exposition of the Whole Book of Canticles*, 198–202.

68. Stievermann, "Reading Canticles in the Tradition of New England Millennialism," 222.

69. Stievermann, "Reading Canticles in the Tradition of New England Millennialism," 232. On Cotton Mather and his retreat from the "Brightmanian" approach to the Song of Songs, see also Middlekauff, *The Mathers*; Silverman, *The Life and Times of Cotton Mather*; Stadler, "Ejaculating Tongues: Poe, Mather, and the Jewish Penis"; Smolinski, "'Eager Imitators of the Egyptian Inventions': Cotton Mather's Engagement with John Spencer and the Debate about the Pagan Origin of the Mosaic Laws, Rites, and Customs"; Stievermann, *Prophecy, Piety, and the Problem of Historicity: Interpreting the Hebrew Scriptures in Cotton Mather's "Biblia Americana."*

70. Among numerous others, see Nederveen Pieterse, "The History of a Metaphor: Christian Zionism and the Politics of Apocalypse"; Sizer, *Christian Zionism: Road Map to Armageddon?*; Cohn-Sherbok, *The Politics of Apocalypse: The History and Influence of Christian Zionism*; Lewis, *The Origins of Christian Zionism: Lord Shaftesbury and Evangelical Support for a Jewish Homeland*; Crome, "Historical Understandings in Millennial Studies: A Case Study of Christian Zionism"; Smith, *More Desired than Our Owne Salvation: The Roots of Christian Zionism*; Ariel, "Israel in Contemporary Evangelical Christian Millennial Thought."

Afterword

1. Thornton, "Jews in Early Christian Eschatological Scenarios."

2. Heng, *The Invention of Race in the European Middle Ages*, 19, 55. See also the instructive discussion, advancing what Heng (25–26) terms an ambivalent "agnostic stance," in Nirenberg, "Was There Race before Modernity? The Example of 'Jewish' Blood in Late Medieval Spain," along with other, more recent studies cited in Heng's thorough notes, especially to ch. 1 (45–54).

3. Walliss, *The End All Around Us: Apocalyptic Texts and Popular Culture.*

Bibliography

Primary Sources

ANF	Ante-Nicene Fathers
CCCM	Corpus Christianorum, Continuatio Mediaevalis
CCSL	Corpus Christianorum, Series Latina
CSEL	Corpus Scriptorum Ecclesiasticorum Latinorum
FOC	Fathers of the Church
GCS	Die griechischen christlichen Schriftsteller
LNPNF	Library of Nicene and Post-Nicene Fathers
NRSV	New Revised Standard Version
OTP	*The Old Testament Pseudepigrapha*
PG	Patrologia Graeca
PL	Patrologia Latina
SC	Sources chrétiennes
SLNPNF	Select Library of Nicene and Post-Nicene Fathers

Albert the Great. *Opera omnia*. 38 vols. Paris: Vivès, 1890–1899.

Alexander, Philip S., ed. *The Targum of Canticles*. The Aramaic Bible 17A. Collegeville, MN: Liturgical Press, 2003.

Ambrosiaster. *Commentaries on Romans and 1–2 Corinthians*. Edited by Gerald L. Bray. Downers Grove, IL: IVP Academic, 2009.

Augustine. *The City of God against the Pagans*. Edited by George E. McCracken et al. 7 vols. Loeb Classical Library. Cambridge, MA: Harvard University Press, 1957–1972.

——. *Four Anti-Pelagian Writings*. Trans. John A. Mourant and William A. Collinge. FOC 86. Washington, DC: Catholic University of America Press, 1992.

——. *Letters*. Trans. Wilfrid Parsons. 5 vols. FOC 12, 18, 20, 30, 32. 1951–1956; repr., Washington, DC: Catholic University of America Press, 1964–1967.

——. *Treatises on Marriage and Other Subjects*. Edited by Roy J. Deferrari. FOC 27. New York: Fathers of the Church, 1955.

Beatus of Liebana. *Commentary on the Apocalypse*. Trans. M. S. O'Brien. 2 vols. N.p., 2013–2016.

Bede. *The Reckoning of Time*. Trans. Faith Wallis. Translated Texts for Historians 29. Liverpool: Liverpool University Press, 1999.

Berger, David, ed. *The Jewish-Christian Debate in the High Middle Ages: A Critical Edition of the Niẓẓaḥon Vetus*. Philadelphia: Jewish Publication Society of America, 1979.

Berger, Klaus, ed. *Die griechische Daniel-Diegese: Eine altkirchliche Apokalypse*. Studia Post-Biblica 27. Leiden: Brill, 1976.

Biblia latina cum glossa ordinaria: Facsimile Reprint of the Editio Princeps Adolph Rusch of Strassburg. 4 vols. 1480–1481; repr., Turnhout: Brepols, 1992.

Biblia sacra cum glossis. 6 vols. Venice, 1588.

Boveland, Karin, et al., eds. *Der Antichrist, und Die fünfzehn Zeichen vor dem jüngsten Gericht: Faksimile der ersten typographischen Ausgabe eines unbekannten Strassburger Druckers, um 1480*. 2 vols. Hamburg: Wittig, 1979.

Brightman, Thomas. *A Commentary on the Canticles or the Song of Salomon*. London, 1644.

———. *A most comfortable exposition: of the last and most difficult part of the prophecie of Daniel from the 26. verse of the 11. chap, to the end of the 12. chapter. Wherin the restoring of the Iewes and their callinge to the faith of Christ, after the utter overthrow of their three last enemies, is set forth in livelie coulours, by the labour and studie of that bright and worthie man of God*. London, 1635.

———. *The revelation of St. Iohn illustrated with an analysis & scholions: wherein the sense is opened by the scripture & the euent of things fore-told shewed by histories*. 4th ed. London, 1644.

Calvin, John. *Commentarius in Epistolam Pauli ad Romanos*. Edited by T. H. L. Parker and D. C. Parker. Ioannis Calvini Opera Exegetica 13. Geneva: Librairie Droz, 1999.

Cathcart, Kevin J., and R. P. Gordon, eds. *The Targum of the Minor Prophets*. The Aramaic Bible 14. Wilmington, DE: M. Glazier, 1989.

Charlesworth, James H., ed. *The Old Testament Pseudepigrapha*. 2 vols. Garden City, NY: Doubleday, 1983–1985.

Cornelius à Lapide. *Commentaria in sacram scripturam*. 24 vols. Paris: Vivès, 1866–1874.

Cotton, John. *A Brief Exposition of the Whole Book of Canticles, or, Song of Solomon*. London, 1642.

Draxe, Thomas. *An alarum to the last iudgement. Or An exact discourse of the second comming of Christ: and of the generall and remarkeable signes and fore-runners of it past, present, and to come; soundly and soberly handled, and wholesomely applyed. Wherein diuers deep mysteries are plainly expounded, and sundry curiosities are duely examined, answered and confuted*. London, 1615.

Emmerson, Richard K., and David F. Hult, eds. *Antichrist and Judgment Day: The Middle French "Jour du jugement."* Asheville, NC: Pegasus Press, 1998.

Erasmus of Rotterdam. *New Testament Scholarship: Paraphrases on Romans and Galatians*. Edited by Robert D. Sider. Collected Works of Erasmus 42. Toronto: University of Toronto Press, 1984.

———. *Opera omnia*. 10 vols. 1703–1706; repr., London: Gregg, 1962.

Falk, Gerhard. *The Jew in Christian Theology: Martin Luther's Anti-Jewish "Vom Schem Hamphoras."* Jefferson, NC: McFarland, 1992.

Finch, Henry. *The calling of the Ievves A present to Iudah and the children of Israel that ioyned with him, and to Ioseph (the valiant tribe of Ephraim) and all the house of*

Israel that ioyned with him. The Lord giue them grace, that they may returne and seeke Iehovah their God, and Dauid their King, in these latter dayes. There is prefixed an epistle vnto them, written for their sake in the Hebrue tongue, and translated into English. London, 1621.

Frankfurter, David, ed. *Elijah in Upper Egypt: The Apocalypse of Elijah and Early Egyptian Christianity*. Minneapolis: Fortress Press, 1993.

Fredriksen, Paula, ed. and trans. *Augustine on Romans: Propositions from the Epistle to the Romans, Unfinished Commentary on the Epistle to the Romans*. SBLTT 23/ Early Christian Literature Series 6. Chico, CA: Society for Biblical Literature, 1982.

Henneke, Edgar, et al., eds. *New Testament Apocrypha*. 2 vols. Philadelphia: Westminster Press, 1963–1965.

Herrad of Hohenbourg. *Hortus deliciarum*. Edited by Rosalie Green et al. 2 vols. London: Warburg Institute, 1979.

Hippolytus of Rome. *Commentary on Daniel and "Chronicon."* Edited by T. C. Schmidt. Piscataway, NJ: Gorgias Press, 2017.

Homes, Nathanael. *A Commentary, Literal or Historical, and Mystical or Spiritual, on the Whole Book of Canticles*. London, 1650(?).

Joachim of Fiore. *Adversus Iudeos*. Edited by Arsenio Frugoni. Fonti per la storia d'Italia medievale. Rome: Istituto Storico Italiano, 1957.

——. *Concordia Noui ac Veteris Testamenti*. Edited by Alexander Patschovsky. 4 vols. Fonti per la storia dell'Italia medievale: Antiquitates 49. Rome: Istituto Storico Italiano, 2018.

——. *De ultimis tribulationibus*. Edited by Kurt-Victor Selge. In "Ein Traktat Joachims," *Florensia* 7 (1993): 7–35.

——. *Exhortatorium Iudeorum*. Edited by Alexander Patschovsky. Fonti per la storia dell'Italia medieval: Antiquitates 26. Rome: Istituto Storico Italiano, 2006.

——. *Expositio in Apocalypsim*. 1527; repr., Frankfurt: Minerva, 1964.

——. *Liber de Concordia Noui ac Veteris Testamenti*. Edited by E. Randolph Daniel. *Transactions of the American Philosophical Society* 73, no. 8 (1983): i-lxii, 1–455.

——. *Il libro delle figure dell'abate Gioachino da Fiore*. Edited by Leone Tondelli and Marjorie Reeves. 2nd ed. 2 vols. Turin: Società editrice internazionale, 1953.

——. *Psalterium decem cordarum*. Edited by Kurt-Victor Selge. Monumenta Germaniae Historica: Quellen zur Geistesgeschichte des Mittelalters 20. Hannover: Hahnsche Buchhandlung, 2009.

——. *Tractatus super quatuor evangelia*. Edited by Francesco Santi. Fonti per la storia dell'Italia medievale: Antiquitates 17. Rome: Istituto Storico Italiano, 2002.

John of Rupescissa. *Liber ostensor quod adesse festinant tempora*. Edited by André Vauchez, Clémence Thévenaz Modestin, and Christine Morerod-Fattebert. Sources et documents d'histoire du Moyen Âge 8. Rome: École Francaise de Rome, 2005.

——. *Liber secretorum eventuum*. Edited by Robert Lerner and Christine Morerod-Fattebert. Spicilegium Friburgense 36. Fribourg: Éditions Universitaires Fribourg Suisse, 1994.

——. *Vade mecum in tribulacione (1356): A Late Medieval Eschatological Manual for the Forthcoming Thirteen Years of Horror and Hardship*. Edited by Matthias Kaup. London: Routledge, 2017.

——. *Vade mecum in tribulatione*. Edited by Elena Tealdi. Milan: Vita e Pensiero, 2015.

Johnston, Alexandra F., ed. "Chester Cycle 1572/2010." https://pls.artsci.utoronto.ca/wp-content/uploads/2015/09/chester22.pdf.

Juan de Torquemada. *Tratado contra los madianitas e ismaelita*. Edited by Eloy Benito Ruano et al. Madrid: Aben Ezra Ediciones, 2002.

Lightfoot, J. L., ed. *The Sibylline Oracles: With Introduction, Translation, and Commentary on the First and Second Books*. Oxford: Oxford University Press, 2007.

Litwa, M. David, ed. *Refutation of All Heresies*. Atlanta: SBL Press, 2015.

Luther, Martin. *Lectures on Romans*. Trans. Wilhelm Pauck. Philadelphia: Westminster Press, 1961.

——. *Werke*. 69 vols. Weimar: H. Böhlau, 1883–1983.

Mandeville, John. *The Book of Marvels and Travel*. Trans. Anthony Bale. Oxford: Oxford University Press, 2012.

Martène, Edmund, and Ursinus Durand, eds. *Veterum scriptorum et monumentorum historicorum, dogmaticorum, moralium, amplissima collectio*. 9 vols. Paris, 1724–1733.

Martínez de Ampiés, Martin. *Libro del Anticristo: Declaración . . . del sermón de San Vicente (1496)*. Edited by Françoise Gilbert. Anejos de RILCE 26. Pamplona: Ediciones Universidad de Navarra, 1999.

Mather, Increase. "Increase Mather's 'New Jerusalem': Millennialism in Late Seventeenth-Century New England." Edited by Mason I. Lowance Jr. and David Watters. *Proceedings of the American Antiquarian Society* 87 (1977): 343–408.

——. *The Mystery of Israel's Salvation*. London, 1669.

McGinn, Bernard, ed. *Apocalyptic Spirituality: Treatises and Letters of Lactantius, Adso of Montier-en-Der, Joachim of Fiore, the Franciscan Spirituals, Savonarola*. New York: Paulist Press, 1979.

Melito of Sardis. *On Pascha and Fragments*. Edited by Stuart G. Hall. Oxford: Clarendon Press, 1979.

Musper, H. Theodore, and Manfred von Arnim, eds. *Der Antichrist und die fünfzehn Zeichen: Faksimile-Ausgabe des einzigen erhaltenen chiroxylographischen Blockbuches*. 2 vols. Munich: Prestel-Verlag, 1970.

Origen. *Commentary on the Epistle to the Romans: Books 6–10*. Trans. Thomas P. Scheck. FOC 104. Washington, DC: Catholic University of America Press, 2002.

——. *Der Römerbriefkommentar*. Edited by Caroline P. Hammond Bammel. 3 vols. Vetus Latina 16, 33, 34. Freiburg: Herder, 1990–1998.

Otto of Freising. *Chronica sive historia de duabus civitatibus*. Edited by Adolf Hofmeister and Walther Lammers. Berlin: Rütten & Loenig, 1960.

——. *The Two Cities: A Chronicle of Universal History to the Year 1146 A.D.* Trans. Austin P. Evans and Charles Knapp. New York: Octagon Books, 1966.

Pablo de Santa Maria. *Scrutinium scripturarum*. Edited by Christopher Sanctotis. Burgos, 1591.

——. "La segunda parte del *Scrutinium scripturarum*." Edited by Javier Martínez de Bedoya. Th.D. thesis, Pontificia Universitas Sanctae Crucis, 2002.

Pelagius. *Commentary on St Paul's Epistle to the Romans*. Trans. and ed. Theodore de Bruyn. Oxford: Oxford University Press, 1993.

——. *Expositions of Thirteen Epistles of St. Paul* Edited by Alexander Souter. 3 vols. Texts and Studies: Contributions to Biblical and Patristic Literature 9. Cambridge: Cambridge University Press, 1922–1931.

Peter Abelard. *Commentary on the Epistle to the Romans.* Trans. Stephn R. Cartwright. FOC Medieval Continuation 12. Washington, DC: Catholic University of America Press, 2011.

——. *Expositio in Epistolam ad Romanos.* Edited by Rolf Peppermüller. 3 vols. Fontes Christiani 26. Freiburg: Herder, 2000.

Peter John Olivi. *Commentary on the Apocalypse.* Trans. Warren Lewis. Saint Bonaventure, NY: Franciscan Institute Publications, 2017.

——. *Lectura super Apocalypsim.* Edited by Warren Lewis. Saint Bonaventure, NY: Franciscan Institute Publications, 2015.

Pope, Marvin H. *Song of Songs: A New Translation with Introduction and Commentary.* The Anchor Bible. Garden City, NY: Doubleday, 1977.

Pseudo-Ephrem. "Sermon on the End." Trans. J. Reeves. https://pages.uncc.edu/john-reeves/research-projects/trajectories-in-near-eastern-apocalyptic/pseudo-ephrem-syriac/.

Pseudo-Methodius. *Apocalypse.* Edited by Benjamin Garstad. Cambridge, MA: Harvard University Press, 2012.

Ricke, Joseph Martin, ed. "The Antichrist 'Vita' at the End of the Middle Ages: An Edition of 'The Byrthe and Lyfe of the Moost False and Deceytfull Antechryst.'" Ph.D. dissertation, Rice University, 1982.

Roy, Emile, ed. *Le "Jour du jugement": Mystere français sur le Grand Schism.* 1902; repr., Geneva: Slatkine Reprints, 1976.

Sackur, Ernst, ed. *Sibyllinische Texte und Forschungen: Pseudomethodius, Adso und Die tiburtinische Sibylle.* 1898; repr., Turin: Bottega D'Erasmo, 1963.

Sbaffoni, Fausto, ed. *Testi sull' anticristo.* 2 vols. Florence: Nardini, 1992.

Simonsohn, Shlomo, ed. *The Apostolic See and the Jews—Documents: 492–1404.* Pontifical Institute of Medieval Studies Texts and Studies 94. Toronto: Pontifical Institute of Medieval Studies, 1988.

Staab, Karl, ed. *Pauluskommentare aus der griechischen Kirche.* Münster: Aschendorff, 1933.

Suger of Saint-Denis. *On the Abbey Church of St.-Denis and Its Art Treasures.* Edited by Erwin Panofsky and Gerda Panofsky-Soergel. 2nd ed. Princeton: Princeton University Press, 1977.

Symes, Carol, trans. *The Play about the Antichrist: Ludus de Antichristo.* https://www.academia.edu/31354647/.

Theodore of Mopsuestia. "*Commentary on Romans:* An Annotated Translation." Trans. Charles David Gregory. Ph.D. dissertation, Southern Baptist Theological Seminary, 1992.

Thomas Aquinas. *Commentary on the Letter of Saint Paul to the Romans.* Trans. F. R. Larcher; ed. J. Mortensen and E. Alcarón. Latin/English Edition of the Works of St. Thomas Aquinas 37. Lander, WY: Aquinas Institute, 2012.

——. *Summa theologiae.* Edited by Thomas Gilby et al. 60 vols. Cambridge: Blackfriars, 1964–1976.

Verhelst, Daniel, ed. "Scarpsum de dictis sancti Efrem prope fine mundi." In *Pascua Mediaevalia: Studies voor Prof. J.M. de Smet,* edited by R. Lievens et al. Leuven: Leuven University Press, 1983.

Walberg, Emmanuel, ed. *Deux versions inédites de la légende de l'Antéchrist, en vers français du XIIIe siècle.* Lund: C.W.K. Gleerup, 1928.

William of Saint-Amour. *De periculis novissimorum temporum.* Edited by G. Geltner. Paris: Peeters Press, 2008.

Williram of Ebersberg. *Expositio in Cantica Canticorum.* Edited by Henrike Lähnemann and Michael Rupp. 2004; repr., Berlin: De Gruyter, 2012.

Woodward, Michael Scott, trans. *The Glossa Ordinaria on Romans.* Kalamazoo: Medieval Institute Publications, Western Michigan University, 2011.

Wright, John, trans. *The Play of Antichrist.* Toronto: Pontifical Institute of Medieval Studies, 1967.

Young, Karl, ed. *The Drama of the Medieval Church.* 2 vols. Oxford: Clarendon Press, 1962.

Secondary Sources

Aageson, James W. "Scripture and Structure in the Development of the Argument in Romans 9–11." *Catholic Biblical Quarterly* 48 (1986): 265–89.

——. "Typology, Correspondence, and the Application of Scripture in Romans 9–11." *Journal for the Study of the New Testament* 31 (1987): 51–72.

Abulafia, Anna Sapir. *Christians and Jews in the Twelfth-Century Renaissance.* London: Routledge, 1995.

——. *Christians and Jews in Dispute: Disputational Literature and the Rise of Anti-Judaism in the West (c. 1000–1150).* Aldershot: Ashgate, 1998.

——. "The Conquest of Jerusalem: Joachim of Fiore and the Jews." In *The Experience of Crusading,* vol.1, *Western Approaches,* edited by Marcus Bull and Norman Housely, 1:127–46. Cambridge: Cambridge University Press, 2003.

Achinstein, Sharon. "John Foxe and the Jews." *Renaissance Quarterly* 54 (2001): 86–120.

Adams, Jonathan, and Jussi Hanska. *The Jewish-Christian Encounter in Medieval Preaching.* Routledge Research in Medieval Studies 6. New York: Routledge, 2015.

Affeldt, Werner. "Verzeichnis der Römerbriefkommentare der Lateinischen Kirche bis zu Nikolaus von Lyra." *Traditio* 13 (1957): 369–406.

——. *Die weltliche Gewalt in der Paulus-Exegese: Rom.13, 1–7 in den Römerbriefkommentaren der lateinischen Kirche bis zum Ende des 13. Jahrhunderts.* Forschungen zur Kirchen- und Dogmengeschichte 22. Göttingen: Vandenhoeck & Ruprecht, 1969.

Aichele, Klaus. *Das Antichristdrama des Mittelalters der Reformation und Gegenreformation.* The Hague: M. Nijhoff, 1974.

——. "The Glorification of Anti-Christ in the Concluding Scenes of the Medieval 'Ludus de Antichristo.'" *MLN* 91 (1976): 424–36.

Akbari, Suzanne Conklin. *Idols in the East: European Representations of Islam and the Orient, 1100–1450.* Ithaca, NY: Cornell University Press, 2009.

Alexander, Paul J. *The Byzantine Apocalyptic Tradition,* edited by Dorothy de F. Abrahame. Berkeley: University of California Press, 1985.

Alexander, Philip S. "The Song of Songs as Historical Allegory: Notes on the Development of an Exegetical Tradition." In *Targumic and Cognate Studies: Essays in Honour of Martin McNamara,* 14–29. Sheffield: Sheffield Academic Press, 1996.

Almond, Philip C. "Thomas Brightman and the Origins of Philo-Semitism: An Elizabethan Theologian and the Restoration of the Jews to Israel." *Reformation & Renaissance Review* 9 (2007): 3–25.

———. "John Napier and the Mathematics of the 'Middle Future' Apocalypse." *Scottish Journal of Theology* 63 (2010): 54–69.

———. *The Devil: A New Biography*. Ithaca, NY: Cornell University Press, 2014.

———. *The Antichrist: A New Biography*. Cambridge: Cambridge University Press, 2020.

Ambrus, Gábor. "Love, Number, Symbol: The Figure of the *Rotae Ezekiel* in Joachim of Fiore." *Cristianesimo Nella Storia* 35 (2014): 451–73.

———. "The Eschatological Future of the Jews in the 'Vine Diagram' of Joachim of Fiore." *Irish Theological Quarterly* 81 (2016): 171–94.

Anderson, Andrew Runni. *Alexander's Gate, Gog and Magog, and the Inclosed Nations*. Cambridge, MA: Medieval Academy of America, 1932.

Anderson, Paul N., and R. Alan Culpepper. *Communities in Dispute: Current Scholarship on the Johannine Epistles*. Atlanta: SBL Press, 2014.

Ariel, Yaakov. "Israel in Contemporary Evangelical Christian Millennial Thought." *Numen: International Review for the History of Religions* 59 (2012): 456–85.

Arrighini, Ambrogio. *L'anticristo: Nelle sacre scritture, nella storia, nella letteratura*. 2nd ed. Le metamorfosi del sacro 15. Genoa: I Dioscuri, 1988.

Astell, Ann W. *The Song of Songs in the Middle Ages*. Ithaca, NY: Cornell University Press, 1990.

Awad, Najeeb G. "The Influence of John Chrysostom's Hermeneutics on John Calvin's Exegetical Approach to Paul's Epistle to the Romans." *Scottish Journal of Theology* 63 (2010): 414–36.

Awerbuch, Marianne. *Christlich-jüdische Begegnung im Zeitalter der Frühscholastik*. Munich: Chr. Kaiser, 1980.

Babcock, William S. "Augustine's Interpretation of Romans." *Augustinian Studies* 10 (1979): 55–74.

Bădiliță, Cristian. *Métamorphoses de l'Antichrist chez les Pères de l'Église*. Théologie Historique. Paris: Beauchesne, 2005.

Baer, Yitzhak. *History of the Jews in Christian Spain*. 1961.

Bagby, Stephen. "Volitional Sin in Origen's Commentary on Romans." *Harvard Theological Review* 107 (2014): 340–62.

———. *Sin in Origen's Commentary on Romans*. Lanham, MD: Lexington Books / Fortress Academic, 2018.

Baker, Murray. "Paul and the Salvation of Israel: Paul's Ministry, the Motif of Jealousy, and Israel's Yes." *Catholic Biblical Quarterly* 67 (2005): 469–84.

Bale, Anthony P. *The Jew in the Medieval Book: English Antisemitisms, 1350–1500*. Cambridge Studies in Medieval Literature. Cambridge: Cambridge University Press, 2006.

———. "Christian Anti-Semitism and Intermedial Experience in Late Medieval England." In *The Religions of the Book: Christian Perceptions, 1400–1660*, edited by Matthew Dimmock and Andrew Hadfield, 23–44. Early Modern Literature in History. Basingstoke: Palgrave Macmillan, 2008.

Barclay, John M. G. "A Rereading of Romans: Justice, Jews and Gentiles." *Journal of Theological Studies* 46 (1995): 646–51.

———. *Paul and the Gift*. Grand Rapids, MI: Eerdmans Publishing Company, 2015.

Bärsch, Claus-E. "Antijudaismus, Apokalyptik und Satanologie: Die religiösen Elemente des Nationalsozialistischen Antisemitismus." *Zeitschrift für Religions- und Geistesgeschichte* 40 (1988): 112–33.

———. "Der Jude als Antichrist in der NS-Ideologie: Die kollektive Identität der Deutschen und der Antisemitismus unter religionspolitologischer Perspektive." *Zeitschrift für Religions- und Geistesgeschichte* 47 (1995): 160–88.

Basevi, Claudio. "La justificación en los comentarios de Pelagio, Lutero y Santo Tomás a La Epístola a los Romanos." *Scripta Theologica* 19 (1–2) (1987): 113–76.

Bauckham, Richard, ed. *Tudor Apocalypse: Sixteenth-Century Apocalypticism, Millennarianism, and the English Reformation: From John Bale to John Foxe and Thomas Brightman ; Illustrative Texts from The Lanterne of Lyght . . . [et al.].* Oxford: Sutton Courtenay Press, 1978.

———. "The Two Fig Tree Parables in the Apocalypse of Peter." *Journal of Biblical Literature* 104 (1985): 269–87.

———. "The Apocalypse of Peter: An Account of Research." In *Aufstieg und Niedergang der Römischen Welt* 25,6:4712–50. 2nd ser. Berlin: De Gruyter, 1988.

———. *The Fate of the Dead: Studies on the Jewish and Christian Apocalypses.* Boston: Brill, 1998.

———. "Jews and Jewish Christians in the Land of Israel at the Time of the Bar Kochba War, with Special Reference to the Apocalypse of Peter." In *Tolerance and Intolerance in Early Judaism and Christianity*, edited by Graham Stanton and Guy G. Stroumsa, 228–38. Cambridge: Cambridge University Press, 1998.

Baxter, A. G., and John A. Ziesler. "Paul and the Arboriculture : Romans 11:17–24." *Journal for the Study of the New Testament* 24 (1985): 25–32.

Beker, J. Christiaan. "Romans 9–11 in the Context of the Early Church." *Princeton Seminary Bulletin* 11 (1990): 40–55.

Belkin, Ahuva. "The Antichrist Legend in the Utrecht Psalter." *Rivista di Storia e Letteratura Religiosa* 23 (1987): 279–88.

———. "Antichrist as the Embodiment of the Insipiens in Thirteenth-Century French Psalters." *Florilegium* 10 (1991): 65–82.

Bell, Richard H. *Provoked to Jealousy: The Origin and Purpose of the Jealousy Motif in Romans 9–11.* Wissenschaftliche Untersuchungen zum Neuen Testament. Tubingen: Mohr Siebeck, 1994.

Belli, Filippo. *Argumentation and Use of Scriptures in Romans 9–11.* Analecta Biblica 183. Rome: Gregorian & Biblical Press, 2010.

Benmelech, Moti. "Back to the Future: The Ten Tribes and Messianic Hopes in Jewish Society during the Early Modern Age." In *Peoples of the Apocalypse: Eschatological Beliefs and Political Scenarios*, edited by Wolfram Brandes, Felicitas Schmieder, and Rebekka Voß, 63:193–209. Millennium-Studien/Millennium Studies. Berlin: De Gruyter, 2016.

Ben-Shalom, Ram. "Between Official and Private Dispute: The Case of Christian Spain and Provence in the Late Middle Ages." *AJS Review* 27 (2003): 23–72.

Berg, M. van den, and M. Dircksen. "Mandrake from Antiquity to Harry Potter." *Akroterion* 53 (2008): 67–79.

Berger, David. "Three Typological Themes in Jewish Messianism: Messiah Son of Joseph, Rabbinic Calculations, and the Figure of Antichrist." *Association for Jewish Studies Review* 10 (1985): 141–64.

———. "Mission to the Jews and Jewish-Christian Contacts in the Polemical Literature in the High Middle Ages." *American Historical Review* 91 (1986): 576.

Bietenhard, Hans. *Caesarea, Origenes und die Juden*. Stuttgart: Kohlhammer, 1974.

Bignami Odier, Jeanne. *Jean de Roquetaillade (De Rupescissa)/par Jeanne Bignami-Odier*. Paris: Imprimerie Nationale, 1981.

Birnbaum, Elisabeth. "Sulamit und die Kirchenväter: Wer ist die Geliebte des Hohe-liedes?" In *Biblische Frauen in patristischer Rezeption*, edited by Agnethe Siquans, 127–53. Göttingen: Vandenhoeck & Ruprecht, 2017.

Black, Fiona C. "Unlikely Bedfellows: Allegorical and Feminist Readings of Song of Songs 7.1–8." In *The Song of Songs: A Feminist Companion to the Bible*, edited by Athalya Brenner and Carole R. Fontaine, 104–29. Sheffield: Sheffield Academic Press, 2000.

Blumenfeld-Kosinski, Renate. "Illustration as Commentary in Late Medieval Images of Antichrist's Birth." *Deutsche Vierteljahrsschrift für Literaturwissenschaft und Geistesgeschichte* 63 (1989): 589–607.

Blumenkranz, Bernhard. *Die Judenpredigt Augustins: Ein Beitrag zur Geschichte der jüdisch-christlichen Beziehungen in den ersten Jahrhunderten*. Basler Beiträge zur Geschichtswissenschaft 25. Basel: Helbing & Lichtenhahn, 1946.

——. "Augustin et les Juifs. Augustin et le judaïsme." *Recherches Augustiniennes* 1 (1958): 225–41.

——. *Le juif médiéval au miroir de l'art chrétien*. Paris: Études augustiniennes, 1966.

Bøe, Sverre. *Gog and Magog: Ezekiel 38–39 as Pre-Text for Revelation 19,17 and 20,7–10*. Wissenschaftliche Untersuchungen zum Neuen Testament 2,135. Tübingen: Mohr Siebeck, 2001.

Boguslawski, Steven C. *Thomas Aquinas on the Jews: Insights into His Commentary on Romans 9–11*. Mahwah, NJ: Paulist Press, 2008.

Bonura, Christopher. "When Did the Legend of the Last Emperor Originate? A New Look at the Textual Relationship between the Apocalypse of Pseudo-Methodius and the Tiburtine Sibyl." *Viator* 47 (2016): 47–100.

Bossert, Kathleen Meredith Barker. "The Tudor Antichrists, 1485–1603." Ph.D. dissertation, University of Maryland, 2010.

Bostick, Curtis V. *The Antichrist and the Lollards: Apocalypticism in Late Medieval and Reformation England*. Studies in Medieval and Reformation Thought. Leiden: Brill, 1998.

Bourgel, Jonathan. "Jewish Christians and Other Religious Groups in Judaea from the Great Revolt to the Bar-Kokhba." Ph.D. dissertation, Tel Aviv University, 2009.

Bousset, Wilhelm. *The Antichrist Legend: A Chapter in Jewish and Christian Folklore*. London: Hutchinson, 1896.

Boyarin, Daniel. "The Subversion of the Jews: Moses's Veil and the Hermeneutics of Supersession." *Diacritics* 23 (1993): 16–35.

——. *A Radical Jew: Paul and the Politics of Identity*. Berkeley: University of California Press, 1994.

Bozeman, Theodore Dwight. *To Live Ancient Lives: The Primitivist Dimension in Puritanism*. Chapel Hill: University of North Carolina Press, 1988.

Brady, David. *The Contribution of British Writers between 1560 and 1830 to the Interpretation of Revelation 13.16–18 (The Number of the Beast): A Study in the History of Exegesis*. Beiträge zur Geschichte der biblischen Exegese 27. Tübingen: Mohr Siebeck, 1983.

Brandes, Wolfram, and Felicitas Schmieder, eds. *Antichrist: Konstruktionen von Feind-bildern*. Berlin: Akademie, 2010.

Braude, Benjamin. "'Mandeville's' Jews among Others." In *Pilgrims & Travelers to the Holy Land*, edited by Bryan F. Le Beau and Menachem Mor, 133–58. Studies in Jewish Civilization 7. Omaha, NE: Creighton University Press, 1996.

——. "The Sons of Noah and the Construction of Ethnic and Geographical Identities in the Medieval and Early Modern Periods." *William and Mary Quarterly: A Magazine of Early American History and Culture* 54 (1997): 103–42.

Bray, Gerald L. "Ambrosiaster." In *Reading Romans through the Centuries: From the Early Church to Karl Barth*, edited by Jeffrey P. Greenman and Timothy Larsen, 21–38. Grand Rapids, MI: Brazos, 2005.

Bright, Pamela. "Augustine." In *Reading Romans through the Centuries: From the Early Church to Karl Barth*, edited by Jeffrey P. Greenman and Timothy Larsen, 59–80. Grand Rapids, MI: Brazos, 2005.

Brown, Peter. "Pelagius and His Supporters: Aims and Environment." *Journal of Theological Studies* 19 (1968): 93–114.

Brown, Raymond Edward. *The Epistles of John*. The Anchor Bible, v. 30. Garden City, NY: Doubleday, 1982.

Brunotte, Ulrike. "From Nehemia Americanus to Indianized Jews." *Journal of Modern Jewish Studies* 15 (2016): 188–207.

Buc, Philippe. *The Dangers of Ritual: Between Early Medieval Texts and Social Scientific Theory*. Princeton: Princeton University Press, 2001.

Buchholz, Dennis D. *Your Eyes Will Be Opened: A Study of the Greek (Ethiopic) Apocalypse of Peter*. Atlanta: Scholars Press, 1988.

Buck, Lawrence P. "*Anatomia Antichristi*: Form and Content of the Papal Antichrist." *Sixteenth Century Journal: Journal of Early Modern Studies* 42 (2011): 349–68.

——. *The Roman Monster: An Icon of the Papal Antichrist in Reformation Polemics*. Early Modern Studies Series. Kirksville, MO: Truman State University Press, 2014.

Buitenwerf, Rieuwerd. *Book III of the Sibylline Oracles and Its Social Setting*. Studia in Veteris Testamenti Pseudepigrapha 17. Leiden: Brill, 2003.

——. "The Identity of the Prophetess Sibyl in 'Sibylline Oracles' III." In *Prophets and Prophecy in Jewish and Early Christian Literature*, edited by Jozef Verheyden, Korinna Zamfir, and Tobias Nicklas, 41–55. Wissenschaftliche Untersuchungen zum Neuen Testament, 2,286. Tübingen: Mohr Siebeck, 2010.

Burns, J. Patout. "The Interpretation of Romans in the Pelagian Controversy." *Augustinian Studies* 10 (1979): 43–54.

Burr, David. "The Persecution of Peter Olivi." *Transactions of the American Philosophical Society* 66 (1976): 1–98.

——. "Olivi's Apocalyptic Timetable." *Journal of Medieval and Renaissance Studies* 11 (1981): 237–60.

——. *Olivi's Peaceable Kingdom: A Reading of the Apocalypse Commentary*. Philadelphia: Po, 1993.

——. "The Antichrist and the Jews in Four Thirteenth-Century Apocalyse Commentaries." In *Friars and Jews in the Middle Ages and the Renaissance*, edited by Steven J. McMichael and Susan E. Myers, 23–38. The Medieval Franciscans 2. Leiden: Brill, 2004.

Campbell, Nathaniel. "'Lest He Should Come Unforeseen': The Antichrist Cycle in the *Hortus Deliciarum*." *Gesta* 54 (2015): 85–118.

Campbell, William S. *Paul's Gospel in an Intercultural Context: Jew and Gentile in the Letter to the Romans*. Studies in the Intercultural History of Christianity, vol. 69. Frankfurt: Peter Lang, 1991.

——. *Paul and the Creation of Christian Identity*. London: T&T Clark, 2008.

——. "The Addressees of Paul's Letter to the Romans: Assemblies of God in House Churches and Synagogues?" In *Between Gospel and Election: Explorations in the Interpretation of Romans 9–11*, edited by Florian Wilk and J. Ross Wagner, 171–95. Wissenschaftliche Untersuchungen zum Neuen Testament 257. Tübingen: Mohr Siebeck, 2010.

Capp, Bernard S. *The Fifth Monarchy Men: A Study in Seventeenth-Century English Millenarianism*. London: Faber and Faber, 1972.

——. "Transplanting the Holy Land: Diggers, Fifth Monarchists, and the New Israel." In *Holy Land, Holy Lands, and Christian History: Papers Read at the 1998 Summer Meeting and the 1999 Winter Meeting of the Ecclesiastical History Society*, edited by R. N. Swanson, 288–98. Woodbridge: Ecclesiastical Historical Society, 2000.

Carbó García, Juan Ramón. "La venida de Gog y Magog: Identificaciones de la prole del Anticristo entre la tradición apocalíptica, la Antigüedad tardía y el Medievo." *Arys: Antigüedad: Religiones y Sociedades* 10 (2012): 381–408.

Carlevaris, Angela. "Sie Kamen zu Ihr, um Sie zu Befragen: Hildegard und die Juden." In *Hildegard von Bingen in ihrem historischen Umfeld*, edited by Alfred Haverkamp and Alexander Reberchon, 117–28. Mainz: Philipp von Zabern, 2000.

Carr, Amelia Jane. "Visual and Symbolic Imagery in the Twelfth-Century Tegernsee *Ludus de Antichristo*." Ph.D. dissertation, Northwestern University, 1984.

Carr, David McLain. "The Song of Songs as a Microcosm of the Canonization and Decanonization Process." In *Canonization and Decanonization: Papers Presented to the International Conference of the Leiden Institute for the Study of Religions (LISOR), Held at Leiden 9–10 January 1997*, edited by Arie van der Kooij and Karel van der Toorn, 173–89. Studies in the History of Religions 82. Leiden: Brill, 1998.

Caubet Iturbe, Francisco-Javier. "Et sic omnis israel salvus fieret, Rom 11, 26: Su interpretación por los escritores cristianos de los siglos III–XII." *Estudios Bíblicos* 21 (1962): 127–50.

Caviness, Madeline Harrison. "Suger's Glass at Saint-Denis: The State of Research." In *Abbot Suger and Saint-Denis: A Symposium*, 257–72. New York: Metropolitan Museum of Art, 1986.

Cazanave, Caroline. "Hénoch et Elie: 'Et c'est la fin des temps pour quoi ils sont ensemble . . .'" In *Fin des temps et temps de la fin dans l'univers médiéval*, 125–43. Senefiance. Aix-en-Provence: Presses universitaires de Provence, 2014.

Cerrato, John A. *Hippolytus between East and West: The Commentaries and the Provenance of the Corpus*. Oxford Theological Monographs. Oxford: Oxford University Press, 2002.

——. "Hippolytus and Cyril of Jerusalem on the Antichrist: When Did an Antichrist Theology Emerge in Early Christian Baptismal Catechesis?" In *Apocalyptic*

Thought in Early Christianity, edited by Robert J. Daly, 154–59. Grand Rapids, MI: Baker Academic Press, 2009.

Chazan, Robert. *Daggers of Faith: Thirteenth-Century Christian Missionizing and Jewish Response*. Berkeley: University of California Press, 1989.

——. *Medieval Stereotypes and Modern Antisemitism*. Berkeley: University of California Press, 1997.

Chilton, Bruce. *Studying the Historical Jesus: Evaluations of the State of Current Research*. New Testament Tools and Studies 19. Leiden: Brill, 1998.

Cirafesi, Wally V. "The Johannine Community Hypothesis (1968–Present): Past and Present Approaches and a New Way Forward." *Currents in Biblical Research* 12 (2014): 173–93.

Clark, Elizabeth A. "Origen, the Jews, and the Song of Songs: Allegory and Polemic in Christian Antiquity." In *Perspectives on the Song of Songs = Perspektiven der Hoheliedauslegung*, edited by Anselm C. Hagedorn, 346:274–93. Berlin: De Gruyter, 2005.

Clarke, Elizabeth. *Politics, Religion, and the Song of Songs in Seventeenth-Century England*. New York: Palgrave Macmillan, 2011.

Clopper, Lawrence M. "The History and Development of the Chester Cycle." *Modern Philology: A Journal Devoted to Research in Medieval and Modern Literature* 75 (1978): 219–46.

Coccini, Francesca. "Paul and the Destiny of Israel in Origen's Commentary on the Letter to the Romans." In *Ancient Perspectives on Paul*, edited by Tobias Niklas et al., 279–96. Göttingen: Vandenhoeck & Ruprecht, 2013.

Cockett, Peter. "Staging Antichrist and the Performance of Miracles." In *Spectacle and Public Performance in the Late Middle Ages and the Renaissance*, edited by Robert E. Stillman, 31–50. Studies in Medieval and Reformation Traditions 113. Leiden: Brill, 2006.

Cogley, Richard W. "The Fall of the Ottoman Empire and the Restoration of Israel in the 'Judeo-Centric' Strand of Puritan Millenarianism." *Church History* 72 (2003): 304–32.

——. "'The Most Vile and Barbarous Nation of All the World': Giles Fletcher the Elder's The Tartars or, Ten Tribes (ca. 1610)." *Renaissance Quarterly* 58 (2005): 781–814.

Cohen, Gerson D. "The Song of Songs and the Jewish Religious Mentality." In *Studies in the Variety of Rabbinic Cultures*, 3–17. Philadelphia: Jewish Publication Society of America, 1991.

Cohen, Jeremy. *Be Fertile and Increase, Fill the Earth and Master It: The Ancient and Medieval Career of a Biblical Text*. Ithaca, NY: Cornell University Press, 1989.

——. *Christ Killers: The Jews and the Passion from the Bible to the Big Screen*. New York: Oxford University Press, 2007.

——. *The Friars and the Jews: The Evolution of Medieval Anti-Judaism*. Ithaca, NY: Cornell University Press, 1982.

——, ed. *From Witness to Witchcraft: Jews and Judaism in Medieval Christian Thought*. Wolfenbutteler Mittelalter-Studien 11. Wiesbaden: Harrassowitz 1997.

——. "The Jews as the Killers of Christ in the Latin Tradition, from Augustine to the Friars." *Traditio* 39 (1983): 1–27.

——. *Living Letters of the Law: Ideas of the Jew in Medieval Christianity*. Berkeley: University of California Press, 1999.

——. "The Mystery of Israel's Salvation: Romans 11:25–26 in Patristic and Medieval Exegesis." *Harvard Theological Review* 98 (2005): 247–81.

——. "Revisiting Augustine's Doctrine of Jewish Witness." *Journal of Religion* 89 (2009): 564–78.

——. "Scholarship and Intolerance in the Medieval Academy: The Study and Evaluation of Judaism in European Christendom." *American Historical Review* 91 (1986): 593.

——. "'Slay Them Not': Augustine and the Jews in Modern Scholarship." *Medieval Encounters* 4 (1998): 78–92.

——. "Supersessionism, the Epistle to the Romans, Thomas Aquinas, and the Jews of the Eschaton." *Journal of Ecumenical Studies* 52 (2017): 527–53.

——. "*Synagoga Conversa*: Honorius Augustodunensis, the Song of Songs, and Christianity's 'Eschatological Jew.'" *Speculum* 79 (2004): 309–40.

——. "Tortosa in Retrospect: The Disputation as Reported in Solomon Ibn Verga's *Shevet Yehudah*" [Hebrew]. *Zion* 76 (2011): 417–52.

Cohn-Sherbok, Dan. *The Politics of Apocalypse: The History and Influence of Christian Zionism*. Oxford: Oneworld, 2006.

Collins, Adela Yarbro. "The Early Christian Apocalypses." *Semeia* 14 (1979): 61–121.

Collins, John J. "Pre-Christian Jewish Messianism: An Overview." In *The Messiah in Early Judaism and Christianity*, edited by Magnus Zetterholm, 1–20. Minneapolis: Fortress Press, 2007.

——. *Apocalypse, Prophecy, and Pseudepigraphy: On Jewish Apocalyptic Literature*. Grand Rapids, MI: Eerdmans Publishing Company, 2015.

Collins, John J., Bernard McGinn, and Stephen J. Stein, eds. *The Encyclopedia of Apocalypticism*. 3 vols. New York: Continuum, 1998.

Cook, Michael J. "The Ties That Blind: An Exposition of II Corinthians 3:12–4:6 and Romans 11:7–10." In *When Jews and Christians Meet*, edited by Jackob Josef Petuchowski, 125–39. Albany: State University of New York Press, 1988.

——. "Paul's Argument in Romans 9–11." *Review & Expositor* 103 (2006): 91–111.

Coolman, Holly Taylor. "Romans 9–11: Rereading Aquinas on the Jews." In *Reading Romans with St. Thomas Aquinas*, 101–12. Washington, DC: Catholic University of America Press, 2012.

Cosgrove, Charles H. "The Church with and for Israel: History of a Theological Novum before and after Barth." *Perspectives in Religious Studies* 22 (1995): 259–78.

——. *Elusive Israel: The Puzzle of Election in Romans*. Louisville: Westminster John Knox Press, 1997.

Courtray, Régis. "Nouvelles recherches sur la transmission du *De Antichristo* de Jérôme." *Sacris Erudiri* 43 (2004): 33–53.

——. "La réception du commentaire sur Daniel de Jérôme dans l'occident médiéval chrétien (VIIe–XIIe siècle)." *Sacris Erudiri* 44 (2005): 117–87.

Cranford, Michael. "Election and Ethnicity: Paul's View of Israel in Romans 9.1–13." *Journal for the Study of the New Testament* 50 (1993): 27–41.

Crome, Andrew. "'The Proper and Naturall Meaning of the Prophets': The Hermeneutic Roots of Judeo-Centric Eschatology." *Renaissance Studies* 24 (2010): 725–41.

——. "Historical Understandings in Millennial Studies: A Case Study of Christian Zionism." In *Beyond the End: The Future of Millennial Studies*, edited by Joshua

Searle and Kenneth G. C. Newport, 20–46. The Bible in the Modern World 49. Sheffield: Sheffield Phoenix Press, 2012.

——. *The Restoration of the Jews: Early Modern Hermeneutics, Eschatology, and National Identity in the Works of Thomas Brightman*. Cham, Switzerland: Springer International Publishing, 2014.

——, ed. *Prophecy and Eschatology in the Transatlantic World, 1550–1800*. Christianities in the Trans-Atlantic World, 1500–1800. London: Palgrave Macmillan, 2016.

——. "'Shall They Return to Jerusalem Againe?': Jewish Restoration in Early Modern English Thought." In *Christian Zionism and English National Identity, 1600–1850*, edited by Andrew Crome, 29–66. Cham, Switzerland: Springer International Publishing, 2018.

Crouzel, Henri. *Origen: The Life and Thought of the First Great Theologian*. Translated by A. S. Worrall. San Francisco: Harper & Row, 1989.

Curschmann, Michael. "Imagined Exegesis: Text and Picture in the Exegetical Works of Rupert of Deutz, Honorius Augustodunensis, and Gerhoch of Reichersberg." *Traditio* 44 (1988): 145–69.

Dahan, Gilbert. *Les intellectuels chrétiens et les juifs au Moyen Age*. Paris: Éditions du Cerf, 1990.

——. "Genres, Forms, and Various Methods in Christian Exegesis of the Middle Ages." In *Hebrew Bible/Old Testament: The History of Its Interpretation*, 1,2:196–236. Göttingen: Vandenhoeck & Ruprecht, 2000.

Dan, Joseph. "Armilus: The Jewish Antichrist and the Origins and Dating of Sefer Zerubbavel." In *Toward the Millennium: Messianic Expectations from the Bible to Waco*, edited by Peter Schaefer and Mark R. Cohen, 73–104. Studies in the History of Religions 77. Leiden: Brill, 2001.

Daniel, E. Randolph. "A New Understanding of Joachim: The Concords, the Exile, and the Exodus." In *Gioacchino da Fiore tra Bernardo di Clairvaux e Innocenzo III*, edited by Roberto Rusconi, 5:209–22. Rome: Vielle, 2001.

——. "Abbot Joachim of Fiore and the Conversion of the Jews." In *Friars and Jews in the Middle Ages and Renaissance*, edited by Susan Meyers and Steven J. McMichael, 1–21. The Medieval Franciscans 2. Leiden: Brill, 2004.

——. *Abbot Joachim of Fiore and Joachimism: Selected Articles*. Variorum Collected Studies Series. Farnham: Ashgate, 2011.

——. "Double Antichrist or Antichrists: Abbot Joachim of Fiore." Chapter 7 in *Abbot Joachim of Fiore and Joachimism*. Farnham: Ashgate, 2011.

Darby, Peter. *Bede and the End of Time*. Studies in Early Medieval Britain. Farnham: Ashgate, 2012.

——. "Bede's History of the Future." In *Bede and the Future*, edited by Peter Darby and Faith Wallis, 115–38. Burlington, VT: Ashgate, 2014.

Davies, D. P. "Eschatological Hope in the Early Christian Community." In *The Coming Deliverer: Millennial Themes in World Religions*, 102–18. Cardiff: University of Wales Press, 1997.

De Lange, Nicholas Robert Michael. *Origen and the Jews: Studies in Jewish-Christian Relations in Third-Century Palestine*. Cambridge: Cambridge University Press, 1976.

De Lubac, Henri. *Medieval Exegesis: The Four Senses to Scripture*. Translated by Marc Sebanc and E. M. Macierowski. 3 vols. Grand Rapids, MI: Eerdmans Publishing Company, 1998–2009.

Dendle, Peter. "Review of Philip C. Almond, *The Devil: A New Biography*." *Magic, Ritual & Witchcraft* 11 (2016): 135–38.

Derolez, Albert. *The Autograph Manuscript of the Liber Floridus: A Key to the Encyclopedia of Lambert of Saint-Omer*. Corpus Christianorum, Autographa Medii Aevi 4. Turnhout: Brepols, 1998.

Despres, Denise L. "Cultic Anti-Judaism and Chaucer's Litel Clergeon." *Modern Philology* 91 (1994): 413.

De Toro, José Miguel. "*Exsilium hominum ignorantia est*: Honorius Augustodunensis and Knowledge in the Twelfth Century." *Imago Temporis—Medium Aevum* 13 (2019): 115–33.

Devun, Leah. *Prophecy, Alchemy, and the End of Time: John of Rupescissa in the Late Middle Ages*. New York: Columbia University Press, 2009.

De Winter, Patrick M. "Visions of the Apocalypse in Medieval England and France {Burckhardt-Wildt Apocalypse}." *Bulletin of the Cleveland Museum of Art* 70 (1983): 396–417.

Deyermond, Alan. "Historia universal e ideología nacional en Pablo de Santa María." In *Homenaje a Alvaro Galmés de Fuentes*, 2:313–24. Oviedo: Universidad de Oviedo, 1987.

DiTommaso, Lorenzo. *The Book of Daniel and the Apocryphal Daniel Literature*. Studia in Veteris Testamenti Pseudepigrapha 20. Leiden: Brill, 2005.

——. "The Apocalyptic Other." In *The "Other" in Second Temple Judaism: Essays in Honor of John J. Collins*, edited by Daniel C. Harlow et al., 221–46. Grand Rapids, MI: Eerdmans Publishing Company, 2011.

——. "The Apocryphal Daniel Apocalypses: Works, Manuscripts, and Overview." *Ephemerides Theologicae Lovanienses* 94 (2018): 275–316.

Domanyi, Thomas. *Der Römerbriefkommentar des Thomas von Aquin: Ein Beitrag zur Untersuchung seiner Auslegungsmethoden*. Bern: Lang, 1979.

Donaldson, Terence L. "'Riches for the Gentiles' (Rom 11:12): Israel's Rejection and Paul's Gentile Mission." *Journal of Biblical Literature* 112 (1993): 81–98.

——. "Jewish Christianity, Israel's Stumbling, and the Sonderweg Reading of Paul." *Journal for the Study of the New Testament* 29 (2006): 27–54.

Donfried, Karl Paul, ed. *The Romans Debate: Revised and Expanded Edition*. Edinburgh: T&T Clark, 1991.

Dove, Mary. "Sex, Allegory, and Censorship: A Reconsideration of Medieval Commentaries on the Song of Songs." *Literature and Theology* 10 (1996): 317–28.

——. "Literal Senses in the Song of Songs." In *Nicholas of Lyra: The Senses of Scripture*, edited by Philip D. W. Krey and Lesley Smith, 129–46. Studies in the History of Christian Thought 90. Leiden: Brill, 2000.

Dox, Donnalee. "Representation without Referent: The Jew in Medieval English Drama." Ph.D. dissertation, University of Minnesota, 1995.

Dronke, Peter. "The Song of Songs and Medieval Love-Lyric." In *The Bible and Western Culture*, edited by W. Lourdaux and D. Verhelst, 236–62. Leuven: Leuven University Press, 1979.

Duker Fishman, Rivkha. "The Bar-Kokhva Rebellion in Christian Sources" [Hebrew]. In *The Bar Kokhva Revolt: A New Approach,* edited by Aharon Oppenheimer and Uriel Rappaport, 233–42. Jerusalem: Yad Izhak Ben-Zvi, 1984.

Dunbar, David G. "The Eschatology of Hippolytus of Rome." Ph.D. dissertation, Drew University, 1979.

———. "The Delay of the Parousia in Hippolytus." *Vigiliae Christianae* 37 (1983): 313–27.

———. "Hippolytus of Rome and the Eschatological Exegesis of the Early Church." *Westminster Theological Journal* 45 (1983): 322–39.

Dunn, James D. G., ed. *Paul and the Mosaic Law: The Third Durham-Tübingen Research Symposium on Earliest Christianity and Judaism, Durham, September, 1994.* Tubingen: Mohr Siebeck, 1996.

———. *The Theology of Paul the Apostle.* Grand Rapids, MI: Eerdmans Publishing Company, 1998.

———. *The New Perspective on Paul: Collected Essays.* Rev. ed. Wissenschaftliche Untersuchungen zum Neuen Testament 185. Grand Rapids, MI: Eerdmans Publishing Company, 2008.

———. "A New Perspective on the New Perspective on Paul." *Early Christianity* 4 (2013): 157–82.

Eastman, Susan Grove. "Israel and Divine Mercy in Galatians and Romans." In *Between Gospel and Election: Explorations in the Interpretation of Romans 9–11,* edited by Florian Wilk and J. Ross Wagner, 147–70. Wissenschaftliche Untersuchungen zum Neuen Testament 257. Tübingen: Mohr Siebeck, 2010.

Echevarria, Ana. *The Fortress of Faith: The Attitude towards Muslims in Fifteenth-Century Spain.* Boston: Brill, 1999.

Edwards, John. "New Light on the Converso Debate? The Jewish Christianity of Alonso de Cartagena and Juan de Torquemada." In *Cross, Crescent, and Conversion: Studies on Medieval Spain and Christendom in Memory of Richard Fletcher,* edited by Simon Barton and Peter Linehan, 311–26. Medieval Mediterranean 73. Leiden: Brill, 2008.

Ehrensperger, Kathy, and R. Ward Holder. *Reformation Readings of Romans.* London: T&T Clark, 2008.

Eisenbaum, Pamela. *Paul Was Not a Christian: The Original Message of a Misunderstood Apostle.* New York: Harper Collins, 2009.

Eismeijer, Anne C. *Divina Quaternitas: A Preliminary Study in the Method and Application of Visual Exegesis.* Assen: Van Gorkum, 1978.

Elliott, Mark W. *The Song of Songs and Christology in the Early Church, 381–451.* Studien und Texte zu Antike und Christentum 7. Tübingen: Mohr Siebeck, 2000.

Emmerson, Richard K. "Antichrist as Anti-Saint: The Significance of Abbot Adso's Libellus de Antichristo." *American Benedictine Review* 30 (1979): 175–90.

———. *Antichrist in the Middle Ages: A Study of Medieval Apocalypticism, Art, and Literature.* Seattle: University of Washington Press, 1981.

———. "Antichrist on Page and Stage in the Later Middle Ages." In *Spectacle and Public Performance in the Late Middle Ages and the Renaissance,* edited by Robert E. Stillman, 1–29. Studies in Medieval and Reformation Traditions 113. Leiden: Brill, 2006.

———. *Apocalypse Illuminated: The Visual Exegesis of Revelation in Medieval Illuminated Manuscripts.* University Park: Pennsylvania State University Press, 2018.

——. "Contextualizing Performance: The Reception of the Chester Antichrist." *Journal of Medieval and Early Modern Studies* 29 (1999): 89–119.

——. "Medieval Illustrated Apocalypse Manuscripts." In *A Companion to the Premodern Apocalypse*, edited by Michael A. Ryan, 21–66. Companions to the Christian Tradition 64. Leiden: Brill, 2016.

——. "'Nowe Ys Common This Daye': Enoch and Elias, Antichrist, and the Structure of the Chester Cycle." In *Homo, Memento Finis: The Iconography of Just Judgment in Medieval Art and Drama*, edited by David Bevington, 89–120. Early Drama, Art, and Music Monograph Series 6. Kalamazoo: Medieval Institute Publications, Western Michigan University, 1985.

——. "The Representation of Antichrist in Hildegard of Bingen's *Scivias*: Image, Word, Commentary, and Visionary Experience." *Gesta* 41 (2002): 95–110.

——. "Visualizing Performance: The Miniatures of the Besançon MS 579 *Jour du Jugement*." *Exemplaria* 11 (1999): 245–84.

——. "Wynkyn De Worde's Byrthe and Lyfe of Antechryst and Popular Eschatology on the Eve of the English Reformation." *Mediaevalia* 14 (1988): 281–311.

Enders, Jody. *The Medieval Theater of Cruelty: Rhetoric, Memory, Violence*. Ithaca, NY: Cornell University Press, 1999.

Engstrom, Alfred G. "The Voices of Plants and Flowers and the Changing Cry of the Mandrake." In *Medieval Studies in Honor of Urban Tigner Holmes, Jr.*, 43–52. Chapel Hill: University of North Carolina Press, 1965.

Evans, G. R. (Gillian Rosemary). *Old Arts and New Theology: The Beginnings of Theology as an Academic Discipline*. New York: Oxford University Press, 1980.

Evitt, Regula Meyer. "Eschatology, Millenarian Apocalypticism, and the Liturgical Anti-Judaism of the Medieval Prophet Plays." In *The Apocalyptic Year 1000: Religious Expectation and Social Change, 950–1050*, edited by Richard Landes, Andrew Gow, and David C. Van Meter, 205–29. Oxford: Oxford University Press, 2003.

Fagan, Patricia Claire. "A Critical Edition of Martín Martínez Dampiés's 'Libro Del Antichristo', Zaragoza, 1496." Ph.D. dissertation, Boston College, 2001.

Firth, Katharine R. *The Apocalyptic Tradition in Reformation Britain, 1530–1645*. Oxford: Oxford University Press, 1979.

Flanagan, Sabina. "Twelfth-Century Apocalyptic Imaginations and the Coming of the Antichrist." *Journal of Religious History* 24 (2000): 57–69.

Fleck, Andrew. "Here, There, and In Between: Representing Difference in the Travels of Sir John Mandeville." *Studies in Philology* 97 (2000): 379–400.

Flinker, Noam. *The Song of Songs in English Renaissance Literature: Kisses of Their Mouths*. Studies in Renaissance Literature 3. Cambridge: D.S. Brewer, 2000.

Flint, Valerie I. J. "The Commentaries of Honorius Augustodunensis on the Song of Songs." *Revue Benedictine* 84 (1974): 196–211.

——. *Honorius Augustodunensis of Regensburg*. Authors of the Middle Ages 6 (Historical and Religious Writers of the Latin West). London: Variorum, 1995.

Ford, J. Massyngberde. "The Construction of the Other: The Antichrist." *Andrews University Seminary Studies* 33 (1995): 203–30.

——. "The Physical Features of the Antichrist." *Journal for the Study of the Pseudepigrapha* 14 (1996): 23–41.

Fornari, Giuseppe. "Figures of Antichrist: The Apocalypse and Its Restraints in Contemporary Political Thought." *Contagion: Journal of Violence, Mimesis, and Culture* 17 (2010): 53–85.

Forsyth, Neil. *The Old Enemy: Satan and the Combat Myth*. Princeton: Princeton University Press, 1987.

——. *The Satanic Epic*. Princeton: Princeton University Press, 2003.

Frank, Jacqueline A. "The Quadrige Aminadab Medallion in the 'Anagogical' Window at the Royal Abbey of Saint-Denis." *Gazette des Beaux-Arts* 141 (1999): 219–33.

Frank, Susan. "The Unbelieving Jews in the Epistle of Paul to the Romans, Chapters 9–11: A Study of Selected Latin Commentaries from Atto of Vercelli (885–961) to Giles of Rome (1274–1316)." Ph.D. dissertation, Temple University, 1990.

Franke, Thomas S. "Miracles and Monsters: Gog and Magog, Alexander the Great, and Antichrist in the Apocalypse of the Catalan Atlas (1375)." In *Holy Monsters, Sacred Grotesques: Monstrosity and Religion in Europe and the United States*, edited by Michael E. Heyes, 23–46. Lanham, MD: Lexington Books, 2018.

Fredriksen, Paula. "Allegory and Reading God's Book: Paul and Augustine on the Destiny of Israel." In *Interpretation and Allegory: Antiquity to the Modern Period*, edited by Jon Whitman, 125–49. Brill's Studies in Intellectual History 101. Leiden: Brill, 2000.

——. "Augustine and Israel: *Interpretatio ad litteram*, Jews, and Judaism in Augustine's Theology of History." *Studia Patristica* 38 (2001): 119–35.

——. *Augustine and the Jews: A Christian Defense of Jews and Judaism*. New York: Doubleday, 2008.

——. "Divine Justice and Human Freedom: Augustine on Jews and Judaism, 392–398." In *From Witness to Witchcraft: Jews and Judaism in Medieval Christian Thought*, edited by Jeremy Cohen, 29–54. Wolfenbutteler Mittelalter-Studien 11. Wiesbaden: Harrassowitz, 1996.

——. "*Excaecati occulta justitia Dei*: Augustine on Jews and Judaism." *Journal of Early Christian Studies* 3 (1995): 299–324.

——. *Paul: The Pagans' Apostle*. New Haven: Yale University Press, 2017.

——. "Secundum Carnem: History and Israel in the Theology of St Augustine." In *Limits of Ancient Christianity: Essays on Late Antique Thought and Culture in Honor of R. A. Markus*, edited by William E. Klingshirn and Mark Vessey, 26–41. Ann Arbor: University of Michigan Press, 1999.

——. "Tyconius and Augustine on the Apocalypse." In *The Apocalypse in the Middle Ages*, edited by Richard K. Emmerson and Bernard McGinn, 20–37. Ithaca, NY: Cornell University Press, 1992.

Frey, Joerg, Matthijs den Dulk, and Jan G. Van der Watt, eds. *2 Peter and the Apocalypse of Peter: Towards a New Perspective*. Leiden: Brill, 2019.

Fried, Johannes. "'999 Jahre Nach Christi Geburt der Antichrist': Wie die Zerstörung des heiligen Grabes zum apokalyptischen Zeichen wurde und die denkfigur universaler Judenverfolgung hervorbrachte." In *Konflikt und Bewältigung: Die Zerstörung der Grabeskirche zu Jerusalem im Jahre 1009*, edited by Thomas Pratsch, 97–136. Millennium-Studien zu Kultur und Geschichte des ersten Jahrtausends n. Chr. 32. Berlin: De Gruyter, 2011.

Froehlich, Karlfried. "Romans 8:1–11: Pauline Theology in Medieval Interpretation." In *Faith and History: Essays in Honor of Paul W Meyer*, 239–60. Grand Rapids, MI: Eerdmans, 1990.

——. *Sensing the Scriptures: Aminadab's Chariot and the Predicament of Biblical Interpretation*. Grand Rapids, MI: Eerdmans Publishing Company, 2014.

Fulton, Rachel. "The Virgin Mary and the Song of Songs in the High Middle Ages." Ph.D. dissertation, Columbia University, 1994.

——. "Mimetic Devotion, Marian Exegesis, and the Historical Sense of the Song of Songs." *Viator: Medieval and Renaissance Studies* 27 (1996): 85–116.

Gager, John G. *The Origins of Anti-Semitism: Attitudes toward Judaism in Pagan and Christian Antiquity*. New York: Oxford University Press, 1983.

——. *Reinventing Paul*. New York: Oxford University Press, 2000.

Gantner, Clemens. "Hoffnung in der Apokalypse? Die Ismaeliten in den älteren lateinischen Fassungen der Revelationes des Pseudo-Methodius." In *Abendländische Apokalyptik: Kompendium zur Genealogie der Endzeit*, 521–48. Berlin: Akademie, 2012.

Garlington, Don. *Studies in the New Perspective on Paul: Essays and Reviews*. Eugene, OR: Wipf & Stock Publishers, 2008.

Garrigues, Marie-Odile. "Qui était Honorius Augustodunensis?" *Angelicum* 50 (1973): 20–49.

——. "Quelques recherches sur l'oeuvre d'Honorius Augustodunensis." *Revue d'Histoire Ecclésiastique* 70 (1975): 388–425.

——. "L'oeuvre d'Honorius Augustodunensis: Inventaire critique." *Abhandlungen der Braunschweigischen Wissenschaftlichen Gesellschaft* 38–40: 38 (1986): 7–136; 39 (1987) 123–28; 40 (1988): 129–90.

Garroway, Joshua D. "The Law-Observant Lord: John Chrysostom's Engagement with the Jewishness of Christ." *Journal of Early Christian Studies* 18 (2010): 591–615.

——. *Paul's Gentile-Jews: Neither Jew nor Gentile, but Both*. New York: Palgrave Macmillan, 2012.

Garstad, Benjamin. "Alexander's Gate and the Unclean Nations: Translation, Textual Appropriation, and the Construction of Barriers." *Transcultural: A Journal of Translation and Cultural Studies* 8 (2016): 5–16.

Gaston, Lloyd. *Paul and the Torah*. Vancouver: University of British Columbia Press, 1987.

Gathercole, Simon. "Locating Christ and Israel in Romans 9–11." In *God and Israel: Providence and Purpose in Romans 9–11*, edited by Todd D. Still, 123–48. Waco, TX: Baylor University Press, 2017.

Gatto, Alfred. "The Life and Works of Joachim of Fiore—An Overview." In *A Companion to Joachim of Fiore*, edited by Matthias Riedl, 73:20–40. Leiden: Brill, 2017.

Geissler, Klaus. "Die Juden in mittelalterlichen Texten Deutschlands: Eine Untersuchung zum Minoritätenproblem anhand literarischer Quellen." *Zeitschrift für bayerische Landesgeschichte* 38 (1975): 163–226.

Geltner, G. "William of St. Amour's 'De Periculis Novissimorum Temporum': A False Start to Medieval Antifraternalism?" In *Defenders and Critics of Franciscan Life: Essays in Honor of John V. Fleming*, edited by M. F. Cusato and G. Geltner, 127–43. Leiden: Brill, 2009.

———. *The Making of Medieval Antifraternalism: Polemic, Violence, Deviance, and Remembrance.* Oxford: Oxford University Press, 2012.

George, Timothy. "Modernizing Luther, Domesticating Paul: Another Perspective." In *Justification and Variegated Nomism*, vol. 2, *The Paradoxes of Paul*, edited by D.A. Carson, Peter T. O'Brien, and Mark A. Seifrid, 437–63. Tubingen: Mohr Siebeck, 2004.

Gersh, Stephen. "Honorius Augustodunensis and Eriugena: Remarks on the Method and Content of the Clavis Physicae." In *Eriugena Redivivus: Zur Wirkungsgeschichte seines denkens im Mittelalter und im Übergang zur Neuzeit*, edited by Walter Beierwaltes, 165–72. Vorträge des V. Internationalen Eriugena-Colloquiums, Werner-Reimers-Stiftung Bad Homburg, 26.–30. August 1985. Heidelberg: C. Winter, 1987.

Getty, Mary Ann. "Paul and the Salvation of Israel: A Perspective on Romans 9–11." *Catholic Biblical Quarterly* 50 (1988): 456–69.

Ginsburg, Christian David. *The Song of Songs and Coheleth (Commonly Called the Book of Ecclesiastes).* New York: Ktav Publishing House, 1857.

Glaser, Eliane. *Judaism without Jews: Philosemitism and Christian Polemic in Early Modern England.* New York: Palgrave Macmillan, 2007.

Glorieux, P. *Pour revaloriser Migne: Tables rectificatives.* Lille: Facultés catholiques, 1952.

Goff, Matthew. "Antichrist and His Predecessors: The Incorporation of Jewish Traditions of Evil into Christian End-Time Scenarios." In *Millennialism from the Hebrew Bible to the Present*, ed. Leonard J. Greenspoon and Ronald Simkins, 91–113. Studies in Jewish Civilization 12. Lincoln: University of Nebraska Press, 2002.

González Martínez, Eusebio. "Interdependencia entre Judíos y Gentiles en Rm 11,25–27." *Scripta Theologica* 43 (2011): 125–42.

Goodrich, John K. "Until the Fullness of the Gentiles Comes In: A Critical Review of Recent Scholarship on the Salvation of 'All Israel' (Romans 11:26)." *Journal for the Study of Paul and His Letters* 6 (2016): 5–32.

Gorday, Peter J. *Principles of Patristic Exegesis: Romans 9–11 in Origen, John Chrysostom, and Augustine.* Studies in the Bible and Early Christianity 4. New York: Edwin Mellen Press, 1983.

Gordis, Lisa M. *Opening Scripture: Bible Reading and Interpretive Authority in Puritan New England.* Chicago: University of Chicago Press, 2003.

Gottschall, Dagmar. *Das "Elucidarium" des Honorius Augustodunensis: Untersuchungen zu seiner Überlieferungs- und Rezeptionsgeschichte im deutschsprachigen Raum mit Ausgabe der niederdeutschen Übersetzung.* Tübingen: M. Niemeyer, 1992.

Gow, Andrew Colin. *The Red Jews: Antisemitism in an Apocalyptic Age, 1200–1600.* Studies in Medieval and Reformation Thought 55. Leiden: Brill, 1995.

———. "The Jewish Antichrist in Medieval and Early Modern Germany." *Medieval Encounters* 2 (1996): 249–85.

Gribben, Crawford. *The Puritan Millennium: Literature & Theology, 1550–1682.* Dublin: Four Courts Press, 2000.

Griffith, Karlyn. "Illustrating Antichrist and the Day of Judgment in the Eighty-Nine Miniatures of Besançon, Bibliothèque Municipale MS 579." Master's thesis, Florida State University, 2008.

——. "Performative Reading and Receiving a Performance of the *Jour du Jugement* in MS Besançon 579." *Comparative Drama* 45 (2011): 99–126.

Griffiths, Fiona J. *The Garden of Delights: Reform and Renaissance for Women in the Twelfth Century.* Philadelphia: University of Pennsylvania Press, 2007.

Grindheim, Sigurd. *The Crux of Election: Paul's Critique of the Jewish Confidence in the Election of Israel.* Wissenschaftliche Untersuchungen zum Neuen Testament 2,202. Tübingen: Mohr Siebeck, 2005.

Grodecki, Louis. "The Style of the Stained-Glass Windows of Saint-Denis." In *Abbot Suger and Saint-Denis: A Symposium,* 273–81. New York: Metropolitan Museum of Art, 1986.

——. *Études sur les vitraux de Suger à Saint Denis (XIIe siècle).* Paris: Presses de l'Université de Paris-Sorbonne, 1995.

Gromacki, Robert. "Israel: Her Past, Present, and Future in Romans 9–11." *Journal of Ministry & Theology* 18 (2014): 47–76.

Guibbory, Achsah. *Christian Identity, Jews, and Israel in Seventeenth-Century England.* Oxford: Oxford University Press, 2010.

Gumerlock, Francis X. "Nero Antichrist: Patristic Evidence for the Use of Nero's Naming in Calculating the Number of the Beast (Rev 13:18)." *Westminster Theological Journal* 68 (2006): 347–60.

Günther, Gerhard. *Der Antichrist: Der staufisches Ludus de Antichristo.* Translated by Gottfried Hasenkamp. Hamburg: F. Wittig, 1970.

Haacker, Klaus. *The Theology of Paul's Letter to the Romans.* New York: Cambridge University Press, 2003.

Hafemann, S. J. "Paul and His Interpreters." In *Dictionary of Paul and His Letters,* edited by Gerald F. Hawthorne, Ralph P. Martin, and Daniel G. Reid, 666–79. Downers Grove, IL: InterVarsity Press, 1993.

Hakola, Raimo. "The Johannine Community as Jewish Christians? Some Problems in Current Scholarly Consensus." In *Jewish Christianity Reconsidered: Rethinking Ancient Groups and Texts,* edited by Matt Jackson-McCabe, 181–201. Minneapolis: Fortress Press, 2007.

——. "The Reception and Development of the Johannine Tradition in 1, 2, and 3 John." In *Legacy of John: Second-Century Reception of the Fourth Gospel,* 17–47. Supplements to Novum Testamentum 132. Leiden: Brill, 2010.

——. *Reconsidering Johannine Christianity: A Social Identity Approach.* Bible World (London). New York: Routledge, 2015.

Hall, Christopher A. "John Chrysostom." In *Reading Romans through the Centuries: From the Early Church to Karl Barth,* edited by Jeffrey P. Greenman and Timothy Larsen, 39–57. Grand Rapids, MI: Brazos Press, 2005.

Hall, Michael G. (Michael Garibaldi). *The Last American Puritan: The Life of Increase Mather, 1639–1723.* Middletown, CT: Wesleyan University Press, 1988.

Hammond, Jeffrey A. "The Bride in Redemptive Time: John Cotton and the Canticles Controversy." *New England Quarterly: A Historical Review of New England Life and Letters* 56 (1983): 78–102.

Hammond Bammel, Caroline P. *Der Römerbrieftext des Rufin und seine Origenes-Übersetzung.* Vetus Latina: Aus der Geschichte der Altlateinischen Bible 10. Freiburg: Herder, 1985.

———. "Die Juden im Römerbriefkommentar des Origenes." In *Christlicher Antijudaismus und jüdischer Antipaganismus: Ihre Motive und Hintergründe in den ersten drei Jahrhunderten*, edited by Herbert Frohnhofen, 145–51. Hamburg: Steinmann & Steinmann, 1990.

———. "Augustine, Origen, and the Exegesis of St. Paul." *Augustinianum* 32 (1992): 341–68.

Hannam, Walter Andrew. "The 'Inevitabile' of Honorius Augustodunensis: A Study in the Textures of Early Twelfth-Century Augustianisms." Ph.D. dissertation, Boston College, 2014.

Harding, Mark. "The Salvation of Israel and the Logic of Romans 11:11–36." *Australian Biblical Review* 46 (1998): 55–69.

Harrill, James Albert. *Paul the Apostle: His Life and Legacy in Their Roman Context*. New York: Cambridge University Press, 2012.

Harris, Jennifer A. "Enduring Covenant in the Christian Middle Ages." *Journal of Ecumenical Studies* 44 (2009): 563–86.

Haynes, Stephen R. "'Recovering the Real Paul': Theology and Exegesis in Romans 9–11." *Ex Auditu* 4 (1988): 70–84.

Hays, Richard B. *Echoes of Scripture in the Letters of Paul*. New Haven: Yale University Press, 1989.

———. *The Conversion of the Imagination: Paul as Interpreter of Israel's Scripture*. Grand Rapids, MI: Eerdmans Publishing Company, 2005.

Hayward, C. T. R. *Interpretations of the Name Israel in Ancient Judaism and Some Early Christian Writings: From Victorious Athlete to Heavenly Champion*. Oxford: Oxford University Press, 2005.

Heckart, Jennifer L. "Sympathy for the Devil? Origen and the End." *Union Seminary Quarterly Review* 60 (2007): 49–63.

Heil, Johannes. *Kompilation oder Konstruktion? Die Juden in den Pauluskommentaren des 9. Jahrhunderts*. Hannover: Hahnsche, 1998.

Heil, John Paul. "From Remnant to Seed of Hope for Israel: Romans 9:27–29." *Catholic Biblical Quarterly* 64 (2002): 703–20.

Heimann, Heinz-Dieter. "Antichristvorstellungen im Wandel der Mittelalterlichen Gesellschaft." *Zeitschrift für Religions- und Geistesgeschichte* 47 (1995): 99–113.

Hempel, Wolfgang. "Ludus Typologicus: Die allegorische Struktur des *Ludus de Antichristo*." In *Momentum Dramaticum: Festschrift for Eckehard Catholy*, 55–74. Waterloo, ON: University of Waterloo Press, 1990.

Heng, Geraldine. *The Invention of Race in the European Middle Ages*. Cambridge: Cambridge University Press, 2018.

Hesselink, I. John. "Calvin's Understanding of the Relation of the Church and Israel Based Largely on His Interpretation of Romans 9–11." *Ex Auditu* 4 (1988): 59–69.

Higgins, Iain Macleod. *Writing East: The "Travels" of Sir John Mandeville*. Philadelphia: University of Pennsylvania Press, 1997.

Hill, Charles E. "Antichrist from the Tribe of Dan." *Journal of Theological Studies* 46 (1995): 99–117.

———. *Regnum Caelorum: Patterns of Millennial Thought in Early Christianity*. Grand Rapids, MI: Eerdmans Publishing Company, 2001.

Hill, Christopher. *Antichrist in Seventeenth-Century England*. London: Oxford University Press, 1971.

———. *The English Bible and the Seventeenth-Century Revolution*. London: Allen Lane, 1993.

Hills, Julian V. "Parables, Pretenders, and Prophecies: Translation and Interpretation in the 'Apocalypse of Peter' 2." *Revue Biblique* 98 (1991): 560–73.

Himmelfarb, Martha. *Jewish Messiahs in a Christian Empire: A History of the Book of Zerubbabel*. Cambridge, MA: Harvard University Press, 2017.

Hirsch-Reich, Beatrice. "Joachim von Fiore und das Judentum." In *Joachim of Fiore in Christian Thought: Essays on the Influence of the Calabrian Prophet*, edited by Delno C. West, 473–510. New York: B. Franklin, 1975.

Hirshman, Marc G. *A Rivalry of Genius: Jewish and Christian Biblical Interpretation in Late Antiquity*. Albany: State University of New York Press, 1996.

Hoffmann, Konrad. "Sugers 'Anagogisches Fenster' in St. Denis." *Wallraf-Richartz-Jahrbuch* 30 (1968): 57–88.

Hofius, Otfried. "Das Evangelium und Israel: Erwägungen zu Römer 9–11." *Zeitschrift für Theologie und Kirche* 83 (1986): 297–324.

———. "'All Israel Will Be Saved': Divine Salvation and Israel's Deliverance in Romans 9–11." *Princeton Seminary Bulletin* 11 (1990): 19–39.

Hogeterp, Albert L. A. "The Mystery of Israel's Salvation: A Re-Reading of Romans 11:25–32 in Light of the Dead Sea Scrolls." In *Flores Florentino: Dead Sea Scrolls and Other Early Jewish Studies in Honour of Florentino García Martínez*, edited by Anthony Hilhorst, Emile Peuch, and Eibert Tigchelaar, 653–66. Supplements to the *Journal for the Study of Judaism* 122. Leiden: Brill, 2007.

———. *Expectations of the End: A Comparative Traditio-Historical Study of Eschatological, Apocalyptic, and Messianic Ideas in the Dead Sea Scrolls and the New Testament*. Studies on the Texts of the Desert of Judah 83. Leiden: Brill, 2009.

Holliday, Lisa R. "Will Satan Be Saved? Reconsidering Origen's Theory of Volition in *Peri Archon*." *Vigiliae Christianae* 63 (2009): 1–23.

Holtz, Traugott. "Das Gericht über die Juden und die Rettung Ganz Israels (1 Thess 2,15f und Röm 11,25f)." In *Wissenschaft und Kirche*, 119–31. Bielefeld: Luther-Verlag, 1989.

Hood, John Y. B. *Aquinas and the Jews*. Philadelphia: University of Pennsylvania Press, 1995.

Horbury, William. "Antichrist among Jews and Gentiles." In *Jews in a Graeco-Roman World*, edited by Martin Goodman, 113–33. Oxford: Clarendon Press, 1998.

———. *Messianism among Jews and Christians: Twelve Biblical and Historical Studies*. Edinburgh: T&T Clark, 2003.

———. "Messianism among Jews and Christians in the Second Century." *Augustinianum* 28 (2008): 71–88.

Horst, Pieter W van der. "Jews and Christians in Antioch at the End of the Fourth Century." In *Christian-Jewish Relations through the Centuries*, 228–38. Sheffield: Sheffield Academic Press, 2000.

Hoyland, Robert G. *Seeing Islam as Others Saw It: A Survey and Evaluation of Christian, Jewish, and Zoroastrian Writings on Early Islam*. Princeton, NJ: Darwin Press, 1997.

Hübner, Hans. *Gottes Ich und Israel: Zum Schriftgebrauch der Psalmen in Römer 9–11.* Gottingen: Vandenhoeck & Ruprecht, 1984.

——. *Biblische Theologie des Neuen Testaments.* Vol. 2, *Die Theologie des Paulus und ihre Neutestamentliche Wirkungsgeschichte.* Gottingen: Vandenhoeck & Ruprecht, 1993.

——. "New Testament Interpretation of the Old Testament." In *Hebrew Bible/Old Testament: The History of Its Interpretation,* 1,1:332–72. Gottingen: Vandenhoeck & Ruprecht, 1996.

Huey, Caroline. *Hans Folz and Print Culture in Late Medieval Germany: The Creation of Popular Discourse.* New York: Routledge, 2016.

Hughes, Kevin L. *Constructing Antichrist: Paul, Biblical Commentary, and the Development of Doctrine in the Early Middle Ages.* Washington, DC: Catholic University of America Press, 2005.

Hummel, Leonard M. "'Wrath against the Unrighteous': The Place of Luther's Lectures on Romans in His Understanding of Judaism." *Seminary Ridge Review* 11 (2008): 64–82.

Hunter, David G. "'On the Sin of Adam and Eve': A Little-Known Defense of Marriage and Childbearing by Ambrosiaster." *Harvard Theological Review* 82 (1989): 283–99.

Hutchins, Zachery McLeod. *Inventing Eden: Primitivism, Millennialism, and the Making of New England.* New York: Oxford University Press, 2014.

Hvalvik, Reidar. "A 'Sonderweg' for Israel: A Critical Examination of a Current Interpretation of Romans 11:25–27." *Journal for the Study of the New Testament* 12 (1990): 87–107.

Iogna-Prat, Dominique. *Order and Exclusion: Cluny and Christendom Face Heresy, Judaism, and Islam, 1000–1150.* Ithaca, NY: Cornell University Press, 2002.

Ivanov, Sergey. "A Text on Antichrist in St. Petersburg, National Library of Russia Lat. Q.v.IV.3 and the Liber Floridus." *Mediaeval Studies* 75 (2013): 93–108.

Izbicki, Thomas M. "Juan de Torquemada's Defense of the Conversos." *Catholic Historical Review* 85 (1999): 195–207.

Jacoff, Michael. *The Horses of San Marco and the Quadriga of the Lord.* Princeton: Princeton University Press, 1993.

Jenks, Gregory C. *The Origins and Early Development of the Antichrist Myth.* Beihefte zur die Zeitschrift für die Neutestamentliche Wissenschaft 59. Berlin: De Gruyter, 1991.

Johnson, Clinton Andrew, Jr. "Paul's 'Anti-Christology' in 2 Thessalonians 2:3–12 in Canonical Context." *Journal of Theological Interpretation* 8 (2014): 125–43.

Johnson, Dan G. "The Structure and Meaning of Romans 11." *Catholic Biblical Quarterly* 46 (1984): 91–103.

Johnson, David W. "Purging the Poison: The Revision of Pelagius' Pauline Commentaries by Cassiodorus and His Students." Ph.D. dissertation, Princeton Theological Seminary, 1989.

Johnson, S. Lewis. "Paul and 'the Israel of God': An Exegetical and Eschatological Case-Study." *Master's Seminary Journal* 20 (2009): 41–55.

Johnson Hodge, Caroline E. *If Sons, Then Heirs: A Study of Kinship and Ethnicity in the Letters of Paul.* New York: Oxford University Press, 2007.

Johnston, Warren. *Revelation Restored: The Apocalypse in Later Seventeenth-Century England*. Woodbridge: Boydell Press, 2011.

Jones, Gareth Lloyd. "Paul of Burgos and the 'Adversus Judaeos' Tradition." *Henoch* 21 (1999): 313–29.

Jordan, William C. "Judaizing the Passion: The Case of the Crown of Thorns in the Middle Ages." In *New Perspectives on Jewish-Christian Relations in Honor of David Berger*, edited by Elisheva Carlebach and Jacob Joseph Schacter, 51–63. Brill Reference Library of Judaism 33. Leiden: Brill, 2012.

Joyner, Danielle. *Painting the Hortus Deliciarum: Medieval Women, Wisdom, and Time*. University Park: The Pennsylvania State University Press, 2016.

Judant, Denise. *Judaïsme et Christianisme: Dossier Patristique*. Paris: Cèdre, 1969.

Jue, Jeffrey K. *Heaven upon Earth: Joseph Mede (1586–1638) and the Legacy of Millenarianism*. Dordrecht: Springer, 2006.

———. "Puritan Millenarianism in Old and New England." In *The Cambridge Companion to Puritanism*, 259–76. Cambridge: Cambridge University Press, 2008.

Kallas, Endel. "Martin Luther as Expositor of the Song of Songs." *Lutheran Quarterly* 2 (1988): 323–41.

Kalleres, Dayna S. *City of Demons: Violence, Ritual, and Christian Power in Late Antiquity*. Berkeley: University of California Press, 2013.

Kampling, Rainer. *Das Blut Christi und die Juden: Mt 27,25 bei den lateinischsprachigen christlichen Autoren bis zu Leo dem Grossen*. Münster: Aschendorff, 1984.

Katz, David S. *Philo-Semitism and the Readmission of the Jews to England, 1603–1655*. Oxford: Clarendon Press, 1982.

———. "Millenarianism, the Jews, and Biblical Criticism in Seventeenth-Century England." *Pietismus und Neuzeit*, no. 14, 1989, 166–84.

Keen, Karen R. "Song of Songs in the Eyes of Rashi and Nicholas of Lyra: Comparing Jewish and Christian Exegesis." *Conversations with the Biblical World* 35 (2015): 212–35.

Kelley, Erin E. "Doubt and Religious Drama across Sixteenth-Century England, or Did the Middle Ages Believe in Their Plays?" In *The Chester Cycle in Context, 1555–1575 (Religion, Drama, and the Impact of Change)*, edited by Jessica Dell, David Klausner, and Helen Ostovich, 47–63. Farnham: Ashgate, 2012.

Kelly, Henry Ansgar. *Satan: A Biography*. Cambridge: Cambridge University Press, 2006.

Kelly, J. N. D. *Golden Mouth: The Story of John Chrysostom, Ascetic, Preacher, Bishop*. Ithaca, NY: Cornell University Press, 1995.

Kim, Dongsu. "Reading Paul's Καὶ Οὕτως Πα^ς Ἰσραὴλ Σωθήσεται (Rom. 11:26a) in the Context of Romans." *Calvin Theological Journal* 45 (2010): 317–34.

Kim, Seyoon. "The 'Mystery' of Rom 11.25–6 Once More." *New Testament Studies* 43 (1997): 412–29.

Kirk, J. R. Daniel. "Why Does the Deliverer Come in Ek Siōn (Romans 11.26)?" *Journal for the Study of the New Testament* 33 (2010): 81–99.

Kitzinger, Beatrice Ellen. "Judgment on Parchment: Illuminating Theater in Besançon MS 579." *Gesta* 55 (2016): 49–78.

Kjær, Jonna. "Une lecture du mystère du *Jour du Jugement* portant sur l'imagination allégorique." *Orbis Litterarum* 62 (2007): 110–38.

Klauck, Hans-Josef. "Do They Never Come Back? Nero Redivivus and the Apocalypse of John." *Catholic Biblical Quarterly* 63 (2001): 683.

Knibbs, Eric. "Berengaudus on the Apocalypse." In *The End of the World in Medieval Thought and Spirituality*, edited by Eric Knibbs, Jessica A. Boon, and Erica Gelser, 135–62. Cham, Switzerland: Palgrave Macmillan, 2019.

Koester, Craig R. "The Antichrist Theme in the Johannine Epistles and Its Role in Christian Tradition." In *Communities in Dispute: Current Scholarship on the Johannine Epistles*, edited by Paul N. Anderson and R. Alan Culpepper, 187–96. Society of Biblical Literature: Early Christianity and Its Literature 13. Atlanta: SBL Press, 2014.

Konrad, Robert. *De ortu et tempore Antichristi: Antichristvorstellungen und Geschichtsbild des Abtes Adso von Montier-en-Der*. Münchener Historische Studien: Abteilung Mittelalterliche Geschichte 1. Kallmünz: Michael Lassleben, 1964.

Kreitzer, Larry J. *The New Testament in Fiction and Film: On Reversing the Hermeneutical Flow*. Biblical Seminar 17. Sheffield: Journal for the Study of the Old Testament Press, 1993.

Kriegel, Maurice. "Autour de Pablo de Santa Maria et d'Alfonso de Cartagena: Alignement culturel et originalité 'converso.'" *Revue d'Histoire Moderne et Contemporaine* 41 (1994): 197–205.

——. "The Reckonings of Nahmanides and Arnold of Villanova: On the Early Contacts between Christian Millenarianism and Jewish Messianism." *Jewish History* 26 (2012): 17–40.

——. "Paul de Burgos et Profiat Duran déchiffrent 1391." In *The Jews of Europe around 1400; Disruption, Crisis, and Resilience*, edited by Lukas Clemens and Christoph Cluse, 235–57. Wiesbaden: Harrassowitz, 2018.

Krummel, Miriamne Ara. *Crafting Jewishness in Medieval England: Legally Absent, Virtually Present*. New York: Palgrave Macmillan, 2011.

Kucicki, Janusz. *Eschatology of the Thessalonian Correspondence: A Comparative Study of 1 Thess 4, 13–5, 11 and 2 Thess 2, 1–12 to the Dead Sea Scrolls and the Old Testament Pseudepigrapha*. Alte Testament im Dialog 7. Bern: Peter Lang, 2014.

Kühnel, Bianca. *The End of Time in the Order of Things: Science and Eschatology in Early Medieval Art*. Regensburg: Schnell & Steiner, 2003.

Kupfer, Marcia. "'. . . Lectres . . . plus Vrayes': Hebrew Script and Jewish Witness in the Mandeville Manuscript of Charles V." *Speculum* 83 (2008): 58–111.

Kyrychenko, Alexander. "The Consistency of Romans 9–11." *Restoration Quarterly* 45 (2003): 215–27.

LaCocque, André. "La Shulamite et les chars d'Aminadab: Un essai herméneutique sur Cantique 6,12–7,1." *Revue Biblique* 102 (1995): 330–47.

Landes, Richard. "Lest the Millennium Be Fulfilled: Apocalyptic Expectations and the Pattern of Western Chronography 100–800 CE." In *The Use and Abuse of Eschatology in the Middle Ages*, edited by Werner Verbeke, Daniel Verhelst, and Andries Welkenhuysen, 137–211. Leuven: Leuven University Press, 1988.

——. "The Fear of an Apocalyptic Year 1000: Augustinian Historiography, Medieval and Modern." *Speculum* 75 (2000): 97–145.

——. "What Happens When Jesus Doesn't Come? Jewish and Christian Relations in Apocalyptic Time." *Terrorism & Political Violence* 14 (2002): 241–74.

Landes, Richard, Andrew Gow, and David C. Van Meter, eds. *The Apocalyptic Year 1000: Religious Expectation and Social Change, 950–1050*. Oxford: Oxford University Press, 2003.

Lasker, Daniel J. "Proselyte Judaism, Christianity, and Islam in the Thought of Judah Halevi." *Jewish Quarterly Review* 81 (1990): 75–91.

Latteri, Natalie E. "A Dialogue on Disaster: Antichrists in Jewish and Christian Apocalypses and Their Medieval Recensions." *Quidditas* 38 (2017): 61–82.

Lawrence, John M. "Nero Redivivus." *Fides et Historia* 11 (1978): 54–66.

Lerner, Robert E. "Refreshment of the Saints: The Time after Antichrist as a Station for Earthly Progress in Medieval Thought." *Traditio* 32 (1976): 97–144.

——. "Antichrists and Antichrist in Joachim of Fiore." *Speculum* 60 (1985): 553–70.

——. "The Medieval Return to the Thousand-Year Sabbath." In *The Apocalypse in the Middle Ages*, edited by Richard K. Emmerson and Bernard McGinn, 51–71. Ithaca, NY: Cornell University Press, 1992.

——. "Peter Olivi on the Conversion of the Jews." In *Pierre de Jean Olivi (1248–1298): Pensée scolastique, dissidence spirituelle et société*, edited by Alain Boureau and Sylvain Piron, 207–16. Etudes de Philosophie Médiévale 79. Paris: Vrin, 1999.

——. *The Feast of Saint Abraham: Medieval Millenarians and the Jews*. Philadelphia: University of Pennsylvania Press, 2001.

Leshock, David B. "Religious Geography: Designating Jews and Muslims as Foreigners in Medieval England." In *Meeting the Foreign in the Middle Ages*, edited by Albrecht Classen, 202–25. New York: Routledge, 2002.

Levering, Matthew, and Michael Dauphinais, eds. *Reading Romans with St. Thomas Aquinas*. Washington, DC: Catholic University of America Press, 2012.

Lewis, Donald M. *The Origins of Christian Zionism: Lord Shaftesbury and Evangelical Support for a Jewish Homeland*. New York: Cambridge University Press, 2009.

Lewis, Suzanne. "*Tractatus adversus Judaeos* in the Gulbenkian Apocalypse." *Art Bulletin* 68 (1986): 543–66.

——. "Exegesis and Illustration in Thirteenth-Century English Apocalypses." In *The Apocalypse in the Middle Ages*, edited by Richard K. Emmerson and Bernard McGinn, 259–75. Ithaca, NY: Cornell University Press, 1992.

——. *Reading Images: Narrative Discourse and Reception in the Thirteenth-Century Illuminated Apocalypse*. Cambridge: Cambridge University Press, 1995.

Lietaert Peerbolte, L. J. *The Antecedents of Antichrist: A Traditio-Historical Study of the Earliest Christian Views on Eschatological Opponents*. Supplements to the *Journal for the Study of Judaism* 49. Leiden: Brill, 1996.

Lipton, Sara. *Images of Intolerance: The Representation of Jews and Judaism in the Bible Moralisée*. Berkeley: University of California Press, 1999.

——. "Isaac and Antichrist in the Archives." *Past & Present* 232 (2016): 3–44.

Lobrichon, Guy. "L'ordre de ce temps et les désordres de la fin: Apocalypse et société, du IXe à la fin du XIe siècle." In *The Use and Abuse of Eschatology in the Middle Ages*, edited by Werner Verbeke, Daniel Verhelst, and Andries Welkenhuysen, 221–41. Leuven: Leuven University Press, 1988.

——. "Stalking the Signs: The Apocalyptic Commentaries." In *The Apocalyptic Year 1000: Religious Expectation and Social Change, 950–1050*, edited by Richard Landes, Andrew Gow, and David C. Van Meter, 67–79. Oxford: Oxford University Press, 2003.

Lodge, John G. *Romans 9–11: A Reader-Response Analysis.* International Studies in Formative Christianity and Judaism 6. Atlanta: Scholars Press, 1996.

Lomperis, Linda. "Medieval Travel Writing and the Question of Race." *Journal of Medieval and Early Modern Studies* 31 (2001): 147–64.

Longenecker, Richard N. *Introducing Romans: Critical Issues in Paul's Most Famous Letter.* Grand Rapids, MI: Eerdmans Publishing Company, 2011.

——. *The Epistle to the Romans: A Commentary on the Greek Text.* Grand Rapids, MI: Eerdmans Publishing Company, 2016.

Longman, Tremper. *Song of Songs.* Grand Rapids, MI: Eerdmans Publishing Company, 2001.

Lopez, Davina C. "Grafting Rhetoric: Myth and Methodological Multivalence in Romans 11." In *God and Israel: Providence and Purpose in Romans 9–11*, edited by Todd D. Still, 49–93. Waco, TX: Baylor University Press, 2017.

Lorein, G. W. *The Antichrist Theme in the Intertestamental Period. Journal for the Study of the Pseudepigrapha* Supplement Series 44. London: T&T Clark, 2003.

Lowance, Mason I., Jr. *The Language of Canaan: Metaphor and Symbol in New England from the Puritans to the Transcendentalists.* Cambridge, MA: Harvard University Press, 1980.

Lucken, Linus Urban. *Antichrist and the Prophets of Antichrist in the Chester Cycle.* Washington, DC: Catholic University of America Press, 1940.

Luke, Murray. "Jesuit Hebrew Studies after Trent: Cornelius à Lapide (1567–1637)." *Journal of Jesuit Studies* 4 (2017): 76–97.

MacLean, Simon. "Reform, Queenship, and the End of the World in Tenth-Century France: Adso's 'Letter on the Origin and Time of the Antichrist' Reconsidered." *Revue Belge de Philologie et d'Histoire/Belgisch Tijdschrift voor Filologie en Geschiedenis* 86 (3–4) (2008): 645–75.

Madden, Joshua E. "A Rapprochement between Origen and the 'New Perspective' on Paul: Christ and the Law in Origen's Commentary on Romans." *Heythrop Journal* 57 (2016): 638–48.

Magdalino, Paul. "'All Israel Will Be Saved'? The Forced Baptism of the Jews and Imperial Eschatology." In *Jews in Early Christian Law: Byzantium and the Latin West, 6th–11th Centuries*, edited by N. R. M. De Lange et al., 2:231–42. Turnhout: Brepols, 2014.

Mähl, Sibylle. *Quadriga Virtutum: Die Kardinaltugenden in den Geistesgeschichte der Karolingerzeit.* Beihefte zum *Archiv für Kulturgeschichte* 9. Cologne: Böhlau, 1969.

Malaise, Isabelle. "L'iconographie biblique du Cantique des Cantiques au XIIe siècle." *Scriptorium* 46 (1992): 67–73.

Manselli, Raoul. "I popoli immaginari: Gog e Magog." In *Popoli e paesi nella cultura altomedievale*, 2:487–517. Spoleto: Centro Italiano di Studi sull'alto Medioevo, 1983.

Margolin, Jean Claude. "The Epistle to the Romans (Chapter 11) According to the Versions and/or Commentaries of Valla, Colet, Lefèvre, and Erasmus." In *The Bible in the Sixteenth Century*, edited by David Curtis Steinmetz, 136–66. Duke Monographs in Medieval and Renaissance Studies 11. Durham, NC: Duke University Press, 1990.

Markish, Shimon. *Erasmus and the Jews.* Chicago: University of Chicago Press, 1986.

Markus, Robert Austin. "The Legacy of Pelagius: Orthodoxy, Heresy, and Conciliation." In *The Making of Orthodoxy: Essays in Honour of Henry Chadwick*, edited by Rowan William, 214–34. Cambridge: Cambridge University Press, 1989.

Marshall, Bruce D. "'Quasi in Figura': A Brief Reflection on Jewish Election, after Thomas Aquinas." *Nova et Vetera* 7 (2009): 477–84.

Martin, J. "Commodianus." *Traditio* 13 (1957): 1–71.

Martin, John D. "Dramatized Disputations: Late Medieval German Dramatizations of Jewish-Christian Religious Disputations, Church Policy, and Local Social Climates." *Medieval Encounters* 8 (2002): 209–27.

——. "The Depiction of Jews in the Carnival Plays and Comedies of Hans Folz and Hans Sachs in Early Modern Nuremberg." *Baylor Journal of Theatre and Performance* 3 (2006): 43–65.

——. *Representations of Jews in Late Medieval and Early Modern German Literature*. 2nd ed. Studies in German Jewish History 5. New York: Peter Lang, 2006.

Martin, Leslie H. "Comic Eschatology in the Chester Coming of Antichrist." *Comparative Drama* 5 (1971): 163–76.

Martyn, J. Louis. "The Covenants of Hagar and Sarah." In *Faith and History: Essays in Honor of Paul W Meyer*, edited by John T. Carroll, Charles H. Cosgrove, and E. Elizabeth Johnson, 160–92. Atlanta: Scholars Press, 1990.

Mason, Stephen. "Paul, Classical Anti-Jewish Polemic and the Letter to the Romans." In *Self-Definition and Self-Discovery in Early Christianity: A Study in Changing Horizons; Essays in Appreciation of Ben F. Meyer from Former Students*, edited by David J. Hawkins and Tom Robinson, 181–223. Studies in the Bible and Early Christianity 26. New York: E. Mellen Press, 1983.

Matar, Nabil I. "The Idea of the Restoration of the Jews in English Protestant Thought, 1661–1701." *Harvard Theological Review* 78 (1985): 115–48.

Matter, E. Ann. *The Voice of My Beloved: The Song of Songs in Western Medieval Christianity*. Philadelphia: University of Pennsylvania Press, 1990.

——. "The Apocalypse in Early Medieval Exegesis." In *The Apocalypse in the Middle Ages*, edited by Richard K. Emmerson and Bernard McGinn, 38–50. Ithaca, NY: Cornell University Press, 1992.

——. "The Love Song of the Millennium: Medieval Christian Apocalyptic and the Song of Songs." In *Scrolls of Love: Ruth and the Song of Songs*, edited by Peter S. Hawkins and Leslie Cushing Stahlberg, 228–43. New York: Fordham University Press, 2006.

——. "Wandering to the End: The Medieval Christian Context of the Wandering Jew." In *Transforming Relations: Essays on Jews and Christians throughout History in Honor of Michael A Signer*, edited by Franklin T. Harkins, 224–40. Notre Dame, IN: University of Notre Dame Press, 2010.

McClymond, Michael J. *The Devil's Redemption: A New History and Interpretation of Christian Universalism*. Grand Rapids, MI: Baker Academic, 2018.

McConnell, John F. "Communis Omnium Patria." *Catholic Biblical Quarterly* 17 (1955): 217–32.

McGavin, John J., and Greg Walker. *Imagining Spectatorship: From the Mysteries to the Shakespearean Stage*. Oxford Textual Perspectives 7. Oxford: Oxford University Press, 2016.

McGinn, Bernard. *The Calabrian Abbot: Joachim of Fiore in the History of Western Thought*. New York: Macmillan, 1985.

———. "Portraying Antichrist in the Middle Ages." In *The Use and Abuse of Eschatology in the Middle Ages*, edited by Werner Verbeke, Daniel Verhelst, and Andries Welkenhuysen, 1–48. Mediaevalia Lovaniensa; Ser. 1, Studia 15. Leuven: Leuven University Press, 1988.

———. *Visions of the End: Apocalyptic Traditions in the Middle Ages*. 2nd ed. New York: Columbia University Press, 1998.

———. *Antichrist: Two Thousand Years of the Human Fascination with Evil*. New York: Columbia University Press, 2000.

———. "Apocalypticism and Mysticism in Joachim of Fiore's *Expositio in Apocalypsim*." In *The End of the World in Medieval Thought and Spirituality*, edited by Eric Knibbs, Jessica A. Boon, and Erica Gelser, 163–96. Cham, Switzerland: Palgrave Macmillan, 2019.

McGuckin, John A. "Origen on the Jews." In *Christianity and Judaism*, edited by Diana Wood, 1–13. Studies in Church History 29. Oxford: Blackwell, 1992.

McMichael, Steven J. *Was Jesus of Nazareth the Messiah? Alphonso de Espina's Argument against the Jews in the "Fortalitium Fidei" (c.1464)*. South Florida Studies in the History of Judaism 96. Atlanta: Scholars Press, 1994.

———. "The Sources for Alfonso de Espina's Messianic Argument against the Jews in the *Fortalitium Fidei*." In *Iberia and the Mediterranean World of the Middle Ages: Essays in Honor of Robert I. Burns, S.J.*, edited by Paul E. Chevedden, 72–95. Leiden: Brill, 1995.

———. "Did Isaiah Foretell Jewish Blindness and Suffering for Not Accepting Jesus of Nazareth as Messiah? A Medieval Perspective." *Biblical Theology Bulletin* 26, no. 4 (1996): 144–51.

———. "Alfonso de Espina on the Mosaic Law." In *Friars and Jews in the Middle Ages and Renaissance*, edited by Steven J. McMichael and Susan E. Myers, 199–223. The Medieval Franciscans 2. Leiden: Brill, 2004.

———. "The End of the World, Antichrist, and the Final Conversion of the Jews in the *Fortalitium Fidei* of Friar Alonso de Espina (d. 1464)." *Medieval Encounters* 12 (2006): 224–73.

McNabb, Cameron Hunt. "Night of the Living Bread: Unstable Signs in Chester's Antichrist." *Early Theatre: A Journal Associated with the Records of Early English Drama* 19 (2016): 9–30.

Meeks, Wayne A. *The Prophet-King: Moses Traditions and the Johannine Christology*. Leiden: Brill, 1967.

———. "On Trusting an Unpredictable God: A Hermeneutical Meditation on Romans 9–11." In *Faith and History: Essays in Honor of Paul W. Meyer*, edited by John T. Carroll, Charles H. Cosgrove, and E. Elizabeth Johnson, 105–24. Atlanta: Scholars Press, 1990.

Meeks, Wayne A., and Robert L. Wilken. *Jews and Christians in Antioch in the First Four Centuries of the Common Era*. Society for Biblical Literature Sources for Biblical Study 13. Missoula, MT: Scholars Press, 1978.

Menhardt, Hermann. "Der Nachlass des Honorius Augustodunensis." *Zeitschrift für deutsches Altertum und deutsche Literatur* 89 (1958): 23–69.

———. "Die Mandragora im millstätter Physiologus, bei Honorius Augustodunensis und im St. Trudperter Hohenliede." In *Festschrift für Ludwig Wolff zum 70. Geburtstag*, edited by Werner Schröde, 173–94. Neumünster: Karl Wachholtz, 1962.

Merkle, Benjamin L. "Romans 11 and the Future of Ethnic Israel." *Journal of the Evangelical Theological Society* 43 (2000): 709–21.

Mesler, Katelyn. "John of Rupescissa's Engagement with Prophetic Texts in the Sexdequiloquium." *Oliviana: Mouvements et Dissidences Spirituels XIIIe–XIVe Siècles* 3 (2009): 1–8.

Meuthen, Erich. *Kirche und Heilsgeschichte bei Gerhoh von Reichersberg.* Leiden: Brill, 1959.

Meyuhas Ginio, Alisa. "La polémica cristiana *Adversus Judaeos* en España a fines de la Edad Media." *El Olivo* 37 (1993): 5–23.

———. "An Appeal in Favor of the Judeoconversos: Juan de Torquemada and His *Tractatus contra Madianitas et Ismaelitas*" [Hebrew]. *Zion* 60 (1995): 301–33.

———. "The Fortress of Faith—at the End of the West: Alonso de Espina and His *Fortalitium Fidei.*" In *Contra Iudaeos: Ancient and Medieval Polemics between Christians and Jews*, edited by Ora Limor and Guy G. Stroumsa, 215–37. Tübingen: Mohr Siebeck, 1996.

———. "Expectations of the End of Time in Alonso de Espina's *Fortalitium Fidei* (Castile, 1464)" [Hebrew]. In *Fin de Siècle—End of Ages*, edited by Yosef Kaplan, 99–109. Jerusalem: Zalman Shazar Center for Jewish History, 2005.

Middlekauff, Robert. *The Mathers: Three Generations of Puritan Intellectuals, 1596–1728.* New York: Oxford University Press, 1971.

Mihoc, V. "Saint Paul and the Jews According to Saint John Chrysostom's Commentary on Romans 9–11." *Sacra Scripta* 6 (2008): 123–38.

Milikowsky, Chaim Joseph. "Elijah and the Messiah." *Jerusalem Studies in Jewish Thought* 2 (1983): 491–96.

———. "Trajectories of Return, Restoration, and Redemption in Rabbinic Judaism: Elijah, the Messiah, the War of Gog, and the World to Come." In *Restoration: Old Testament, Jewish, and Christian Perspectives*, edited by James M. Scott, 265–80. Leiden: Brill, 2001.

Minnis, A. J. *Medieval Theory of Authorship: Scholastic Literary Attitudes in the Later Middle Ages.* Philadelphia: University of Pennsylvania Press, 1988.

Mitchell, Margaret Mary. "'A Variable and Many-Sorted Man': John Chrysostom's Treatment of Pauline Inconsistency." *Journal of Early Christian Studies* 6 (1998): 93–111.

Mittman, Asa Simon. "Mandeville's Jews, Colonialism, Certainty, and Art History." In *Postcolonising the Medieval Image*, edited by Eva Frojmovic and Catherine E. Karkov, 91–119. London: Routledge, 2017.

Möhring, Hannes. *Der Weltkaiser der Endzeit: Entstehung, Wandel und Wirkung einer tausendjährigen Weissagung.* Stuttgart: Thorbecke, 2000.

Monroe, Elizabeth. "Images of Synagoga as Christian Discourse (1000–1215)." Ph.D. dissertation, University of Southern California, 2003.

———. "'Fair and Friendly, Sweet and Beautiful': Hopes for Jewish Conversion in Synagoga's Song of Songs Imagery." In *Beyond the Yellow Badge: Anti-Judaism and*

Antisemitism in Medieval and Early Modern Visual Culture, edited by M. B. Merback, 31–62. Leiden: Brill, 2007.

———. "Dangerous Passages and Spiritual Redemption in the *Hortus Deliciarum*." In *Push Me, Pull You*, edited by Sarah Blick and Laura Deborah Gelfand, 39–74. Studies in Medieval and Reformation Traditions 156. Leiden: Brill, 2011.

Moo, Douglas J. *The Epistle to the Romans*. Grand Rapids, MI: Eerdmans Publishing Company, 1996.

———. "Paul's Universalizing Hermeneutic in Romans." *Southern Baptist Journal of Theology* 11 (2007): 62–90.

———. "John Barclay's *Paul and the Gift* and the New Perspective on Paul." *Themelios* 41 (2016): 279–88.

Moore, R. I. "Anti-Semitism and the Birth of Europe." In *Christianity and Judaism: Papers Read at the 1991 Summer Meeting and the 1992 Winter Meeting of the Ecclesiastical History Society*, edited by Diana Wood, 33–57. Oxford: Blackwell, 1992.

———. *The Formation of a Persecuting Society: Authority and Deviance in Western Europe, 950–1250*. Oxford: Blackwell, 2007.

Moore, Stephen D. "The Song of Songs in the History of Sexuality." *Church History* 69 (2000): 328–49.

Müller, Ulrich B. "Der Apokalyptische Prophet Johannes als Judenchrist: Judenchristliche Traditionen in der Johannesoffenbarung." *Zeitschrift für die Neutestamentliche Wissenschaft und die Kunde der Älteren Kirche* 104 (2013): 98–117.

Mussner, Franz. "Ganz Israel wird gerettet werden (Röm 11:26)." *Kairos* 18 (1976): 241–55.

Nanos, Mark D. *The Mystery of Romans: The Jewish Context of Paul's Letter*. Minneapolis: Fortress Press, 1996.

———. "'The Gifts and the Calling of God Are Irrevocable' (Romans 11:29): If So, How Can Paul Declare That 'Not All Israelites Truly Belong to Israel' (9:6)?" *Studies in Christian-Jewish Relations* 11 (2016): 1–17.

Nederveen Pieterse, Jan. "The History of a Metaphor: Christian Zionism and the Politics of Apocalypse." *Archives de Sciences Sociales des Religions* 36 (75) (1991): 75–103.

Netanyahu, B. *The Origins of the Inquisition in Fifteenth-Century Spain*. New York: Random House, 1995.

Nirenberg, David. "Was There Race before Modernity? The Example of 'Jewish' Blood in Late Medieval Spain." In *The Origins of Racism in the West*, edited by Miriam Eliav-Feldon, Benjamin Isaac, and Joseph Ziegler, 232–64. Cambridge: Cambridge University Press, 2009.

Norelli, Enrico. "Un 'testimonium' sur l'Antichrist (Hippolyte, *L'Antichrist* 15 et 54)." In *Poussières de Christianisme et de Judaïsme antiques: Études réunies en l'honneur de Jean-Daniel Kaestli et Éric Junod*, edited by Albert Frey and Rémi Gounelle, 245–70. Prahins, Switzerland: Éditions du Zèbre, 2007.

Novenson, Matthew V. *The Grammar of Messianism: An Ancient Jewish Political Idiom and Its Users*. New York: Oxford University Press, 2017.

Oberman, Heiko Augustinus. "Three Sixteenth-Century Attitudes to Judaism: Reuchlin, Erasmus, and Luther." In *Jewish Thought in the Sixteenth Century*, edited by Bernard Dov Cooperman, 329–64. Cambridge, MA: Harvard University Press, 1983.

——. *The Roots of Anti-Semitism: In the Age of Renaissance and Reformation*. Translated by James I. Porter. Philadelphia: University of Pennsylvania Press, 1984.

O'Connor, Donal J. "St. Thomas's Commentary on Romans." *Irish Theological Quarterly* 34 (1967): 329–43.

O'Hear, Natasha F. H. *Contrasting Images of the Book of Revelation in Late Medieval and Early Modern Art: A Case Study in Visual Exegesis*. Oxford: Oxford University Press, 2011.

——. *Picturing the Apocalypse: The Book of Revelation in the Arts over Two Millennia*. Oxford: Oxford University Press, 2015.

O'Leary, Joseph S. "The Recuperation of Judaism." In *Origeniana Sexta: Origène et La Bible/Origen and the Bible*, edited by Gilles Dorival and Alain Le Boulluec, 373–79. Leuven: Leuven University Press, 1993.

Oliver, Isaac W. "Jewish Followers of Jesus and the Bar Kokhba Revolt: Re-Examining the Christian Sources." In *Winning Revolutions: The Psychosocial Dynamics of Revolts for Freedom, Fairness, and Rights*, edited by J. Harold Ellens, 109–27. Santa Barbara: Praeger, 2013.

Olsen, V. Norskov (Viggo Norskov). *John Foxe and the Elizabethan Church*. Berkeley: University of California Press, 1973.

Orbe, Antonio. *Antropología de San Ireneo*. Biblioteca de Autores Cristianos 286. Madrid: Editorial Catolica, 1969.

——. "San Ireneo y el régimen del milenio." *Studia Missionalia* 32 (1983): 345–72.

Osborn, Eric Francis. *Irenaeus of Lyons*. Cambridge: Cambridge University Press, 2001.

Ovitt, George. "Christian Eschatology and the Chester 'Judgment.'" *Essays in Literature* 10 (1983): 3–16.

Pabel, Hilmar M. "Erasmus of Rotterdam and Judaism: A Reexamination in the Light of New Evidence." *Archiv für Reformationsgeschichte* 87 (1996): 9–37.

Pagels, Elaine H. "The Social History of Satan, the 'Intimate Enemy': A Preliminary Sketch." *Harvard Theological Review* 84 (1991): 105–28.

——. "The Social History of Satan, Part II: Satan in the New Testament Gospels." *Journal of the American Academy of Religion* 62 (1994): 17–58.

Palmer, James T. *The Apocalypse in the Early Middle Ages*. Cambridge: Cambridge University Press, 2014.

Parker, John. *The Aesthetics of Antichrist: From Christian Drama to Christopher Marlowe*. Ithaca, NY: Cornell University Press, 2007.

Parmentier, M. F. G. "Greek Church Fathers on Romans 9." *Bijdragen* 49 (1989): 139–54; 50: 2–20.

Patschovsky, Alexander, ed. *Der Passauer Anonymus: Ein Sammelwerk ueber Ketzer, Juden, Antichrist aus der Mitte des 13. Jahrhunderts*. Schriften der Monumenta Germaniae Historica 22. Stuttgart: Hiersemann, 1968.

Patte, Daniel. "A Post-Holocaust Biblical Critic Responds." In *Reading Israel in Romans: Legitimacy and Plausibility of Divergent Interpretations*, edited by Cristina Grenholm and Daniel Patte, 225–45. Valley Forge, PA: Trinity Press International, 2000.

Payne, John B. "Erasmus: Interpreter of Romans." *Sixteenth Century Journal* 2 (1971): 1–35.

——. "Erasmus on Romans 9:6–24." In *The Bible in the Sixteenth Century*, edited by David Curtis Steinmetz, 119–35. Duke Monographs in Medieval and Renaissance Studies 11. Durham, NC: Duke University Press, 1990.

Pelikan, Jaroslav. *The Christian Tradition: A History of the Development of Doctrine.* 5 vols. Chicago: University of Chicago Press, 1971–1989.

Pelletier, Anne-Marie. *Lectures du Cantique des Cantiques: De l'enigme du sens aux figures du lecteur.* Analecta Biblica 121. Rome: Editrice Pontificio Istituto Biblico, 1989.

Penna, Romano. "The Evolution of Paul's Attitude toward the Jews." In *Paul the Apostle,* edited by Romano Penna, 1:290–321. Collegeville, MN: Michael Glazier Books, 1996.

Petersen, Rodney Lawrence. *Preaching in the Last Days: The Theme of "Two Witnesses" in the Sixteenth and Seventeenth Centuries.* New York: Oxford University Press, 1993.

Phelan, Helen. "*Hortus Deliciarum/Garden of Delights*: A Somatic Interpretation." *Nature, Culture & Literature* 13 (2017): 60–75.

Philip, Lotte Brand. "The Prado 'Epiphany' by Jerome Bosch." *Art Bulletin* 35 (1953): 267–93.

Piper, John. *The Justification of God: An Exegetical and Theological Study of Romans 9:1–23.* 2nd ed. Grand Rapids, MI: Baker Academic, 1993.

Pitts, Andrew W. "Unity and Diversity In Pauline Eschatology." In *Paul: Jew, Greek, and Roman,* edited by Stanley E. Porter, 65–91. Leiden: Brill, 2009.

Poesch, Jessie. "Antichrist Imagery in Anglo-French Apocalypse Manuscripts." Ph.D. dissertation, University of Pennsylvania, 1966.

Pomplun, Trent. "'Quasi in Figura': A Cosmological Reading of the Thomistic Phrase." *Nova et Vetera* 7 (2009): 505–22.

Pope, Marvin H. *Song of Songs: A New Translation with Introduction and Commentary.* Garden City, NY: Doubleday, 1977.

Potestà, Gian Luca. "The *Vaticinium of Constans*: Genesis and Original Purposes of the Legend of the Last World Emperor." *Millennium* 8 (2011): 271–89.

Potestà, Gian Luca, and Marco Rizzi, eds. *L'anticristo.* 3 vols. Rome: Fondazione Lorenzo Valla, 2005–2019.

Prest, Wilfrid R. "The Art of Law and the Law of God: Sir Henry Finch (1558–1625)." In *Puritans and Revolutionaries: Essays in Seventeenth-Century History Presented to Christopher Hill,* edited by Donald Pennington and Keith Thomas, 94–117. Oxford: Clarendon Press, 1978.

Prinzivalli, Emanuela. "A Fresh Look at Rufinus as a Translator." In *Origeniana undecima: Origen and Origenism in the History of Western Thought,* edited by Anders-Christian Jacobsen, 247–75. Bibliotheca Ephemeridum Theologicarum Lovaniensium 279. Leuven: Peeters, 2016.

Quasten, Johannes. *Patrology.* 4 vols. Belmont, MA: Christian Classics, 1950–1986.

Ragotzky, Hedda. "Fastnacht und Endzeit: Zur Funktion der Antichrist-Figur im nürnberger Fastnachtspiel des 15. Jahrhunderts." *Zeitschrift für deutsche Philologie* 121 (2002): 54–71.

Rahner, Hugo. *Greek Myths and Christian Mystery.* New York: Harper & Row, 1971.

Rainini, Marco. *Disegni dei tempi: Il "Liber figurarum" e la teologia figurativa di Gioacchino da Fiore.* Rome: Viella, 2006.

Räisänen, Heikki. *Paul and the Law.* Tübingen: Mohr Siebeck, 1987.

——. "Paul, God, and Israel: Romans 9–11 in Recent Research." In *Social World of Formative Christianity and Judaism: Essays in Tribute to Howard Clark Kee,* edited by Jacob Neusner, 178–206. Philadelphia: Fortress Press, 1988.

——. "Torn between Two Loyalties: Romans 9–11 and Paul's Conflicting Convictions." In *Nordic Paul*, edited by Lars Aejmelaeus and Antti Mustakallio, 19–39. London: T&T Clark, 2008.

Ramelli, Ilaria. *The Christian Doctrine of Apokatastasis: A Critical Assessment from the New Testament to Eriugena*. Supplements to *Vigiliae Christianae* 120. Boston: Brill, 2013.

Rangheri, Maurizio. "La Epistola ad Gerbergam Reginam *De ortu et tempore Antichristi* di Adsone di Montier-en-Der e le sue fonti." *Studi Medievali* 14 (1973): 677–732.

Rauh, Horst Dieter. *Das Bild des Antichrist im Mittelalter: Von Tyconius zum deutschen Symbolismus*. 2nd ed. Beiträge zur Geschichte der Philosophie und Theologie des Mittelalters, n.s. 9. Münster: Aschendorff, 1979.

Reasoner, Mark. *Romans in Full Circle: A History of Interpretation*. Louisville: Westminster John Knox Press, 2005.

——. "Romans 9–11 Moves from Margin to Center, from Rejection to Salvation: Four Grids for Recent English-Language Exegesis." In *Between Gospel and Election: Explorations in the Interpretation of Romans 9–11*, edited by Florian Wilk and J. Ross Wagner, 73–89. Wissenschaftliche Untersuchungen zum Neuen Testament 257. Tübingen: Mohr Siebeck, 2010.

Reed, Annette Yoshiko. "Messianism between Judaism and Christianity." In *Rethinking the Messianic Idea in Judaism*, edited by Michael L. Morgan and Steven Weitzman, 25–53. Bloomington: Indiana University Press, 2015.

Rees, B. R. *Pelagius: Life and Letters*. Woodbridge: Boydell Press, 1998.

Reeves, Marjorie, and Beatrice Hirsch-Reich. *The "Figurae" of Joachim of Fiore*. Oxford: Clarendon Press, 1972.

Refoulé, François. ". . . *Et ainsi tout Israël sera sauvé": Romains 11, 25–32*. Paris: Éditions du Cerf, 1984.

——. "Cohérence ou incohérence de Paul en Romains 9–11." *Revue Biblique* 98 (1991): 51–79.

Reinhartz, Adele. "Rabbinic Perceptions of Simeon Bar Kosiba." *Journal for the Study of Judaism in the Persian, Hellenistic and Roman Period* 20 (1989): 171–94.

Reinink, Gerrit J. "Pseudo-Methodius und die Legende vom römischen Endkaiser." In *The Use and Abuse of Eschatology in the Middle Ages*, edited by Werner Verbeke, Daniel Verhelst, and Andries Welkenhuysen, 82–111. Leuven: Leuven University Press, 1988.

——. "Pseudo-Methodius: A Concept of History in Response to the Rise of Islam." In *The Byzantine and Early Islamic Near East*, edited by Averil Cameron and Lawrence I. Conrad, 149–87. Princeton, NJ: Darwin Press, 1992.

——. "Pseudo-Methodius and the Pseudo-Ephremian 'Sermo de fine mundi.'" In *Media Latinitas: A Collection of Essays to Mark the Occasion of the Retirement of L. J. Engels*, edited by R. I. A. Nip et al., 317–21. Instrumenta Patristica 28. Turnhout: Brepols, 1996.

——. "From Apocalyptics to Apologetics: Early Syriac Reactions to Islam." In *Endzeiten: Eschatologie in den monotheistischen Weltreligionen*, edited by Wolfram Brandes and Felicitas Schmieder, 75–87. Berlin: De Gruyter, 2008.

Rémy, Gérard. "Jean Chrysostome, Interprète de Romains 9–11: Un regard chrétien sur les Juifs et les Gentils." In *Judaïsme et Christianisme chez les Pères*, edited by

Marie-Anne Vannier, 253–75. Judaïsme ancien et origines du Christianisme 8. Turnhout: Brepols, 2015.

Rensberger, David. "Conflict and Community in the Johannine Letters." *Interpretation—Journal of Bible and Theology* 60 (2006): 278–90.

Resnick, Irven M. "Talmud, Talmudisti, and Albert the Great." *Viator: Medieval and Renaissance Studies* 33 (2002): 69–86.

——. *Marks of Distinction: Christian Perceptions of Jews in the High Middle Ages*. Washington, DC: Catholic University of America Press, 2012.

Rhoads, Bonita, and Julia Reinhard Lupton. "Circumcising the Antichrist: An Ethnohistorical Fantasy." *Jouvert: A Journal of Postcolonial Studies* 3, no. 1–2 (1999). https://legacy.chass.ncsu.edu/jouvert/v3i12/rhoad.htm.

Ridder, Klaus, and Ulrich Barton. "Die Antichrist-Figur im mittelalterlichen Schauspiel." In *Antichrist*, edited by Wolfram Brandes and Felicitas Schmieder, 179–95. Berlin: Akademie Verlag, 2010.

Riedlinger, Helmut. *Die Makellosigkeit der Kirche in den lateinischen Hoheliedkommentaren des Mittelalters*. Beiträge zur Geschichte der Philosophie und Philosophie des Mittelalters 38,3. Münster: Aschendorff, 1958.

Rigaux, Béda. *L'Antéchrist et l'opposition au royaume messianique dans l'Ancien et le Nouveau Testament*. Paris: J. Gabalda, 1932.

Ritter, Adolf M. "John Chrysostom and the Jews: A Reconsideration." In *Ancient Christianity in the Caucasus*, edited by Tamila Mgaloblishvili, 141–54. Richmond: Curzon, 1998.

Rizzi, Marco. "Some Reflections on Origen, Celsus, and Their Views on the Jews." In *Jews and Christians in Antiquity: A Regional Perspective*, edited by Pierluigi Lanfranchi and Joseph Verheyden, 37–59. Interdisciplinary Studies in Ancient Culture and Religion 18. Leuven: Peeters, 2018.

Rosenmeier, Jesper. "Eaters and Non-Eaters: John Cotton's A Brief Exposition of . . . Canticles (1642) in Light of Boston's (Linc.) Religious and Civil Conflicts, 1619–22." *Early American Literature* 36 (2001): 149–82.

Rosenstock, Bruce. "Alonso de Cartgena: Nation, Miscegenation, and the Jews in Late-Medieval Castile." *Exemplaria* 12 (2000): 185–204.

——. *New Men: Conversos, Christian Theology, and Society in Fifteenth-Century Castile*. Papers of the Medieval Hispanic Research Seminar 39. London: Department of Hispanic Studies, Queen Mary and Westfield College, 2002.

Rouillard, Linda Marie. *Medieval Considerations of Incest, Marriage, and Penance*. Cham, Switzerland: Palgrave Macmillan, 2020.

Roukema, Riemer. *The Diversity of Laws in Origen's Commentary on Romans*. Amsterdam: Free University Press, 1988.

——. "Origen, the Jews, and the New Testament." In *The "New Testament" as a Polemical Tool: Studies in Ancient Christian Anti-Jewish Rhetoric and Beliefs*, edited by Riemer Roukema and Hagit Amirav, 241–53. Novum Testamentum et orbis antiquus 118. Göttingen: Vandenhoeck & Ruprecht, 2018.

Rowe, Nina. *The Jew, the Cathedral, and the Medieval City: Synagoga and Ecclesia in the Thirteenth Century*. New York: Cambridge University Press, 2011.

Rubenstein, Jay. *Armies of Heaven: The First Crusade and the Quest for Apocalypse*. New York: Basic Books, 2011.

——. *Nebuchadnezzar's Dream: The Crusades, Apocalyptic Prophecy, and the End of History.* Oxford: Oxford University Press, 2019.

Rubin, Miri. "Ecclesia and Synagoga: The Changing Meanings of a Powerful Pairing." In *Conflict and Religious Conversation in Latin Christendom: Studies in Honour of Ora Limor,* edited by Israel Jacob Yuval and Ram Ben-Shalom, 55–86. Cultural Encounters in Late Antiquity and the Middle Ages 17. Turnhout: Brepols, 2014.

Rudolph, Conrad. "Inventing the Exegetical Stained-Glass Window: Suger, Hugh, and a New Elite Art." *Art Bulletin* 93 (2011): 399–422.

Rusconi, Roberto. *Profezia e profeti alla fine del Medioevo.* Rome: Viella, 1999.

Russell, Jeffrey Burton. *The Devil: Perceptions of Evil from Antiquity to Primitive Christianity.* Ithaca, NY: Cornell University Press, 1977.

——. *Satan: The Early Christian Tradition.* Ithaca, NY: Cornell University Press, 1981.

——. *Lucifer: The Devil in the Middle Ages.* Ithaca, NY: Cornell University Press, 1984.

Ruud, Jay. "The Jews in the Chester Play of Antichrist." *Geardagum: Essays on Old and Middle English* 26 (2006): 53–71.

Ryan, Thomas F. "The Love of Learning and the Desire for God in Thomas Aquinas's Commentary on Romans." In *Medieval Readings of Romans,* edited by William S. Campbell et al., 101–14. New York: T&T Clark International, 2007.

Sanders, E. P. *Paul and Palestinian Judaism: A Comparison of Patterns of Religion.* Philadelphia: Fortress Press, 1977.

——. *Paul, the Law, and the Jewish People.* Philadelphia: Fortress Press, 1983.

——. *Comparing Judaism and Christianity: Common Judaism, Paul, and the Inner and the Outer in Ancient Religion.* Minneapolis: Fortress Press, 2016.

Satran, David. "The Salvation of the Devil: Origen and Origenism in Jerome's Biblical Commentaries." *Studia Patristica* 23 (1989): 171–77.

Schaaf, Judy. "The Christian-Jewish Debate and the 'Catalan Atlas.'" In *Jews in Medieval Christendom: Slay Them Not,* edited by Kristine T. Utterback and Merrall L. Price, 245–74. Leiden: Brill, 2013.

Schäfer, Peter. *Der Bar Kokhba-Aufstand: Studien zum zweiten jüdischen Krieg gegen Rom.* Tübingen: Mohr Siebeck, 1981.

——, ed. *The Bar Kokhba War Reconsidered: New Perspectives on the Second Jewish Revolt against Rome.* Texts and Studies in Ancient Judaism 100. Tübingen: Mohr Siebeck, 2003.

Scheck, Thomas P. *Origen and the History of Justification: The Legacy of Origen's Commentary on Romans.* Notre Dame, IN: University of Notre Dame Press, 2008.

——. "Origen's Interpretation of Romans." In *A Companion to St. Paul in the Middle Ages,* edited by Steven R. Cartwright, 15–49. Boston: Brill, 2013.

——. "Pelagius's Interpretation of Romans." In *A Companion to St. Paul in the Middle Ages,* edited by Steven R. Cartwright, 79–113. Boston: Brill, 2013.

Schelkle, Karl Hermann. *Paulus, lehrer der Väter: Die altkirchliche Auslegung von Römer 1–11.* 2nd ed. Düsseldorf: Patmos-Verlag, 1959.

Schenk, Richard. "Covenant Initiation: Thomas Aquinas and Robert Kilwardy on the Sacrament of Circumcision." In *Ordo sapientiae et amoris: Image et message de Saint Thomas d' Aquin à travers les récentes études historiques, herméneutiques et doctrinales; Hommage au professeur Jean-Pierre Torrell O.P., à l'occasion de son 65e,* edited by Carlos-Josaphat Pinto de Oliveira, 555–93. Studia friburgensia, n.s. 78. Fribourg: Éditions universitaires, 1993.

Scheper, George L. "Reformation Attitudes toward Allegory and the Song of Songs." *Publications of the Modern Language Association* 89 (1974): 551–62.

Scherb, Victor I. "Assimilating Giants: The Appropriation of Gog and Magog in Medieval and Early Modern England." *Journal of Medieval and Early Modern Studies* 32 (2002): 59–84.

Schlageter, Johannes. *Das Heil der Armen und das Verderben der Reichen: Petrus Johannis Olivi OFM, die Frage nach der höchsten Armut.* Franziskanische Forschungen 34. Werl/Westfalen: Dietrich-Coelde-Verlag, 1989.

Schmidt, Andrea B. "Die 'Brüste des Nordens' und Alexanders Mauer gegen Gog und Magog." In *Endzeiten: Eschatologie in den monotheistischen Weltreligionen*, edited by Wolfram Brandes and Felicitas Schmieder, 89–100. Berlin: De Gruyter, 2008.

Schmieder, Felicitas. "Prophetische Propaganda in der Politik des 14. Jahrhunderts: Johannes von Rupescissa." In *Endzeiten: Eschatologie in den monotheistischen Weltreligionen*, edited by Wolfram Brandes and Felicitas Schmieder, 249–60. Berlin: De Gruyter, 2008.

Schmuck, Stephan. "The 'Turk' as Antichrist in John Foxe's *Acts and Monuments* (1570)." *Reformation* 10 (2005): 21–44.

Schoeps, Julius H., Christoph Schulte, and Christine Stumpfe, eds. "Der Antichrist." *Zeitschrift für Religions- und Geistesgeschichte* 47 (1995): 97–188.

Schreckenberg, Heinz. *The Jews in Christian Art: An Illustrated History.* New York: Continuum, 1996.

———. *Die Christlichen Adversus-Judaeos-Texte (11.–13. Jh.): Mit einer Ikonographie des Judenthemas bis zum 4. Laterankonzil.* New York: Peter Lang, 1997.

Scott, James Morgan, ed. "'And Then All Israel Will Be Saved' (Rom 11–26): Introduction." In *Restoration: Old Testament, Jewish, and Christian Perspectives*, 489–526. Supplements to the *Journal for the Study of Judaism* 72. Leiden: Brill, 2001.

Seiferth, Wolfgang S. *Synagogue and Church in the Middle Ages: Two Symbols in Art and Literature.* Translated by Lee Chadeayne and Paul Gottwald. New York: Ungar, 1970.

Shacham-Rosby, Chana. "Elijah the Prophet in Medieval Franco-German (Ashkenazi) Jewish Culture" [Hebrew]. Ph.D. dissertation, Ben-Gurion University of the Negev, 2018.

Shalev-Enyi, Sarit. "Iconography of Love: Illustrations of Bride and Bridegroom in Ashkenazi Prayerbooks of the Thirteenth and Fourteenth Century." *Studies in Iconography* 26 (2005): 27–57.

Sievers, Joseph. "A History of the Interpretation of Romans 11:29." *Annali di Storia dell'Esegesi* 14 (1997): 381–442.

———. "'God's Gifts and Call Are Irrevocable': The Reception of Romans 11:29 through the Centuries and Jewish-Christian Relations." In *Reading Israel in Romans: Legitimacy and Plausibility of Divergent Interpretations*, edited by Cristina Grenholm and Daniel Patte, 127–73. Harrisburg, PA: Trinity Press International, 2000.

Signer, Michael A., and John Van Engen, eds. *Jews and Christians in Twelfth-Century Europe.* Notre Dame, IN: University of Notre Dame Press, 2001.

Silverman, Kenneth. *The Life and Times of Cotton Mather.* New York: Harper & Row, 1984.

Sizer, Stephen. *Christian Zionism: Road Map to Armageddon?* Leicester: Inter-Varsity Press, 2004.

Smalley, Beryl. *The Study of the Bible in the Middle Ages*. 3rd ed. Oxford: Blackwell, 1983.

Smith, Christopher R. "Chiliasm and Recapitulation in the Theology of Irenaeus." *Vigiliae Christianae* 48 (1994): 313–31.

Smith, Robert O. *More Desired than Our Owne Salvation: The Roots of Christian Zionism*. New York: Oxford University Press, 2013.

Smolinski, Reiner. "Israel Redivivus: The Eschatological Limits of Puritan Typology in New England." *New England Quarterly: A Historical Review of New England Life and Letters* 63 (1990): 357–95.

——. "'The Way to Lost Zion': The Cotton-Williams Debate on the Separation of Church and State in Millenarian Perspective." In *Millennial Thought in America: Historical and Intellectual Contexts, 1630–1860*, edited by Bernd Engler, Joerg O. Fichte, and Oliver Scheiding, 61–96. Mosaic: Studien und Texte zur Amerikanischen Kultur und Geschichte 15. Tübingen: Wissenschaft Verlag, 2002.

——. "'Eager imitators of the Egyptian Inventions': Cotton Mather's Engagement with John Spencer and the Debate about the Pagan Origin of the Mosaic Laws, Rites, and Customs." In *Cotton Mather and Biblia Americana—America's First Bible Commentary: Essays in Reappraisal*, edited by Reiner Smolinski, Jan Stievermann, and Harry S. Stout, 295–335. Tübingen: Mohr Siebeck, 2010.

Snyder, Graydon F. "Major Motifs in the Interpretation of Paul's Letter to the Romans." In *Celebrating Romans: Template for Pauline Theology—Essays in Honor of Robert Jewett*, edited by Sheila E. McGinn, 42–63. Grand Rapids, MI: Eerdmans Publishing Company, 2004.

Sordi, Marta. "Commodianus, *Carmen apologeticum* 892 ss.: Rex ab oriente." *Augustinianum* 22 (1982): 203–10.

Soulen, R Kendall. "'They Are Israelites': The Priority of the Present Tense for Jewish-Christian Relations." In *Between Gospel and Election: Explorations in the Interpretation of Romans 9–11*, edited by Florian Wilk and J. Ross Wagner, 497–504. Wissenschaftliche Untersuchungen zum Neuen Testament 257. Tübingen: Mohr Siebeck, 2010.

Souter, Alexander. *A Study of Ambrosiaster*. Texts and Studies 7,4. Cambridge: Cambridge University Press, 1905.

——. *The Earliest Latin Commentaries on the Epistles of St. Paul*. Repr. ed., 1999. Oxford: Oxford University Press, 1927.

Spector, Stephen. "Anti-Semitism and the English Mystery Plays." In *The Drama of the Middle Ages: Comparative and Critical Essay*, edited by Clifford Davison, 328–41. New York: AMS Press, 1982.

Speller, Lydia. "Ambrosiaster and the Jews." *Studia Patristica* 17 (1982): 72–78.

Spencer, F Scott. "Metaphor, Mystery, and the Salvation of Israel in Romans 9–11: Paul's Appeal to Humility and Doxology." *Review & Expositor* 103 (2006): 113–38.

Spicq, Ceslas. *Esquisse d'une histoire de l'exégèse latine au moyen âge*. Bibliothèque thomiste 26. Paris: Vrin, 1944.

Stadler, Gustavus. "Ejaculating Tongues: Poe, Mather, and the Jewish Penis." In *The Puritan Origins of American Sex: Religion, Sexuality, and National Identity in American Literature*, edited by Tracy Fessenden, Nicholas F. Radel, and Magdalena J. Zaborowska, 109–26. New York: Routledge, 2001.

Stanley, Christopher D. "'The Redeemer Will Come *Ek Siōn*': Romans 11.26–27 Revisited." In *Paul and the Scriptures of Israel*, edited by Craig Alan Evans and James Alvin Sanders, 118–42. Sheffield: Sheffield Academic Press, 1993.

Staples, Jason A. "What Do the Gentiles Have to Do with 'All Israel'? A Fresh Look at Romans 11:25–27." *Journal of Biblical Literature* 130 (2011): 371–90.

Steenberg, Irenaeus M. C. *Irenaeus on Creation, the Cosmic Christ, and the Saga of Redemption*. Supplements to *Vigiliae Christianae* 91. Leiden: Brill, 2008.

Steer, Georg. *Hugo Ripelin von Strassburg: Zur Rezeptions- und Wirkungsgeschichte des "Compendium theologicae veritatis" im deutschen Spätmittelalter*. Tübingen: Niemeyer, 1981.

Stevens, Martin. *Four Middle English Mystery Cycles: Textual, Contextual, and Critical Interpretations*. Princeton: Princeton University Press, 1987.

Stevenson, Jill. "Poised at the Threatening Edge: Feeling the Future in Medieval Last Judgment Performances." *Theatre Journal* 67 (2015): 273–93.

Stievermann, Jan. *Prophecy, Piety, and the Problem of Historicity: Interpreting the Hebrew Scriptures in Cotton Mather's "Biblia Americana."* Beiträge zur historischen Theologie 179. Tübingen: Mohr Siebeck, 2016.

——. "Reading Canticles in the Tradition of New England Millennialism: John Cotton and Cotton Mather's Commentaries on the Song of Songs." In *Prophecy and Eschatology in the Transatlantic World, 1550–800*, edited by Andrew Crome, 213–38. London: Palgrave MacMillan, 2016.

Still, Todd D., ed. *God and Israel: Providence and Purpose in Romans 9–11*. Waco, TX: Baylor University Press, 2017.

Stow, Kenneth R. "Agobard of Lyons and the Origins of the Medieval Conception of the Jew." *Conservative Judaism* 29 (1974): 58–65.

Stowers, Stanley K. *A Rereading of Romans: Justice, Jews, and Gentiles*. New Haven: Yale University Press, 1994.

Streett, Daniel R. *They Went Out from Us: The Identity of the Opponents in First John*. Beihefte zur Zeitschrift für die Neutestamentliche Wissenschaft und die Kunde der Älteren Kirche 177. Berlin: De Gruyter, 2011.

Strickland, Debra Higgs. *Saracens, Demons & Jews: Making Monsters in Medieval Art*. Princeton: Princeton University Press, 2003.

——. "Antichrist and the Jews in Medieval Art and Protestant Propaganda." *Studies in Iconography* 32 (2011): 1–50.

——. *The Epiphany of Hieronymus Bosch: Imagining Antichrist and Others from the Middle Ages to the Reformation*. London: Harvey Miller Publishers, 2016.

Stuczynski, Claude B. "Pro-'Converso' Apologetics and Biblical Exegesis." In *The Hebrew Bible in Fifteenth-Century Spain: Exegesis, Literature, Philosophy, and the Arts*, edited by Jonathan Decter and Arturo Prats, 151–76. Leiden: Brill, 2012.

Synan, Edward A. "Some Medieval Perceptions of the Controversy on Jewish Law." In *Understanding Scripture: Explorations of Jewish and Christian Traditions of Interpretation*, edited by Clemens Thoma and Michael Wyschogrod, 102–24. New York: Paulist Press, 1987.

Szittya, Penn R. *The Antifraternal Tradition in Medieval Literature*. Princeton: Princeton University Press, 1986.

Szpiech, Ryan. "Scrutinizing History: Polemic and Exegesis in Pablo de Santa María's *Siete edades del mundo*." *Medieval Encounters: Jewish, Christian and Muslim Culture in Confluence and Dialogue* 16 (2010): 96–142.

——. "A Father's Bequest: Augustinian Typology and Personal Testimony in the Conversion Narrative of Solomon Halevi/Pablo de Santa María." In *The Hebrew Bible in Fifteenth-Century Spain: Exegesis, Literature, Philosophy, and the Arts*, edited by Jonathan Decter and Arturo Prats, 177–98. Leiden: Brill, 2012.

——. *Conversion and Narrative: Reading and Religious Authority in Medieval Polemic*. Philadelphia: University of Pennsylvania Press, 2013.

Talbert, Charles H. "Paul, Judaism, and the Revisionists." *Catholic Biblical Quarterly* 63 (2001): 1–22.

Tapie, Matthew A. *Aquinas on Israel and the Church: The Question of Supersessionism in the Theology of Thomas Aquinas*. Eugene, OR: Pickwick Publications, 2014.

Taylor, John W. "The Freedom of God and the Hope of Israel: Theological Interpretation of Romans 9." *Southwestern Journal of Theology* 56 (2013): 25–41.

Thatcher, Tom. "Cain the Jew the AntiChrist: Collective Memory and the Johannine Ethic of Loving and Hating." In *Rethinking the Ethics of John: "Implicit Ethics" in the Johannine Writings*, edited by Jan G. van der Watt and Ruben Zimmermann, 350–73. Wissenschaftliche Untersuchungen zum Neuen Testament 291. Tübingen: Mohr Siebeck, 2012.

Thielman, Frank. *From Plight to Solution: A Jewish Framework for Understanding Paul's View of the Law in Galatians and Romans*. Leiden: Brill, 1989.

Thomas, David, Barbara Roggema, and Juan Pedro Monferrer Sala. *Christian-Muslim Relations: A Bibliographical History*. Vol. 1, *600–900*. Christian-Muslim Relations: A Bibliographical History 1. Leiden: Brill, 2009.

Thomas, Robert L. "Hermeneutics of the New Perspective on Paul." *Master's Seminary Journal* 16 (2005): 293–316.

Thornton, Timothy C. G. "Jews in Early Christian Eschatological Scenarios." *Studia Patristica* 34 (2001): 656–71.

Tinkle, Theresa. "God's Chosen Peoples: Christians and Jews in *The Book of John Mandeville*." *Journal of English and Germanic Philology* 113 (2014): 443–71.

Toit, Philip la Grange du. "The Salvation of 'All Israel' in Romans 11:25–27 as the Salvation of Inner-Elect, Historical Israel in Christ." *Neotestamentica* 49 (2015): 417–52.

Tonstad, Sigve K. "Appraising the Myth of Nero Redivivus in the Interpretation of Revelation." *Andrews University Seminary Studies* 46 (2008): 175–99.

Toon, Peter, ed. *Puritans, the Millennium, and the Future of Israel: Puritan Eschatology 1600 to 1660*. Cambridge: J. Clarke, 1970.

Tournay, R. "Les Chariots d'Aminadab (Cant. vi 12): Israël, Peuple théophore." *Vetus Testamentum* 9 (1959): 288–309.

Trakatellis, Demetrios. "Being Transformed: Chrysostom's Exegesis of the Epistle to the Romans." *Greek Orthodox Theological Review* 36 (1991): 211–29.

Travassos Valdez, Maria Ana. *Historical Interpretations of the "Fifth Empire": The Dynamics of Periodization from Daniel to António Vieira, S.J.* Leiden: Brill, 2011.

Traver, Andrew. "The *Liber de Antichristo* and the Failure of Joachite Expectations." *Florensia* 14 (2001): 87–98.

Trigg, Joseph Wilson. *Origen: The Bible and Philosophy in the Third-Century Church*. Atlanta: John Knox Press, 1983.

——. *Origen*. Early Church Fathers 3. London: Routledge, 1998.

Trudinger, Paul. "The 'Nero Redivivus' Rumour and the Date of the Apocalypse of John." *St Mark's Review* 131 (1987): 43–44.

Tsirpanlis, Constantine N. "The Antichrist and the End of the World in Irenaeus, Justin, Hippolytus, and Tertullian." *Patristic and Byzantine Review* 9 (1990): 5–17.

Turner, Denys. *Eros and Allegory: Medieval Exegesis of the Song of Songs.* Cistercian Studies Series 156. Kalamazoo: Cistercian Publications, 2001.

Tzamalikos, Panayiotis. *Origen: Philosophy of History and Eschatology.* Supplements to *Vigiliae Christianae* 85. Leiden: Brill, 2007.

Uddin, Mohan. "Paul, the Devil and 'Unbelief' in Israel (with Particular Reference to 2 Corinthians 3–4 and Romans 9–11)." *Tyndale Bulletin* 50 (1999): 265–80.

Van de Water, Rick. "Bar Kokhba and Patristic Interpretations of the 'Antichrist.'" In *Bible et Terre Sainte: Mélanges Marcel Beaudry,* edited by José Enrique Aguilar Chiu, Kieran J. O'Mahony, and Maurice Roger, 483–92. New York: Peter Lang, 2008.

Van Henten, Jan Willem. "Nero Redivivus Demolished: The Coherence of the Nero Traditions in the Sibylline Oracles." *Journal for the Study of the Pseudepigrapha* 21 (2000): 3–17.

Van Liere, Frans. "Christ or Antichrist? The Jewish Messiah in Twelfth-Century Christian Eschatology." In *From Knowledge to Beatitude: St. Victor, Twelfth-Century Scholars, and Beyond; Essays in Honor of Grover A. Zinn, Jr.,* edited by E. Ann Matter and Lesley Smith, 342–57. Notre Dame, IN: University of Notre Dame Press, 2013.

Venema, Cornelis P. "'In This Way All Israel Will Be Saved': A Study of Romans 11:26." *Mid-America Journal of Theology* 22 (2011): 19–40.

Verhelst, Daniel. "La préhistoire des conceptions d'Adson concernant l'Antéchrist." *Recherches de Théologie Ancienne et Médiévale* 40 (1973): 52–103.

——, ed. "Introduction: Adson; Sa vie et ses oeuvres." In *De ortu et tempore Antichristi necnon et tractatus qui ab eo dependunt,* by Adso Deruensis. CCCM 45. Turnhout: Brepols, 1976.

——. "Adso of Montier-en-Der and the Fear of the Year 1000." In *The Apocalyptic Year 1000: Religious Expectation and Social Change, 950–1050,* edited by Richard Landes, Andrew Gow, and David C. Van Meter, 81–92. Oxford: Oxford University Press, 2003.

Vicchio, Stephen. *The Legend of the Anti-Christ: A History.* Eugene, OR: Wipf & Stock, 2009.

Vidal Doval, Rosa. *Misera Hispania: Jews and Conversos in Alonso de Espina's "Fortalitium Fidei."* Oxford: The Society for the Study of Medieval Languages and Literature, 2013.

Villiers, Pieter G. R. de. "The Future Existence of the Believers According to 2 Thessalonians." *Hervormde Teologiese Studies* 67 (2011): 1–9.

Visser, Derk. *Apocalypse as Utopian Expectation (800–1500): The Apocalypse Commentary of Berengaudus of Ferrières and the Relationship between Exegesis, Liturgy, and Iconography.* New York: Brill, 1996.

Vlach, Michael J. *The Church as a Replacement of Israel: An Analysis of Supersessionism.* Frankfurt am Main: Peter Lang, 2009.

Wagner, J. Ross. *Heralds of the Good News: Isaiah and Paul "in Concert" in the Letter to the Romans.* Boston: Brill, 2002.

Walliss, John. *The End All Around Us: Apocalyptic Texts and Popular Culture*. Hoboken, NJ: Taylor and Francis, 2014.

Walsh, Martin William. "Demon or Deluded Messiah? The Characterization of Antichrist in the Chester Cycle." *Medieval English Theatre* 7 (1985): 13–24.

Ward, Rowland S. "A Passion for God and a Passion for Jews: The Basis and Practice of Jewish Mission 1550–1850." *Reformed Theological Review* 70 (2011): 1–25.

Warner, J. Christopher. "John Bale: Bibliographer between Trithemius and the Four Horsemen of the Apocalypse." *Reformation* 18 (2013): 36–47.

Wasserberg, Günter. "Romans 9–11 and Jewish-Christian Dialogue: Prospects and Provisos." *Society of Biblical Literature Seminar Papers* 37 (1998): 1–11.

Waters, Benjamin Victor. "The Two Eschatological Perspectives of the Book of Daniel." *SJOT: Scandinavian Journal of the Old Testament* 30 (2016): 91–111.

Watt, Jack. "Parisian Theologians and the Jews: Peter Lombard and Peter Cantor." In *The Medieval Church: Universities, Heresy, and the Religious Life; Essays in Honour of Gordon Leff*, 55–76. Studies in Church History Subsidia 11. Woodbridge: Ecclesiastical History Society, 1999.

Weaver, Joel A. *Theodoret of Cyrus on Romans 11:26: Recovering an Early Christian Elijah Redivivus Tradition*. American University Studies 7,249. New York: Peter Lang, 2007.

Wechsler, Judith Glatzer. "A Change in the Iconography of the Song of Songs in Twelfth- and Thirteenth-Century Latin Bibles." In *Texts and Responses: Studies Presented to Nahum N. Glatzer on the Occasion of His Seventieth Birthday by His Students*, edited by Michael A. Fishbane and Paul R. Mendes-Flohr, 73–93. Leiden: Brill, 1975.

Weinrich, William C. "Antichrist in the Early Church." *Concordia Theological Quarterly* 49 (2–3) (1985): 135–47.

Westerholm, Stephen. "The 'New Perspective' at Twenty-Five." In *Justification and Variegated Nomism*, 140:2:1–38. Wissenschaftliche Untersuchungen zum Neuen Testament 2. Tübingen: Mohr Siebeck, 2001.

———. *Perspectives Old and New on Paul: The "Lutheran" Paul and His Critics*. Grand Rapids, MI: Eerdmans, 2004.

———. "The New Perspective on Paul in Review." *Direction* 44 (2015): 4–15.

Westrem, Scott D. "Against Gog and Magog." In *Text and Territory: Geographical Imagination in the European Middle Ages*, edited by Sylvia Tomasch and Sealy Gilles, 54–75. Philadelphia: University of Pennsylvania Press, 1998.

Whalen, Brett Edward. *Dominion of God: Christendom and Apocalypse in the Middle Ages*. Cambridge, MA: Harvard University Press, 2009.

———. "Joachim of Fiore, Apocalyptic Conversion, and the 'Persecuting Society.'" *History Compass* 8 (vii) (2010): 682–91.

———. "Joachim the Theorist of History and Society." In *A Companion to Joachim of Fiore*, edited by Matthias Riedl, 88–108. Leiden: Brill, 2017.

Wilk, Florian, and J. Ross Wagner, eds. *Between Gospel and Election: Explorations in the Interpretation of Romans 9–11*. Wissenschaftliche Untersuchungen zum Neuen Testament 257. Tübingen: Mohr Siebeck, 2010.

Wilken, Robert L. *John Chrysostom and the Jews: Rhetoric and Reality in the Late Fourth Century*. Berkeley: University of California Press, 1983.

Williams Boyarin, Adrienne. *Miracles of the Virgin in Medieval England: Law and Jewishness in Marian Legends*. Cambridge: D.S. Brewer, 2010.

Williamson, Arthur H. *Apocalypse Then: Prophecy and the Making of the Modern World*. Westport, CT: Praeger, 2008.

Wills, Garry. *What Paul Meant*. New York: Viking, 2006.

Wim, François. "Grace, Free Will, and Predestination in the Biblical Commentaries of Cornelius a Lapide." *Annali di Storia dell'Esegesi* 34 (2017): 175–97.

Woodward, Michael Scott, ed. *The Glossa Ordinaria on Romans*. Kalamazoo: Medieval Institute Publications, Western Michigan University, 2011.

Wright, N. T. "Romans 9–11 and the 'New Perspective.'" In *Between Gospel and Election: Explorations in the Interpretation of Romans 9–11*, edited by Florian Wilk and J. Ross Wagner, 37–54. Wissenschaftliche Untersuchungen zum Neuen Testament 257. Tübingen: Mohr Siebeck, 2010.

Wright, Rosemary Muir. *Art and Antichrist in Medieval Europe*. Manchester: Manchester University Press, 1995.

Yisraeli, Yosi. "Constructing and Undermining Converso Jewishness: Profiat Duran and Pablo de Santa María." In *Religious Conversion: History, Experience, and Meaning*, edited by Ira Katznelson and Miri Rubin, 185–215. London: Routledge, 2014.

——. "Between Jewish and Christian Scholarship in the Fifteenth Century: The Consolidation of a 'Converso Doctrine' in the Theological Writings of Pablo de Santa María." Ph.D. dissertation, Tel Aviv University, 2015.

——. "A Christianized Sephardic Critique of Rashi's 'Peshaṭ' in Pablo de Santa María's 'Additiones ad Postillam Nicolai de Lyra.'" In *Medieval Exegesis and Religious Difference: Commentary, Conflict, and Community in the Premodern Mediterranean*, edited by Ryan Szpiech, 128–41, 246–53. New York: Fordham University Press, 2015.

——. "From Christian Polemic to a Jewish-Converso Dialogue: Jewish Skepticism and Rabbinic-Christian Traditions in the *Scrutinium Scripturarum*." *Medieval Encounters: Jewish, Christian and Muslim Culture in Confluence and Dialogue* 24 (2018): 160–96.

Zakai, Avihu. "Puritan Millennialism and Theocracy in Early Massachusetts." *History of European Ideas* 8 (1987): 309–18.

——. "Thomas Brightman and English Apocalyptic Tradition." In *Menasseh Ben Israel and His World*, edited by Yosef Kaplan, Henry Méchoulan, and Richard H. Popkin, 15:31–44. Brill's Studies in Intellectual History. Leiden: Brill, 1989.

——. *Exile and Kingdom: History and Apocalypse in the Puritan Migration to America*. Cambridge: Cambridge University Press, 1992.

——. "Theocracy in Massachusetts: The Puritan Universe of Sacred Imagination." *Studies in the Literary Imagination* 27 (1994): 23.

——. "The Poetics of History and the Destiny of Israel: The Role of the Jews in English Apocalyptic Thought during the 16th-Century and 17th-Century." *Journal of Jewish Thought and Philosophy* 5 (1996): 313–50.

Zarcone, Thierry. "The Myth of the Mandrake, the 'Plant-Human.'" *Diogenes* 52 (2005): 115–29.

Zetterholm, Magnus. *Approaches to Paul: A Student's Guide to Recent Scholarship*. Minneapolis: Fortress Press, 2009.

Zoccali, Christopher. "'And So All Israel Will Be Saved': Competing Interpretations of Romans 11.26 in Pauline Scholarship." *Journal for the Study of the New Testament* 30 (2008): 289–318.

Zumkeller, Adolar. "Der Terminus 'Sola Fides' bei Augustinus." In *Christian Authority: Essays in Honour of Henry Chadwick*, edited by G. R. Evans, 86–100. Oxford: Clarendon Press, 1988.

INDEX

Page numbers in *italics* indicate illustrations. Authored works will be found under the name of the author.

Aaron (brother of Moses), 181, 183, 184
Abelard. *See* Peter Abelard
Abingdon Apocalypse, 144, *147*, 185
Abner of Burgos, 191
Abraham (biblical patriarch): descendants of, and definition/delimitation of Israel, 11, 28, 44, 60, 63, 189; Gentiles and, 39, 45, 120; Joachim of Fiore on, 115
Abulafia, Anna Sapir, 119
Adam and Eve, 85
Adam of Persigne, 250n94
Adso of Montier-en-Der, 72–73, 100–106; on conception and birth of Antichrist, 101–2; *De ortu et tempore Antichristi*, 100–104, 148; Herrad of Hohenburg's *Hortus deliciarum* and, 109, 111, 112; Honorius Augustodunensis breaking with tradition of, 176; Hugo Ripelin of Strasbourg and, 105, 112; influence of, 100–101, 104–5; Joachim of Fiore and, 249n80; *Ludus de Antichristo* and, 109; on place of Antichrist's birth, 102–3; on rise and fall of Antichrist, 103–4; twelfth and thirteenth century reflections of, 105–6; vernacular works influenced by, 133, 135, 138, 139
adversus Judaeos tradition, 19, 172
Agobard of Lyons, *On the Superstitions of the Jews*, 94
Akbari, Suzanne Conklin, 132
Akiba (Akiva) ben Joseph, 80, 130
Alexander the Great, Gog and Magog/Jews associated with tribes confined by, 97, 112–13, 125–28, *127*, 128–30, 198
Algasia, letter of Jerome to, 91
allegorical understanding of biblical texts: Antichrist/the Jews and, 115, 128, 152;

Honorius Augustodunensis on Song of Songs and, 160, 161, 164, *166*, 168, 170–72, 181, 184, 186; Origen on, 39; Pablo de Santa María and, 189; Puritan move away from, 201, 204, 212
Alonso de Cartagena, 196, 198, 199, 224; *Defensorium unitatis christianae*, 196
Alonso de Espina, 223; *Fortalitium fidei*, 198–99
Amazons, queen of, 113, 131, 133, *151*, 152, 198, 253n9
Ambrose of Milan, 41, 179, 259n11, 263n64
Ambrosiaster: Augustine influenced by, 51–52; later Western medieval influence of, 54, 56; on order of conversion of Gentiles and Jews, 175; Origen compared, 41–42, 43, 45; on salvation of Israel, 8, 41–46; Thomas Aquinas compared, 65, 238n61
American Indians linked with ten lost tribes of Israel, 205
Aminadab, quadriga/chariots of, 163, *165*, 167, 171, 172, 178–79, *179*, 181, *183*, 183–85
anagogical window, abbey of Saint-Denis, 181–84, *182*, *183*, *185*, 264n68
Andrew of St. Victor, 173
Angelom of Luxeuil, 171
Annes/Annas, in late medieval vernacular drama, 138–39
Anselm of Canterbury, 161, 173; *Cur Deus homo*, 173
Anselm of Havelberg, 161
Anselm of Laon, 261n41
The Antichrist (1450–1500), 133